Predictive Analytics

for dŭmmies®

A Wiley Brand

2nd edition

by Anasse Bari, Ph.D.,
Mohamed Chaouchi, and
Tommy Jung

for dŭmmies®
A Wiley Brand

Predictive Analytics For Dummies®, 2nd Edition

Published by: **John Wiley & Sons, Inc.,** 111 River Street, Hoboken, NJ 07030-5774, www.wiley.com

Copyright © 2017 by John Wiley & Sons, Inc., Hoboken, New Jersey

Media and software compilation copyright © 2017 by John Wiley & Sons, Inc. All rights reserved.

Published simultaneously in Canada

For general information on our other products and services, please contact our Customer Care Department within the U.S. at 877-762-2974, outside the U.S. at 317-572-3993, or fax 317-572-4002. For technical support, please visit https://hub.wiley.com/community/support/dummies.

Wiley publishes in a variety of print and electronic formats and by print-on-demand. Some material included with standard print versions of this book may not be included in e-books or in print-on-demand. If this book refers to media such as a CD or DVD that is not included in the version you purchased, you may download this material at http://booksupport.wiley.com. For more information about Wiley products, visit www.wiley.com.

Library of Congress Control Number: 2016951998

ISBN 978-1-119-26700-3 (pbk); 978-1-119-26701-0 (epub); 978-1-119-26702-7 (epdf)

Manufactured in the United States of America

10 9 8 7 6 5 4 3

Table of Contents

Introduction

Predictive Analytics is the art and science of using data to make better informed decisions. Predictive analytics helps you uncover hidden patterns and relationships in your data that can help you predict with greater confidence what may happen in the future, and provide you with valuable, actionable insights for your organization.

About This Book

Our goal was to make this complex subject as practical as possible, in a way that appeals to everyone from technical experts to non-technical level business strategists.

The subject is complex because it is not really just one subject. It is the combination of at least a few multifaceted fields: data mining, statistics, and mathematics.

Data mining requires an understanding of machine learning and information retrieval. On top of this, mathematics and statistics must be applied to your business domain; be it marketing, actuary service, fraud, crime, or banking.

Most of the current materials on predictive analytics are pretty difficult to read if you don't already have a background in some of the aforementioned subjects. They are filled with complex mathematical equations and modeling techniques. Or, they are at a high level with specific use cases but with little guidance regarding implementation. We include both, while trying to keep a wide spectrum of readers engaged.

The focus of this book is developing a roadmap for implementing predictive analytics within your organization. Its intended audience is the larger community of business managers, business analysts, data scientists, and information technology professionals.

Maybe you are a business manager and you have heard the buzz about predictive analytics. Maybe you've been working with data mining and you want to add predictive analytics to your skill set. Maybe you know R or Python, but you're totally new to predictive analytics. If this sounds like you, then this book will be a good fit. Even if you have no experience analyzing data, but want or need to derive greater value from your organization's data, you can also find something of value in this book.

Foolish Assumptions

Without oversimplifying, we have tried to explain technical concepts in non-technical terms, tackling each topic from the ground up.

Even if you are an experienced practitioner, you should find something new, and at the very least, you will gain validation for what you already know, and guidance for establishing best practices.

We also hope to have contributed a few concepts and ideas for the very first time in a major publication like this. For example we explain how you can apply biologically inspired algorithms to predictive analytics.

We assume that the reader will not be a programmer. The code presented in this book is very brief and easy to follow. Readers of all programming levels will benefit from this book, because it is more about learning the process of predictive analytics rather than learning a programming language.

Icons Used in This Book

The following icons in the margins indicate highlighted material that we think could be of interest to you. Next, we describe the meaning of each icon that is used in this book.

The tips are ideas we would like you to take note of. This is usually practical advice you can apply for that given topic.

This icon is rarely used in this book. We may have used it only once or twice in the entire book. The intent is to save you time by bringing to your attention some common pitfalls that you are better off avoiding.

TECHNICAL STUFF

We have made sincere efforts to steer away from the technical stuff. But when we have no choice we make sure to let you know. So if you don't care too much about the technical stuff you can easily skip this part and you won't miss much. If the technical stuff is your thing, then you may find these sections fascinating.

REMEMBER

This is something we would like you to take a special note of. This is a concept or idea we think is important for you know and remember. An example of this would be a best practice we think it is noteworthy.

Beyond the Book

A lot of extra content that is not in this book is available at www.dummies.com. Go online to find the following:

>> **The Cheat Sheet for this book is at**

> www.dummies.com/cheatsheet/predictiveanalytics

Here you'll find the necessary steps needed to build a predictive analytics model and some cases studies of predictive analytics.

>> **Updates to this book, if we have any, are also available at**

> www.dummies.com/extras/predictiveanalytics

Where to Go from Here

Let's start making some predictions! You can apply predictive analytics to virtually every business domain. Right now there is explosive growth in predictive analytics' market, and this is just the beginning. The arena is wide open, and the possibilities are endless.

1

Getting Started with Predictive Analytics

IN THIS PART . . .

Exploring predictive analytics

Identifying uses

Classifying data

Presenting information

Chapter 1

Entering the Arena

Predictive analytics is a bright light bulb powered by your data.

You can never have too much insight. The more you see, the better the decisions you make — and you never want to be in the dark. You want to see what lies ahead, preferably before others do. It's like playing the game "Let's Make a Deal" where you have to choose the door with the hidden prize. Which door do you choose? Door 1, Door 2, or Door 3? They all look the same, so it's just your best guess — your choice depends on you and your luck. But what if you had an edge — the ability to see through the keyhole? Predictive analytics can give you that edge.

Exploring Predictive Analytics

What would you do in a world where you know how likely you are to end up marrying your college roommate? Where you can predict what profession will best suit you? Where you can predict the best city and country for you to live in?

In short, imagine a world where you can maximize the potential of every moment of your life. Such a life would be productive, efficient, and powerful. You will (in effect) have superpowers — and a lot more spare time. Well, such a world may seem a little boring to people who like to take uncalculated risks, but not to a profit-generating organization. Organizations spend millions of dollars managing risk. And if there is something out there that helps them manage their risk, optimize their operations, and maximize their profits, you should definitely learn about it. That is the world of predictive analytics.

Mining data

Big data is the new reality. In fact, data is only getting bigger, faster, and richer. It's here to stay and you'd better capitalize on it.

Data is one of your organization's most valuable assets. It's full of hidden value, but you have to dig for it. *Data mining* is the discovery of hidden patterns of data through machine learning — and sophisticated algorithms are the mining tools. *Predictive analytics* is the process of refining that data resource, using business knowledge to extract hidden value from those newly discovered patterns.

Data mining + business knowledge = predictive analytics => value

Today's leading organizations are looking at their data, examining it, and processing it to search for ways to better understand their customer base, improve their operations, outperform their competitors, and better position themselves in the marketplace. They are looking into how they can use that information to increase their market share and sharpen their competitive edge. How can they drive better sales and more effectively target marketing campaigns? How can they better serve their customers and meet their needs? What can they do to improve the bottom line?

But these tools are useful in realms beyond business. As one major example, government law enforcement agencies are asking questions related to crime detection and prevention. Is this a person of interest? Will this criminal be a repeat offender? Where will the next crime happen?

Other industries, notably those with financial responsibility, could use a trustworthy glimpse into the future. Companies are trying to know whether the transaction they're currently processing is fraudulent, whether an insurance claim is legitimate, whether a credit card purchase is valid, whether a credit applicant is worthy of credit . . . the list goes on.

Governments, companies, and individuals are (variously) looking to spot trends in social movements, detect emerging healthcare issues and disease outbreaks, uncover new fashion trends, or find that perfect lifetime partner.

These — and plenty more — business and research questions are topics you can investigate further to find answers to by mining the available data and building predictive analytics models to guide future decisions.

Data + predictive analytics = light.

Highlighting the model

A *model* is a mathematical representation of an object or a process. We build models to simulate real-world phenomena as a further investigative step, in hopes of understanding more clearly what's really going on. For example, to model our customers' behavior, we seek to mimic how our customers have been navigating through our websites:

>> Which products did they look at before they made a purchase?

>> Which pages did they view before making that purchase?

>> Did they look at the products' descriptions?

>> Did they read users' reviews?

>> How many reviews did they read?

>> Did they read both positive and negative reviews?

>> Did they purchase something else in addition to the product they came looking for?

We collect all that data from past occurrences. We look at those historical transactions between our company and our customers — and try to make consistent sense of them. We examine that data and see whether it holds answers to our questions. Collecting that data — with particular attention to the breadth and depth of the data, its quality level, and its predictive value — helps to form the boundaries that will define our model and its outputs.

This process isn't to be confused with just reporting on the data; it's also different from just visualizing that data. Although those steps are vital, they're just the beginning of exploring the data and gaining a usable understanding of it.

We go a lot deeper when we're talking about developing predictive analytics. In the first place, we need to take a threefold approach:

>> Thoroughly understand the business problem we're trying to solve.

>> Obtain and prepare the data we want our model to work with.

>> Run statistical analysis, data-mining, and machine-learning algorithms on the data.

In the process, we have to look at various *attributes* — data points we think are relevant to our analysis. We'll run several *algorithms*, which are sets of mathematical instructions that get machines to do problem-solving. We keep running through possible combinations of data and investigate what-if scenarios. Eventually we build our model, find our answers, and prepare to deploy that model and reap its benefits.

What does a model look like? Well, in programming terms, a predictive analytics model can be as simple as a few `if ... then` statements that tell the machine, "If this condition exists, then perform this action."

Here are some simple rule-based trading models:

>> If it's past 10:00a.m. ET and the market is up, then buy 100 shares of XYZ stock.

>> If my stock is up by 10 percent, then take profits.

>> If my portfolio is down by 10 percent, then exit my positions.

Here's a simple rule-based recommender system (for more about recommender systems, see Chapter 2):

>> If a person buys a book by this author, then recommend other books by the same author.

>> If a person buys a book on this topic, then recommend other books on the same and related topic.

>> If a person buys a book on this topic, then recommend books that other customers have purchased when they bought this book.

Adding Business Value

In an increasingly competitive environment, organizations always need ways to become more competitive. Predictive analytics found its way into organizations as one such tool. Using technology in the form of machine-learning algorithms, statistics, and data-mining techniques (Chapter 3 shows how these disciplines differ and overlap), organizations can uncover hidden patterns and trends in their data that can aid in operations and strategy and help fulfill critical business needs.

Embedding predictive analytics in operational decisions improves return on investment because organizations spend less time dealing with low-impact, low-risk operational decisions. Employees can focus more of their time on high-impact, high-risk decisions. For example, most standard insurance claims can be automatically paid out. However, when the predictive model comes across a claim that's unusual (an outlier), or when the claim exhibits the same pattern as a fraudulent claim, the system can flag the claim automatically and send it to the appropriate person to take action.

By using predictive analytics to predict a future event or trend, the company can create a strategy to position itself to take advantage of that insight. If your predictive model is telling you (for example) that the trend in fashion is toward black turtlenecks, you can take appropriate actions to design more black-colored turtlenecks or design more accessories to go with the fashionable item. Tom Khabaza's Eighth Law of Data Mining summarizes this perfectly. "The value of a predictive model arises in two ways:

The model's predictions drive improved (more effective) action, and

The model delivers insight (new knowledge) which leads to improved strategy."

Endless opportunities

Organizations around the world are striving to improve, compete, and be lean. They're looking to make their planning process more agile. They're investigating how to manage inventories and optimize the allocations of their human resources to best advantage. They're looking to act on opportunities as they arise in real time.

Predictive analytics can make all those goals more reachable. The domains to which predictive analytics can be applied are unlimited; the arena is wide open and everything is fair game. Let the mining start. Let the analysis begin.

Go to your analytics team and have them mine the data you've accumulated or acquired, with an eye toward finding an advantageous niche market for your product; innovate with data. Ask the team to help you gain confidence in your decision-making and risk management.

Albert Einstein once said, "Know where to find information and how to use it; that is the secret of success." If that's the secret to success, then you will succeed by using predictive analytics: The information is in your data and data mining will find it. The rest of the equation relies on your business knowledge of how to interpret that information — and ultimately use it to create success.

Finding value in data equals success. Therefore we can rewrite our predictive analytics equation as

Data mining + business knowledge = predictive analytics => success

Empowering your organization

Predictive analytics empowers your organization by providing three advantages:

>> Vision

>> Decision

>> Precision

Vision

Predictive analytics will lead you to see what is invisible to others — in particular, useful patterns in your data.

Predictive analytics can provide you with powerful hints to lend direction to the decisions you're about to make in your company's quest to retain customers, attract more customers, and maximize profits. Predictive analytics can go through a lot of past customer data, associate it with other pieces of data, and assemble all the pieces in the right order to solve that puzzle in various ways, including

>> Categorizing your customers and speculating about their needs.

>> Knowing your customers' wish lists.

>> Guessing your customers' next actions.

>> Categorizing your customers as loyal, seasonal, or wandering.

Knowing this type of information beforehand shapes your strategic planning and helps optimize resource allocation, increase customer satisfaction, and maximize your profits.

Decision

A well-made predictive analytics model provides analytical results free of emotion and bias. The model uses mathematical functions to derive forward insights from numbers and text that describe past facts and current information. The model provides you with consistent and unbiased insights to support your decisions.

Consider the scenario of a typical application for a credit card: The process takes a few minutes; the bank or agency makes a quick, fact-based decision on whether to extend credit, and is confident in their decision. The speed of that transaction is possible thanks to predictive analytics, which predicted the applicant's creditworthiness.

Precision

Imagine having to read a lot of reports, derive insights from the past facts buried in them, go through rows of Excel spreadsheets to compare results, or extract information from a large array of numbers. You'd need a staff to do these time-consuming tasks. With predictive analytics, you can use automated tools to do the job for you — saving time and resources, reducing human error, and improving precision.

For example, you can focus targeted marketing campaigns by examining the data you have about your customers, their demographics, and their purchases. When you know precisely which customers you should market to, you can zero in on those most likely to buy.

Starting a Predictive Analytic Project

For the moment, let's forget about algorithms and higher math; predictions are used in every aspect of our lives. Consider how many times you have said (or heard people say), "I told you that was going to happen."

When you want to predict a future event with any accuracy, however, you'll need to know the past and understand the current situation. Doing so entails several processes:

» Extract the facts that are currently happening.

» Distinguish present facts from those that just happened.

» Derive possible scenarios that could happen.

» Rank the scenarios according to how likely they are to happen.

Predictive analytics can help you with each of these processes, so that you know as much as you can about what has happened and can make better-informed decisions about the future.

Companies typically create predictive analytics solutions by combining three ingredients:

» Business knowledge

» Data-science team and technology

» The data

Though the proportion of the three ingredients will vary from one business to the next, all are required for a successful predictive analytic solution that yields actionable insights.

Business knowledge

Because any predictive analytics project is started to fulfill a business need, business-specific knowledge and a clear business objective are critical to its success. Ideas for a project can come from anyone within the organization, but it's up to the leadership team to set the business goals and get buy-in from the needed departments across the whole organization.

Be sure the decision-makers in your team are prepared to act. When you present a prototype of your project, it needs an in-house champion — someone who's going to push for its adoption.

The leadership team or domain experts must also set clear *metrics* — ways to quantify and measure the outcome of the project. Appropriate metrics keep the departments involved clear about what they need to do, how much they need to do, and whether what they're doing is helping the company achieve its business goals.

The *business stakeholders* are those who are most familiar with the domain of the business. They'll have ideas about which correlations — relationships between features — of data work and which don't, which variables are important to the model, and whether you should create new variables — as in derived features or attributes — to improve the model.

Business analysts and other domain experts can analyze and interpret the patterns discovered by the machines, making useful meaning out of the data patterns and deriving actionable insights.

This is an *iterative* (building a model and interpreting its findings) process between business and science. In the course of building a predictive model, you have to try successive versions of the model to improve how it works (which is what data experts mean when they say *iterate the model over its lifecycle*). You might go through a lot of revisions and repetitions before you can prove that your model is bringing real value to the business. Even after the predictive models are deployed, the business must monitor the results, validate the accuracy of the models and improve upon the models as more data is being collected.

Data-science team and technology

The technology used in predictive analytics will include at least some (if not all) of these capabilities:

>> Data mining

>> Statistics

>> Machine-learning algorithms

>> Software tools to build the model

The business people needn't understand the details of all the technology used or the math involved — but they should have a good handle on the process that model represents, and on how it integrates with the overall infrastructure of your organization. Remember, this is a collaborative process; the data scientists and business people must work closely together to build the model.

By the same token, providing a good general grasp of business knowledge to the data scientists gives them a better chance at creating an accurate predictive model, and helps them deploy the model much more quickly. After the model is deployed, the business can start evaluating the results right away — and the teams can start working on improving the model. Through testing, the teams will learn together what works and what doesn't.

The combination of business knowledge, data exploration, and technology leads to a successful deployment of the predictive model. So the overall approach is to develop the model through successive versions and make sure the team members have enough knowledge of both the business and the data science that everyone is on the same page.

Some analytical tools — specialized software products — are advanced enough that they require people with scientific backgrounds to use them; others are simple enough that any business person within the organization can use them. Selecting the right tool(s) is also a decision that must be taken very carefully. Every company will have different needs and not any one tool can address all those needs. But one thing is certain; every company will have to use some sort of tool to do predictive analytics.

Selecting the right software product for the job depends on such factors as

>> The cost of the product

>> The complexity of the business problem

- >> The complexity of data

- >> The source(s) of the data

- >> The velocity of the data (the speed by which the data changes)

- >> The people within the organization who will use the product

The Data

All else being equal, you'd expect a person who has more experience to be better at doing a job, playing a game, or whatever than someone who has less experience. That same thinking can be applied to an organization. If you imagine an organization as a person, you can view the organization's data as its equivalent of experience. By using that experience, you can make more insightful business decisions and operate with greater efficiency. Such is the process of turning data into business value with predictive analytics.

It's increasingly clear that data is a vital asset for driving the decision-making process quick, realistic answers and insights. Predictive analytics empower business decisions by uncovering opportunities such as emerging trends, markets, or customers before the competition.

Data can also present a few challenges in its raw form. It can be distributed across multiple sources, mix your own data with third-party data, and otherwise make the quality of incoming data too messy to use right away. Thus you should expect your data scientists to spend considerable time exploring your data and preparing it for analysis. This process of *data cleansing* and *data preparation* involves spotting missing values, duplicate records, and outliers, generating derived values, and normalization. (For more about these processes, see Chapters 9 and 15.)

Big data has its own challenging properties that include volume, velocity, and variety: In effect, too much of it comes in too fast, from too many places, in too many different forms. Then the main problem becomes separating the relevant data from the noise surrounding it.

In such a case, your team has to evaluate the state of the data and its type, and choose the most suitable algorithm to run on that data. Such decisions are part of an exploration phase in which the data scientists gain intimate knowledge of your data while they're selecting which attributes have the most predictive power.

Ongoing Predictive Analytics

Predictive analytics should never be about implementing one project or two, even if those two projects are very successful. It should be an ongoing process that feeds into, and is enforced by, the governing body overseeing strategy and operational planning at your organization.

You should put data at the forefront of the decision-making process at your organization. Data must support any major initiatives. After collecting and acquiring all relevant data, have your data-science team make sense of it, and propose a way forward based on their findings. The outcomes of these efforts should reach the entire organization by fostering a cultural change that embraces the analytical work as an accepted way to make informed decisions.

Your work on predictive models doesn't stop at the moment you deploy them. That only gets your foot in the door. You should actually be constantly looking for ways to improve that model. Models tend to decay over time. So refreshing the model is a necessary step in building predictive analytics solutions. The model should be undergoing continuous improvement.

Additionally, you may have several models deployed, and each one of them may have undergone several revisions. In such case, it's imperative to have processes in place to manage the models' lifecycle, overseeing the creation, updating, and retiring of each model. Depending on the line of the business you're in, you may need to audit all changes and be very granular in your documentation of all steps involved in this process.

Your belief in the promise of predictive analytics should never stop you from questioning the results of a predictive analytics project. You can't just go ahead and implement blindly. You should make sure that the results make sense businesswise. Also, when the results are too good to be true, they probably are. Verify the correctness and accuracy of all steps followed to generate those models. Scrutinizing the models' results and asking the hard questions will only further your confidence in the decisions you will finally make based on those findings.

Sometimes the results of a predictive analytics project can be so obvious that business stakeholders may dismiss them altogether on the pretense that "we already knew that". Keep in mind, however, that making the effort to thoroughly understand the outputs of a model can be rewarding, no matter how obvious the results may seem at first.

When (for example) a model shows you that 90 percent of your customers are urban, and are between the ages of 25 and 45, the results may seem obvious. You may feel you wasted time and resources to only find out what you already knew.

It may be far more important, however, to ask *what the other 10% are made of.* How can you increase *their* percentages? You may need to build a new model to find out more about that segment of your customers. Or you may want to learn more about what attracts 90 percent of your customers to your product.

Building predictive analytics models should be an ongoing process and the results should be shared across the organization. You should always be looking to improve your models; never shy away from both experimenting and asking the hard questions. With relevant data, a talented data-science team, and the buy-in from the business stakeholders, the possibilities are endless.

Forming Your Predictive Analytics Team

A successful predictive analytics team blends the necessary skills and attitude. We'll bet you can find them in your organization.

Hiring experienced practitioners

The data-science team should be composed of experienced practitioners. Experienced data scientists know their way around data. They know what models work best for which business problems and data types.

It should be required for your data science team to have members with professional knowledge and proven experience in statistics, data mining, and machine learning. These three disciplines should be mandatory for any data science team; the idea is that these skills must exist within the team, not necessarily that every team member needs all three. However, hiring team members from diverse backgrounds can spice up and enrich your team. Other experiences and knowledge of other disciplines can make the overall team more rounded and can broaden its horizons.

Among the team members you hire to join your data-science team should be data scientists who have knowledge of your specific business domain. That business knowledge could come from past experience working on projects in your business domain or in fields or related to it. The more the team members know about your line of business, the easier it will be for them to work with your data and build analytical solutions.

There are many powerful tools provided by many vendors, in addition to great open source tools available to you. Your team members should have working knowledge with these tools. This will facilitate the life cycle of building analytical solutions. Also, that knowledge will facilitate collaboration across the team members and between business analysts and data scientists.

Demonstrating commitment and curiosity

Senior management should show their commitment to the analytical efforts. They should meet with the team members and follow the progress of their projects. They should allocate time to be briefed about the projects, their progress, and their final findings.

Your data science team members should believe in the mission and be committed to finding answers to the business questions they are after. Keeping the team members motivated and engaged will help allow them to thrive to deliver the best solutions. Team members should be curious and excited to achieve the business goals.

Your team members should be able to communicate their findings in a language understood by your business stakeholders. When the team members are able to communicate with the business stakeholders, they will be able to gather support for the new solutions and get the necessary buy-in. This is especially important when the business users will need to change the way they have been doing their work when they start applying the new findings.

The team members should be curious, always asking questions, and trying to learn as much as they can about their projects. By not shying away from asking the toughest questions about the data, methods used and models outputs, and not shying away from trying even the wackiest scenarios, the team members will deliver optimal solutions.

Collaboration among team members and across the rest of the organization is important to the success of these projects. Team members should be able to help each other and answer each other's questions. Also they should be able to share the results and get immediate feedback.

Surveying the Marketplace

Big data and predictive analytics are bringing equally big changes to academia, the job market, and virtually every competitive company out there. Everybody will feel the impact. The survivors will treat it as an opportunity.

Responding to big data

Numerous universities offer certificates and master's degrees in predictive analytics or big-data analytics; some of these degree programs have emerged within the past year or two. This reflects the amazing growth and popularity of this field. The occupation of "data scientist" is now being labeled as one of the sexiest jobs in America by popular job journals and websites.

This demand in job growth is expected to grow; the projection is that job positions will outnumber qualified applicants. Some universities are shifting their program offerings to take advantage of this growth and attract more students. Some offer analytics programs in their business schools; while others provide similar offerings in their science and engineering schools. Like the real-world applications that handle big data and predictive analytics, the discipline that makes use of them spans departments — you can find relevant course offerings in business, mathematics, statistics, and computer science. The result is the same: more attractive and relevant degree programs for today's economy, and more students looking for a growing occupational field.

Working with big data

We read stories every day about how a hot new company is springing up using predictive analytics to solve specific problems — from predicting what you will do at every turn throughout the day to scoring how suitable you are as a boyfriend. Pretty wild. No matter how outrageous the concept, someone seems to be doing it. People and companies do it for a straightforward reason: There is a market for it. There is a huge demand for social analytics, people analytics, *everything data* analytics.

Statisticians and mathematicians — whose primary task once consisted primarily of sitting at desks and crunching numbers for drug and finance companies — are now in the forefront of a data revolution that promises to predict nearly everything about nearly everyone — including you.

So why are we witnessing this sudden shift in analytics? After all, mathematics, statistics and their derivatives, computer science, machine learning, and data mining have been here for decades. In fact, most of the algorithms in use today to develop predictive models were created decades ago. The answer has to be "data" — lots of it.

We gather and generate huge amounts of data every day. Only recently have we been able to mine this data effectively. Processing power and data storage have increased exponentially while getting faster and cheaper. We've figured out how to use computer hardware to store and process large amounts of data.

AMAZING GROWTH

Throughout this book, we highlight several case studies that illustrate the successful use of predictive analytics. In this section, we'd like to highlight the crème de la crème of predictive analytics: Amazon.

As one of the largest online stores, Amazon is probably one of the best-known businesses associated with predictive analytics. Amazon analyzes endless streams of customer transactions in the quest to discover hidden purchasing patterns, as well as associations among products, customers, and purchases. When you want to see an effective recommender system in action, you'll find it working away on Amazon. Predictive analytics enabled Amazon to recommend products that are the exact product you always wanted, even that elusive "holy grail," the product you didn't realize you wanted. This is the power of analytics and predictive modeling seeing patterns in enormous amounts of data.

To create its recommender system, Amazon uses *collaborative filtering* — an algorithm that looks at information on its users and on its products. By looking at the items currently in a user's shopping cart, as well as at items they've purchased, rated, and liked in the past — and then linking them to what other customers have purchased — Amazon cross-sells customers with those one-line recommendations we're all familiar with, such as

Frequently Bought Together

Customers Who Bought This Item Also Bought

Amazon goes even farther in its use of data: Besides generating more money by cross-selling and making marketing recommendations to its customers, Amazon uses the data to build a relationship with its customers — customized results, customized web pages, and personalized customer service. Data fuels every level of the company's interaction with its customers. And customers respond positively to it; Amazon revenues continue to soar every quarter.

The field that comprises computers, software development, programming, and making profitable use of the Internet has opened up an environment where everyone can be creatively involved. Most people on earth are now connected via the World Wide Web, social networking, smartphones, tablets, apps, you name it. We spend countless hours on the Internet daily — and generate data every minute while we're at it. With that much online data, it was only natural that companies would start seeing it as a resource to be mined and refined, seeking patterns in our online behavior and exploiting what they find in hopes to capitalizing on this new opportunity. Amazon (see the accompanying sidebar) is a famous example.

In short, this is only the beginning.

Chapter 2

Predictive Analytics in the Wild

redictive analytics sounds like a fancy name, but we use much the same process naturally in our daily decision-making. Sometimes it happens so fast that most of us don't even recognize when we're doing it. We call that process "intuition" or "gut instinct": In essence, it's quickly *analyzing* a situation to *predict* an outcome — and then making a decision.

When a new problem calls for decision-making, natural gut instinct works most like predictive analytics when you've already had some experience in solving a similar problem. Everyone relies on individual experience, and so solves the problem or handles the situation with different degrees of success.

You'd expect the person with the most experience to make the best decisions, on average, over the long run. In fact, that is the most likely outcome for simple problems with relatively few influencing factors. For more complex problems, complex external factors influence the final result.

A hypothetical example is getting to work on time on Friday morning: You wake up in the morning 15 minutes later than you normally do. You predict — using data gathered from experience — that traffic is lighter on Friday morning than during the rest of the week. You know some general factors that influence traffic congestion:

>> How many commuters are going to work at the same time

>> Whether popular events (such as baseball games) are scheduled in the area you're driving through

>> Emerging events like car accidents and bad weather

Of course, you may have considered the unusual events (*outliers*) but disregarded them as part of your normal decision-making. Over the long run, you'll make a better decision about local traffic conditions than a person who just moved to the area. The net effect of that better decision mounts up: Congratulations — you've gained an extra hour of sleep every month.

But such competitive advantages don't last forever. As other commuters realize this pattern, they'll begin to take advantage of it as well — and also sleep in for an extra 15 minutes. Your returns from analyzing the Friday traffic eventually start to diminish if you don't continually *optimize* your get-to-work-on-Fridays *model*.

A model built with predictive analytics could handle far more than the few variables (influencing factors) that a human can process. A predictive model built with decision trees can find patterns with as many independent variables as can access, and may lead to a discovery that a certain variable is more influential than you initially thought. If you're a robot and can follow the rules of the decision tree, you can probably shave more time from the commute.

More complex problems lead, of course, to more complex analysis. Many factors contribute to the final decision, besides (and beyond) what the specific, immediate problem is asking for. A good example is predicting whether a stock will go up or down. At the core of the problem is a simple question: Will the stock go up or down? A simple answer is hard to get because the stock market is so fluid and dynamic. The *influencers* that affect a particular stock price are potentially unlimited in number.

Some influencers are logical; some are illogical. Some can't be predicted with any accuracy. Regardless, Nasim Taleb operates a hedge fund that bets on *black swans* — events that are very unlikely to happen, but when they do happen, the rewards can be tremendous. In his book *Black Swan*, he says that he only has to be right once in a decade. For the most of us, that investment strategy probably wouldn't work; the amount of capital required to start would have to be substantially more than most of us make — because it would diminish while waiting for the major event to happen.

After the market closes, news reporters and analysts will try to explain the move with one reason or another. Was it a *macro event* (say, the whole stock market going up or down) or a smaller, company-specific event (say, the company released some bad news or someone tweeted negatively about its products)? Either way, be careful not to read too much into such factors; they can also be used to explain when the exact opposite result happened. Building an accurate model to predict a stock movement is still very challenging.

Predicting the correct direction of a stock with consistency has a rigid outcome: Either you make money or lose money. But the market isn't rigid: What holds true one day may not hold true the very next day. Fortunately, most such *predictive modeling* tasks aren't quite as complicated as predicting a stock's move upward or downward on a given trading day. Predictive analytics are more commonly used to find insights into nearly everything from marketing to law enforcement:

>> People's buying patterns

>> Pricing of goods and services

>> Large-scale future events such as weather patterns

>> Unusual and suspicious activities

These are just a few (highly publicized) examples of predictive analytics. The potential applications are endless.

Online Marketing and Retail

Companies that have successfully used predictive analytics to improve their sales and marketing include Target Corporation, Amazon, and Netflix. Recent reports by Gartner, IBM, Sloan, and Accenture all suggest that many executives use data and predictive analytics to drive sales.

Recommender systems

You've probably already encountered one of the major outgrowths of predictive analytics: *recommender systems*. These systems try to predict your interests (for example, what you want to buy or watch) and give you recommendations. They do this by matching your preferences with items or other like-minded people, using statistics and machine learning algorithms.

If you're an online cruiser, you often see prompts like these on web pages:

>> People You May Know . . .

>> People Who Viewed This Item Also Viewed . . .

>> People Who Viewed This Item Bought . . .

>> Recommended Based on Your Browsing History . . .

>> Customers Who Bought This Item Also Bought . . .

These are examples of recommendation systems that were made mainstream by companies like Amazon, Netflix, and LinkedIn.

Obviously, these systems weren't created only for the user's convenience — although that reason is definitely one part of the picture. No, recommender systems were created to maximize company profits. They attempt to personalize shopping on the Internet, with an algorithm serving as the salesperson. They were designed to sell, up-sell, cross-sell, keep you engaged, and keep you coming back. The goal is to turn each personalized shopper into a repeat customer. (The sidebar "The personal touch" explores one of the successful techniques.)

Personalized shopping on the Internet

A software recommender system is like an online salesperson who tries to replicate the personal process we experienced at the trade shows. What's different about a recommender system is that it's data-driven. It makes recommendations in volume, with some subtlety (even stealth), with a dash of unconventional wisdom and without a feeling of bias. When a customer buys a product — or shows interest in a product (say, by viewing it), the system recommends a product or service that it considers highly relevant to that customer — automatically. The goal is to generate more sales — sales that wouldn't happen if the recommendation(s) weren't given.

Amazon is a very successful example of implementing a recommender system; their success story highlights its importance. When you browse for an item on the Amazon website, you always find some variation on the theme of related items — "Customers who viewed this also viewed" or "Customers who bought items in your recent history also bought."

This highly effective technique is considered one of Amazon's "killer" features — and a big reason for their huge success as the dominant online marketplace. Amazon brilliantly adapted a successful offline technique practiced by salespeople — and perfected it for the online world.

THE PERSONAL TOUCH

One of the authors used to work for a speech-recognition company that made order-handling systems for the top Wall Street firms. Every day the company would have to analyze a huge number of trade messages for accuracy and speed. The company came up with a system that was extremely accurate and fast. Using millions of trade messages, they constantly trained and fine-tuned the speech engine to adapt to each user's unique speech profile. The key concept was the use of text analytics and machine learning to predict what the user (in this case, a trader) was going to do (trade) based on what the user was saying:

- How the grammar was formed

- Quantifiable attributes such as the size of the trade

- Whether the trader was buying or selling

The predictive model, created with an ensemble of machine-learning algorithms, would spot patterns in the user's orders — and assign weights to each word that could potentially come next. Then, after the speech engine parsed each word, the system would start predicting which word would come next. The model worked much like an auto-complete feature, using a recommender system.

The company also made noise-cancelling microphones and headsets to compensate for high-noise environments such as trade shows where the products were demonstrated. We would consistently be a convention favorite; our booths would be packed with attendees waiting to participate in our demos. We started selling the products directly at the booth, and we'd have lines of buyers throughout the day.

We had a lot of fun interacting with customers instead of the normal daily routine in front of the computer, programming or analyzing data. We cross-sold accessories and up-sold more expensive microphones and headsets. But the demos and direct selling at the trade shows taught us important lessons: We were so successful not only because we gave great product demos, but also because we were recommending products of ours that would best suit the customers' needs — based on the information they gave us. We weren't only presenters but also salespeople; we were the "live-action" recommender system.

Amazon popularized recommender systems for e-commerce. Their successful example has made recommender systems so popular and important in e-commerce that other companies are following suit.

Implementing a Recommender System

There are three main approaches to creating a recommender system: collaborative filtering, content-based filtering, and a combination of both called the hybrid approach. The collaborative filtering approach uses the collective actions of the user to achieve the goal of predicting the user's future behavior. The content-based approach attempts to match a particular user's preferences to an item without regard to other users' opinions. There are challenges to both the collaborative and content-based filtering approaches, which the hybrid approach attempts to solve.

Collaborative filtering

Collaborative filtering focuses on user and item characteristics based on the actions of the community. It can group users with similar interests or tastes, using classification algorithms such as *k-nearest neighbor* — k-NN for short (see Chapter 6 for more on k-NN). It can compute the similarity between items or users, using similarity measures such as cosine similarity (discussed in the next section).

The general concept is to find groups of people who like the same things: If person A likes X, then person B will also like X. For example: If Tiffany likes watching *Frozen*, then her *neighbor* (person with similar taste) Victoria will also like watching *Frozen*.

Collaborative filtering algorithms generally require

>> A community of users to generate data

>> Creating a database of interests for items by users

>> Formulas that can compute the similarity between items or users

>> Algorithms that can match users with similar interests

Collaborative filtering uses two approaches: item-based and user-based.

Item-based collaborative filtering

One of Amazon's recommender systems uses *item-based collaborative filtering* — doling out a huge inventory of products from the company database when a user views a single item on the website.

TIP

You know you're looking at an item-based collaborative filtering system (or, often, a content-based system) if it shows you recommendations at your very first item view, even if you haven't created a profile.

Looks like magic, but it's not. Although your profile hasn't been created yet (because you aren't logged in or you don't have any previous browser history on that site) the system takes what amounts to a guess: It bases its recommendation on *the item itself* and *what other customers viewed or bought after (or before) they purchased that item*. So you'll see some onscreen message like

Customers who bought this item also bought . . .

Customers who bought items in your recent history also bought . . .

Which other items do customers buy after viewing this item?

In essence, the recommendation is based on how similar the currently viewed item is to other items, based on the actions of the community of users.

Table 2-1 shows a sample matrix of customers and the items they purchased. It will be used as an example of item-based collaborative filtering.

TABLE 2-1   ## Item-Based Collaborative Filtering

Customer	Item 1	Item 2	Item 3	Item 4	Item 5	Item 6
A	X	X	X			
B	X	X				
C			X		X	
D			X	X	X	
E		X	X			
F	X	X		X	X	
G	X		X			
H	X					
I						X

Table 2-2 shows a table of item similarity calculated using the cosine similarity formula. The formula for *cosine similarity* is $(A \cdot B) / (\|A\| \|B\|)$, where A and B are items to compare. To read the table and find out how similar a pair of items are, just locate the cell where the two items intersect. The number will be between 0 and 1. A value of 1 means the items are perfectly similar; 0 means they aren't similar.

The system can provide a list of recommendations that are above a certain similarity value or can recommend the top *n* number of items. In this scenario, we can say that any value greater than or equal to 0.40 is similar; the system will recommend those items.

TABLE 2-2   **Item Similarity**

	Item 1	Item 2	Item 3	Item 4	Item 5	Item 6
Item 6	0	0	0	0	0	–
Item 5	0.26	0.29	0.52	0.82		0
Item 4	0.32	0.35	0.32		0.82	0
Item 3	0.40	0.45		0.32	0.52	0
Item 2	0.67		0.45	0.35	0.29	0
Item 1		0.67	0.40	0.32	0.26	0

For example, the similarity between item 1 and item 2 is 0.67. The similarity between item 2 and item 1 is the same. Thus the table is a mirror image across the diagonal from lower-left to upper-right. You can also see that item 6 isn't similar to any other items because it has a value of 0.

This implementation of an item-based recommendation system is simplified to illustrate how it works. For simplicity, we only use one criterion to determine item similarity: whether the user purchased the item. More complex systems could go into greater detail by

» Using profiles created by users that represent their tastes

» Factoring in how much a user likes (or highly rates) an item

» Weighing how many items the user purchased that are similar to the potential recommended item(s)

» Making assumptions about whether a user likes an item on the basis of whether the user has simply viewed the item, even though no purchase was made

Here are two common ways you could use this recommender system:

» **Offline** via an e-mail marketing campaign or when the user is on the website while logged in.

  The system could send marketing ads or make these recommendations on the website:

  • **Item 3 to Customer B**

    Recommended because Customer B purchased Items 1 and 2, and both items are similar to Item 3.

  • **Item 4, then Item 2, to Customer C**

Recommended because Customer C purchased Items 3 and 5. Item 5 is similar to Item 4 (similarity value: 0.82). Item 2 is similar to Item 3 (similarity value: 0.45).

- **Item 2 to Customer D**

  Recommended because Customer D purchased Items 3, 4, and 5. Item 3 is similar to Item 2.

- **Item 1 to Customer E**

  Recommended because Customer E purchased Items 2 and 3, both of which are similar to Item 1.

- **Item 3 to Customer F**

  Recommended because Customer F purchased Items 1, 2, 4, and 5. Items 1, 2, and 5 are similar to Item 3.

- **Item 2 to Customer G**

  Recommended because Customer G purchased Items 1 and 3. They are both similar to Item 2.

- **Item 2, then Item 3, to Customer H**

  Recommended because Customer H purchased Item 1. Item 1 is similar to Items 2 and 3.

- **Undetermined item to Customer A**

  Ideally, you should have a lot more items and users. And there should be some items that a customer has purchased that are similar to other items that he or she hasn't yet purchased.

- **Undetermined item to Customer I**

  In this case, the data is insufficient to serve as the basis of a recommendation. This is an example of the cold-start problem (more about this problem later in this chapter).

» **Online** via a page view while the user isn't logged in.

Order matters — the recommendations must start from highest similarity, unless there are other overriding factors, such as inventory or profitability.

The system would recommend similar items when the user is viewing one of its items:

- If Item 1 is being viewed, the system recommends Items 2 and 3.

- If Item 2 is being viewed, the system recommends Items 1 and 3.

- If Item 3 is being viewed, the system recommends Items 5, 2, and 1.

- If Item 4 is being viewed, the system recommends Items 5.

- If Item 5 is being viewed, the system recommends Items 4 and 3.

- If Item 6 is being viewed, there is insufficient data to make a recommendation. This is an example of the cold-start problem (as described later in this chapter).

REMEMBER

Whether the user is logged in will affect the recommendation that the system makes. After all, you want to avoid recommending an item that the customer has already purchased. When the user is logged in, the system will use the profile that the user created (or it created for the user). Within that profile, the system will have a record of previous purchases; it removes already-purchased items from the recommendation list.

In the example, Customer H only purchased a single item (Item 1). However, the item she purchased was similar to other items that show up in data from other customer purchases.

A customer viewing Item 6 is an example of the cold-start problem: Item 6 hasn't been purchased by enough people yet, perhaps because it's new or it isn't very popular. Either way, the system doesn't have enough to go on. Collaborative filtering takes a little training with data before it can be effective. In that case, the system can take the approach of making the most purchased (or profitable, or liked) item the default recommendation.

Initially, of course, these data tables will be sparse until enough data points come in. As more data points are included in the collaborative filtering algorithm, the recommender system becomes more accurate.

User-based collaborative filtering

With a user-based approach to collaborative filtering, the system can calculate similarity between pairs of users by using the cosine similarity formula, a technique much like the item-based approach. Usually such calculations take longer to do, and may need to be computed more often, than those used in the item-based approach. That's because

>> You'd have a lot more users than items (ideally anyway).

>> You'd expect items to change less frequently than users.

>> With more users and less change in the items offered, you can use many more attributes than just purchase history when calculating user similarity.

A user-based system can also use machine-learning algorithms to group all users who have shown that they have the same tastes. The system builds neighborhoods of users who have similar profiles, purchase patterns, or rating patterns. When a person in a neighborhood buys and likes an item, the recommender system can recommend that item to everyone else in the neighborhood.

As with item-based collaborative filtering, the user-based approach requires sufficient data on each user to be effective. Before the system can make recommendations, it must create a user profile — so it also requires that the user create an account and be logged in (or store session information in the browser via cookies) while viewing a website. Initially the system can ask the user explicitly to create a profile, flesh out the profile by asking questions, and then optimize its suggestions after the user's purchase data has accumulated.

Netflix is an example of quickly building a profile for each customer. Here's the general procedure:

1. Netflix invites its customers to set up queues of the movies they'd like to watch.
2. The chosen movies are analyzed to learn about the customer's tastes in movies.
3. The predictive model recommends more movies for the customer to watch, based on the movies already in the queue.

TIP

Netflix has discovered that the more movies you have in your queue, the more likely you are to stay a customer.

Table 2-3 — a sample matrix of customers and their purchased items — is an example of user-based collaborative filtering. For simplicity, we will use a rule that a user neighborhood is created from users who bought at least two things in common.

TABLE 2-3   ## User-Based Collaborative Filtering

Customer	Item 1	Item 2	Item 3	Item 4	Item 5	Item 6
A - N1	X	X	X			
B - N1	X	X				
C - N2			X		X	
D - N2			X	X	X	
E - N1		X	X			
F - N1	X	X		X	X	
G - N1	X		X			
H - N3	X					
I - N3						X

There are three user neighborhoods formed: N1, N2, and N3. Every user in neighborhoods N1 and N2 has purchased at least 2 items in common with someone else in the same neighborhood. N3 are users that haven't yet met the criteria and will not receive recommendations until they purchase other items to meet the criteria.

Here's an example of how you could use this recommender system:

Offline via an e-mail marketing campaign or when the user is on the website while logged in. The system could send marketing ads or make recommendations on the website as follows:

>> **Item 3 to Customer B**

>> **Item 4 to Customer C**

>> **Item 1 to Customer E**

>> **Item 3 to Customer F**

>> **Item 2 to Customer G**

>> **Undetermined item to Customers A and D**

TIP

Ideally you should have a lot more items than six. And there should always be some items in a customer's neighborhood that the customer hasn't purchased yet.

>> **Undetermined item to Customers H and I**

In this case, there is insufficient data to serve as the basis of a recommendation.

Initially, this system can recommend all items that other members of the group already have that each individual member doesn't have. In this simple example, the recommendations are similar to those produced by the item-based collaborative filter approach. You should expect the recommendations to diverge between approaches as more users, items, and data points come in.

TIP

One very important difference is that since each customer belongs to a group, any future purchases that a member makes will be recommended to the other members of the group until the filter is retrained. So customers A and D will start getting recommendations very quickly since they already belong to a neighborhood and surely the other neighbors will buy something soon.

For example: If Customer B buys Item 6, then the recommender system will recommend item 6 to everyone in N1 (Customer A, B, E, F and G).

Customer F can potentially belong to either neighborhood N1 or N2 depending how the collaborative filtering algorithm is implemented. We have chosen to group Customer F with neighborhood N1 because the user is most similar to Customer B (which belongs to N1) using cosine similarity measure. Either way, Item 3 will be recommended under this scenario.

Customers H and I provide examples of the *cold-start problem:* The customer just hasn't generated enough data to be grouped into a user neighborhood. In the absence of a user profile, a new customer with very little or no purchase history — or who only buys obscure items — will always pose the cold-start problem to the system, regardless of which collaborative filtering approach is in use.

Customer I illustrates an aspect of the cold-start problem that's unique to the user-based approach. The item-based approach would start finding other items similar to the item that the customer bought; then, when other users start purchasing Item 6, the system can start making recommendations. No further purchases need be made by the user; the item-based approach can start recommending. In a user-based system, however, Customer I has to make additional purchases in order to belong to a neighborhood of users; the system can't make any recommendations yet.

Okay, there's an assumption at work in these simple examples — namely, that the customer not only purchased the item but liked it enough to make similar purchases. What if the customer didn't like the item? The system needs, at very least, to produce better precision in its recommendations. You can add a criterion to the recommender system to group people who gave similar ratings to the items they purchased. When the system finds customers who like and dislike the same items, then the assumption of high precision is valid. In other words, there is a high probability that the customers share the same tastes.

User-based versus item-based collaborative filtering

In general, item-based collaborative filtering for large-scale e-commerce systems is faster and more scalable. Finding similar users, however — especially users with lots of features — takes longer than finding similar items.

TIP

Building user neighborhoods may be too time-consuming for large datasets, and may not be appropriate for large e-commerce sites that depend on real-time recommendations.

The user-based system also suffers more acutely than the item-based system from two other challenges: the cold-start problem (mentioned earlier) and *sparsity* — essentially the fact that even the most prolific customers can't be expected to purchase even a fraction of a percent of the whole product catalog.

So building user neighborhoods based on limited purchase histories may not produce very accurate recommendations.

The user-based approach also comes with a key restriction: Each user has to be logged in (or have a profile in his or her browser history) for user-based filtering to work. Before the system can make a recommendation, it has to know something about the prospective customer.

Content-based filtering

Content-based recommender systems mostly match *features* (tagged keywords) among similar items and the user's profile to make recommendations. When a user purchases an item that has tagged features, items with features that match those of the original item will be recommended. The more features match, the higher the probability the user will like the recommendation. This degree of probability is called *precision.*

Content-based filtering uses various techniques to match the attributes of a particular item with a user's profile. These techniques include machine-learning algorithms to determine a user's profile without having to ask. This technique is called *implicit data gathering.* A more direct approach is to use *explicit data gathering:* Use a questionnaire to ask the users what features they like in an item. An example of that would be asking what genre of movie or which actresses they like when they first sign up for a movie subscription.

Tagging to describe items

In general, the company doing the selling (or the manufacturer) usually tags its items with keywords. In the Amazon website, however, it's fairly typical never to see the tags for any items purchased or viewed — and not even to be asked to tag an item. Customers can review the items they've purchased, but that isn't the same as tagging.

Tagging items can pose a scale challenge for a store like Amazon that has so many items. Additionally, some attributes can be subjective and may be incorrectly tagged, depending on who tags it. One solution that solves the scaling issue is to allow customers or the general public to tag the items. (Photos are a good example of user-based tagging.) To keep tags manageable and accurate, an acceptable set of tags may be provided by the website. Only when an appropriate number of users agree (that is, use the same tag to describe an item), will the agreed-upon tag be used to describe the item.

User-based tagging, however, turns up other problems for a content-based filtering system (and collaborative filtering):

>> **Credibility:** Not all customers tell the truth (especially online), and users who have only a small rating history can skew the data. In addition, some vendors may give (or encourage others to give) positive ratings to their own products while giving negative ratings to their competitors' products.

>> **Sparsity:** Not all items will be rated or will have enough ratings to produce useful data.

>> **Inconsistency:** Not all users use the same keywords to tag an item, even though the meaning may be the same. Additionally, some attributes can be subjective. For example, one viewer of a movie may consider it short while another says it's too long.

Attributes need clear definitions. An attribute with too few boundaries is hard to evaluate; imposing too many rules on an attribute may be asking users to do too much work, which will discourage them from tagging items.

TIP

Attributes with vague or undefined boundaries can result from offering the user free-form input fields on e-commerce shopping forms. When you restrict the user to selecting tag values from a set range of possible inputs, the resulting data is easier to analyze; you won't have to cleanse "dirty data" of irrelevant content. Of course, many existing systems were built without analytics in mind, so cleansing the data is a large part of data preparation. You can save some of that cleansing time by building predictive analytic solutions into your system. One way to do so is to carefully consider and define the allowable inputs when you're (re)building your e-commerce site.

Tagging most items in a product catalog can help solve the cold-start problem that plagues collaborative filtering. For a while, however, the precision of the system's recommendations will be low until it creates or obtains a user profile.

Table 2-4, a sample matrix of customers and their purchased items, shows an example of content-based filtering.

TABLE 2-4 **Content-Based Filtering**

Items	Feature 1	Feature 2	Feature 3	Feature 4	Feature 5
Item 1	X	X			
Item 2		X	X		
Item 3	X		X	X	
Item 4		X		X	X
Item 5	X		X		X

Here, when a user likes Feature 2 — and that's recorded in her profile — the system will recommend all items that have Feature 2 in them: Item 1, Item 2, and Item 4.

This approach works even when the user has never purchased or reviewed an item. The system will just look in the product database for any item that has been tagged with Feature 2. If (for example) a user who's looking for movies with Audrey Hepburn — and that preference shows up in the user's profile — the system will recommend all the movies that feature Audrey Hepburn to this user.

This example, however, quickly exposes a limitation of the content-based filtering technique: The user probably already knows about all the movies that Audrey Hepburn has been in, or can easily find out — so, from that user's point of view, the system hasn't recommended anything new or of value. In this case, the system should recommend something relevant that the user wouldn't have thought of. In the absence of telepathy, what's needed is greater precision.

Improving precision with constant feedback

One way to improve the precision of the system's recommendations is to ask customers for feedback whenever possible. Collecting customer feedback can be done in many different ways, through multiple channels. Some companies ask the customer to rate an item or service after purchase. Other systems provide social-media-style links so customers can "like" or "dislike" a product. Constant interaction between customers and companies may make the customer feel more fully engaged.

For example, Netflix asks its customers to rate movies they've watched so that the company can use that data to train their systems (models) to make more precise movie recommendations. Amazon sends you an e-mail asking you to rate items you've purchased after you've had enough time to evaluate the product and the buying experience.

Such data points constantly improve the recommendation models — and they're possible because Amazon and Netflix make a point of convincing customers that their feedback benefits all customers. Such continuous interaction with customers to collect feedback not only increases the precision of the system's recommendations, it can also make customers happier, reduce churn (subscription cancellation), and generate repeat business. This is a type of cycle that results in more product sales that generate more revenue for the company.

Measuring the effectiveness of system recommendations

The success of a system's recommendations depends on how well it meets two criteria: *precision* (think of it as a set of perfect matches — usually a small set) and *recall* (think of it as a set of possible matches — usually a larger set). Here's a closer look:

>> **Precision** measures how accurate the system's recommendation was. Precision is difficult to measure because it can be subjective and hard to quantify. For example, when a user first visits the Amazon site, can Amazon know for sure whether its recommendations are on target? Some recommendations may connect with the customer's interests but the customer may still not buy. The highest confidence that a recommendation is precise comes from clear evidence: The customer buys the item. Alternatively, the system can explicitly ask the user to rate its recommendations.

>> **Recall** measures the set of possible good recommendations your system comes up with. Think of recall as an inventory of possible recommendations, but not all of them are perfect recommendations. There is generally an inverse relationship to precision and recall. That is, as recall goes up, precision goes down, and vice versa. You can't expect to have a large inventory of items that a customer *will* buy. You may expect to have a large inventory of items that a customer *might* consider buying. But a large inventory is only half the battle; see the cautionary sidebar, "Precision versus recall."

>> The ideal system has both high precision and high recall. But realistically, the best outcome is to strike a delicate balance between the two. Emphasizing precision or recall really depends on the problem you're trying to solve.

WARNING

One major problem with content-based recommender systems is that it's easy to give them too narrow a focus. They make recommendations based on past purchases, likes, and dislikes. They may fall short for customers who want to try new things and experiences. Those customers want to hear about something totally different from what they've already bought or seen. People can be unpredictable that way.

Hybrid recommender systems

The best implementation may be a *hybrid* approach to creating a recommender system. By combining content-based and collaborative filtering into a single approach, the system can try to overcome each one's shortcomings.

A major problem with the content-based approach is its accuracy and narrow focus. The recommendations may not be very interesting or unique. Many of the recommendations may have already been known to the user, so the system isn't providing anything new from the user's perspective. However, the implementation is much simpler than that of collaborative filtering. The content-based approach requires only that a profile be created for the items (keyword tagging). The user's profile can be implicitly or explicitly created. This system can start working right away.

PRECISION VERSUS RECALL

The relationship between precision and recall is best described through an example: A recommendation system generally recommends a list of several items (the top *n*), not just one or two. Let's assume that the recommendation list only contains two precise recommendations. So the system can recommend those two items and it will have perfect precision. However, what if you need to show recommendations for an e-mail campaign that has 10 slots? You must include 8 other possible recommendations that aren't perfectly precise. Those additional 8 recommendations bring down the precision. In contrast, recall has gone up because the system determined that there were 20 possible recommendations, of which the system initially only showed the top two. Recall has gone up from 2/20 to 10/20.

Having a large inventory of recommendations seems an advantage, but what if they keep failing to stimulate a sale? Well, one problem is the customers' reaction if they perceive the system's recommendations as poor: They lose interest and go elsewhere. Thus offering everything and anything just to fish for possible sales can cause more damage than good: Repeated off-target recommendations can irritate customers; future attempts to market to those customers may end up in the spam folder.

Take, for example, a job-listing site sends a customer even one advertisement for a job that is completely inappropriate for the customer — say, advertising an opening in heavy construction to a person whose experience and expertise are in running a florist's shop. The customer will probably consider the recommendation poor, even crazy. If the company doesn't boost the precision of its recommendation algorithm, there goes the job seeker to a competing job-listing site.

A major problem with collaborative filtering is that it suffers from the cold-start problem. Many users who are just starting out won't receive accurate recommendations — or any recommendations at all — until enough data is gathered from the community of users. The data collection will require time to complete — and that collection depends on how active the website is. It may also require users to create accounts in their systems (in order to create a profile) before they can start receiving recommendations.

A hybrid recommender system can try to solve both these problems. It can start by using the content-based approach to avoid the cold-start problem. After enough data is collected from the community of users, the system can then use the collaborative filtering approach to produce more interesting and personalized recommendations.

Target Marketing

Predictive analytics make your marketing campaigns more customer-oriented. The idea is to customize your advertisements to target a segment of your total customer base — not the whole. If you send only the ads that are relevant to a segment of customers, you increase the likelihood that those particular visitors will perform the action that you hope for — buying. When you can determine which segment of your customer base will respond best to your message, you save money on the cost of convincing a customer to make the purchase (acquisition costs) and improve overall efficiency.

For example, when you pay an online ad network — for example, Google AdWords — to display your ads, typically you pay for each click that sends traffic to your website through a sponsored ad that appears in response to a search. Getting the visitor ultimately to do what you hope she'll do while she's on your website — become a paying customer — should be part of your marketing strategy. This type of marketing cost structure is called *pay per click*. You pay the network (in this case, Google) for each click, whether or not the visitor converts into a sale.

Because you're paying for each click with no guarantee of converting each visit into a sale, you'll want to create some sort of filter to ensure that those likeliest to become customers receive your advertisement. No point displaying your ad to just anyone — a shotgun strategy is far from optimal, and your acquisition costs would be through the roof. Your ad's target audience should be those visitors who have the highest chance of conversion.

This is where predictive analytics can come to your aid for target marketing. By creating an effective predictive model that ranks the customers in your database according to who is most likely to buy, subscribe, or meet some other organizational goal, you have the potential to increase the return on your marketing investment. Specifically, predictive analytics for marketing can

>> Increase profitability

>> Increase your conversion ratio

>> Increase customer satisfaction by reducing unwanted contact

>> Increase operational efficiencies

>> Learn what works (or doesn't) in each marketing campaign

Targeting using predictive modeling

Traditional marketing targets a group of customers without applying such modern techniques as predictive modeling using data-mining, and machine-learning algorithms to the dataset. Predictive modeling, in the area of direct marketing is called *response modeling using predictive analytics* (or simply *response modeling* from here on). Sometimes analysts create filters to apply to the dataset, thereby creating a select group to target. But that select group may not be optimally configured. Response modeling, on the other hand, seeks to discover patterns in the data that are present but not immediately apparent (in part because the number of variables being considered is nearly always greater than the number of variables that would be present in a marketer's segment or "filter"); the result is an optimized group to target.

Table 2-5 uses a small sample to compare the profit generated by direct mailings — traditional marketing versus response modeling.

TABLE 2-5   ## Comparing Direct Mailing Results (Small Sample)

	Traditional Marketing	Response Modeling
Number of customers targeted	1000	100
Cost per customer targeted (assume $2)	$2	$2
Number of responses	20	10
Response rate	2 percent	10 percent
Total revenue (assume $100 per response)	$2,000	$1,000
Total cost of campaign	$2,000	$200
Total profit	$0	$800

In Table 2-5, response modeling has targeted 10 percent of the traditional number of customers (100 instead of 1000) to an optimized subset. The response rate should be higher with response modeling — 10 percent instead of the 2 percent that is typical for traditional marketing. The net result is a profit of $800 under response modeling; traditional marketing breaks even. Also, as per-customer targeting costs increase, response modeling's value gets even better — without even taking into account the implicit benefits of not targeting unqualified customers.

When you make constant contact with a customer without providing any benefit, you run the risk of being ignored in the future.

TIP

Table 2-6 is an example that shows the profit comparison between direct mailings using traditional marketing and response modeling with a larger sample size.

TABLE 2-6   **Comparing Direct Mailing Results (Larger Sample)**

	Traditional Marketing	Response Modeling
Number of customers targeted	10000	1000
Cost per customer targeted	$2	$2
Number of responses	200	100
Response rate	2 percent	10 percent
Total revenue (assume $100 per response)	$20,000	$10,000
Total cost of campaign	$20,000	$2000
Total profit	$0	$8,000

In Table 2-6, response modeling has (again) targeted only 10 percent of the 10,000 prospective customers traditionally targeted. In an optimized subset of 1,000, the response rate should be higher. We assumed a response rate of 2 percent for a traditional direct-mailing marketing campaign; with response modeling, the response rate is 10 percent because the customers are likelier to buy in the first place.

Response modeling creates a profit of $8,000 under this scenario; traditional marketing breaks even. As in the preceding scenario, any revenue earned using traditional marketing is consumed by marketing costs. Thus, as the accuracy of customers targeted, increases, the value of response modeling also increases.

Response modeling also applies to email marketing campaigns, even though the production costs are much cheaper than other channels. Fatigue from constant email contact will diminish the value of future marketing campaigns for all other channels.

Uplift modeling

So how do you know that the customer you targeted wouldn't have purchased anyway? To clarify this question, you can restate it in a couple different ways:

>> How do you know the customer wouldn't have purchased even when she didn't get the marketing contact from you?

>> How do you know that what you sent to the customer influenced her to make the purchase?

Some modelers claim that the problems with response modeling are as follows:

>> You're taking a subset of your customers whom you've predicted will have some interest in the product or service already.

>> You're wasting marketing dollars on customers who don't need the extra influence to convert.

>> You may be decreasing your net margins because the discounts you're using to entice the customer to buy may be unnecessary.

>> You may be reducing your customer satisfaction because some customers don't want to be (constantly) contacted.

>> You're incorrectly taking credit for the response in your evaluation of the model.

Uplift modeling, also called *true lift modeling* and *net modeling* among other terms, aims to answer those criticisms by predicting which customers will *only* convert when contacted.

Uplift modeling works by generating predictive scores that aim at ranking individuals by their ability to be influenced. Abstractly, there are four possible groupings of customers:

>> **Persuadables:** Customers who can be persuaded to purchase — but will only buy when contacted.

>> **Sure Things:** Customers who will buy, regardless of contact.

>> **Lost Causes:** Customers who will not buy, regardless of contact.

>> **Do Not Disturbs:** Customers whom you shouldn't contact. Contacting them may cause a negative response like provoking them to cancel a subscription, return a product, or ask for a price adjustment.

Uplift modeling is designed to target the Persuadables. The Persuadables get a high predictive score, while the Do Not Disturbs get a low predictive score.

In the middle of the range are the Sure Things and Lost Causes.

Uplift models have proven to be effective, but they are more difficult to create than a response model. Here's why:

>> It generally is more complex to find a group of Persuadables than Sure Things. Sure Things usually are easier to identify, because they are customers who may have already purchased before or have shown interest in the product. Persuadables may have purchased a similar product or exhibit similar features as customers that have purchased. With a potentially smaller target size of Persuadables, complexity of building the uplift model, the operating effort, and cost, companies may not justify the use over response modeling.

In the case of voters, many undecided voters may fall into the group of Persuadables and can be switched to your candidate and motivated to vote when given a particular treatment.

>> It's more difficult to measure the success of the model because it's attempting to measure the influence that the treatment caused to change a customer's behavior, not the concrete action of whether the customer purchased after receiving contact. A customer may have been influenced by other factors between the time they received contact and took action.

To truly measure whether a customer can be or has been influenced accurately, you would (in effect) have to clone her and split the identical clones into a separate group. The first (treated/cloned group) would receive the advertisement; the second (control/original group) would not. Setting aside such sci-fi scenarios, you have to make some concessions to reality and employ an alternative method to get a useful measurement of the model's success.

Measuring uplift modeling requires having two test sets: a randomized control group and a treatment group. The treatment group gets the specially designed treatment (or contact), while the control group gets the default experience (no treatment or no contact). The positive difference in response rate between the treatment group and the control group is the uplift.

Even with these difficulties, some modelers argue that uplift modeling provides true marketing impact. They consider it more efficient than response modeling because it doesn't include the Sure Things in the targeting (which artificially inflates response rates). For that reason, uplift modeling is the choice for target marketing using predictive analytics.

Uplift modeling is still a relatively new technique in target marketing. More companies are starting to use it and have found success using it in their customer retention, marketing campaigns, and even presidential campaigns. For companies with large customer lists, uplift modeling is worth exploring.

Some pundits are crediting uplift modeling for President Obama's 2012 presidential campaign win. The campaign's data analyst used uplift modeling to heavily target voters who were most likely to be influenced by contact. They used personalized messages via several channels of contact: social media, television, direct mail, and telephone. They concentrated their efforts to influence the group of Persuadables. They invested heavily in this strategy; apparently it paid off.

Personalization

You may have noticed that websites remember what you did or which pages you looked at on their website last week or last month. Such websites are tracking your behavior, from clicks on certain parts of the page to the order of the pages you viewed for a session, to offer you the most relevant advertisements, products, or news articles.

Online customer experience

These websites are attempting to personalize your online experience to influence you and make it easier for you to take the action the companies that operate the websites want. The desired outcomes or goals these companies are usually looking for include

>> Filling out a registration or an appointment form

>> Clicking on a product link

>> Reading another news article

>> Watching a video

>> Buying a product

After the company has collected enough data for customers that successfully meet the goal, they can try to learn from the patterns those customers did before the action was taken, then apply the patterns to similar customers. Finding customers that are similar is by no means a simple task. Sure, an analyst can easily identify a single to a few customer attributes to manually segment the data by and see whether there are any patterns. But this process becomes exponentially more difficult as the number of transactions gets bigger and the customer attributes get wider.

Using machine learning algorithms, the machine can find micro-segments of similar customers so companies can target a group of customers more precisely with personalized content and offers.

Retargeting

Your web surfing behavior tracking isn't limited to the current website you're on. It can be tracked across multiple websites. This technology is possible through browser cookies and advertising networks that share data with its affiliates. When you visit one website and view a product page, then move on to another new website and see an advertisement for the product on the banner or side rail, this is *retargeting*.

By itself, retargeting isn't predictive analytics. But this gives you the knowledge that the data is out there and can be shared across websites. The ad networks share the data with their affiliates, and much of this data is available through data management platforms. By combining this third-party data with the company's own data, they can create more advanced predictive models.

Implementation

Personalized websites can be created in several ways. It really depends on which types of data that are available and whether the customer is logged in or not. Having profile data on the customer adds many more attributes to create a predictive model.

These are some data types and sources that can be used to create personalization models:

>> Customer's profile data, when she is logged in.

Profile data can include such attributes as age and gender.

>> Content on the page.

Using text mining techniques like TF-IDF, we can find important keywords.

>> The referring webpage.

The referring webpage may have keywords in its website address (URL).

>> The websites and pages you visited before.

When this data is available, it can show interest in a product or subject.

>> The geolocation of the web browser.

The physical location of the browser accessing the website, using its Internet Protocol address.

>> Temporal data, such as time of day.

Time of day and day of week are common temporal segmentation attributes.

Optimizing using personalization

Optimizing an e-commerce site using personalization is a great example of improving customer experience and satisfaction. By providing individualized content, customers see relevant offers, encounter fewer distractions, and build trust in the system, which will ultimately drive sales. Here's an illustration of how personalization increases sales.

Suppose we are operating a travel booking website. We want to optimize the experience for our two biggest markets: California and Florida travelers. Our analysts know that Californians like to travel to Nevada and Floridians like to travel to Georgia. So we use a simple rule to personalize the home page by geolocation.

We show a hero image of Las Vegas to IP addresses belonging to California; for Floridians, we show a hero image of downtown Atlanta. (A hero image is a big banner placed on the top or center of the web page.) We're using the hero image to personalize, inspire, and influence the site visitor to make a booking. Some visitors will make the booking regardless of the personalized image, because that was their original intention. Others may be inspired and influenced into further researching and planning a trip to Las Vegas or Atlanta, thus increasing your booking rate.

Using predictive modeling, we can use every available attribute to create sophisticated models that target specific segments of the California and Florida markets. For example, the model could have discovered that northern Californians with children like to travel to Lake Tahoe, while the ones without children like to fly to Waikiki Beach in Hawaii. Meanwhile, southern Californians like to go to Las Vegas. Northern Floridians may like Atlanta, while southerners may prefer the Caribbean Islands.

Predictive modeling allows you to be as granular as you like in segmenting data to make personalized offers. It can detect patterns in micro-segments that would normally be very difficult. A rule-based system may start with a few simple rules, but eventually turn into a complex and convoluted set of rules. The constant manual updating and deploying may make a rule-based system unmanageable. Using machine learning to algorithmically produce content presentation for personalization is a scalable and cost-effective solution. Personalization has great potential to increase ROI.

Similarities of Personalization and Recommendations

Personalization is similar to recommendations, and they are often used together. In addition, some websites use the term *personalized recommendations*. Recommendation implementations are easy to identify because they are often called out specifically with "Recommended for you" or "Customers that bought this also bought that." When you read an article on a news site, the recommendation engine will recommend other relevant articles for you to read. When you buy a product, the recommendation engine will recommend other products that may interest you to buy.

One type of personalization can refer to how you like the content of the website to be presented to you:

» The website's arrangement:

- Main navigation on the top or the left panel?

- Content groupings by vertical columns or horizontal rows?

- Text lists or thumbnail images?

» The colors of CTA (call to action) buttons and links:

- Colors matter, and they often mean different things and exude different feelings to different people. Some research has shown orange to be the color that converts the best, because orange contrasts well with typical websites.

- Most people are accustomed to Google search links being blue for unvisited and red for visited. But the default colors on browsers could be different. People with color blindness may prefer different colors for links.

» The flow of the checkout process.

High-frequency customers may prefer one-click ordering from the product page, while standard customers may prefer a one-page checkout process after clicking the product to review their order.

Another type of personalization refers to which type of content on the website should be presented to the customer according to their profile. This can be in the form of personalized recommendations.

» Relevant ads and offerings.

For example, it may not make sense for an apparel company to show ads for men's clothes when the customer is female and have no history of purchasing men's clothes. They should be showing ads for women's clothes in similar price point categories as their purchase history.

» Relevant items.

Based on your profile, purchase history, reading history, and similarity to other like-minded customers, show relevant products or articles on your personalized home page.

Content and Text Analytics

There's no shortage of information out there these days — but your success demands that you find and gather only the useful stuff. Valuable content is scattered across a massive number of files throughout your company. Harvesting that content and making sense of it can provide valuable insight — but doing that is challenging. The approach that meets the challenge is *content analytics* — analyzing content found in various types of documents and from a variety of sources. For example, the correct analysis of content from Word documents, system files, presentations, e-mails, and websites can illuminate a question from various angles.

Most content from such data sources is unstructured, at least as far as your business purposes are concerned. Content analytics can help you organize it into a structure that makes it easier to access, query, analyze, or feed directly into a traditional predictive analytic model.

Some common uses for content analytics and text analytics include

>> **Summarizing documents:** Reducing a document to its most import features or concepts can give the reader quick overview, saving time.

>> **Analyzing sentiment:** Determining the mood or opinion of a person as evident in the content — say, regarding a product after it's launched or the campaigns or policies of a political figure — can help clarify what the response should be.

>> **Scoring essays:** Automatic scoring of essays for exams can help universities filter applications.

>> **Categorizing news:** Categorizing news articles according to content can enable a recommender system to link recommended news articles to users.

>> **Retrieving information:** Finding and gathering content of interest from various data sources.

Chapter 3

Exploring Your Data Types and Associated Techniques

I n this information age, data is being accumulated at such a rapid pace that it can be overwhelming. That data is usually stored in a database, or scattered across documents, e-mails, and text or audiovisual files.

Knowing your data types — whether attitudinal or behavioral, structured or unstructured, static or streamed — will position you to have a deeper and broader understanding of your data. Learning how to categorize your data can bring you the rest of the way to that deeper understanding — which in turn can facilitate your predictive analytics efforts.

The handiest way to define those efforts is in terms of the tools they use: *Predictive analytics* is an approach to business data that uses the techniques, tools, and algorithms of three disciplines — data mining, statistics, and machine learning — to develop a predictive model. This chapter covers these disciplines, but first it explores data types. When carefully built, that model can help decision-makers spot trends and patterns that represent enhanced business opportunities. Understanding the connection between predictive analytics and the three disciplines that provide its primary tools will strengthen your analysis.

There are two major ways to implement predictive analytics:

>> **Data-driven:** This approach is based solely on your data.

>> **User-driven:** This approach explores ideas you have — say, for example, about your customers and their behavior — and examines whether your data supports those ideas.

Recognizing Your Data Types

If your company is like most others, you've gathered a large amount of data through the years — simply as a result of operating a business. Some of this data can be found in your databases; some may be scattered across hard drives on your company's computers or in its online content.

Your raw data may consist of presentations, individual text files, images, audio and video files, and e-mails — for openers.

REMEMBER

The sheer amount of this data can be overwhelming. When you categorize it, however, you create the core of any predictive analytics effort. The more you learn about your data, the better able you are to analyze and use it. You can start by getting a good working knowledge of your data types — in particular, structured versus unstructured data, and streamed versus static data. The upcoming sections give you a closer look at these data types.

Structured and unstructured data

Data contained in databases, documents, e-mails, and other data files can be categorized either as structured or unstructured data.

Structured data is well organized, follows a consistent order, is relatively easy to search and query, and can be readily accessed and understood by a person or a computer program.

A classic example of structured data is an Excel spreadsheet with labeled columns. Such structured data is consistent; column headers — usually brief, accurate descriptions of the content in each column — tell you exactly what kind of content to expect. In a column labeled *e-mail address,* for example, you can count on finding a list of (no surprise here) e-mail addresses. Such overt consistency makes structured data amenable to automated data management.

Structured data is usually stored in well-defined schemas such as databases. It's usually tabular, with columns and rows that clearly define its attributes.

Unstructured data, on the other hand, tends to be free-form, non-tabular, dispersed, and not easily retrievable; such data requires deliberate intervention to make sense of it. Miscellaneous e-mails, documents, web pages, and files (whether text, audio, and/or video) in scattered locations are examples of unstructured data.

It's hard to categorize the content of unstructured data. It tends to be mostly text, it's usually created in a hodgepodge of free-form styles, and finding any attributes you can use to describe or group it is no small task.

The content of unstructured data is hard to work with or make sense of programmatically. Computer programs can't analyze or generate reports on such data directly without processing, simply because it lacks structure, has no underlying dominant characteristic, and individual items of data have no common ground. However, now there are more technologies and new tools that can make sense of unstructured data.

In general, there's a higher percentage of unstructured data than structured data in the world. Unstructured data requires more work to make it useful, so it gets more attention — thus tends to consume more time. No wonder the promise of a processing capability that can swiftly make sense of huge bodies of unstructured data is a major selling point for predictive analytics.

TIP

Don't underestimate the importance of structured data and the power it brings to your analysis. It's far more efficient to analyze structured data than to analyze unstructured data. Unstructured data can also be costly to preprocess for analysis as you're building a predictive analytics project. The selection of relevant data, its cleansing, and subsequent transformations can be lengthy and tedious. The resultant newly organized data from those necessary preprocessing steps can then be used in a predictive analytics model. The wholesale transformation of unstructured data however, may have to wait until you have your predictive analytics model up and running.

It might be more rewarding to quickly get full value from your structured data than worry too soon about processing unstructured data and risk further delays to your projects.

Tagging documents and text analytics are two approaches to structuring text documents, linking their contents, grouping and summarizing their data, and uncovering patterns in that data. Both disciplines provide a rich framework of algorithms and techniques to mine the text scattered across a sea of documents.

It's also worth noting that search engine platforms provide readily available tools for indexing data and making it searchable.

Table 3-1 compares structured and unstructured data.

TABLE 3-1   ## Characteristics of Structured and Structured Data

Characteristics	Structured	Unstructured
Association	Organized	Scattered and dispersed
Appearance	Formally defined	Free-form
Accessibility	Easy to access and query	Hard to access and query
Availability	Percentagewise lower	Percentagewise higher
Analysis	Efficient to analyze	Additional preprocessing is needed

Unstructured data doesn't completely lack structure — you just have to ferret it out. Even the text inside digital files still has some structure associated with it, often showing up in the metadata — for example, document titles, dates the files were last modified, and their authors' names. The same thing applies for e-mails: The contents may be unstructured, but structured data is associated with them — for example, the date and time they were sent, the names of their senders and recipients, whether they contain attachments.

It may be worthwhile to conduct a preliminary analysis on the structured components of your data to estimate the potential value of a full analysis of the overall unstructured data. When the analysis yields little, that should be weighed in determining resources you will allocate to that portion of the unstructured data.

The idea here is that you can still find some order you can use while you're going through all that "unstructured data". Of course, you may have to do some digging. The content of a thread of 25 e-mails shooting back and forth between two recipients may wander away from the subject line of the first original e-mail, even when the subject line stays the same. Additionally, the very first subject line in that e-mail thread may not accurately reflect even the content of that very first e-mail. (For example, the subject line may say something as unhelpful as "Hi, there!")

The separation line between the two data types isn't always clear. In general, you can always find some attributes of unstructured data that can be considered structured data. Whether that structure is reflective of the content of that data — or useful in data analysis — is unclear at best. For that matter, structured data can hold unstructured data within it. In a web form, for example, users may be asked to give feedback on a product by choosing an answer from multiple choices — but also presented with a comment box where they can provide additional feedback. The answers from multiple choices are structured; the comment field is unstructured because of its free-form nature. Such cases are best understood as a mix of structured and unstructured data. Most data is a composite of both.

Technically speaking, there will always be some exceptions in defining data categories; the lines between the two can be blurry. But the idea is to make a useful distinction between structured and unstructured data — and that is almost always possible.

TIP

For a successful predictive analytics project, both your structured and unstructured data must be combined in a logical format that can be analyzed.

One of the authors once found himself with a few folders, each holding hundreds of PDF files. To save time, instead of looking at each file to try to understand its content, he used a few lines of programming and a free software tool to get a quick idea of the data contained in those files:

1. A few lines of Java allowed him to open the files, extract the embedded text, and save that content into a new text file in a separate folder.

2. He fired up RapidMiner Studio and used its text processing package to gain some insights.

   Using "Process Documents" (from the Files operator), he specified the path to my text files, the document types to process, and the type of vector to create (TF, TF-IDF, and others).

TECHNICAL STUFF

TF stands for *term frequency* (the count of words across the documents). TF-IDF is the term *frequency inverse document frequency.* Some words are more frequent than others; as a weighing mechanism to gauge the relative importance of a word, its frequency is offset by the number of the documents where the word appears.

3. He defined text processing for those documents:

   - A tokenizer operator chops the text into "tokens," or individual words.

   - A filter excludes English stop words (common words, such as "like", "and", and "the").

   - A filter eliminates one- and two-letter words.

   - A filter operator transforms all words to lower case.

   - A stemmer operator breaks words down to their stems or roots. For example, the words *anticipate, anticipating,* and *anticipation* are grouped under one root, *anticipate.*

These operators come in a friendly user interface. Figure 3-1 shows the user interface for the different operators described as they appear in RapidMiner Studio 6.4.

FIGURE 3-1:
Text processing
operators in
RapidMiner
Studio.

With a matter of minutes, he clicked "run," and a data matrix was generated, consisting of all the words that fit the specified criteria. The various words were displayed in the rows of the matrix, and the columns showed total occurrences and the document occurrences. A quick sort on the occurrence column lists the most important words, or *terms* (a term consists of one word or more if you specify any to track) inside the universe of the documents. Just like that, a daunting task is rendered simple and quick insights of the pile unstructured data are gained. This type of analysis can help you identify terms that are most descriptive in a document, and it can come handy when you're trying to find the similarity between two documents. Of course, further and more complex analysis will need to take place later, but this gets you started.

These are the top words for the first edition of *Predictive Analytics For Dummies:* data, model, predictive, analytics, business, customer, cluster, and algorithm.

TECHNICAL
STUFF

Static and streamed data

Data can also be identified as streamed, static, or a mix of the two. *Streamed data* changes continuously; examples include the constant stream of Facebook updates, tweets on Twitter, and the constantly changing stock prices while the market is still open.

Streamed data is continuously changing; *static data* is self-contained and enclosed. The problems associated with static data include gaps, outliers, or incorrect data, all of which may require some cleansing, preparation, and preprocessing before you can use static data for an analysis.

As with streamed data, other problems may arise. Volume can be a problem; the sheer amount of non-stop data constantly arriving can be overwhelming. And the faster the data is streaming in, the harder it is for the analysis to catch up.

The two main models for analyzing streamed data are as follows:

>> **Examine only the newest data points and make a decision about the state of the model and its next move.** This approach is incremental — essentially building up a picture of the data as it arrives.

>> **Evaluate the entire dataset, or a subset of it, to make a decision each time new data points arrive.** This approach is inclusive of more data points in the analysis — what constitutes the "entire" dataset changes every time new data is added.

Depending on the nature of your business and the anticipated impact of the decision, one model is preferable over the other.

Some business domains, such as the analysis of environmental, market, or intelligence data, prize new data that arrives in real time. All this data must be analyzed as it's being streamed — and interpreted not only correctly but right away. Based on the newly available information, the model redraws the whole internal representation of the outside world. Doing so provides you with the most up-to-date basis for a decision you may need to make and act upon quickly.

For example, a predictive analytics model may process a stock price as a data feed, even while the data is rapidly changing, analyze the data in the context of immediate market conditions existing in real time, and then decide whether to trade a particular stock.

Clearly, analyzing streamed data differs from analyzing static data. Analyzing a mix of both data types can be even more challenging.

TECHNICAL
STUFF

Generally, the learning and the building of a model mostly is performed on static data. When that model is deployed to production, it will process streamed data. Even static data is constantly refreshed through regular updates; streamed data should be understood in light of its real-time aspect.

Identifying Data Categories

As a result of doing business, companies have gathered masses of data about their business and customers, often referred to as *business intelligence*. To help you develop categories for your data, what follows is a general rundown of the types of data that are considered business intelligence:

Behavioral data derives from transactions, and can be collected automatically:

>> Items bought

>> Methods of payment

>> Whether the purchased items were on sale

>> The purchasers' access information:

- Address

- Phone number

- E-mail address

All of us have provided such data when making a purchase online (or even when buying at a store or over the phone).

TIP

Other types of data can be collected from customers with their co-operation:

>> Data provided by customers when they fill out surveys

>> Customers' collected answers to polls via questionnaires

>> Information collected from customers who make direct contact with companies

- In a physical store

- Over the phone

- Through the company website

In addition, the type of data that a business collects from its operations can provide information about its customers. Common examples include the amount of time that customers spend on company websites, as well as customers' browsing histories. All that data combined can be analyzed to answer some important questions:

>> How can your business improve the customer experience?

>> How can you retain existing customers and attract new ones?

>> What would your customer base like to buy next?

>> Which purchases can you recommend to particular customers?

The first step toward answering these questions (and many others) is to collect and use all customer-related operations data for a comprehensive analysis. The data types that make up such data can intersect and could be described and/or grouped differently for the purposes of analysis.

TIP

Some companies collect these types of data by giving customers personalized experiences. For example, when a business provides its customers with the tools they need to build personalized websites, it not only empowers customers (and enriches their experience of dealing with the company), it also allows the company to learn from a direct expression of its customers' wants and needs: the websites they create.

REMEMBER

The ability to combine various types of data from different sources (usually for the first time) is one of the reasons that predictive analytics can yield insights and useful results.

Attitudinal data

Any information that can shed light on how customers think or feel is considered *attitudinal data*.

When companies put out surveys that ask their customers for feedback and their thoughts about their line of businesses and products, the collected data is an example of attitudinal data.

Attitudinal data has a direct impact on the type of marketing campaign a company can launch. It helps shape and target the message of that campaign. Attitudinal data can help make both the message and the products more relevant to the customers' needs and wants — allowing the business to serve existing customers better and attract prospective ones.

REMEMBER

The limitation of attitudinal data is a certain imperfection: Not everyone objectively answers survey questions, and not everyone provides all the relevant details that shaped their thinking at the time of the survey.

Many customers use social media to express their opinions about a product, service, or company. Their opinions reflect their experiences and their interactions with the company. As a result, many companies are gathering that data, and applying various analyses to make sense of it. One popular technique is the application of sentiment analysis, (sometimes referred to as *opinion mining*). Facebook posts, or tweets, are analyzed to determine whether the attitude, mood, or opinion of their authors is negative, neutral, or positive. The result of that analysis can help companies improve their marketing strategies and offer better customer service.

It may be a challenge to find attitudinal data for everyone in your analysis, and it can also be difficult to match the customer transactional data with social media data. In general, linking various data sources, in a meaningful way, is a very hard task and can take time.

Behavioral data

Behavioral data derives from what customers do when they interact with the business; it consists mainly of data from sales transactions. Behavioral data tends to be more reliable than attitudinal data because it represents what actually happened.

Businesses know, for example, what products are selling, who is buying them, and how customers are paying for them.

Behavioral data is a by-product of normal operations, so is available to a company at no extra cost. Attitudinal data, on the other hand, requires conducting surveys or commissioning market research to get insights into the minds of the customers.

REMEMBER

Attitudinal data is analyzed to understand *why* customers behave the way they do, and details their views of your company. Behavioral data tells you *what* is happening and records customers' real actions. Attitudinal data provides insight into motivations; behavioral data provides the who-did-what — the overall context that led to customers' particular reactions. Your analysis should include groups for both types of data; they are complementary.

Combining both attitudinal and behavioral data can make your predictive analytics models more accurate by helping you define the segments of your customer base, offer a more personalized customer experience, and identify the drivers behind the business.

Table 3-2 compares attitudinal and behavioral data.

TABLE 3-2	Comparing Attitudinal and Behavioral Data	
Characteristics	Attitudinal data	Behavioral data
Data Source	Customers' thoughts	Customers' actions
Data Means	Collected from surveys	Collected from transactions
Data Type	Subjective	Objective
Data Cost	May cost extra	No extra cost

Demographic data

Demographic data comprises information including age, race, marital status, education level, employment status, household income, and location. You can get demographic data from the U.S. Census Bureau, other government agencies, or through commercial entities.

The more data you have about your customers, the better the insight you'll have into identifying specific demographic and market trends as well as how they may affect your business. Measuring the pulse of the demographic trends will enable you to adjust to the changes and better market to, attract, and serve those segments.

REMEMBER

Different segments of the population are interested in different products.

Small businesses catering to specific locations should pay attention to the demographic changes in those locations. All of us have witnessed populations changing over time in certain neighborhoods. Businesses must be aware of such changes; they may affect business significantly.

Demographic data, when combined with behavioral and attitudinal data, allows marketers to paint an accurate picture of their current and potential customers, allowing them to increase satisfaction, retention, and acquisition.

Demographic data is static data, so it's hard to use to predict a change of behavior when the underlying input variables aren't changing. Therefore, demographics data only is useful when combined with transactional data.

Generating Predictive Analytics

There are two ways to go about generating or implementing predictive analytics: purely on the basis of your data (with no prior knowledge of what you're after) or with a proposed business hypothesis that the data may or may not support. You don't have to choose one or the other; the two approaches can be complementary. Each has its advantages and disadvantages.

REMEMBER

Whether you're coming up with hypotheses to test, analyzing the results that come out of your data analysis (and making sense of them), or starting to examine your data with no prior assumptions of what you may find, the goal of your analysis is always the same: to decide whether to act on what you find. You have an active role in implementing the process needed for either approach to predictive analytics. Both approaches to predictive analytics have their limitations; keep risk management in mind as you cross-examine their results. Which approach do you find to be both promising of good results and relatively safe?

Combining both types of analysis empowers your business and enables you to expand your understanding, insight, and awareness of your business and your customers. It makes your decision process smarter and subsequently more profitable.

Data-driven analytics

If you're basing your analysis purely on existing data, you can use internal data — accumulated by your company over the years — or external data (often purchased from a source outside your company) that is relevant to your line of business.

To make sense of that data, you can employ data-mining tools to overcome both its complexity and size; reveal some patterns you weren't aware of; uncover some associations and links within your data; and use your findings to generate new categorizations, new insights and new understanding. Data-driven analysis can even reveal a gem or two that can radically improve your business — all of which gives this approach an element of surprise that feeds on curiosity and builds anticipation.

REMEMBER

Data-driven analysis is best suited for large datasets because it's hard for human beings to wrap their minds around huge amounts of data. Data-mining tools and visualization techniques help us get a closer look and cut the overwhelming mass of data down to size. Keep these general principles in mind:

>> The more complete your data is, the better the outcome of data-driven analytics. If you have extensive data that has key information to the variables you're measuring, and spans an extended period of time, you're guaranteed to discover something new about your business.

- » Data-driven analytics is neutral because
  - No prior knowledge about the data is necessary.
  - You aren't after a specific hypothesis. You're analyzing the data for the sake of it, or with a general goal in mind.

- » The nature of this analysis is broad and it doesn't concern itself with a specific search or validation of a preconceived idea. This approach to analytics can be viewed as sort of random and broad data mining.

- » If you conduct such data analysis, and if you learn something about your business from the analysis, you'll still need to decide whether the results you're getting are worth implementing or acting upon.

- » Relying solely on data-driven analytics adds some risk to the resulting business decisions. You can, however, limit that risk by incorporating some of the realism that characterizes user-driven analytics (described in the next section). When real-world data proves (or at least supports) the correctness of your original ideas, then the appropriate decision is practically already made. When an informed hunch is validated by the data, the whole analysis shows itself as driven by strategic ideas that were worth pursuing and verifying.

The following story is very interesting. It's about the importance of having data help you decide instead of letting data be the sole driver for the decision-making process. Amazon and Netflix look at massive data in their quests to create the best, most entertaining show in the business. Based on these insights, Amazon created the show *Alpha House*, which did okay, while Netflix produced *House of Cards*, which generated tremendous success. What made the difference in the outcome for these two companies who rely on, and heavily use, data science in their daily operations? It turned out, as detailed by Sebastian Wernicke in his TED Talk ("How to use data to make a hit TV show"), that Netflix took the results from the data analysis to understand what their audience wants to watch, and then the team of experts who took the risk and made a decision to create a show they thought would fit that criteria. Amazon stuck to the data and data analysis in all aspects of the process, and managed to produce a show that their audience liked; the result was a successful show, but not a blockbuster.

REMEMBER

Data can only help so much in the success of the decision-making process. At a certain point, management must make the best decision based on what they have learned from the data.

User-driven analytics

The *user-driven* approach to predictive analytics starts with you (or your managers) conceiving of ideas and then taking refuge in your data to see whether those ideas have merit, would stand testing, and are supported by the data.

The test data doesn't have to be big; it's something you define and choose as you deem relevant for testing your ideas.

The process of picking the right datasets and designing accurate testing methods — in fact, the whole process from inception to adoption — has to be guided by careful consideration and meticulous planning.

Selecting the variables with predictive power can be daunting and time consuming. Preparing your data is a crucial aspect of the predictive analytics process. Chapter 9 highlights the challenges, and provides guidance and tips to prepare your data; it also details algorithms that specialize in features selection and extraction.

User-driven analytics requires not only strategic thinking but also enough in-depth knowledge of the business domain to back up the hypothesis. Vision and intuition can be very helpful here; you're looking for how the data lends specific support to ideas you deemed important and strategic. This approach to predictive analytics is defined (and limited) by the scope of the ideas you're probing. Decision-making becomes easier when the data supports your ideas.

REMEMBER

Relying only on user-driven analytics can cost you in terms of insight; you may miss the hidden connections that may lurk in your data. Your ideas may miss the subtle changes that have been occurring in your business over time — which can only come to light when you apply data-driven analytics to complete the picture.

In short, your ideas should also include an awareness of the unknowns that surround your business, and probe them by looking for interconnected variables in the many aspects of your business. This is hard to achieve but data-driven analysis can help. For example, you may analyze the importance of the cost of raw material you need to create your product, the demand for the product, and how the costs affect your price. But you may miss hidden and other correlated factors that have influence on the pricing — such as the state of the economy as a whole, the turnover rate of employees at your company, and subtle changes in how your product is being consumed.

WARNING

The process of probing your ideas may not be as straightforward as analyzing whole datasets. It can also be affected by your bias to prove the correctness of your initial assumptions.

Table 3-3 compares data-driven and user-driven data.

TABLE 3-3   **Data-Driven and User-Driven Analytics**

Characteristics	Data-driven data	User-driven data
Business Knowledge Needed	No prior knowledge	In-depth domain knowledge
Analysis and Tools Used	Broad use of data-mining tools	Specific design for analysis and testing
Big Data	Suited for large-scale data	Can work on smaller datasets
Analysis Scope	Open scope	Limited scope
Analysis Conclusion	Needs verification of results	Easier adoption of analysis results
Data Pattern	Uncovers patterns and associations	May miss hidden patterns and associations

Connecting to Related Disciplines

Predictive analytics makes heavy use of three related disciplines: data mining, statistics, and machine learning. All four disciplines intersect to such a large degree that their names are often used interchangeably. Just to keep the record straight, there are some distinctions: predictive analytics combines many of the techniques, tools, and algorithms that data mining, statistics, and machine learning have in common. Its goal, however, is to use those tools to understand the data, analyze it, learn from it, and create a mathematical model that can make useful business predictions. That futuristic orientation is what differentiates predictive analytics as it combines aspects of the other three disciplines in the various steps and or stages required to develop a predictive model.

It's the predictive capability that sets apart this specialized use of statistics, data mining, and machine learning. The upcoming sections examine the contributions of each discipline.

Statistics

Statistics are numbers that result from measuring empirical data over time. As a discipline, statistics concerns itself with gathering and analyzing data — often to tell a story in numbers.

Statistics can infer relationships within data; thus it plays an active role in presenting data and helping us understand it. Using only a sample of the data, statistics can give us a basis for inferring hypotheses about the data as a whole. Thus the discipline is both *descriptive* and *inferential*.

Inferential statistics is concerned with making inferences or predictions about the characteristics of a whole population from a sample dataset. Sample data for analysis is chosen at random, in a way that represents (but doesn't include) the whole population, which is hard to have access to. When the sample dataset is well chosen, analyzing it allows the investigator to project the findings of the analysis onto the whole population with a measurable degree of accuracy.

Statistics relies, of course, on mathematics to analyze the data by verifying a hypothesis or theory, determining its accuracy, and drawing a conclusion.

It is the statisticians' job to prove or disprove, with a single sample, whether their hypothesis about the population is true. The fact that a hypothesis precedes the analysis is a clear distinction for statistics, and a hallmark that differentiates it from other techniques.

Unlike data mining, statistics doesn't involve data cleansing or preprocessing. But descriptive statistics and data mining do have data grouping in common; both aim to describe data and define the processes used to categorize it.

REMEMBER

A common denominator among all these disciplines is the underlying mathematics. The math is at the heart of statistics, and all algorithms and programming used in data mining, machine learning, and predictive analytics. Another common denominator is data analysis, a quest for better-informed, smarter decisions about future outcomes.

Data mining

Data mining is concerned mainly with analyzing data through describing, summarizing, classifying, and clustering the data so as to find useful patterns, links, or associations within it.

TIP

Data mining is often used interchangeably with *machine learning* but there are some distinctions between the two terms. For example: data miners are familiar with the use of machine learning to perform some tasks involving large amounts of data. However, they can also create a sophisticated and optimized query on a database without the use of machine learning — which would still be considered data mining. This is similar to *knowledge discovery in databases*, (KDD). It finds knowledge in data and emphasizes a broad application of particular data mining techniques.

For more about the specific use of data mining in predictive analytics, see Chapters 6 and 7.

Machine learning

Machine learning is another discipline that focuses on analyzing the data and making sense of it — but does so by teaching a computer program to do the work. The more data is analyzed, the more the system can learn about it, what to expect from it, and what to do with it. Data analysis becomes a source of continuous feedback to the system, which promptly analyzes data, attempts to understand and make sense of it, and gets better at those tasks.

When a new special case, usually an exception or a new behavior, is processed for the first time, the knowledge base of the system is incremented to include the new case. The more special cases are handled, the better equipped the system is to make decisions that produce the most useful outcome. This is the nature of the learning that the machine is programmed to do.

Machine learning is the equivalent of teaching a system the rules of a game, and then getting the system to practice the game by playing at elementary and intermediate levels. After that preparation, the system can play at advanced levels in real time.

IBM Watson uses natural language processing and machine learning to reveal insights from large amounts of unstructured data. Watson was used in a 2011 *Jeopardy!* match, and it won. Before that, IBM's Deep Blue beat world champion Gary Kasparov in chess. In 2016, Google's AlphaGo beat the world champion, Lee Sedol, in Go (a much harder game to conquer, because Go is exponentially more complex than chess).

Machine learning is perfectly suited for

» Complex data

» Data in various forms

» Data collected from diverse sources

» Data in large amounts

Data mining can uncover previously unknown connections and associations in the data. Machine learning can categorize the new and upcoming unknowns, learn from them based on its previous processing of the data, and get better at incorporating them into the known data. Both techniques lead to greater insight and understanding of the data.

Chapter 4
Complexities of Data

Your Google search log, Uber trips logs, Tweets, Facebook status updates, Airbnb stays, and bank statements tell a story about your life. Your geographical locations logged by your cellphone carrier, your most frequent places visited, and your online purchases can define your habits, your preferences, and your personality.

This avalanche of data, being generated at every moment, is referred to as *big data*, and it's the main driver of many predictive analytics models. Capturing all different types of data together in one place and applying analytics to it is a highly complex task. However, you might be surprised that in most cases only about a small percent of that data is used for analysis that results in real, valuable results. This small percent of big data is often referred as *smart data or small data* — the nucleus that makes sense out of big data. Only this small representative portion of big data will make it into the elevator pitch that justifies your analytical results.

REMEMBER

The secret recipe for a truly successful predictive analytics project starts with filtering out the dirt, noise, invalid data, irrelevant data, and misleading data. When you've done that task, then ultimately you can extract smart data from big data. Analyzing smart data leads to extracting the value of predictive analytics.

So how do we go from big data to smart data to tangible value? At what rate must data be captured, considering how fast it's being generated? Can visualization of raw data give you a clue as to what to correct, exclude, or include? Relax. This chapter addresses all those questions.

Finding Value in Your Data

Any successful journey takes serious preparation. Predictive analytics models are essentially a deep dive into large amounts of data. When the data isn't well prepared, the predictive analytics model will emerge from the dive with no fish. The key to finding value in predictive analytics is to prepare the data — thoroughly and meticulously — that your model will use to make predictions.

Processing data beforehand can be a stumbling block in the predictive analytics process. Gaining experience in building predictive models — and, in particular, preparing data — teaches the importance of patience. Selecting, processing, cleaning, and preparing the data is laborious. It's the most time-consuming task in the predictive analytics lifecycle. However, proper and systematic preparing of the data will significantly increase the chance that your data analytics will bear fruit.

Although it takes both time and effort to build that first predictive model, after you take the first step — building the first model that finds value in your data — then future models will be less resource-intensive and time-consuming, even with completely new datasets. Even when you don't use the same data for the next model, your data analysts will have gained valuable experience with the first model.

Delving into your data

Using a fruit analogy, you not only have to remove the bad peel or the cover, but dig into it to get to the endocarp; as you get closer to the endocarp, you get to the best part of the fruit. The same rule applies to big data, as shown in Figure 4-1.

Data validity

Data isn't always valid when you first encounter it. Most data are either *incomplete* (missing some attributes or values) or *noisy* (containing outliers or errors). In the biomedical and bioinformatics fields, for example, outliers can lead the analytics to generate incorrect or misleading results. Outliers in cancer data, for example, can be a major factor that skews the accuracy of medical treatments: Gene-expression samples may appear as false cancer positives because they were analyzed against a sample that contained errors.

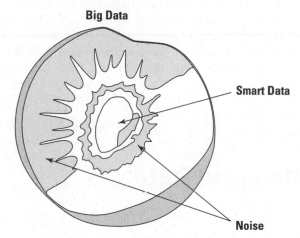

Big Data

Smart Data

Noise

FIGURE 4-1:
Big data and smart data.

Inconsistent data is data that contains discrepancies in data attributes. For example, a data record may have two attributes that don't match: say, a zip code (such as 20037) and a corresponding state (Delaware). Invalid data can lead to wrong predictive modeling, which leads to misleading analytical results that will cause bad executive decisions. For example, sending coupons for diapers to people who have no children is a fairly obvious mistake. But it can happen easily if the marketing department of a diaper company ends up with invalid results from their predictive analytics model. Gmail might not always suggest the right people if you're trying to fill in the prospective customers you might have forgotten to include in a group e-mail list. Facebook, to give another example, may suggest friends who might not be the type of friends you're looking for.

In such cases, it's possible that there's a large margin of error in the models or algorithms. In some cases, the flaws and anomalies are in the data initially selected to power the predictive model — but the algorithms that power the predictive model might end up being applied to large chunks of invalid data. Invalid data is just one example that can lead to poor predictions.

Data variety

The absence of uniformity in data is another big challenge known as *data variety*. From the endless stream of unstructured text data (generated through e-mails, presentations, project reports, texts, tweets) to structured bank statements, geo-location data, Uber trips logs and customer demographics, companies are starving for this variety of data.

Aggregating this data and preparing it for analytics is a complex task. How can you integrate data generated from different systems such as Twitter, Opentable. com, Google search, and a third party that tracks customer data? Well, the answer is that there is no common solution. Every situation is different, and the data scientist usually has to do a lot of maneuvering to integrate the data and prepare it for analytics. Even so, a simple approach to standardization can support data integration from different sources: You agree with your data providers to a standard data format that your system can handle — a framework that can make all your data sources generate data that's readable by both humans and machines. Think of it as a new language that all big-data sources will speak every time they're in the big-data world.

Constantly Changing Data

This section presents two main challenges of big data: velocity and volume. These are (respectively) the rate at which data is being generated, received, and analyzed, and the growing mass of data.

Data velocity

Velocity is the speed of an object moving in a specific direction. *Data velocity* refers to another challenge of big data: the rate at which data is being generated, captured, or delivered. The challenge is figuring out how to keep up.

Think of the data being generated by a cellphone provider. It includes all customers' cellphone numbers, call durations, and GPS locations (for openers). This data is growing all the time, making the task of capturing smart data from big data even more challenging.

So how do you overcome this challenge? There isn't one simple solution available yet. However, your team can (in fact, must) decide

>> How often you can capture data

>> What you can afford in resources and finances

>> Which type of data you're going to model (for example, streaming or one-time data)

>> Whether you're modeling streaming data or only deriving prediction scores of one or multiple records

If (for example) you own a supercomputer and you have the funds, then you should capture as much data as you can — but you might also need to take into consideration how often that data is changing. In Chapters 16 and 17, we outline some of the widely used tools to handle streams of data.

High volume of data

A common mistake that people make when they talk about big data is to define it as merely a large amount of data. Big data isn't just about large volumes of data; it's more about a wide *variety* of data (yes, in huge amounts) generated at high speed and frequency. In Figure 4-2, big data spans three dimensions in spiral exponential fashion; it looks like a tornado.

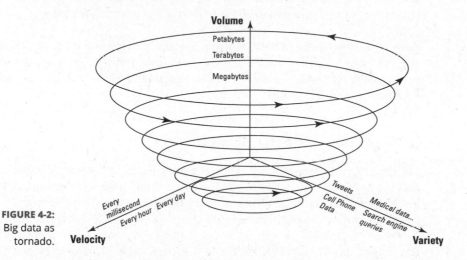

FIGURE 4-2: Big data as tornado.

Big data is "big" not only because of its large volume (such as numbers of rows, or columns, or comprehensiveness); it's also — and mainly — about those other three dimensions: volume, velocity and variety.

Complexities in Searching Your Data

This section presents the three main concepts of searching unstructured text data in preparation for using it in predictive analytics:

>> Getting ready to go beyond the basic keyword search

>> Making your data semantically searchable

>> Adding context to the users' search experience

Keyword-based search

Imagine if you were tasked with searching large amounts of data. One way to approach the problem is to issue a search query that consists (obviously) of words. The search tool looks for matching words in the database, the data warehouse, or goes rummaging through any text in which your data resides. Assume you're issuing the following search query: *the President of the United States visits Africa*. The search results will consist of text that contains exactly one or a combination of the words *President, United States, visits, Africa*. You might get the exact information you're looking for, but not always.

How about the documents that don't contain any of the words previously mentioned, but some combination of the following: *Obama's trip to Kenya*.

None of the words you initially searched for are in there — but the search results are *semantically* (meaningfully) useful. How can you prepare your data to be semantically retrievable? How can you go beyond the traditional keyword search? Your answers are in the next section.

Semantic-based search

An illustration of how semantic-based search works is a proof of value project that Dr. Bari led during his tenure at the World Bank Group in Washington, DC, an international organization whose primary mission is to fight poverty around the world. The project aimed to investigate existing large-scale enterprise search and analytics capabilities in the market and build a prototype for a cutting-edge framework that would organize the World Bank data — most of which was an unstructured collection of documents, publications, project reports, briefs, and case studies. This massive valuable knowledge is a resource used toward the Bank's main mission of reducing world poverty. But the fact that it's unstructured makes it challenging to access, capture, share, understand, search, data-mine, and visualize.

The World Bank is an immense organization, with many offices around the globe. During the feasibility study, we found out that like in any other large organization, divisions used several terms and concepts that had the same overall meaning but different nuances. For example, terms such as *climatology, climate change, gas ozone depletion,* and *greenhouse emissions* were all semantically related but not identical in meaning. The goal was to engineer a search capability that is smart enough to extract documents that contained related concepts when someone searched any of these terms.

The very initial architecture for that capability that the Bari's team adopted was the Unstructured Information Management Architecture (UIMA), a software-based solution. Originally designed by IBM Research, UIMA is available in IBM software such as IBM Content Analytics, one of the tools that powers IBM Watson, the famous computer that won the Jeopardy game. Bari's team joined forces with engineers and data scientists from IBM Content Management and Enterprise Search, and later with an IBM Watson team, to collaborate on this project.

TECHNICAL STUFF

An *Unstructured Information Management (UIM)* solution is a software system that analyzes large volumes of unstructured information (text, audio, video, images, and so on) to discover, organize and deliver relevant knowledge to the client or the application end-user.

The *ontology* of a domain is an array of concepts and related terms particular to a domain. A UIMA-based solution uses ontologies to provide semantic tagging, which allows enriched searching independent of data format (text, speech, PowerPoint presentation, e-mail, video, and so on). UIMA appends another layer to the captured data, and then adds *metadata* to identify data that can be structured and semantically searched.

Semantic search is based on the contextual meaning of search terms as they appear in the searchable data space that UIMA builds. Semantic search is more accurate than the usual keyword-based search because a user query returns search results of not only documents that contain the search terms, but also of documents that are semantically relevant to the query.

For example, if you're searching for *biodiversity in Africa*, a typical (keyword-based) search will return documents that have the exact words *biodiversity* and *Africa*. A UIMA-based semantic search will return not only the documents that have those two words, but also anything that is semantically relevant to "biodiversity in Africa" — for example, documents that contain such combinations of words as "plant resources in Africa," "animal resources in Morocco," or "genetic resources in Zimbabwe." Semantic capabilities can go beyond correlation between words and leverage the grammatical structure of the search query to give better search results. Semantic capabilities are mainly based on complex natural-language processing algorithms.

Through semantic tagging and use of ontologies, information becomes semantically retrievable, independent of the language or the medium in which the information was created (Word, PowerPoint, e-mail, video, and so on). This solution provides a single hub where data can be captured, organized, exchanged, and rendered semantically retrievable.

Dictionaries of synonyms and related terms are open-source (freely available) — or you can develop your own dictionaries specific to your domain or your data. You can build a spreadsheet with the root word and its corresponding related words, synonyms, and broader terms. The spreadsheet can be uploaded into a search tool such as IBM Content Analytics (ICA) to power the enterprise search and content analytics.

Contextual search

In the world of search engines, the goal is to display *the right results for the right user.* Contextual search is about discovering that right time to display the right results and to the right user. Indeed, a search engine that uses contextual search attempts to understand its users algorithmically, by learning users' preferences from their behaviors on the web and other users' online experiences. Contextual search, when implemented right, will deliver the most relevant results that the user needs to see at the right time.

Major search engines like Google and Bing have been building the next generation of search. That web search is mainly based on actualizing the concept of contextual search. Contextual search engines try to frame the user search experience within a meaningful context. As an example, consider a user searching for "Good coffee shops in New York City," A contextual search most likely will return search results according the user location. If the user's location at the time of searching was SoHo in New York City, then the results will be ranked based on both public coffee shop ratings or popularity (because the user specified the word "good" in the query) and proximity to the user's location. The location of the user automatically is detected by the search engine, and an algorithm optimizes the search results to display the web pages about coffee shops in order of proximity to the user's current location.

Further, if the same user searching for a good coffee place in New York City also is known to be a guru in predictive analytics, big data, and data science, then the ads on the search engine's results or the pages of the coffee shops should display relative ads (such as an ad for *Predictive Analytics For Dummies*).

A search engine that uses contextual search learns and builds a user profile that encapsulates the users' preferences through logging the most visited web pages by the user, the keywords used by the user in past search queries and even in some cases personal information about a user like occupation, address, and gender among others. Further, for the same user who searched for "Good coffee shops in New York City," the results might not only be ranked based on the user location and user's preferences, but also on predicted users' social status so the coffee shops presented in the search results are within the user's budget that was algorithmically predicted: A diner or a five-star hotel.

User's location, user's profile, and other factors add context to the user search experience. For the same query, a search engine returns different results depending on who is searching, location, and time. The result might even be shaped by what mood the user is in at the time of search (sentiment analysis component) and many other factors.

The next-generation contextual search will span over a multi-dimensional space of users attributes that can be learned from the digital prints we leave on the cyberspace:

>> Places we go (for example, through Uber and online reservations)

>> Web pages we visit

>> E-commerce sites where we shop

>> Products we buy (or return)

>> Sequences of our activities

>> Workout activities we do

>> Food we eat

>> Entertainment we like

All of this information will sketch a digital profile of you in cyberspace. The user profiles will be the backbone for the recommendation systems that power contextual search.

Recommender systems and predictive models are the heart of a contextual based search engine. In essence, a recommender system will be suggesting relevant search results to the user by using term-based recommendation, similar-users recommendation, or both. Recommender systems are covered in details in Chapter 2.

The challenge for building such a recommender system is creating a knowledge base. The knowledge base is simply the data about users' information and their online behavior. If you're building a search engine for your organization with contextual search, you need to architect a data hub where you will store your users' information, the clickstream (clicks logs on your site) and search queries that are happening every time a user is on your site.

As an example, consider a case where you build a search engine to serve your company's employees for documents, such as project reports and publications.

One of the first things that you would need to do is to locate the employees' data, such as the departments they work for, their interests, and their past projects, then build their biographies. This data usually is available in the human resources department. Then you may want to join this data with logs from the search engine web application in your organization about employee's query performed in the site, the time the queries were issued, and the time spent on every page or search results. This information will allow you to build profiles of your employees based on their behavior and personal information. These data sources are a possible way to feed the knowledge base of your system. You might expand it later to other data sources that will help build richer profiles about your users.

Additionally, you may want to build a recommender system that will match users to documents. To be able to merge the results from the recommender system to your search engine platform, you may need to design an algorithm that will serve for that purpose. You may need to apply keyword-based search and semantic search that will give you a larger set of results that you may expand or narrow by using the results from contextual search.

In fact, the search results generated by the keyword-based search are documents where the keywords being searched appear the most.

Natural-language processing algorithms and ontologies that will power semantic-based search will expand the search result through query expansion to semantically related keywords (for example, searching for "Car" will be expanded to searching for "Vehicle"). The recommender system will bring another set of results that matches the users who is performing the search query. One way to create an optimal search results is to filter the search results given by the semantic and keyword based search, then apply high-ranking score to those documents that were recommended by the recommendation system to the user performing the search.

Consider a scenario where the user is searching for "solar power plants projects". Assume that Document#1, Document#2, and Document#3 are the top three documents returned in the search results page. These documents appear on the top search results according to keyword-based search mainly because they have the words solar, power, plants and projects mentioned relatively frequently in those documents and in important sections in those documents (such as title, introduction, and conclusion). When the search engine supports semantic search, then the results may change; for example, Document#5 may outrank Document#2 or Document#3 and appear in the search results page because Document#5 contains several related terms to the search query (such as energy, climate change, carbon emissions, and fossil fuels), in addition to high frequency of the words solar, plant and project. In addition, because the user who is searching for "solar power plants projects" is known to the search engine to be interested in projects in Africa, the recommender system built into the search engine might give a high relevancy score to Document#3. In fact, Document#3 is about a project that describes the world's largest concentrated solar plant (which was recently developed in Morocco, which is located in north Africa). Notice that a context of user's interests in projects in African countries played a role in the search results.

Let us consider another scenario where a user is searching for the same query "solar power plants projects". Unlike the preceding scenario, the search results for the same search query for this particular user are different and it's showing a document that appears first in the search results page that talks about a recent giant solar plant in the town of Beloit.

The reason behind this document appearing first in the search result could be that this particular user clicked on U.S. based solar plants projects document in the past, and it could also be that the user is an energy specialist interested specifically in solar projects in the United States of America.

Information about the user's interests can be captured either at initial registration for the search engine, or can be gathered from the human resources department, or captured as the user navigated through the search engine website in the past. In summary, the search results will be adjusted according to the user's predicted interests at the time she or he is searching.

Differentiating Business Intelligence from Big-Data Analytics

Be sure to make a clear distinction between business intelligence and data mining. Here are the basics of the distinction:

>> **Business intelligence (BI)** is about building a model that answers specific business questions. You start with a question or a set of questions, gather data and data sources, and then build a computer program that uses those resources to provide answers to the business questions you've targeted. Business intelligence is about providing the infrastructure for searching your data and building reports. Business intelligence uses *controlled data* — predefined, structured data, stored mainly in data-warehousing environments. BI uses *online analytical processing (OLAP)* techniques to provide some analytical capabilities — enough to construct dashboards you can use to query data, as well as create and view reports. BI is different from data mining and doesn't discovered hidden insights.

>> **Data mining (DM)** is a more generalized data-exploration task: You may not necessarily know exactly what you're looking for, but you're open to all discoveries. Data mining can be the first step in the analytics process that allows you to dive into the collected and prepared data to unveil insights that could have gone undiscovered otherwise. Big data Analytics rely on newer technologies that allow deeper knowledge discovery in large bodies of data of any type (structured, unstructured, or semi-structured); technologies designed for such work include Hadoop, Spark, and MapReduce (introduced in Chapter 3).

Predictive Analytics emerged to complement, rather than compete with, business intelligence and data mining. You can co-ordinate your pursuit of analytics with business intelligence by using BI to preprocess the data you're preparing for use in your predictive analytics model. You can point BI systems to different data sources — and use the visualizations that BI produces from raw data — to give you an overview of your data even before you start designing your analytics model. This approach leads to the visualization of large amounts of raw data, as discussed in the next section.

Exploration of Raw Data

A picture is worth a thousand words — especially when you're trying to get a good handle on your data. At the pre-processing step, while you're preparing your data, it's a best practice to visualize what you have in hand before getting into predictive analytics.

You start by using a spreadsheet such as Microsoft Excel to create a data matrix — which consists of candidate data *features* (also referred to as *attributes*). Several business intelligence software packages (such as Tableau) can give you a preliminary overview of the data to which you're about to apply analytics.

Identifying data attributes

In programming terms, data is a collection of objects and their corresponding attributes. A *data object* is also called a *record, item, observation, instance,* or *entity.* A data object can be described by a collection of attributes that describe it. A data *attribute* is also known as *feature, field,* or *characteristic.* Attributes can be nominal, ordinal, or interval:

>> **Nominal attributes** are numbers (for example, zip codes) or nouns (for example, gender).

>> **Ordinal attributes,** in most cases, represent ratings or rankings (for example, degree of interest in buying Product A, ranked from 1 to 10 to represent least interest to most interest).

>> **Interval attributes** represent data ranges, such as calendar dates.

One motivation behind visualizing raw data is to select that subset of attributes that will potentially be included in the analytics. Again, this is one of the tasks that will lead you to the nucleus — the smart data to which you'll apply analytics.

Your data scientist might be applying predictive models to a database or data warehouse that stores terabytes (or more) of data. Don't be surprised when it takes a very long time to run models over the whole database. You'll need to select and extract a good representative sample of your large body of data — one that produces nearly the same analytical results as the whole body. Another helpful step, called *dimension reduction*, starts when you select the data attributes that are most important — and here visualization can be of help. Visualization might be able to give you an idea of the dispersion of the attributes in your data. For example, taking a spreadsheet of numerical data and with a few clicks in Excel, you can identify the maximum, minimum, variance, and median. You can picture spikes in your data that might lead you to quickly find those outliers that are easy to capture. The next sections illustrate examples of visualizations that you can apply to raw data to detect outliers, missing values, and (in some cases) early insights.

Exploring common data visualizations

When you request a cleaning service come to your house and the company you hire has never been to your house, naturally you'd expect the company to ask you about (you guessed it) your house. They might also ask about structural features such as the number of rooms and baths, the current overall state of the house, and when they can visit the house to see it before they start cleaning — or even give you an estimate of the cost. Well, getting your data in order is similar to getting your house in order.

Suppose you've captured a large amount of data. You'd like to see it before you even start building your predictive analytics model. Visualizing your data will help you in the very first steps of data preparation by

>> Guiding you to where to start cleaning your data

>> Providing clues to which values you need to fill

>> Pointing you to easy outliers and eliminating them

>> Correcting inconsistent data

>> Eliminating redundant data records

Tabular visualizations

Tables are the simplest, most basic pictorial representation of data. Tables (also known as *spreadsheets*) consist of rows and columns — which correspond, respectively, to the objects and their attributes mentioned earlier as making up your data. For example, consider online social network data. A data object could represent a user. Attributes of a user (data object) can be headings of columns: Gender, Zip Code, or Date of Birth.

The cells in a table represent values as shown in Figure 4-3. Visualization in tables can help you easily spot missing attribute values of data objects.

Data Source#1: Online Social Network Data

Social Network User ID	Date of Birth	Gender	Zip Code	Friends Count	Relationship Status
556694901	6/3/1985	M	21036	859	In relationship
556694902	8/1/1977	F	94024	332	Married
556694903	9/5/1978	F	21794	754	In relationship
556694904	3/9/1986	M	21737	20	Single
556694905	2/7/1984	F	33109	169	Single
556694906	4/7/1983	F	21131	-63	Married
556694907	9/1/1982	M	21042	12	Married
556694908	1/3/1981	F	92067	185	In relationship
556694909	4/5/1980	M	92662	123	Single
556694910	5/3/2029	F	93108	174	Married
556694911	6/9/1994	F	94027	1236	In relationship
556694912	8/1/1978	F	90402	963	Single
556694913	9/8/1980	F	92661	414	Married
556694914	2/3/1982	F	94024	795	Single
556694915	6/6/1981	F	94957	1186	In relationship
556694916	8/8/1994	M	94028	367	Complicated
556694917	2/7/1989	R	33109	45	Complicated
556694918	5/2/1996	M	11962	1247	In relationship
...	...	...	...	...	...

FIGURE 4-3: Example of online social network data in tabular format.

Tables can also provide the flexibility of adding new attributes that are combinations of other attributes. For example, in social network data, you can add another column called Age, which can be easily calculated — as a derived attribute — from the existing Date of Birth attribute. In Figure 4-4, the tabular social network data shows a new column, Age, created from another existing column (Date of Birth).

Data Source#1: Online Social Network Data

Social Network User ID	Date of Birth	Gender	Zip Code	Friends Count	Relationship Status	Age
556694901	6/3/1985	M	21036	859	In relationship	28
556694902	8/1/1977	F	94024	332	Married	36
556694903	9/5/1978	F	21794	754	In relationship	35
556694904	3/9/1986	M	21737	20	Single	27
556694905	2/7/1984	F	33109	169	Single	29
556694906	4/7/1983	F	21131	-63	Married	30
556694907	9/1/1982	M	21042	12	Married	31
556694908	1/3/1981	F	92067	185	In relationship	32
556694909	4/5/1980	M	92662	123	Single	33
556694910	5/3/2029	F	93108	174	Married	-16
556694911	6/9/1994	F	94027	1236	In relationship	19
556694912	8/1/1978	F	90402	963	Single	35
556694913	9/8/1980	F	92661	414	Married	33
556694914	2/3/1982	F	94024	795	Single	31
556694915	6/6/1981	F	94957	1186	In relationship	31
556694916	8/8/1994	M	94028	367	Complicated	19
556694917	2/7/1989	R	33109	45	Complicated	24
556694918	5/2/1996	M	11962	1247	In relationship	17
...	...	...	...	...	...	...

FIGURE 4-4: Example of derived attributes.

Word clouds

Consider a list of words or concepts arranged as a *word cloud* — a graphic representation of all words on the list, showing the size of each word as proportional to a metric that you specify. For example, when you have a spreadsheet of words and occurrences and you'd like to identify the most important words, try a word cloud.

Word clouds work because most organizations' data is text; a common example is Twitter's use of trending terms. Every term in Figure 4-5 (for example) has a weight that affects its size as an indicator of its relative importance. One way to define that weight could be by the number of times a word appears in your data collection. The more frequently a word appears, the "heavier" its weight — and the larger it appears in the cloud.

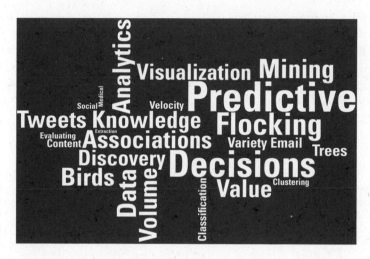

FIGURE 4-5: Word importance represented as weight and size in a word cloud.

Flocking birds as a novel data representation

"Birds of a feather flock together" is a traditional saying that provides instant insight as a way of visualizing data: Individuals of similar tastes, interests, dreams, goals, habits, and behaviors tend to congregate in groups.

Natural flocking behavior in general is a self-organizing system in which objects (in particular, living things) tend to behave according to (a) the environment they belong to and (b) their responses to other existing objects. The flocking behavior of natural societies such as those of bees, flies, birds, fish, and ants — or, for that matter, people — is also known as *swarm intelligence*.

Birds follow natural rules when they behave as a flock. *Flock-mates* are birds located with a certain distance from each other; those birds are considered similar. Each bird moves according to the three main rules that organize flocking behavior.

>> **Separation:** Flock-mates mustn't collide with each other.

>> **Alignment:** Flock-mates move in the same average direction as their neighbors.

>> **Cohesion:** Flock-mates move according to the average position or location of their flock-mates.

Modeling these three rules can enable an analytical system to simulate flocking behaviors. That's because biologically inspired algorithms, in particular those derived from bird-flocking behavior, offer a simple way to model social network data. Using the self-organized natural behavior of flocking birds, you can convert a straightforward spreadsheet into visualization, such as Figure 4-6. The key is to define the notion of similarity as part of your data — and construct a mathematical function that supports that similarity. Start with a couple of questions:

>> What makes two data objects in your data similar?

>> Which attributes can best drive the similarity between two data records?

FIGURE 4-6:
A simple, novel way to visualize big data: natural bird-flocking behavior.

For example, in social network data, the data records represent individual users; the attributes that describe them can include Age, Zip Code, Relationship Status, List of Friends, Number of Friends, Habits, Events Attended, Books Read, and other groups of particular interests (Sports, Movies, and so on).

You can define the similarity for your group according to nearly any attribute. For example, you can call two members of a social network *similar* when they read the same books, have a large number of common friends, and have attended the same events. Those two similar members will flock together if birds flocking in a virtual space represent them.

In the healthcare and biomedical fields, the data object could be patient data. And you could base the attributes on the patient's personal information, treatments, and information related to diagnosis. Then, by plotting the data as a visualization based on the flocking of birds, you might be able to visualize and discern insights before you even apply data analytics. Some interesting patterns in your data would become apparent, including some characteristic groupings — and even data anomalies.

Flocking behavior is iterative because behavior, while consistent, isn't static. At each iteration (or round), birds move. Using flocking birds as a visualization technique is an especially relevant way to represent streamed data. With streaming data, at each point the visualization of data objects can change according to the new incoming data. In Figure 4-6, shown earlier, a flocking bird in a virtual space represents a data object (such as an individual user) in the dataset in question (such as the social network). Similar birds in the virtual space that represent similar data objects in real life will flock together and appear next to each other in the visualization.

We invite you to read more on bird flocking algorithms; here are some references to explore the nature inspired predictive analytics field:

Bellaachia, A., & Bari, A. (2012, June). Flock by leader: a novel machine learning biologically inspired clustering algorithm. Springer Berlin Heidelberg.

Cui, X., Gao, J., & Potok, T. E. (2006). A flocking based algorithm for document clustering analysis. Journal of systems architecture, 52(8), 505-515.

Graph charts

Graph theory provides a set of powerful algorithms that can analyze data structured and represented as a graph. In computer science, a *graph* is data structure, a way to organize data that represents relations between pairs of data objects. A graph consists of two main parts:

>> Vertices, also known as *nodes*

>> Edges, which connect pairs of nodes

Edges can be directed (drawn as arrows) and can have weights, as shown in Figure 4-7. You can decide to place an edge (arrow) between two nodes (circles) — in this case, the members of the social network who are connected to other members as friends:

The arrow's direction indicates who "friends" whom first, or who initiates interactions most of the time.

The weight assigned to a particular edge (the numerical value of the edge, as shown in Figure 4-7) can represent the level of social interaction that two social network members have. This example uses a scale of 10: The closer the value is to 10, the more the network members interact with one another.

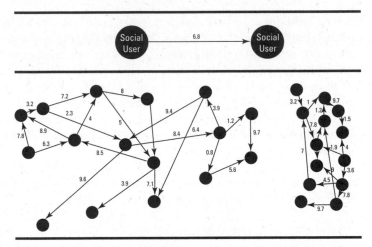

FIGURE 4-7: Online social graph.

Here a *social interaction* is the process in which at least two members of a social network act and or respond to each other. The interaction can be offline and go beyond just the online interactions that are happening on the network. For example, offline interactions can include meetings, conference calls, "live" social gatherings, group travel, social events, mobile communications, and text messaging. All such interactions can be represented as numbers, each with a *score* (a weighted sum of all types of interactions).

The weight on the graph can also represent the *influence rate.* How influential is one member on another? Several algorithms can calculate influence rate between two social network members, based on their online posts, common friends, and other criteria.

In Figure 4-7, social network members are represented with black circles; each relationship represented by an edge shows a level of interaction, which is in turn represented as number on the edge. From an initial view, you can spot two disconnected groups — a quick insight that crops up even before you apply analytics.

You might want to focus on either or both of these two groups; you may want to include one of them in the data you're preparing as a resource for when you build your predictive model. Applying your analytics to one of the groups may enable you to dive into the data and extract patterns that aren't obvious.

Common visualizations

Bar charts are well known type of visualization that can be used to spot spikes or anomalies in your data. You can use it for each attribute to quickly picture minimum and maximum values. Bar charts can be also used to start a discussion of how to normalize your data. *Normalization* is the adjustment of some — or all — attribute values on a scale that makes the data more usable.

A Pie chart is another popular visualization. Pie charts are used mainly to show percentages. They can easily illustrate the distribution of several items, and highlight the most dominant.

Line graphs are a traditional way of representing data that enable you to visualize multiple series or multiple attributes (columns) in the same graph. One advantage of line graphs is flexibility: You can combine different series in one line graph for several purposes. One such graph could depict a correlation between different series.

In Chapter 18 and Chapter 19, we introduce most widely used tools that you can use to visualize data.

2

Incorporating Algorithms in Your Models

Chapter 5

Applying Models

Big data is like an engine that drives our lives. It includes everything about us. Predictive analytics can use big data to foresee our future moves and make predictions about our likely actions — especially when we're someone's prospective customers. Hypothetically, a predictive analytics model can know when you're asleep and can predict the time you'll wake up.

Companies are capturing and storing information at every opportunity. They store every purchase you make, every online search you do, every website you visit, and your preferences. Everything is closely monitored and analyzed. This has become the new norm in our lives. Your doctor, your employer, your next-door grocer will be all analyzing data about you soon, if they aren't already.

TIP

The rule for using all this data is clear: Whichever company can accurately find patterns in your data, analyze them, and use them effectively, will profit from it.

So what are some of the business implications of using predictive analytics on big data? And how can businesses or organizations make profit or make their own success stories from your data? For that matter, how can you do the same? To clarify that picture, this chapter introduces different types of models and highlights some recent case studies from different domains, including healthcare, social media, marketing, and politics. The chapter also highlights domains that correlate with predictive analytics.

Modeling Data

Most predictive analytics tools come equipped with common algorithms, the underlying mathematical formulas, to help you build your model. A completed model can be applied in a few minutes. In fact, a business analyst with no specific background in statistics, data mining, or machine learning can run powerful algorithms on the data relatively quickly, using available predictive analytics tools.

Suppose a business analyst at a retail company would like to know which customer segments to upsell to. She can load each customer's data, purchase history, preferences, demographics, and any other type of relevant data; run a few models to determine the likely segments of interest, and put the results to use right away in a sales campaign.

Those of us who do this type of work for a living (such as data scientists) tend to seek the ultimate results — to build the all-powerful model to wow the business stakeholders and to showcase the wealth of our knowledge.

In pursuit of this goal, the model-building may take a little longer than in the retailer example. Instead of aiming for a quick victory, we want to optimize performance by building a model with the highest accuracy possible.

A lot of tweaking and experimentation is needed. We may start with a large number of variables or features that are available in our dataset, and funnel our way through until we get to the very few variables that have the most predictive power. This process requires running as many simulations as possible while changing the values of the parameters and plotting the results.

Another common technique is to build an ensemble model (see Chapter 7), evaluate the results of the models that make it up, and present the user with the highest-scoring model among them. Or (at the very minimum) we can run multiple and separate techniques on the data, compare results, and eventually pick the one model that consistently scores higher for most of our simulations and what-if scenarios.

REMEMBER

Building a model is part science and part art. The science refers to well-established statistical techniques, machine learning, and data-mining algorithms. Tweaking is the art.

Models and simulation

A model is nothing but a mathematical representation of a segment of the world we are interested in. A model can mimic behavioral aspects of our customers. It can represent the different customer segments. A well-made, well-tuned model can *forecast* — predict with high accuracy — the next outcome of a given event.

From this definition, you can already deduce that it's possible to build a model to mimic and represent virtually about anything you want to analyze. As you might imagine, this process can quickly and easily become very complex and difficult.

To start with the potential complexity, imagine you're working with dataset that has many associated variables with a wide range of values. Going through all the possible values and permutations across the entire dataset can be time-consuming.

The standard approach is to run *what-if scenarios* — hypothetical situations that your simulations investigate. The general outline of running a what-if scenario looks like this:

1. Build the model.

2. Start changing the values of parameters and examining the new results, or use a *tool* — a specialized software program that automates that whole process for you.

3. Look at the report that the model generates.

4. Evaluate the result and pick the most important predictors; if you've run multiple models, pick the right model.

The process looks simpler on the page than it is in practice. Certain tasks lend themselves easily to canned solutions. Others can be very hard to solve — two notoriously hard examples are predicting extended weather conditions or stock-market performance. The farther into the future you try to predict, the faster the accuracy of the predictions diminishes. It may be possible to say (for example) that it will snow within the next 12 hours, but it's hard to come up with an accurate prediction that it will snow in three weeks from now.

Similar uncertainty crops up when predicting a hurricane's path; it's difficult to know with certainty the exact path the farther out into the future one gets. That's why new data is immediately made available for these models, and the forecast is continuously updated.

Simulating the stock market is also extremely difficult, for a simple reason: The market can be affected by virtually everything.

Complex problems require clever solutions, constant tweaking, and continuous refreshment of the deployed models.

>> **Clever solutions**: One way to smarten up the model is to include variables not usually associated with the field you're investigating. To analyze the stock market, for example, you might include data about parking activities at malls, or analyze data about daily local newspapers from around the country.

Another clever solution involves divorce lawyers acquiring data from credit card companies. Apparently those companies know couples are headed for divorce, about two years before the actual divorce dates. And they know that with an accuracy of 98 percent — mainly based on the spending habits of the couples.

>> **Tweaking is a process of many parts**: Going through what-if scenarios, running multiple algorithms, and including or excluding certain variables as you step through the analysis. You get the most from this process if you always re-evaluate and try to understand your data in light of the business problem at hand, ask the hard questions, explore the data, and experiment with the different approaches.

>> **Continuous refreshing of the model**: Updating your model periodically, in light of new information, is recommended to counteract the model's tendency to decay over time.

When new data becomes available, preserve your competitive edge by updating the model; to keep this process relevant, closely track and monitor your model's performance in real time.

When all companies are doing the same thing, exploring the same gaps, and competing in the same space, you have to stay ahead of the curve. One way to do so is to vary your tactics, spice up your campaigns, and hone your ability to detect the changing trends, positioning your business and to take full advantage of them.

In short, building a predictive model is an ongoing process, not a set-it-and-forget-it solution. Getting a business to think that way represents a cultural shift for most organizations, but that's what current market conditions demand.

One other form of complexity is the multiple directions your model-building can go. You can build a model about anything and everything — where do you start? The next section helps clear up the potential confusion by categorizing the different types of models.

Categorizing models

You have various ways to categorize the models used for predictive analytics. In general, you can sort them out by

>> The business problems they solve and the primary business functions they serve (such as sales, advertising, human resources, or risk management).

>> The mathematical implementation used in the model (such as statistics, data mining, and machine learning).

Every model will have some combination of these aspects; more often than not, one or the other will dominate. The intended function of the model can take one of various directions — predictive, classification, clustering, decision-oriented, or associative — as outlined in the following sections.

Predictive models

Predictive models analyze data and predict the next outcome. This is the big contribution of predictive analytics, as distinct from business intelligence. Business intelligence monitors what's going on in an organization now. Predictive models analyze historical data to make an informed decision about the likelihood of future outcomes.

Given certain conditions (recent number and frequency of customers complaints, the date of renewal of service approaching, and the availability of cheaper options by the competition) how likely is this customer to churn?

The output of the predictive model can also be a binary, yes/no or 0/1 answer: whether a transaction is fraudulent, for example. A predictive model can generate multiple results, sometimes combining yes/no results with a probability that a certain event will happen. A customer's creditworthiness, for example, could be rated as yes or no, and a probability assigned that describes how likely that customer is to pay off a loan on time.

Clustering and classification models

When a model uses clustering and classification, it identifies different groupings within existing data. You can still build a predictive model on top of the output of your clustering model using the clustering to classify new data points. If, for example, you run a clustering algorithm on your customers' data and thereby separate them into well-defined groups, you can then use classification to learn about a new customer and clearly identify his group. Then you can tailor your response (for example, a targeted marketing campaign) and your handling of the new customer.

Classification uses a combination of characteristics and features to indicate whether an item of data belongs to a particular class.

Many applications or business problems can be formulated as classification problems. At the very basic level, for example, you can classify outcomes as desired and undesired. For example, you can classify an insurance claim as legitimate or fraudulent.

Decision models

Given a complex scenario, what is the best decision to make — and if you were to take that action, what would the outcome be? Decision-oriented models (simply called *decision models*) address such questions by building strategic plans so as to identify the best course of action, given certain events. Decision models can be risk mitigations strategies, helping to identify your best response to unlikely events.

Decision models probe various scenarios and select the best of all courses. To make an informed decision, you need deep understanding of the complex relationships in the data and the context you're operating in. A decision model serves as a tool to help you develop that understanding.

Association models

Associative models (called *association models*) are built on the underlying associations and relationships present in the data. If (for example) a customer is subscribed to a particular service, it's most likely that she will order another specific service. If a customer is looking to buy Product A (a sports car), and that product is associated with Product B (say, sunglasses branded by the carmaker), he is more likely to buy Product B.

Some of these associations can easily be identified; others may not be so obvious. Stumbling over an interesting association, previously unknown, can lead to dramatic benefits.

Another way of finding an association is to determine whether a given event increases the probability that another event will take place. If, for example, a company that leads a certain industrial sector just reported stellar earnings, what is the probability that a basket of stocks in that same sector to go up or down in value?

Describing and summarizing data

At the start of a predictive analytics project, the data scientist and the business analyst aren't fully familiar with the data yet, and don't know what analysis will work best. Substantial time must be spent exploring that data with the sole goal of gaining familiarity. Visualization tools can help with this.

Describing your data can provide a precise summary of the characteristics and underlying structure that make the data relevant and useful. For example, identifying different groupings within the data is an essential step toward building a model that accurately represents your data — which makes a useful analytical result more likely.

Making better business decisions

Business leaders use predictive analytics, first and foremost, to empower business decision-making. The value of data to an organization is, essentially, how well it drives decision-making toward the organization's success.

Data-driven decisions give your business and managerial processes a solid footing, enhance your customers' satisfaction, and increase your return on investment. In a world marketplace full of ever-changing variables — governed by complex rules and immensely interdependent global systems — organizations can navigate more successfully by using predictive analytics to replace guesswork with actions based on real data.

Predictive analytics can transform your business by generating useful new insights that can serve as the basis of sound strategies and effective decision-making based on facts.

Healthcare Analytics Case Studies

The healthcare domain offers examples of predictive analytics in action. This section offers two case studies. In one, Google search queries attempted to build a predictive model to predict flu outbreak that made good predictions at some point in time, then it failed to continue predicting outbreaks in subsequent years. In the other, cancer data predicts the survival rate of breast cancer patients.

Google Flu Trends

People use Google to search for nearly everything, nearly all the time — their next destination, the name of the person they just met, topics they want to learn about, and even the symptoms of some disease they might think they have. That's where online searches become medically relevant.

Google researchers found that certain search terms may be good indicators that an outbreak of a disease — in particular, influenza — is in progress.

This insight first appeared in a research paper by Jeremy Ginsberg and several others, published in *Nature*. The title sums up the unlikely-sounding premise: "Detecting Influenza Epidemics Using Search Engine Query Data". The results, however, were real for some period of time, then the discovered insights didn't hold for so long. Google has been using search terms attempting to predict the current flu activity, almost in real time, around the world.

Ginsberg and his colleagues discovered a strong correlation between the number of individuals who search for flu-related terms and the number of individuals who actually *have* the flu. Although an Internet search for information about a disease may seem an obvious action to take when you're feeling ill, consider why it seems obvious: An underlying pattern of behavior exists. The pattern shows up in the data.

Google insights derived from search terms reveal patterns that emerge from similar search queries and real-life phenomena. As stated on Google's site, "[there are] more allergy-related searches during allergy season, and more sunburn-related searches during the summer".

Google attempted to utilize those search queries to extract trends. The aim was to build a model that can predict real-life events such as outbreaks in certain regions of the world, in real time.

The clinical data traditionally used for disease surveillance includes number of visits to hospitals, patients' symptoms, and patients' treatments. Such data elements can be used to detect or predict the spread of an epidemic. The Centers for Disease Control and Prevention (CDC) uses traditional surveillance systems with up to a two-week "reporting lag," according to Google. In fact, because flu victims used Google when they first got sick, before they went to the doctor, the hope was that the Google flu approach would shorten the lag time.

The government data that Google used — readily available from the CDC website (www.cdc.gov/flu/weekly) — consists of how many patients' visits were flu-related across the nine regions of the United States. Based on a training dataset that encompassed five years of search queries and publicly available government data on influenza, Google attempted to build a model for the international surveillance of influenza that worked for some point in time, then failed at subsequent years.

The project is known as Google Flu Trends. After its initial success of predicting flu outbreaks with around 97 percent accuracy over the CDC data in 2008, Google reported failure of the same project to report incorrect predictions on subsequent years. In fact, a few months after Google announced its success of building a model that can predict a flu epidemic, Google failed to predict the 2009 swine flu caused by H1N1 influenza.

The predictions Google produced were inaccurate and the CDC remains the only credible source for predicting flu outbreaks. In fact, at some point between 2012 and 2013, Google Flu trends inaccurately predicted the number of flu cases, a number as twice the number of doctors' visits that were originally reported by the CDC. Google Flu Trends is now suspended and is no longer publishing predictions. However, what can we learn from this failure?

Some flu symptoms are

>> Headaches

>> Fever

>> Coughing

>> Vomiting

>> Runny nose

>> Sore throat

>> Tiredness

>> Aching joints

It isn't very clearly cited what exact keywords Google uses to collect related search queries, but most likely the Google search queries are filtered by the preceding symptoms.

The major cause of inaccuracies in Google predictions comes from the fact that many of people who were using Google to search such flu symptoms don't know what influenza is, and most of them don't have it.

If you search Google for "frequent headaches in the morning" you may not necessarily have flu. The same thing applied to other symptoms, such as tiredness and sore throat.

In fact, CDC data shows that the majority of people visiting doctors were thinking that they have influenza. The reality is that they don't end up having it. The CDC reported that about 10 percent of doctor's visits were positive flu cases. The rest were similar illness to influenza.

Of the other 90 percent of doctors' visitors who thought they had the flu but did not, many were searching in Google and weren't excluded from the Google Flu Trend predictive model, although they didn't have a flu. Hence, Google Flu Trends' results were inaccurate.

Lesson learned: Big data inspires and can lead to phenomenal results, but only when it's good quality data.

Cancer survivability predictors

The medical uses of predictive analytics include the use of algorithms to predict the survivability rate among breast cancer patients. According to American Cancer

Society Surveillance Research, breast cancer was the leading type of cancer in 2013. An estimated 232,340 new cases of breast cancer were expected to be diagnosed among American women in 2013, with 39,620 deaths expected from breast cancer in the same year.

Professor Abdelghani Bellaachia and his team at George Washington University made a powerful connection between predictive analytics and human benefit in a research paper published by the Society of Industrial and Applied Mathematics (SIAM): "Predicting Breast Cancer Survivability Using Data Mining Techniques."

In the course of developing the results described in this paper, the team used publicly available historical data about breast cancer survivability to build the model. That data can be downloaded from National Cancer Institute's Surveillance Epidemiology and End Results website, SEER for short (http://seer.cancer.gov).

SEER's database encapsulated historical data about different types of cancer. The collected data on breast cancer included several attributes such as survival time, vital status, and cause of death.

The predictive analytics model adopted for this case study was classification-based. Three algorithms were used — Naïve Bayes, Neural Network, and Decision Trees. (See Chapter 7 for more on these algorithms.) Researchers compared their accuracy and ultimately selected the best for use in their model.

Because this was a classification-based prediction, the model had to be trained by using clusters or classes of data. The pre-classification step requires organizing the data into categories: survived and not survived. Thus the dataset represents two groups of patients. Each row or record corresponds to a breast cancer patient; each can be labeled as survived or not survived.

The training set contains the records of patient data used to build the model; the rest of the records (test data) were used to test the model.

In the case study, a model was selected for breast cancer survivability after comparing all three algorithms' outputs. For this specific application in this specific study, the Decision Trees model performed better by accurately classifying the test data and labeling the target group.

For more details about this use case, see the original publication: Bellaachia, Abdelghani, and Erhan Guven. "Predicting breast cancer survivability using data mining techniques." Age 58.13 (2006): 10-110. http://www.siam.org/meetings/sdm06/workproceed/Scientific%20Datasets/bellaachia.pdf.

Social and Marketing Analytics Case Studies

On a whole different note, social and marketing analytics provide further evidence of startling-but-useful connections between online activity and useful predictions. The next sections examine several examples: the use of shopping data over time to predict pregnancy status of the customer; the use of Twitter to predict the stock market; the use of news articles to speculate the variations of stock prices; the use Twitter to predict earthquakes and election outcomes; and the potential of New York City biker's data. Relax. It only looks like magic.

Target store predicts pregnant women

In an unintentionally invasive instance, the Target store chain used predictive analytics on big data to predict which of its customers were likely to be pregnant. (Charles Duhigg, a reporter at *The New York Times*, initially covered this story.) Target collected data on some specific items that couples were buying, such as vitamins, unscented lotions, books on pregnancy, and maternity clothing.

Using that data, Target developed predictive models for pregnancy among its customers. The models scored the likelihood of a given customer to be pregnant.

Keep in mind that predictive analytics models don't rely on only one factor (such as purchasing patterns) to predict the likelihood of an event. Target probably didn't rely on only one factor to make its predictions. Rather, the model looked at factors that included purchase patterns of pregnancy-related products, age, relationship status, and websites visited. Most important, the resulting predictions were based on events that happened over a period of time, not on isolated events. For example, a couple buys vitamins at some point in time, a pregnancy-guide magazine at another point in time, hand towels at yet another time, and maternity clothes at a still different time. Further, the same couple could have visited websites related to pre-pregnancy, or could have visited websites to look for baby names or lessons for couples on how to cope with the first days of pregnancy. (This information could have been saved from search queries done by the couple.) After Target identified potential customers as probably pregnant, it could then send specialized coupons for products such as lotion and diapers to those customers.

Details of the exact model that Target used to predict customer pregnancy aren't available. One way to build such a model, however, is to use classification-based prediction. (Note that this isn't the only possible way, and may not be the approach used at Target.) The general procedure would look like this:

1. Collect data about past, current, or potential Target customers, and including their purchases over time in the cyberspace (such as search data from Target's website)

2. Collect transactional data from Target customers who actually purchase the products you're interested in, some of which are pregnancy-related.

3. Select training data that will be used to build your classification-based model, and set aside some of the past data to use in testing your model.

4. Test the model until it's validated and you're happy with the accuracy of its performance on historical data.

5. Deploy your model. As new incoming data for a given customer arrives, your model will classify that customer as either potentially pregnant or not.

Twitter-based predictors of earthquakes

Another astonishing use of predictive analytics is to detect earthquakes. Yes, earthquakes. Researchers Sakaki, Okazaki, and Matsuo from the University of Tokyo — situated in a region known for seismic activity — used postings on the Twitter microblog social network to detect an earthquake in real time. A summary of their 2010 research ("Earthquake Shakes Twitter Users: Real-Time Event Detection by Social Sensors") was published in the proceedings of the 2013 International Conference on World Wide Web.

The researchers' approach was to utilize Twitter users as sensor that can signal an event through tweets. Because Twitter users tend to tweet several times daily, the researchers could capture, analyze and categorize tweets in real time. They sought to predict the occurrence of earthquakes of Intensity three or more by monitoring those tweets. One result of the research was an earthquake-based Twitter monitoring system that sends e-mails to registered users to notify them of an earthquake in progress. Apparently the registered users of this system received notification much faster than from the announcements broadcasted by the Japan Meteorological Agency. The Twitter-based system was based on a simple idea:

1. The earthquake-detection application starts collecting tweets about an event that's happening in real time.

2. The collected tweets would be used to trace the exact location of the earthquake.

One problem: Tweets containing the word *earthquake* may or may not be about an actual earthquake. The data collected was originally focused on tweets consisting of words directly related to an earthquake event — for example, such phrases as "Earthquake!" or "Now it's shaking!" The problem was that the meanings of such words might depend on context. *Shaking* crops up in phrases such as "someone is shaking hands with my boss" — and even *earthquake* might mean a topic rather than an event (as in, "I am attending an earthquake conference"). For that matter, the verb tense of the tweet might refer to a past event (as in a phrase such as, "the earthquake yesterday was scary").

To cut through these ambiguities, the researchers developed a classification-based predictive model based on the Support Vector Machine (see Chapter 7).

>> A tweet would be classified as positive or negative on the basis of a simple principle: A positive tweet is about an actual earthquake; a negative tweet is not.

>> Each tweet was represented by using three groups of features:

The number of words in the tweet and the position of the query word within the tweet.

The keywords in the tweet.

The words that precede and follow a query word such as *earthquake* in the tweet.

>> The model makes these assumptions:

That a tweet classified as positive contains the tweeter's geographical location.

That a tweeter who sends a positive tweet can be interpreted as a virtual sensor.

That such a tweeter is actively tweeting about actual events that are taking place.

Twitter-based predictors of political campaign outcomes

In a relatively short time, political activity has saturated online social media — and vice versa — even at the higher levels of government.

At the United States House of Representatives, for example, it's common to see congressional staffers in the House gallery, busily typing tweets into their mobile phones while attending a session. Every senator and congressman or congresswoman has a Twitter page — and they (or their staffers) have to keep it active, so they tweet about everything happening inside the House.

Even so, some things never change: A successful political campaign still focuses on making its candidate popular enough to get elected. A winning candidate is the one who can make a lot of people aware of him or her — and (most importantly) get people talking positively about him or her. That's where politics and social media grab hold of each other.

An Indiana University study has shown a statistically significant relationship between Twitter data and U.S. election results. DiGrazia et al. published a paper titled "More Tweets, More Votes: Social Media as a Quantitative Indicator of Political Behavior". (An electronic copy is available at: `http://ssrn.com/abstract=2235423`.) The study found a correlation between the number of times a candidate for the House of Representatives was mentioned on Twitter in the months before an election and that candidate's performance in that election. The conclusion: The more a candidate is mentioned on Twitter, the better.

According to a *Washington Post* article, the sentiments expressed in tweets as reactions to the political events of the 2012 elections matched the balance of public opinion (as indicated by a random-sample survey) about 25 percent of the time.

As Nick Kolakowski relates in an article published online (`http://insights.dice.com/2012/11/06/twitter-experiment-predicts-obama-election-win`), a team at the Oxford Internet Institute, led by Mark Graham, investigated the relationship between Twitter and election results. They collected thirty million Tweets in October 2012, and counted how many tweets mentioned the two presidential candidates. They found that Obama was mentioned in 132,771 tweets; Romney was mentioned in 120,637 tweets. The Institute translated the count into projected percentages of the popular vote — 52.4 percent for Obama versus 47.6 percent for Romney. At least in terms of popular votes, those figures predicted Obama's victory.

However, a certain ambiguity tended to cloud the picture: The user who tweeted *about* a candidate might not vote *for* that candidate. One way to unveil the intention of such a Twitter user would be to apply sentiment analysis to the text of the tweet. In fact, Graham admitted that they should have analyzed the sentiments of the tweets. Clearly, sentiment analysis plays a major role in building a predictive analytics model for such situations.

So, if you're building a model that seeks to predict victory or defeat for the next prominent political candidate, here's a general approach:

1. Start by collecting a comprehensive training dataset that consists of data about past political campaigns, and present data about all current candidates.

   TIP

   Data should be gathered from microblogs such as Twitter or Tumblr, and also from news articles, YouTube videos (include the number of views and viewer comments), and other sources.

2. Count the mentions of the candidates from your sources.

3. Use sentiment analysis to count the number of positive, negative, and neutral mentions for each candidate.

4. As you iterate through the development of your model, make sure your analysis includes other criteria that affect elections and voting.

TIP

Such factors include scandals, candidates' interviews, debates, people's views as determined by opinion mining, candidates' visits to other countries, sentiment analysis on the candidates' spouses, and so on.

5. *Geocode* — record the geographical coordinates of — your criteria so you can predict by locations.

One or more of the features you identify will have predicting power; those are the features that indicate whether a candidate won a past election. Such results are relevant to your model's predictions.

When your training data has been gathered and cleaned, then a suitable model can be based on classification. At this point, you can use Support Vector Machines, decision trees, or an ensemble model (see Chapter 7 for more on these algorithms) that would base predictions on a set of current criteria *and* past data for each of the political candidates. The idea is to score the results; the higher score should tell you whether the candidate in question will win.

Tweets as predictors for the stock market

Twitter can be a surprisingly valuable source of data when you're building a predictive model for the stock market. A paper by Johan Bollen and his colleagues, "Twitter Mood Predicts the Stock Market," summarizes an analysis of about ten million tweets (by about three million users), which were collected and used to predict the performance of the stock market, up to six days in advance.

The study aggregated tweets by date, and limited its scope to only those tweets that explicitly contained sentiment-related expressions such as "I feel, I am feeling, I'm feeling, I don't feel" were considered in the analysis. The researchers used two tools in this classic example of opinion mining:

>> **Opinion Finder** is a sentiment-analysis tool developed by researchers at the University of Pittsburgh, Cornell University, and the University of Utah. The tool mines text and provides a value that reflects whether the mood discovered in the text is negative or positive.

>> **GPOMS (Google Profile of Mood States)** is a sentiment analysis tool provided by Google. The tool can analyze a text and generate six mood values that could be associated with that text: calm, happy, alert, sure, vital, and kind.

The research followed this general sequence of steps:

1. By aggregating the collected tweets by date and tracking the seven values of the discovered moods, the study generated a *time series* — a sequence of data points taken in order over time. The purpose was to discover and represent public mood over time.

2. For comparison, the researchers downloaded the time series for the Dow Jones Industrial Average (DIJA) closing values (posted on Yahoo! Finance) for the period of time during which they collected the tweets.

3. The study correlated the two time series, using *Granger causality analysis* — a statistical analysis that evaluates whether a time series can be used to forecast another time series — to investigate the hypothesis that public mood values can be used as indicators to predict future DJIA value over the same time period.

4. The study used a Fuzzy Neural Network model (see Chapter 7) to test the hypothesis that including public mood values enhances the prediction accuracy of DJIA.

Although the research didn't provide a complete predictive model, this preliminary correlation of public mood to stock market performance identifies a quest worth pursuing.

Predicting variation of stock prices from news articles

Can we predict the variation of today's stock prices from online news reports? Can we use algorithms to predict the influence of daily news on stock prices? These are just some of the questions asked by those who wish to understand stock valuations and profit from them.

In Dr.Bari's predictive analytics class, graduate students Hongzhi Ren, Lin-Yu Tai, and Yen-Cheng Liu started a research project to apply deep-learning algorithms specifically convolutional neural networks (CNN) and multi-layer perceptron algorithms to predict the influence of news articles on stock prices. (Chapter 7 presents an overview of deep learning.)

The question is whether news articles in text format can be applied to develop a predictive analytics framework to classify how much news articles influence a stock price.

Large of amount of text data from news articles published from 2011 to 2015 were collected from Bloomberg News. Data on stock prices during the same period was collected from Google Finance and Yahoo Finance.

News articles were tagged with the companies' names being mentioned in the articles. During the data preparation phase, each article was assigned a label. The label represented the percent change that occurred to the stock price of the company mentioned in the article. For example, a price change from +1 percent to –1 percent was labeled as "1", a price change +1 percent to +5 percent and –1 percent to –5 percent articles were labeled as "2", from percent change +5 percent to +10 percent and –5 percent to –10 percent articles were labeled as "3", and changes of more than 10 percent were labeled as "4".

After labeling articles with labels that represented their influence on stock prices of the companies mentioned in them, the next phase in building the model was applying feature extraction algorithms to the news articles. (Chapter 9 introduces feature extraction.) Feature extraction from text documents aims at extracting the vocabulary and words that best represent a set of documents. A deep-learning feature extraction algorithm known as word2vec algorithm was applied to take a corpus of news articles as an input and produce a collection of learned word vectors as output. Word2vec is a two-layer neural network that is good for processing text. It's an algorithm that takes a text as input and outputs a set of vectors. Those vectors are considered featured vectors for words in the input text dataset.

For more details and implementation of word2vec, visit `http://deeplearning4j.org/word2vec`. Chapter 7 introduces neural networks and deep learning.

In the modeling phases, two deep learning algorithms knows as multi-layer perceptron (MLP) and convolutional neural network (CNN) (see Chapter 7) were applied to the word vectors generated in the preceding phase to learn from labeled four categories of news articles (1,2,3, and 4) mentioned earlier.

Running multiple experiments and using cross validation as model validation technique, experimental results reported an accuracy of 65.3 percent using MLP model and 71.2 percent for the CNN model to predict the influence label (1 to 4) of a news article. This is an on-going research project and one of the learning outcomes from the early experimental results was that online news articles have the potential to predict the stock future movement. This is an on-going research project that aims at expending the data sources being used to a larger dataset of news to extend the predictive analytics framework.

Analyzing New York City's bicycle usage

If you happen to spend one day in New York City you will encounter a large number of bicyclists interspersed with the pedestrian and vehicle traffic. According to the *New York Daily News*, New York City's bicyclists made a record-breaking ten million trips in 2015.

Early in 2016, Dr. Bari and his graduate students Liyang Yan, Yifu Zhao, and Xingye Zhang began work on a research project to analyze a dataset created by CitiBike. The purpose of the project is to discover valuable insights that could provide solutions to a number of different problems, including congestion on bike lanes, and delivering essential city services where they are needed most.

The genesis of this research project came from the following questions:

>> Can we predict where the city's hotspots will be by mapping people to places within the city?

>> If you work in the financial district in downtown NYC, where would you most likely be living?

>> Where will you most likely spend your time after work?

The potential for such insights to be used as a knowledge base to influence decision making is what drives this research.

The team has been developing a data science framework that has the potential to discover insights from the city's hot spots at any given time of the day. This framework could also be used to reveal potential correlations between workplaces and residential neighborhoods to power recommendation systems for real estate searching.

We considered the following attributes from the dataset:

>> Trip duration

>> Start time and date

>> Stop time and date

>> Start station name

>> End station name

>> Station ID

>> Station latitude and longitude

TECHNICAL STUFF

The dataset website has detailed information about the attributes:

www.citibikenyc.com/system-data

After preprocessing the data, data clustering algorithms such as K-means, DBscan, and hierarchical clustering were applied to the dataset of nearly 300 bicycle stations (Chapter 6 has a detailed explanation of data clustering and algorithms).

Most clustering algorithms came to the same insight: two groups of bicycle stations. Upon closer inspection, the two groups of stations shared many intriguing characteristics:

>> One group of stations was located near work sites, such as banks and insurance companies. A similar number of bikes arrived between 8 A.M. and 11 A.M., and a similar number departed between 5 P.M. and 8 P.M. on the same day.

>> The second group of stations was located near residential areas. Like the first group, these stations happened to have the same number of bikes on average depart between 8 A.M. and 11 A.M., then arrive at the station between 5 P. M. and 8 P. M.

Next, we applied data clustering algorithms to about eight million bike trip records during 2014. Similar trips were grouped based on source station, the destination station's longitude and latitude, time, and duration. A traffic pattern emerged: similar trips between 8 A.M. and 11 A.M. These trips probably were bicyclists traveling from home to work. The same analysis was done for evening trips to discover evening hotspots.

The discovered insights can be summarized like this:

Many cyclists who work in the financial district in New York City probably live in the following areas: Battery Park, Five Points, Chelsea, Hell's Kitchen, and East Village. These cyclists take bikes after work to spend time in one of these areas: Upper Westside, Times Square, or Greenwich Village.

Similarly, many cyclists who travel to SoHo commute from Little Italy, Greenwich Village, Gramercy, Williamsburg, or Fort Greene. They ride bicycles in the evening to spend time in Little Italy, East Village, or Tribeca.

Similar insights were discovered for other parts of the city. These results were only relevant when the weather was convenient for biking. Results also showed that that some cyclists travel to stations that are nearby restaurants, bars, and subway stations. In these cases, it was harder to tell whether the individual took the trip to go to a restaurant or to commute by an alternative method.

There is a lot of potential in the insights from the dataset that can be used to recommend neighborhoods for living, ease bicycle traffic, deliver services to the city, and more. The future of this research will focus on expanding the time frame to look at subsequent years. Additionally, it will aim to take into account alternative data, such as weather and taxi trip data, to develop a smarter predictive analytics framework.

Predictions and responses

In his book *Predictive Analytics: The Power to Predict Who Will Click, Buy, Lie, or Die* (Wiley), Dr. Eric Siegel illustrates that each application of predictive analytics can be outlined by two questions:

>> *What is predicted?*

   The kind of behavior (action, event, or happening) to predict each individual, stock, or other kind of element.

>> *What is done about it?*

   These are the decisions derived by prediction; the action taken by the organization in response to or informed by each prediction.

For example, in the case where Target Stores predicted pregnant women, Dr. Siegel models the predictive analytics application using these two questions:

>> What is predicted?

   Which female customers will have a baby in coming months

>> What is done about it?

   Market relevant offers for soon-to-be parents of newborns

On another instance, Dr. Siegel sums up the targeted direct marketing predictive analytics application as follows:

>> What is predicted?

   Which customers will respond to marketing contact

>> What is done about it?

   Contact customers more likely to respond

Being able to answer these two questions will not only help you view and identify application of predictive analytics, but will also direct you in defining the purpose or the problem of your next predictive analytics application.

Dr. Siegel's book is ideal if you want to read more beyond this chapter on applications of predictive analytics.

The next three sections illustrate important fields that correlate with predictive analytics: data compression, prognostics and open data analytics.

Data compression

Prof.Abdou Youssef is a data compression expert and renowned computer scientist who was awarded a gold medal from the United States National Institute of Standards and Technology (NIST) for his efforts for development of the NIST Digital Library of Mathematical Functions. He has been an advocate and an early proponent of data compression and its role in data analytics before the big data era. Data compression is becoming an important step in the data analytics process. Data compression is the process reducing the size of data. It reduces data storage requirements and can play an important role in improving the performance of the predictive analytics model.

There are many types of data compression. One is known as *lossless compression*. As the name implies, lossless compression algorithms can compress and decompress files with no loss of data during the process. These algorithms are based primarily on statistical modeling techniques that aim to reduce redundant information in a file.

Lossy compression is another type of data compression. Lossy compression algorithms can compress and decompress files into an *approximated* representation of the original data. Lossy compression reduces bits in the data representation by identifying and removing unnecessary and redundant information in the data. This method is often used on multimedia files.

In most cases, data compression algorithms are mathematically complex and require a lot of time to process. Major vendors, such as IBM, offer tools and services for large-scale operations.

It is important for data scientists to understand both the need for data compression algorithms and how to use them. This section provided an overview on the topic of data compression with the goal of inviting the audience to learn more about a subject that will come to have a great impact on our lives.

Here are some useful resources for learning more about data compression:

>> *Data Compression by* Abdou Youssef: `https://www.seas.gwu.edu/~ayoussef/cs6351/`

>> *Introduction to Data Compression* by Guy E. Blelloch, Carnegie Mellon University: `https://www.cs.cmu.edu/~guyb/realworld/compression.pdf`

Prognostics and its Relation to Predictive Analytics

Prognostics is an engineering field that aims at predicting the future state of a system. Prognostics improves the process of scheduling maintenance, ordering parts, and using resources. Prof. David Nagel, a renowned expert in nuclear energy, educator and researcher derived an interesting correlation between the field of Predictive Analytics and the old field of *Prognostics*.

Prognostics and Health Management of Machinery (PHM)

The design, production and operation of machinery are multi-trillion dollar global industries. Anticipation of the needs for machinery maintenance and replacement is of great value to manufacturers of all types. Hence, the field of Prognostic and Health Management (PHM) developed over the past few decades. A good example is the book *Intelligent Fault Diagnosis and Prognosis for Engineering Systems* by G. Vachtsevanos (Wiley).

The core idea is to service machines in production lines when they need it, not according to an overly conservative time-based schedule. With the development and commercial availability of cheap microelectromechanical systems (MEMS) and other small sensors, and the realization of sophisticated real-time computations, the field of PHM developed rapidly. It takes historical and current data, and uses them to predict when machines will require expensive and disruptive attention. That permits cost-effective planning for the care of critical machinery in diverse production lines. The PHM Society serves such work: www.phmsociety.org.

Similarly, predictive analytics (PA), a relatively new field that emerged in recent years, takes big data from many sources, often across complete enterprises or fields. PA processes data with a wide variety of algorithms on diverse computers to predict the times and conditions when actions should be taken. The developed field of PHM and the newer field of PA share common methodologies and goals. Currently, PA and PHM remain distinct from each other. It's possible that PHM will remain separate from PA. It might be more likely that the two fields will interact to their mutual benefit in the coming years. The economic benefits of such interactions could be substantial for both arenas.

In fact, in 2015 General Motors announced the creation of a prognostic technology that aims to determine whether certain vehicle components need attention and maintenance because of possible future failure.

It is important to note that a prognostics system consists of sensors, data acquisition system, prediction algorithms to perform sensor fusion, and predictive model to interpret the results. Data sources involved in building a Prognostic Health Management System mainly include

>> Manufacturer's data:

- Manufacturer engineering data based on computer models and field experience from other or similar systems.

- Represents the nominally expected performance baseline.

- Data updates accomplished by downloading the latest prognostic routines from a central analysis site database through automated means (telemetry).

>> Additional sensor data:

- Oil temperature, air pressures, vibrations.

- Sensor data that include noise as noise could be indicative of the underlying problem.

- Platform CPU data

>> Many algorithms have been used in prognostic systems:

- Linear Regression.

- Time series analysis.

- Bayesian Dynamic linear models.

- Non-linear regression.

The Rise of Open Data

Bob Lytle, the CEO of rel8ed.to (`www.rel8ed.to`), and most recently known as the former CIO of TransUnion Canada, is leading efforts on the use of public information as an alternative and strategic data source for predictive modeling in the financial services and insurance sectors.

Open Data originated from the idea that access to government data should be free and available for everyone to use. Here some examples of open data:

» United States federal agency data: www.data.gov

» Canada's Federal open data: http://open.canada.ca

» World Bank open data: http://data.worldbank.org

The movement of Open Data was part of a simple theory, as Bob says: "We as citizens are the government, and therefore have a right to understand and even reuse the information generated by municipal, regional, and federal entities." However, some data will remain private. Another reality about open data is that open data is dirty data.

Public data is often incomplete, missing many values. The rel8ed.to team is building a platform for cleaning and reducing public data that will be ready to use for modelers across multiple business segments. Bob's team is also using public data to generate open data-driven predictions to find the bottom 10 percent of businesses that will likely fail in 2017, and the top 10 percent that are almost sure to grow and extend. Predictive models using Open Data information can be used by financial institutions to check portfolio trends and take action much earlier in the cycle, before adverse risk or churn events occur.

Chapter 6 and Chapter 9 present several techniques for cleaning and reducing data.

Chapter 6

Identifying Similarities in Data

There is so much data around us that it can feel overwhelming. Large amounts of information are constantly being generated, organized, analyzed, and stored. *Data clustering* is a process that can help you make sense of this flood of data by discovering hidden groupings of similar data items. Data clustering provides a description of your data that says, in essence, *your data contains x number of groups of similar data objects.*

Clustering — in the form of grouping similar things — is part of our daily activities. You use clustering any time you group similar items together. For example, when you store groceries in your fridge, you group the vegetables by themselves in the crisper, put frozen foods in their own section (the freezer), and so on. When you organize currency in your wallet, you arrange the bills by denomination — larger with larger, smaller with smaller. Clustering algorithms achieve this kind of order on a large scale for businesses or organizations — where datasets can comprise thousands or millions of data records associated with thousands of customers, suppliers, business partners, products, services, and so on.

In short, data clustering is an intelligent separation of data into groups of similar data items. The algorithms that do this task have been applied in fields such as biology, marketing, information retrieval, and the analysis of online social networks.

This chapter guides you through the mechanics of data clustering and outlines its importance in predictive analytics.

Explaining Data Clustering

A *dataset* (or data collection) is a set of items. For example, a set of documents is a dataset where the data items are documents. A set of social network users' information (name, age, list of friends, photos, and so on) is a dataset where the data items are profiles of social network users.

Data clustering is the task of dividing a dataset into subsets of similar items. Items can also be referred to as instances, observation, entities, data objects, or data items. In most cases, a dataset is represented in table format — *a data matrix*. A data matrix is a table of numbers, documents, or expressions, represented in rows and columns as follows:

>> Each row corresponds to a given item in the dataset.

   Rows are sometimes referred to as *items, objects, instances, or observations.*

>> Each column represents a particular characteristic of an item.

   Columns are referred to as *features or attributes.*

Applying data clustering to a dataset generates groups of similar data items. These groups are called *clusters* — collections of similar data items.

Similar items have a strong, measurable relationship among them — fresh vegetables, for example, are more similar to each other than they are to frozen vegetables or to fresh fruits — and clustering techniques use that relationship to group the items.

The strength of a relationship between two or more items can be quantified as a *similarity measure:* A mathematical function that computes the similarity between two data items. The results of that computation, called *similarity values,* essentially compare a particular data item to all other items in the dataset. Those other items will be either more similar or less similar in comparison to that specific item.

Computed similarities play a major role in assigning items to groups (*clusters*). Each group has an item that best represents it; this item is referred to as a *cluster representative.*

Consider a dataset that consists of several types of fruits in a basket, as shown in Figure 6-1. The basket has fruits of different types such as apples, bananas, lemons, and pears. In this case, fruits are the data items. The data clustering algorithm extracts groups of similar fruits out of this dataset (basket of different fruits), assuming that the type of the fruit is unknown to the clustering algorithm.

Dataset

Data Clustering

Data Clusters

Clusters' Representatives

FIGURE 6-1:
Data clustering applied to a fruit dataset.

Imagine a robot or a technology that examines every fruit in the basket, and then automatically determines the weight and length for every fruit. Other possible features of fruits could include shape, size, color, and price among others. This step in the data analytics lifecycle is often referred as *feature extraction and feature selection*.

The robot doesn't know the names of fruits, and it will try to group similar fruits together by their features. Later in this process, a human being (such as a fruit expert) can label the discovered groups by looking at some of the data elements of each group. Or, if we leverage previous knowledge of some of the fruits in the basket, we can name the discovered groupings.

The results of the data clustering can be used to automatically assign new fruits to groups as they are added to the basket, and relatively predict their type just from knowing their features. This process in the data analytics lifecycle is often referred as data classification that will be covered in Chapter 7.

The first step in a data clustering process is to translate this dataset into a data matrix: One way to model this dataset is to have the rows represent the items in the dataset (fruits); and the columns represent characteristics, or features, that describe the data items. There are algorithms that can be used specifically to extract and select features from raw data. Chapter 9 covers the details.

In most cases, applying a data clustering technique to the fruit dataset as described above allows you to

>> **Retrieve groups (clusters) of similar items.** You can tell that your fruit is of N number of groups. After that, if you pick a random fruit, you will be able to make a statement about that item as being part of one of the N groups.

>> **Retrieve cluster representatives of each group.** In this example, a cluster representative would be picking one fruit type from the basket and putting it aside. The characteristics of this fruit are such that that fruit best represents the group of similar fruits it belongs to.

When you're done clustering, your dataset is organized and divided into natural groupings.

Motivation

Data clustering reveals structure in the data by extracting natural groupings from a dataset. Therefore, discovering clusters is an essential step toward formulating ideas and hypotheses about the structure of your data and deriving insights to better understand it.

Data clustering can also be a way to model data: It represents a larger body of data by clusters or cluster representatives.

In addition, your analysis may seek simply to partition the data into groups of similar items — as when *market segmentation* partitions target-market data into groups such as

>> Consumers who share the same interests (such as Mediterranean cooking)

>> Consumers who have common needs (for example, those with specific food allergies)

Identifying clusters of similar customers can help you develop a marketing strategy that addresses the needs of specific clusters.

Moreover, data clustering can also help you identify, learn, or predict the nature of new data items — especially how new data can be linked with making predictions. For example, in *pattern recognition*, analyzing patterns in the data (such as buying patterns in particular regions or age groups) can help you develop predictive analytics — in this case, predicting the nature of future data items that can fit well with established patterns.

The fruit basket example uses data clustering to distinguish between different data items. Suppose your business assembles custom fruit baskets, and a new exotic fruit is introduced to the market. You want to learn or predict which cluster the new item will belong to if you add it to the fruit basket. Because you've already applied data clustering to the fruit dataset, you have four clusters — which makes it easier to predict which cluster (specific type of fruit) is appropriate for the new item. All you have to do is to relatively compare the unknown fruit's features (such as weight, length, size, price, and shape) to the other four clusters' representatives and identify which cluster is the best match. Although this process may seem obvious for a person working with a small dataset, it isn't so obvious at a larger scale especially when you have large number of features. The complexity becomes exponential when the dataset is large, diverse, and relatively incoherent — which is why clustering algorithms exist: Computers do that type of work best.

A similar, common, and practical example is the application of data clustering to e-mail messages, dividing a dataset of e-mails into spam and non-spam clusters. An ideal spam-detection tool would need to first divide a dataset (all past e-mails) into two types (groups): spam and non-spam. Then the tool predicts whether unknown incoming e-mail is spam or non-spam. This second step, often referred to as data classification, is covered in detail in Chapter 7.

The goal would be to minimize the number of spam e-mails that end up in your inbox and also minimize the number of legitimate e-mails that end up in your spam folder. (As you've no doubt noticed, this kind of clustering and classification isn't quite perfected yet.)

Data clustering is used in several fields:

>> **Computer imaging:** Data clustering is part of *image segmentation* — the process of dividing a digital image into multiple segments in order to analyze the image more easily. Applying data clustering to an image generates segments (clusters) of contours that represent objects — aiding the detection of threatening health conditions in medical diagnosis and in the screening of airport baggage for suspicious materials.

>> **Information retrieval:** Here the aim is to search and retrieve information from a collection of data, for example a set of documents. Dividing a collection of documents into groups of similar documents is an essential task in information retrieval. Data clustering of documents by topic improves information search.

>> **Medicine:** Applying data clustering to a matrix of gene expression (often known as *microarray gene expression data*) from different cancer-diagnosed patients can generate clusters of positively and negatively diagnosed cancer patients, which can help predict the nature of new cases.

>> **Marketing:** Using data clustering to group customers according to similar purchase behavior improves the efficiency of targeted marketing.

>> **Law enforcement:** In social network analysis, the same data-clustering techniques that can help detect communities of common interests can also help identify online groups involved in suspicious activity.

Converting Raw Data into a Matrix

Before you can extract groups of similar data items from your dataset, you might need to represent your data in a tabular format known as a *data matrix*. This is a preprocessing step that comes before data clustering.

Creating a matrix of terms in documents

Suppose the dataset that you're about to analyze is contained in a set of Microsoft Word documents. The first thing you need to do is to convert the set of documents into a data matrix. Several commercial and open-source tools can handle that task, producing a matrix (often known as a *document–term matrix*), in which each row corresponds to a document in the dataset. Examples of these tools include RapidMiner, and R text-mining packages such as *tm* that can convert unstructured text data into a form that the clustering algorithm can use to discover clusters.

The next section explains one possible way to how documents can be converted into a data matrix.

A *document* is, in essence, a sequence of words. A *term* is a set of one or multiple words.

Every term that a document contains is mentioned either once or several times in the same document. The number of times a term is mentioned in a document can be represented by *term frequency* (TF), a numerical value.

We construct the matrix of terms in the document as follows:

>> The terms that appear in all documents are listed across the top row.

>> Document titles are listed down the leftmost column.

>> The numbers that appear inside the matrix cells correspond to each term's frequency.

For example, in Table 6-1, Document A is represented as a set of numbers (5,16,0,19,0,0.) where 5 corresponds to the number of times the term *predictive analytics* is repeated, 16 corresponds to the number of times *computer science* is repeated, and so on. This is the simplest way to convert a set of documents into a matrix.

TABLE 6-1   **Converting a Collection of Documents into a Matrix**

	Predictive Analytics	Computer Science	Learning	Clustering	2013	Anthropology
Document A	5	16	0	19	0	0
Document B	8	6	2	3	0	0
Document C	0	5	2	3	3	9
Document D	1	9	13	4	6	7
Document E	2	16	16	0	2	13
Document F	13	0	19	16	4	2

Term selection

One challenge in clustering text documents is determining how to select the best terms to represent all documents in the collection. How important a term is in a collection of documents can be calculated in different ways. If, for example, you count the number of times a term is repeated in a document and compare that total with how often it recurs in the whole collection, you get a sense of the term's importance relative to other terms.

Basing the relative importance of a term on its frequency in a collection is often known as *weighting*. The weight you assign can be based on multiple principles, of which two common examples are

>> Terms that appear several times in a document are favored over terms that appear only once.

>> Terms that are used in relatively few documents are favored over terms that are mentioned in all documents.

If (for example) the term *century* is mentioned in all documents in your dataset, then you might not consider assigning it enough weight to have a column of its own in the matrix. There are many weighting techniques that are widely used in practical text mining, such as *term frequency-inverse document frequency* (TF-IDF). TF-IDF tries to measure the importance of a word to both a document and a collection of documents. Similarly, if you're dealing with a dataset of users of an online social network, you can easily convert that dataset into a matrix. User IDs or names will occupy the rows; the columns will list features that best describe those users. (An example of a data matrix of social network users appears later in this chapter.)

Identifying Groups in Your Data

An *algorithm* is a step-by-step process used for solving a problem. One of the most popular and simple algorithm used in data clustering, *K-means*, is named after the algorithm's input and output: **K** is an input to the algorithm; it stands for the number of groupings that the algorithm must extract from a dataset, expressed algebraically as K-means, are outputs of the algorithm; they refer to the set of representatives that represent *k* clusters. A *cluster representative* is the statistical mean of all the data items in the same cluster. The next section explains in detail how to derive a cluster representative (that is, a mean).

K-means clustering algorithm

A K-means algorithm divides a given dataset into *k* clusters. The algorithm performs the following operations:

1. Pick *k* random items from the dataset and label them as initial cluster representatives. In order to improve the performance of the clustering algorithm, it's preferable that the k random items you pick as initial representatives that are well spaced in distance.

2. Associate each remaining item in the dataset with the nearest cluster representative, using a distance measure (such as Euclidean distance, explained later in this chapter).

3. Recalculate the new clusters' representatives.

4. Repeat Steps 2 and 3 until the clusters don't change.

A representative of a cluster is the mathematical *mean* (average) of all items that belong to the same cluster. This representative is also called a *cluster centroid*.

Table 6-2 shows some features of three fruits (data points) from the fruits' dataset. We will assume that the items in Table 6-2 are assigned to the same cluster so we show you how you can calculate a cluster representative of items belonging to the same cluster. In this example we only consider the length and weight as features of these similar fruits for simplicity.

TABLE 6-2   **Three Items from the Fruit Dataset**

Item	Feature#1 Weight (Ounces)	Feature#2 Length (Inches)
1	6.5	6
2	5.5	7
3	6	6.5

Table 6-3 shows the calculations of a cluster representative of three items (for example, bananas) that belong to the same cluster. The cluster representative is a vector of two attributes. Its attributes are the average of the attributes of the items in the cluster in question.

TABLE 6-3

Calculating the Representative of Three Items

Item	Feature#1 Weight (Ounces)	Feature#2 Length (Inches)
1	6.5	6
2	5.5	7
3	6	6.5
Cluster Representative (Centroid Vector)	(6.5+5.5+6)/3=6	(6+7+6.5)/3=6.5

The dataset shown in Table 6-4 consists of seven customers' ratings of two products, A and B. The ranking represents the number of points (between 0 and 20) that each customer has given to a product — the more points given, the higher the product is ranked. Using a K-means algorithm and assuming that k is equal to 2, the dataset will be partitioned into two groups.

TABLE 6-4

Dataset of Customer Ratings for Products A and B

Customer ID	Customer Ratings of Product A	Customer Ratings of Product B
1	2	2
2	3	4
3	6	8
4	7	10
5	10	14
6	9	10
7	7	9

The rest of the procedure looks like this:

1. **Pick two random items (preferably far apart from each other in distance) from the dataset and label them as cluster representatives (as shown in Table 6-5).**

   Table 6-6 shows the initial step of selecting random centroids from which the K-means clustering process begins. The initial centroids are selected randomly from the data that you're about to analyze. In this case, you're looking for two clusters, so two data items are randomly selected: Customers 1 and 5. At first, the clustering process builds two clusters around those two initial (randomly selected) cluster representatives. Then the cluster representatives are recalculated; the calculation is based on the items in each cluster.

TABLE 6-5 ## Selecting Random Initial Cluster Representatives

	Cluster Representative Centroid Vector)
Cluster 1	Customer ID#1 (2, 2)
Cluster 2	Customer ID#5 (10,14)

TABLE 6-6 ## First Iteration of Applying a K-Means Algorithm to the Dataset of Customer Ratings

Iteration#1	Customer Cluster 1		Customer Cluster 2	
Customer to be examined	Customer IDs belonging to Cluster 1	Cluster Representative	Customer IDs belonging to Cluster 2	Cluster Representative
	1	(2, 2)	5	(10, 14)
2	1, 2	(2.5, 3)	5	(10, 14)
3	1, 2, 3	(3.67, 4.67)	5	(10, 14)
4	1, 2, 3	(3.67, 4.67)	4, 5	(8.5, 12)
6	1, 2, 3	(3.67, 4.67)	4, 5, 6	(8.67, 11.33)
7	1, 2, 3	(3.67, 4.67)	4, 5, 6, 7	(8.25, 10.75)

2. **Inspect every other item (customer) and assign it to the cluster representative to which it is most similar.**

   Use the *Euclidean distance* to calculate how similar an item is to a group of items:

   Similarity of Item I to Cluster X $= \sqrt{(f_1 - x_1)^2 + (f_2 - x_2)^2 + \cdots + (f_n - x_n)^2}$

The values $f_1, f_2 \ldots f_n$ are the numerical values of the features that describe the item in question. The values $x_1, x_2 \ldots x_n$ are the features (mean values) of the cluster representative (centroid), assuming that each item has n features.

For example, consider the item called Customer 2 (3, 4): The customer's rating for Product A was 3 and the rating for Product B was 4. The cluster representative feature, as shown in Table 6-6, is (2, 2). The similarity of Customer 2 to Cluster 1 is calculated as follows:

Similarity of Item 2 to Cluster 1 $= \sqrt{(3-2)^2 + (4-2)^2} = 2.24$

Here's what the same process looks like with Cluster 2:

Similarity of Item 2 to $= \sqrt{(3-10)^2 + (4-14)^2} = 12.21$

Comparing these results, you assign Item 2 (that is, Customer 2) to Cluster 1 because the numbers say Item 2 is more similar to Cluster 1.

3. **Apply the same similarity analysis to every other item in the dataset.**

   Every time a new member joins a cluster, you must recalculate the cluster representative, following the example shown in Table 6-3.

REMEMBER

   The use of K-means is an iterative process. At each iteration, the algorithm steps shown here are repeated until the clusters show no further changes. Tables 6-6 and 6-7 show these iterations and assignments of items to clusters. At the end of Iteration 1, Cluster 1 contains Items 1, 2, and 3; Cluster 2 contains Items 4, 5, 6 and 7. The new cluster representatives are (3.67, 4.67) for Cluster 1 and (8.25, 10.75) for Cluster 2.

   Table 6-6 depicts the results of the first iteration of K-mean algorithm. Notice that k equals 2, so you're looking for two clusters, which divides a set of customers into two meaningful groups. Every customer is analyzed separately and is assigned to one of the clusters on the basis of the customer's similarity to each of the current cluster representatives. Note that cluster representatives are updated each time a new member joins a cluster.

4. **Iterate the dataset again, going through every element; compute the similarity between each element and its current cluster representative.**

   Notice that Customer 3 has moved from Cluster 1 to Cluster 2. This is because Customer 3's distance to the cluster representative of Cluster 2 is closer than to the cluster representative of Cluster 1.

Table 6-7 shows a second iteration of K-means algorithm on customer data. Each customer is being re-analyzed. Customer 2 is being assigned to Cluster 1 because Customer 2 is closer to the representative of Cluster 1 than Cluster 2. The same scenario applies to Customer 3. Notice that a cluster representative is being recalculated (as in Table 6-3) each time a new member is assigned to a cluster.

TABLE 6-7 **Second Iteration of Applying a K-Means Algorithm to the Dataset of Customer Ratings**

| Iteration#2 | Customer Cluster 1 | | Customer Cluster 2 | |
Customer to be examined	Customer IDs belonging to Cluster 1	Cluster Representative	Customer IDs belonging to Cluster 2	Cluster Representative
1	1, 2, 3	(3.67, 4.67)	4, 5, 6, 7	(8.25, 10.75)
2	1, 2, 3	(3.67, 4.67)	4, 5, 6, 7	(8.25, 10.75)
3	1, 2	(2.5, 3)	3, 4, 5, 6, 7	(7.8, 10.2)
4	1, 2	(2.5, 3)	3, 4, 5, 6, 7	(7.8, 10.2)
5	1, 2	(2.5,3)	3, 4, 5, 6, 7	(7.8, 10.2)
6	1, 2	(2.5, 3)	3, 4, 5, 6, 7	(7.8, 10.2)
7	1, 2	(2.5, 3)	3, 4, 5, 6, 7	(7.8, 10.2)

Clustering by nearest neighbors

Nearest Neighbors is a simple algorithm widely used to cluster data by assigning an item to a cluster by determining what other items are most similar to it. A typical use of the Nearest Neighbors algorithm follows these general steps:

1. Derive a similarity matrix from the items in the dataset.

This matrix, referred to as the *distance matrix*, will hold the similarity values for each and every item in the data set. (These values are elaborated in detail in the next example.)

2. With the matrix in place, compare each item in the dataset to every other item and compute the similarity value (as shown in the preceding section).

TIP

Initially, every item is assigned to a cluster of one item.

3. Using the distance matrix, examine every item to see whether the distance to its neighbors is less than a value that you have defined.

This value is called the *threshold*.

4. The algorithm puts each element in a separate cluster, analyzes the items, and decides which items are similar, and adds similar items to the same cluster.

5. The algorithm stops when all items have been examined.

Consider, for example, a dataset of eight geographical locations where individuals live. The purpose is to divide these individuals into groups based on their geographical locations, as determined by the Global Positioning System (see Table 6-8).

Table 6-8 shows a simple dataset of individuals' geographic data. For purposes of simplicity, global positional longitude and latitude are depicted as whole numbers. Assume that all the data collected about these eight individuals was collected at a specific point in time.

TABLE 6-8

GPS Dataset

Individual ID	GPS Longitude	GPS Latitude
1	2	10
2	2	5
3	8	4
4	5	8
5	7	5
6	6	4
7	1	2
8	4	9

As with K-means, the first pre-step is to calculate the similarity values for every pair of individuals. One way to calculate a similarity between two items is to determine the Euclidean distance (as described in the preceding section). The similarity value between two points is calculated as shown earlier in Table 6-9.

Similarity between Item A and Item B = $\sqrt{\left(f_{a,1} - f_{b,1}\right)^2 + \left(f_{a,2} - f_{b,2}\right)^2 + \cdots + \left(f_{a,n} - f_{b,n}\right)^2}$

Here $f_{a,1}$ is the first feature of Item A, $f_{a,2}$ is the second feature of Item A, and corresponding values labeled b represent the features of Item B. The variable n is the number of features. In this example, n is 2. For example, the similarity between Item 1 and Item 2 is calculated as follows:

Similarity between Item 1 and Item 2 = $\sqrt{\left(2-2\right)^2 + \left(10-5\right)^2} = 5$

On the basis of this measurement of similarity between items, you can use the Nearest Neighbor algorithm to extract clusters from the dataset of geographical locations.

The first step is to place the individual whose ID is 1, longitude is 2, and latitude is 10 in cluster C1. Then go through all remaining individuals computing how similar each one is to the individual in C1. If the similarity between Individual 1 and another Individual x is less than 4.5 (the user-provided threshold value beyond which an item is too dissimilar — the user of the algorithm can set or choose this value), then Individual x will join C1; otherwise you create a new cluster to accommodate Individual x.

Table 6-9 shows the similarities and numerical relationships between Individuals 1 through 8. The similarity of these data elements is calculated as a Euclidean distance (explained earlier in this chapter); for example, the similarity between Individual 1 and Individual 5 is 7.07. Individuals with similarity values closer to 0 have greater similarity. Half the matrix isn't filled because the matrix is *symmetric* (that is, the similarity between Individuals 1 and 4 is the same as the similarity between Individuals 4 and 1, a property guaranteed by any appropriate similarity measure).

You have now assigned Individual 1 to the first cluster (C1). The similarity between Individual 1 and Individual 2 is equal to 5, which is greater than the threshold value 4.5. A new cluster is generated — and Individual 2 belongs to it. At this stage, you have two clusters of one item each: C1 = {Individual 1} and C2 = {Individual 2}.

Moving the focus to Individual 3, you find that the similarity between Individual 3 and Individual 2 & 1 is larger than the threshold value 4.5. Thus you assign Individual 3 to a new cluster containing one item: C3 = {Individual 3}.

Moving to Individual 4, you calculate how similar Individual 4 is to Individuals 1, 2, and 3. The nearest (most similar) to Individual 4 happens to be Individual 1. The similarity between 4 and 1 is approximately 3.61, which is less than the threshold value 4.5. Individual 4 joins Individual 1 in Cluster C1. The clusters constructed so far are: C1 = {Individual 1, Individual 4}, C2 = {Individual 2} and C3 = {Individual 3}.

Next is to examine Individual 5 and calculate how similar it is to Individuals 1, 2, 3, and 4. The item nearest in distance (most similar) to Individual 5 is Individual 3. The similarity is $\sqrt{2}$ which is less than the threshold value of 4.5. Thus Individual 5 joins C3. The clusters constructed so far are: C1 = {Individual 1, Individual 4}, C2 = {Individual 2} and C3 = {Individual 3, Individual 5}.

When you examine Individual 6 and calculate how similar it is to Individuals 1, 2, 3, 4, and 5, you discover that Individual 5 is nearest (most similar) to Individual 6. Thus Individual 6 joins C3. The clusters constructed so far are: C1 = {Individual 1, Individual 4}, C2 = {Individual 2} and C3 = {Individual 3, Individual 5, Individual 6}.

TABLE 6-9 Determining the Degree of Similarity (Euclidean Distance) Between Individuals

	Individual#1	Individual#2	Individual#3	Individual#4	Individual#5	Individual#6	Individual#7	Individual#8
Individual#1	0	5	8.49	3.61	7.07	7.21	8.06	2.24
Individual#2		0	6.08	4.24	5	4.12	3.16	4.47
Individual#3			0	5	1.41	2	7.28	6.40
Individual#4				0	3.61	4.12	7.21	1.41
Individual#5					0	1.41	6.71	5
Individual#6						0	5.39	5.39
Individual#7							0	7.62
Individual#8								0

When you examine Individual 7 and calculate how similar it is to Individuals 1, 2, 3, 4, 5, and 6, you find that the nearest (most similar) item to Individual 7 is Individual 2. Thus Individual 7 joins C2. The clusters constructed so far are: C1 = {Individual 1, Individual 4}, C2 = {Individual 2, Individual 7} and C3 = {Individual 3, Individual 5, Individual 6}.

When you examine Individual 8, and calculate its similarity to Individuals 1, 2, 3, 4, 5, 6, and 7, you find that the nearest (most similar) item to Individual 8 is Individual 4. Thus Individual 8 joins C1.

The groups of similar data items constructed so far, containing items most similar to each other, are

> C1 = {Individual 1, Individual 4, Individual 8}
>
> C2 = {Individual 2, Individual 7}
>
> C3 = {Individual 3, Individual 5, Individual 6}

Density-based algorithms

Density-based clustering algorithms are a set of machine learning techniques that can discover regions where a number of data elements are relatively close in distance to each other. These areas of data elements create *dense regions of data points*. A density-based algorithm discovers dense areas of data points and starts on building clusters around those dense areas.

One of the most popular density-based algorithms is *density-based spatial clustering of applications with noise* (DBSCAN).

DBSCAN is inspired by the human way of discovering dense areas. In fact, human beings usually detect crowds following dense regions of people. The notion of density in data clustering is based on the fact that data groupings can be discovered by following dense regions.

In order to understand how DBSCAN works, it's important to note that DBSCAN algorithm requires two predefined parameters:

>> ε denotes the radius of a neighborhood.

   A neighborhood of a given point x is the circular region of radius ε that contain data points that are in a distance less than ε.

>> MinPts denotes Minimum points to be considered for a cluster.

DBSCAN is an iterative algorithm; at every iteration it tries to discover the following three types of data points:

>> **Core points:** A point that has more than a minimum points (MinPts) within a radius ε. Those points are said to be *directlyreachable* from core point X.

>> **Border points:** A point that has fewer points than MinPts points within an ε radius, but is in the neighborhood of a core point. A neighborhood of given point X is the set points that are within ε distance from X.

>> **Noise points:** Points that aren't either core points or border points.

In summary, DBSCAN algorithm finds points in the densest regions, known as core points (analogous to cluster representative in K-means). Core points can later be used to generate clusters. Unlike K-means, DBSCAN can explicitly discover noise points.

The main steps of the iterative algorithm can be summarized as follows:

1. Find and label data points as core, border and noise.

2. Report and eliminate noise data points

3. For every core point c that hasn't been assigned to a cluster, create a new cluster with the point C and all the points that are density connected to P.

Consider the following terminologies around the concept of density-connected points:

- Two points X and Y are density connected if there is a point Z such that both X and Y are density reachable from Z.

- We say that a point X is density-reachable from a point Y if there is exist a set of points Q1,. . ., Qn-1, where Qi+1 is directly density-reachable from Qi

4. Assign border points to the cluster of the closest core point.

**TECHNICAL
STUFF**

REMEMBER

It is important to note the following items about DBSCAN algorithm:

>> DBSCAN can handle noise points.

>> DBSCAN doesn't require the number of clusters an input to the algorithm.

>> DBSCAN offers a sense of the density of the data.

>> DBSCAN can handle clusters of different shapes and sizes in most cases.

>> DBSCAN can find to some extent arbitrarily shaped clusters.

>> DBSCAN is very sensitive to the input parameters radius ε and MinPts.

Finding Associations in Data Items

The use of predictive analytics as a data-mining tool also seeks to discover hidden relationships among items in your data. These hidden relationships are called *mining association rules*.

Consider a large dataset of customer transactions, where a *customer transaction* consists of the product(s) purchased by a customer at a given time. In a scenario like this one, the purpose of predictive analytics *as a tool* is to identify associations between products in the dataset. An association between two products is a *relation*, which can help the analyst discern a pattern and derive a rule from the raw data of customer transactions. An example of such a rule could be grocery-buying patterns: If a customer purchases butter and bread, he or she is also likely to buy milk. The rule discovered in this case can be written as

{butter, bread} → {milk}.

In data-mining terms, {butter, bread} is called a *basket*. A real-world basket contains items, of course, and so does this basket: butter and bread. The discovered rule just described is that if a basket contains the items butter and bread, then it's also very likely to contain milk.

Finding such *association rules* in a dataset of customer transactions helps a company (in this case, a grocery store) maximize revenue by deciding which products should be on sale, how to position products in the store's aisles, and how and when to offer promotional pricing.

Analyzing the data generated by past transactions in order to maximize profit is a common practice. Sales data collected regularly (daily, weekly, monthly) from point-of-sale systems such as online stores, supermarkets, bookstores, and restaurants is referred to as *basket data* — which is, in this case, essentially large-scale data about sales transactions. Association rules are generated with a score known as *confidence* — which refers to how likely they are to hold true. For example, if a generated rule shows that 98% of the people who purchased butter and bread also purchased milk, that percentage value (98%) is the *confidence value*.

Other terms associated with a rule are *antecedent* (the "if" part of an "if-then" statement) and the *consequent* (the "then" part of the "if-then"). In the preceding example, the antecedent is butter and bread; milk is the consequent.

In practice, your company will use predictive analytics to retrieve association rules from a customer database. The analyst issues queries whose purpose is to find rules that are either related to the antecedent (what was bought) or rules that can lead to the consequent (what can be expected to be bought).

In another example, consider a coffee shop manager who wants to maximize profit using association rules as a data-mining tool. The store manager would request items like these:

>> Generate all rules that have *croissant* in the antecedent and *café latte* in the consequent.

Such rules would help the manager develop recommendations for which products to sell together with croissants; if café latte is prominent as a consequent, it's highly likely that the recommendation will be to sell café latte with croissants.

>> Generate all rules that have *chocolate chip cookie* as an antecedent.

These rules may help outline and design a plan for increasing sales of chocolate chip cookies.

>> Generate all rules that have *espresso* as an antecedent.

These rules would determine the products whose sales may be affected if the store runs out of espresso.

Apriori algorithm

One of the most popular data mining algorithms for discovering association rules is the *Apriori algorithm.* The algorithm relies on knowledge of frequent itemset properties. It's an iterative algorithm that starts by determining the set of frequent 1-itemset (L1), then it determines the set of frequent two-itemset L2 using L1, and so on. The algorithm is available in major predictive analytics tools, such as R, Apache Mahout, and Weka. For an implementation of Apriori in R, see `https://cran.r-project.org/web/packages/arules/arules.pdf`. For an implementation of Apriori in Weka, view `https://arxiv.org/ftp/arxiv/papers/1406/1406.7371.pdf`

In a recent project, use cases were identified and a roadmap developed for a large financial organization where large-scale predictive analytics frameworks can be leveraged to streamline business operations. One of the subject areas was predictive maintenance (the process of capturing and analyzing system logs as indicators to predict failure in a system). Subsequently, those indicators can be used to develop decisions to act ahead of time to prevent system interruption.

In this case, the Apriori algorithm was applied in the field of predictive maintenance. The purpose of the project was simply to predict software failure before it happens.

Here's how Apriori was used to mine associations that could be used for predictive maintenance.

The first step was a data exploration step to identify the most critical hardware and software failures that the organization had over the past few years:

>> A data dictionary for external and internal data sources was built to help mine frequent items set of event that led to failure.

>> Monitoring tools that are used within the organization for hardware and/or software logs were identified.

Some of the major common software failures can be summarized as

>> Process unable to be started.

>> Processes are started in an incorrect sequence which leads to incorrect process status.

>> Performance degradation/crash due to implementation failure (such as memory leak or incorrect procedure call).

>> Poorly engineered software.

>> Absence of automated patch management systems.

>> License(s) expiration.

>> Distributed denial-of-service attack (DDOS).

   If a service or network is incapable of handling traffic, it may bottleneck the services or machines and make all services on the machine or network inaccessible.

Some of the common hardware failures can be summarized as

>> **Hard drives:** File system corruption, mechanical failure, moisture, and heat.

>> **CPUs:** Heat, over-utilization, overclocking, and surges causing damage to transistors.

>> **Power supplies:** Overloading and overheating (fan failure, dust, dirt, and surges).

>> **Network ports:** Damage.

The second step was to identify data sources, such as

>> **Event logs:** Automated event-logging mechanisms or manual logs.

>> **System Active Reports (SAR):** Reports from API of operating systems.

>> **Self-Monitoring Analysis and Reporting Technology (SMART):** Disk drive health capture of syslog data, hardware agent logging, memory, CPU and memory, fan RPM, and power consumption.

>> **Software logs** (such as Tableau, SharePoint, and SQL servers).

The third step was to assemble a team of data scientists, a data architects, business uses that will be using the framework, a data analytics vendor for Hadoop, and business users who will use the framework. (Chapter 16 has details about Hadoop.)

The data architects designed an ETL process (extract, transform and load) and moved data from data sources into a data hub under Hadoop Distributed File System (HDFS).

After the data was stored into HDFS, it was pre-processed. MapReduce jobs were written to perform these tasks:

>> Convert logs into one common format.

   Syslog, event logs, hardware sensor logging, and environmental logs are semi-structured (for example, per data time: *List<time, List(events>)*).

>> Convert unstructured data from web crawling to capture common hardware, software name, failure type, and severity of the failure.

After the data was pre-processed and harmonized into one data matrix, many possible predictive models for predicting failures were considered. One of the algorithms that was adopted was Apriori. Apriori was able to mine events from the data hub that were correlated. For example, some of the results were in the following format:

{Event A of type Error, Event B of type Error} → {Event C of type Critical}

{Event D of type Critical, Event E of type Error} → {Event F of type System Outage}

From those association rules, several paths to failure were detected that could be used as predictors for impending failure, based on historical events.

Applying Biologically Inspired Clustering Techniques

Nature is a collection of beautiful, simple, and efficient systems. Even a natural process as simple as an apple falling from a tree inspired Newton to identify the law of gravity. But nature is also the best place to look for patterns that suggest solutions to complex problems — natural collective behaviors such as schools of fish, flocking birds, and marching ants have led experts in predictive analytics to design biologically inspired data-clustering algorithms.

Designing a biologically inspired solution involves these steps.

1. Observe and analyze a phenomenon in nature.

2. Mimic or model the behavior and design a representation for it that a computer can comprehend.

3. Use the representation to solve a real-world problem.

In data clustering, two widely-used algorithms purely inspired by nature are based on the flocking of birds and the collective behavior of ant colonies. Both algorithms can model and cluster your data in a simple and natural way.

Birds flocking: Flock by Leader algorithm

Imagine birds' flocking behavior as a model for your company's data. Each data item corresponds to a single bird in the flock; an appropriate visual application can show the flock in action in an imaginary visual space. Your dataset corresponds to the flock. The natural flocking behavior corresponds to data patterns that might otherwise go undiscovered. The aim is to detect swarms (data clusters) among the flocking birds (data elements).

Flocking behavior has been used in real-life applications such as robotics-based rescue operations and computer animation. For example, the producer of the movie *Batman Returns* generated mathematical flocking behavior to simulate bat swarms and penguin flocks.

The use of flocking behavior as a predictive analytics technique — analyzing a company's data as flocks of similar data elements — is based on the dynamics behind flocking behavior as it appears in nature.

Flocking behavior of birds, fish, flies, bees, and ants is a self-organizing system; the individuals tend to move in accordance with both their environment and neighboring individuals.

In a flock of birds, each bird applies three main rules while flocking:

>> **Separation** keeps a bird apart from its nearest flock mates.

>> **Alignment** allows a bird to move along the same average heading as that of its flock mates.

>> **Cohesion** keeps the bird within the local flock.

Each bird in a flock moves according to these rules. A bird's *flock mates* are birds found within a certain distance of the bird, and a certain distance from each other. To avoid collision between birds, a minimum distance must be kept; it can also be mathematically defined. Such are the rules that orchestrate flocking behavior; using them to analyze data is a natural next step.

Consider a dataset of online social network users. Data clustering can identify social communities that share the same interests. Identifying social communities in a social network is a valuable tool that can transform how organizations think, act, operate, and manage their marketing strategies.

Suppose that Zach is an active social network user whose profile has over a thousand friends. If you know who Zach's top ten closest online friends are, who among them he interacts with the most, *and* (from other data analytics sources) that Zach has just bought a book named *Predictive Analytics For Dummies*, you can then target his closest friends (those who are most similar to Zach) and suggest the same book to them, rather than trying to suggest it to all 1,000 of his friends.

In addition, detection of online social clusters can be extremely valuable for intelligence agencies, especially if (say) Zach and some of his closest friends — but not all of his friends — are involved in suspicious activities.

How do you obtain a dataset of social network users? Well, some of the data and tools are already available: Major social networks and micro-blog websites such as Facebook and Twitter provide an application programming interface (API) that allows you to develop programs that can obtain public data posted by users. Those APIs offered by Twitter are referred to as Twitter Streaming APIs. They come in three main types: public, user, and site streams:

>> **Public streams** allow a user to collect public tweets about a specific topic or user, or support an analytics purpose.

>> **User streams** allow a user to collect tweets that are accessible by the user's account.

>> **Site streams** are for large-scale servers that connect to Twitter on behalf of many users.

Now, suppose you use such a program to download users' data and organize it into a tabular format such as the matrix shown in the next figure. Table 6-10 shows a simple matrix that records the online interactions of Zach's online friends over two different weeks. This dataset consists of seven elements and seven features. The features as shown in the table column are the number of interactions between each member and the other members.

For example, the number of online interactions between Mike and John over Week 1 is 10. These interactions include — but aren't limited to — chat conversations, appearances in the same photos, tweets, and e-mail exchanges. After building this dataset, the flocking behavior will be applied to detect communities (clusters) and visualize this data as a flock of data items.

Let us walk you through how a computer applies bird-flocking behavior to detect communities of common interests.

Take an empty piece of paper and imagine you have information about 20 users in a social network that you want to analyze. On that piece of paper, draw 20 dots randomly distributed all around. Each dot represents a user in the social network. If you move dots as if they were birds, they will move according to two central principles:

>> The similarity between those social users in real life

>> The rules that produce flocking behavior as you see it in nature

Let's say you have information about online interactions of those 20 members over a period of 10 days. You can gather information about those daily users on a daily basis, including data about their interactions with one another.

For example, Mike and John appeared in the same photo album, they attended the same event, or they "liked" the same page in an online social network. This information will be processed, analyzed, and converted into a matrix of numbers, with these results:

>> The dots (birds) in representing Mike and John move toward each other (flocking attraction rule).

- >> The dots move with the same speed (flocking alignment and cohesion rules) on that piece of paper (flocking virtual space).

- >> In one day, several real-world interactions will drive the movements of those dots (birds) in your paper.

- >> Applying flocking behavior over 20 days will naturally lead to forming swarms of dots (birds) that are similar in some way.

There are many ways to apply the bird-flocking behavior to discover clusters in large datasets. One of the most recent variations is the Flock by Leader machine-learning clustering algorithm, inspired by the discovery of bird leaders in the pigeon species. The algorithm predicts data elements that could potentially lead another group of data objects. A leader is assigned, and then the leader initiates and leads the flocking behavior. Over the course of the algorithm, leaders can become followers or outliers. In essence, this algorithm works in a way that follows the rules of "survival of the fittest."

The *Flock by Leader* algorithm was first introduced by Prof. Abdelghani Bellaachia and Prof.Anasse Bari in "Flock by Leader: A Novel Machine Learning Biologically Inspired Clustering Algorithm," published as a chapter in the proceedings of the Advances in Swarm Intelligence at Volume 7332 of the series Lecture Notes in Computer Science.

Tables 6-10 and 6-11 show one possible way to represent data generated by online social exchanges over two weeks. Table 6-10 shows that Zach interacted 41 times with Kellie and four times with Arthur.

Figure 6-2 outlines how to apply the bird-flocking algorithm to analyze social network data. As depicted in the figure, each member is represented by a bird in virtual space. Notice that

- >> The birds are initially dispersed randomly in the virtual space.

- >> Each bird has a velocity and a position associated with it.

- >> Velocity and position are calculated for each bird, using three vectors: separation, attraction, and alignment.

- >> Each bird moves according to the three vectors, and this movement produces the flocking behavior seen in nature.

Figure 6-3 illustrates the dynamics of applying flocking behavior to the initial birds shown in Figure 6-2.

TABLE 6-10 Week 1 of a Dataset of a Social Network User's Weekly Interactions

Social Member Network	Interactions with John	Interactions with Mike	Interactions with Zach	Interactions with Emma	Interactions with Kellie	Interactions with Nicole	Interactions with Arthur
John	-	10	10	12	4	4	10
Mike		-	5	5	56	57	5
Zach			-	6	41	4	4
Emma				-	28	8	8
Kellie					-	5	5
Nicole						-	4
Arthur							-

TABLE 6-11   Week 2 of a Dataset of a Social Network User's Weekly Interactions

Social Member Network	Interactions with John	Interactions with Mike	Interactions with Zach	Interactions with Emma	Interactions with Kellie	Interactions with Nicole	Interactions with Arthur
John	-	10	12	10	0	10	8
Mike		-	50	2	0	0	5
Zach			-	9	0	1	3
Emma				-	2	2	1
Kellie					-	4	9
Nicole						-	1
Arthur							-

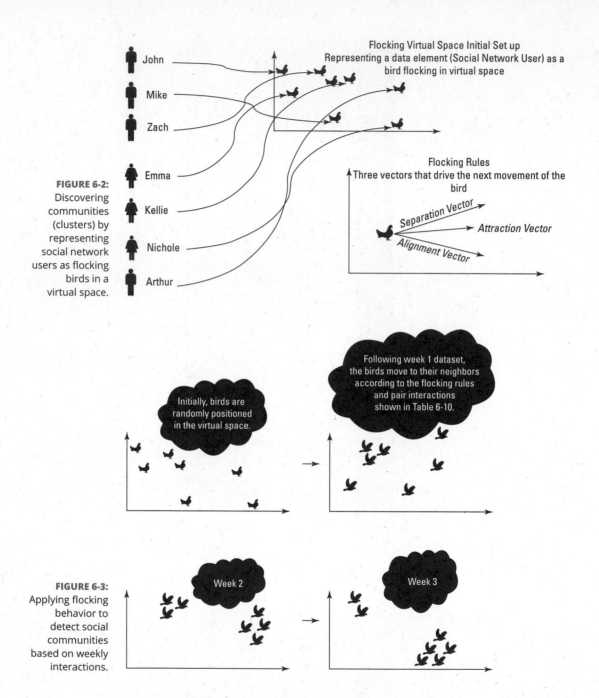

FIGURE 6-2: Discovering communities (clusters) by representing social network users as flocking birds in a virtual space.

Flocking Virtual Space Initial Set up
Representing a data element (Social Network User) as a bird flocking in virtual space

John
Mike
Zach
Emma
Kellie
Nichole
Arthur

Flocking Rules
Three vectors that drive the next movement of the bird

Separation Vector
Attraction Vector
Alignment Vector

Initially, birds are randomly positioned in the virtual space.

Following week 1 dataset, the birds move to their neighbors according to the flocking rules and pair interactions shown in Table 6-10.

FIGURE 6-3: Applying flocking behavior to detect social communities based on weekly interactions.

Week 2

Week 3

Here interaction data is analyzed weekly to find similar social networks' users. Each week the birds can be visualized in a simple grid. The positions of these birds reflect the interactions of actual individuals in the real world.

Ant colonies

Another natural example of self-organizing group behavior is a colony of ants hunting for food. The ants collectively optimize their track so that it always takes the shortest route possible to a food target. Even if you try to disturb a marching colony of ants and prevent them from getting to the food target — say, by blocking their track with a finger — they get back on track quickly and (again) find the shortest way possible to the food target, all of them avoiding the same obstacles while looking for food. This uniformity of behavior is possible because every ant deposits a trail of pheromones on the ground. Okay, how is that related to predictive analytics? Surprisingly closely. Read on.

Consider an army of ants idle in their nest. When they start looking for food, they have absolutely no information about where to find it. They march randomly until an individual ant finds food; now the lucky ant (call it Ant X) has to communicate its find to the rest of the ants — and to do that, it must find its way back to the nest.

Fortunately, Ant X was producing its own pheromones the whole time it was looking for food; it can follow its own trail of pheromones back to the nest. On its way back to the nest, following its own pheromone trail, Ant X puts more pheromones on the same trail. As a result, the scent on Ant X's trail will be the strongest among all the other ants' trails. The strongest trail of pheromones will attract all the other ants that are still searching for food. They'll stop and follow the strongest scent. As more ants join Ant X's trail, they add more pheromones to it; the scent becomes stronger. Pretty soon, all the other ants have a strong scent to follow.

So far, so good: The first ant that discovers food leads the rest of the ants to it by reinforcing scent. But how do the ants discover the shortest path? Well, the trail with the strongest pheromone will attract the most ants — but when large numbers of ants are involved, the shortest trails that reach the food will allow more trips than the longer trails. If several ants have discovered the same source of food, the ants that took the shortest path will do more trips in comparison to ants that follow longer paths — hence more pheromones will be produced on the shortest path. The relationship between individual and collective behavior is an enlightening natural example.

In Figure 6-4, every dot represents a document. Assume that the black dots are documents about predictive analytics and the white dots are documents about anthropology. Dots representing the different types of documents are randomly distributed in the grid of five cells. "Ants" are deployed randomly in the grid to search for similar documents. Every cell with a value in it represents an instance of a "pheromone." Using the document matrix, each cell's "pheromone" value is calculated from the corresponding document.

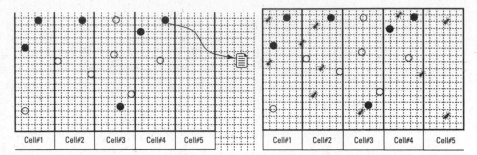

Okay, how does an ant colony's collective intelligence produce a model for effectively clustering data? The answer lies in a simple analogy: Ants are searching for food in their environment, much as we're searching for clusters in a dataset — looking for similar documents within a large set of documents.

Consider a dataset of documents that you want to organize by topic. Similar documents will be grouped in the same cluster. Here's where the ant colony can provide hints on how to group similar documents.

Imagine a two-dimensional (2D) grid where we can represent documents as dots (often referred to as *vectors* with coordinates). The 2D grid is divided into cells. Each cell has a "pheromone" (value) associated with it. (Later in this section, we show how to calculate this value.) Briefly, the "pheromone" value distinguishes each document in a given cell.

The dots are initially distributed randomly — and every dot in the grid represents a unique document. The next step is to deploy other dots randomly on the 2D grid, simulating the ant colony's search for food in its environment. Those dots are initially scattered in the same 2D grid with the documents. Each new dot added to the grid represents an ant. Those "ants," often referred to in the ant-colony algorithm as *agents*, are moving in the 2D grid. Each "ant" will either pick up or drop off the other dots (documents), depending on where the documents best belong. In this analogy, the "food" takes the form of documents sufficiently similar that they can be clustered.

In Figure 6-5, an "ant" walks randomly in the grid; if it encounters a document, it can perform one of two actions: pick or drop. Each cell has a "pheromone intensity" (a relative size of numerical value) that indicates how similar the document is to the other documents (dots) residing near the document in question — the one an "ant" is about to either pick up or drop. Note that the "ant" in Cell 3 will pick up the black-dotted document because the white "pheromone" value is dominating; and move to a cell where the value is close (similar) to what's in Cell 4 (several black dots). The search keeps iterating until the clusters form.

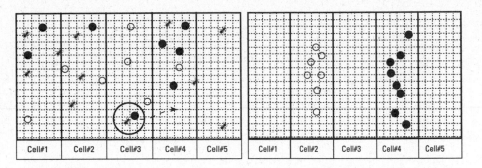

FIGURE 6-5: Deploying "ants" into the documents' virtual space to discover similar documents.

In effect, the "ant" moves documents from one cell to another to form clusters by performing either one of only two actions: picking up a document or dropping a document. When the "ants" started moving randomly on the grid, encountering a dot (document) results in the "ant" picking up a document from its current cell, moving with it, and dropping it into a cell in which it had sufficient similarity to fit.

How would an "ant" determine the best cell in which to drop a document? The answer is that the values in the cells act like "pheromones" — and every cell in the 2D grid contains a numerical value that can be calculated in a way that represents a document in the cell. Remember that each document is represented as a set of numbers or a vector of numerical values. The "intensity of the pheromone" (the numerical value) increases when more documents are dropped into the cell — and that value decreases if the numbers that represent documents are moved out of the cell. There are several publications in the literature about designing data mining algorithms based the swarm intelligence in ant colonies. Here are some related works about ant colonies data mining algorithms:

He, Yulan, Siu Cheung Hui, and Yongxiang Sim. "A novel ant-based clustering approach for document clustering." Asia Information Retrieval Symposium. Springer Berlin Heidelberg, 2006.

Bellaachia, Abdelghani, and Deema Alathel. "Trust-based ant recommender (T-BAR)." 2012 6th IEEE International Conference Intelligent Systems. IEEE, 2012.

Martens, David, et al. "Classification with ant colony optimization." IEEE Transactions on Evolutionary Computation 11.5 (2007): 651-665.

REMEMBER

Most of the clustering algorithms discussed in this chapter are available in the majority of predictive analytics tools, including R, Weka and RapidMiner. They are also available for large-scale data analytics under Apache Mahout and Apache Spark. You will find more details about these technologies in Chapter 16.

Chapter 7

Predicting the Future Using Data Classification

his chapter introduces an easy and widely used concept that can help you predict the future: *data classification*, a data-mining technique used to make sense of overwhelmingly large and humanly unmanageable datasets to uncover hidden patterns in the data. That could be one possible first step in the direction of building a predictive model.

Predictive models that use this technique are called *classification models*, often referred to as *classifiers*. Behind the scenes of these classifiers is a set of sophisticated machine-learning algorithms that learn from experience — as represented by the historical data — to discover hidden patterns and trends in the data. When these unseen relationships come to light, the model can predict the outcome (a category (class label), or numerical value) based on newly input data.

For instance, most financial institutions that issue loans to individuals or corporate entities use *risk modeling* to predict whether the loan will be paid back (or, in the case of mortgage loans, paid back early). Often these models use a classification algorithm. In essence, a classification algorithm predicts the class or category of an unknown event, phenomenon, or future numerical value. The categories or classes are extracted from the data. One way to organize data into categories of similar data objects is by using data clustering (covered in detail in Chapter 6).

Financial analysts, mortgage bankers, and underwriters depend heavily on such predictive models when they decide whether to grant loans. Most people have heard of the *FICO Score* — as noted in the accompanying sidebar, it's a number that represents your credit history and creditworthiness. It's also a classic example of the output you get from a classification model.

Besides providing just a number (or score) as output, a classifier may place a credit applicant in one of several categories of risk — such as risky, not risky, or moderately risky. It's up to the modeler or analyst to determine whether the output will be a discrete number or a category. Thus a classification model may play a major role in whether someone buys that new house or car. The predictive model utilizes historical credit data of the user, labels the user as belonging to a specific category, and speculates on the user's future behavior if his or her loan application is approved.

Classification can be also used in fraud detection, spam e-mail identification, medical diagnosis, image recognition, targeted marketing, text analytics, and many other practical applications.

FICO SCORE AND CREDIT RISK

The FICO Score was initially introduced in 1989 by Fair, Isaac and Company (FICO). Your FICO Score is calculated using several criteria such as length of credit history, bill-payments history, types and balances of credit cards, and also recent applications for credit.

A FICO Score ranges between 300 and 850. The higher the score, the lower the predicted credit risk, and the higher the chances that the applicant will pay back the loan on time. What a high FICO Score means for the applicant is higher chances to be granted a loan.

This chapter explains the underlying concepts behind data classification and illustrates techniques used to build classification-based predictors. You also get a look at a general approach to incorporating data classification into your business.

Explaining Data Classification

In data mining, *data classification* is the process of labeling a data item as belonging to a class or category. A data item is also referred to (in the data-mining vocabulary) as *data object, observation,* or *instance.*

REMEMBER

Data clustering (see Chapter 6) is different from data classification:

>> **Data clustering** is used to describe data by extracting meaningful groupings or categories from a body of data that contains similar elements.

>> **Data classification** is used to predict the category or the grouping that a new and incoming data object belongs to.

You can use data classification to predict new data elements on the basis of the groupings discovered by a data clustering process. The following section walks you through the use of data classification to solve a practical problem.

Lending

A loan can serve as an everyday example of data classification. The loan officer needs to analyze loan applications to decide whether the applicant will be granted or denied a loan.

One way to make such a critical decision is to use a classifier to assist with the decision-making process. In essence, the *classifier* is simply an algorithm that contains instructions that tell a computer how to analyze the information mentioned in the loan application, and how to reference other (outside) sources of information on the applicant. Then the classifier can label the loan application as fitting one of these sample categories, such as "safe," "too risky," or "safe with conditions" assuming that these exact categories are known and labeled in the historical data.

REMEMBER

By removing most of the decision process from the hands of the loan officer or underwriter, the model reduces the human work effort and the company's portfolio risk. This increases return on investment (ROI) by allowing employees to originate more loans and/or get better pricing if the company decides to resell the higher-quality loan.

If the classifier comes back with a result that labels an applicant as "safe with conditions," then the loan processor or officer can request that the applicant fulfill the conditions in order to get the loan. If the conditions are met, then the new data can be run through the classifier again for approval. Using machine learning, the loan application classifier will learn from past applications, leverage current information mentioned in the application, and predict the future behavior of the loan applicant.

As ever, predicting the future is about learning from the past and evaluating the present. Data classification relies on both past and current information — and speeds up decision making by using both faster.

Marketing

To illustrate the use of classifiers in marketing, consider a marketer who has been assigned to design a smart marketing strategy for a specific product. Understanding the customers' demographics drives the design of an effective marketing strategy. Ultimately it helps the company select suitable products to advertise to the customers most likely to buy them.

For instance, one of the criteria you can use to select targeted customers is specific geographical location. You may have an unknown store (or a store that isn't known for selling a particular product — say, a housewares store that could start selling a new food processor) and you want to start a marketing campaign for the new product line.

Using data you collected or bought from a marketing agency, you can build your classifier. You can design a classifier that anticipates whether customers will buy the new product. For each customer profile, the classifier predicts a category that fits each product line you run through it, labeling the customer as (say) "interested," "not interested," or "unknown."

Using the analysis produced by the classifier, you can easily identify the geographical locations that have the most customers who fit the "interested" category. Your model discovers for example that the population of San Francisco includes a large number of customers who have purchased a product similar to what you have for sale.

You jump at this chance to take action on the insight your model just presented to you. You may send an advertisement for that cool new gadget to those customers — and only to them.

To limit operating and marketing costs, you must avoid contacting uninterested customers; the wasted effort would affect your ROI. For that matter, having too much unnecessary contact with customers can dilute the value of your marketing campaigns and increase customer fatigue till your solicitations seem more like a nuisance. You don't want your glossy flyers to land immediately in the garbage can or your e-mails to end up in the spam folder.

TIP

As a marketer, you might want to use data about potential customers' profiles that has been collected from different sources or provided by a third party. Such sources include social media and databases of historical online transactions by customers.

Healthcare

In the medical field, a classifier can help a physician settle on the most suitable treatment for a given patient. It can be designed to analyze the patient data, learn from it, and classify the patient as belonging to a category of similar patients. The classifier can approve recommending the same treatment that helped similar patients of the same category in the past.

As in the examples previously described, the classifier predicts a label or class category for the input, using both past and current data. In the case of healthcare, the predictive model can use more data, more quickly, to help the physician arrive at an effective treatment.

To help physicians prescribe individualized medicine, the classifier would assist them in determining the specific stage of a patient's disease. Hypothetically, the data (say, genetic analysis from a blood sample) could be fed to a trained classifier that could label the stage of a new patient's illness. In the case of cancer (for example), the classifier could have such labels — describing the following classes or groupings — as "healthy," "benign," "early stage," "metastatic," or "terminal."

What's next?

Future uses of classifiers promise to be even more ambitious. Suppose you want to predict how much a customer will spend on a specific date. In such a case, you design a classifier that predicts numerical values rather than specified category names. Of course, numeric predictors can be developed using not only statistical methods such as regression but also other data-mining techniques such as neural networks (covered later in this chapter). Given sufficiently sophisticated designs, classifiers are commonly used in fields such as presidential elections, national security, and climate change. Chapter 5 also presents some current examples of predictive analytics using classification-based modeling.

Introducing Data Classification to Your Business

Getting back down to earth, if your business has yet to use data classification, maybe it's time to introduce it as a way to make better management or operating decisions. This process starts with an investigative step: Identifying a problem area in the business where ample data is available but currently isn't being used to drive business decisions.

One way to identify such a problem area is to hold a meeting with your analysts, managers, and other decision-makers to ask them what risky or difficult decisions they repeatedly make — and what kind of data they need to support their decisions. If you have data that reflects the results of past decisions, be prepared to draw on it. This process of identifying the problem is called the *discovery phase*.

After the discovery phase, you'll want to follow up with individual questionnaires addressed to the business stakeholders. Consider asking the following types of questions:

>> What do you want to know from the data?

>> What action will you take when you get your answer?

>> How will you measure the results from the actions taken?

If the predictive analytical model's results produce meaningful insights, then someone must do something with it — take action. Obviously, you'll want to see whether the results of that action add business value to the organization. So you'll have to find a method of measuring that value — whether in terms of savings from operational costs, increased sales, or better customer retention.

As you conduct these interviews, seek to understand why certain tasks are done and how they're being used in the business process. Asking why things are the way they are may help you uncover unexpected realizations. No point in gathering and analyzing data just for the sake of creating more data. You want to use that data to answer specific business needs.

For the data scientist or modeler, this exercise defines what kinds of data must be classified and analyzed — a step essential to developing a data classification model. A basic distinction to begin with is whether the data you'll use to train the model is internal or external:

>> **Internal data** is specific to your company, usually draws from your company's data sources, and can include many data types — such as structured, semi-structured, or unstructured.

>> **External data** comes from outside the company, often as data bought from other companies.

Regardless of whether the data you use for your model is internal or external, you'll want to evaluate it first. Several questions are likely to crop up in that evaluation:

>> How critical and accurate is the data in question? If it's too sensitive, it may not serve your purposes.

>> How accurate is the data in question? If its accuracy is questionable, then its utility is limited.

>> How do company policy and applicable laws allow the data to be used and processed? You may want to clear the use of the data with your legal department for any legal issues that could arise. (See the accompanying sidebar for a famous recent example)

PREDICTIONS, PRIVACY, AND PROFIT

Legal issues resulting from the use of predictive models are especially relevant if your choice of implementation (or target audience) may raise eyebrows with privacy groups or provoke a negative response from social groups.

Recently, Target Corporation got into a mess with the press when their predictive model targeted pregnant women. According to a *New York Times* article, the model accurately predicted a pregnant teen before her parents knew about it.

Her parents eventually discovered their daughter's pregnancy when the marketing materials sent to their home were filled with items that an expectant mom would receive. In this case, the targeted marketing campaign resulted in an unintended invasion of privacy.

On the other hand, companies like LinkedIn and Netflix use data and predictive analytics very effectively to drive their business decisions. They have turned the data that their customers generate into a money-making machine.

When you've identified data that is appropriate to use in the building of your model, the next step is to classify it — to create and apply useful labels to your data elements. For instance, if you're working on data about customers' buying behavior, the labels could define data categories according to how some groups of customers buy, along these lines:

>> **Seasonal customers** could be those who shop regularly or semi-regularly.

>> **Discount-oriented customers** could be those who tend to shop only when major discounts are offered.

>> **Faithful customers** are those who have bought many of your products over time.

Predicting the category that a new customer will fit can be of great value to the marketing team. The idea is to spend time and money efficiently on identifying which customers to advertise to, determining which products to recommend to them, and choosing the best time to do so. A lot of time and money can be wasted if you target the wrong customers, probably making them less likely to buy than if you hadn't marketed to them in the first place. Using predictive analytics for targeted marketing should aim not only at more successful campaigns, but also at the avoidance of pitfalls and unintended consequences.

Exploring the Data-Classification Process

At a brass-tacks level, data classification consists of two stages:

>> **The learning stage** entails training the classification model by running a designated set of past data through the classifier. The goal is to teach your model to extract and discover hidden relationships and rules — the *classification rules* from historical (training) data. The model does so by employing a classification algorithm.

>> **The prediction stage** that follows the learning stage consists of having the model predict class labels or numerical values that classify data it has not seen before (that is, test data).

To illustrate these stages, suppose you're the owner of an online store that sells watches. You've owned the online store for quite a while, and have gathered a lot of transactional data and personal data about customers who purchased watches from your store. Suppose you've been capturing that data through your site by providing web forms, in addition to the transactional data you've gathered through operations.

You could also purchase data from a third party that provides you with information about your customers outside their interest in watches. That's not as hard as it sounds; there are companies whose business model is to track customers online and collect and sell valuable information about them. Most of those third-party companies gather data from social media sites and apply data-mining methods to discover the relationship of individual users with products. In this case, as the owner of a watch shop, you'd be interested in the relationship between customers and their interest in buying watches.

You can infer this type of information from analyzing, for example, a social network profile of a customer, or a microblog comment of the sort you find on Twitter. To measure an individual's level of interest in watches, you could apply any of several text-analytics tools that can discover such correlations in an individual's written text (social network statuses, tweets, blog postings, and such) or online activity (such as online social interactions, photo uploads, and searches).

After you collect all that data about your customers' past transactions and current interests — the *training data* that shows your model what to look for — you'll need to organize it into a structure that makes it easy to access and use (such as a database).

At this point, you've reached the second phase of data classification: the *prediction stage*, which is all about testing your model and the accuracy of the classification rules it has generated. For that purpose, in many cases you'll need additional historical customer data, referred to as *test data* (which is different from the training data). You feed this test data into your model and measure the accuracy of the resulting predictions. You count the times that the model predicted correctly the future behavior of the customers represented in your test data. You also count the times that the model made wrong predictions.

At this point, you have only two possible outcomes: Either you're satisfied with the accuracy of the model or you aren't:

>> If you're satisfied, then you can start getting your model ready to make predictions as part of a production system.

>> If you're not happy with the prediction, then you'll need to retrain or redesign your model with a new training dataset, revisit the data preparation phase for the original training dataset or try another predictive model.

If your original training data was not representative enough of the pool of your customers — or contained noisy data that threw off the model's results by introducing false signals — then there's more work to do to get your model up and running. Either outcome is useful in its own way.

Using Data Classification to Predict the Future

When your data is divided into clusters of similar objects, your model is in a better position to make reliable predictions. This section examines a handful of common algorithms used to classify data in predictive analytics.

Decision trees

In this section, you will be introduced to the basics of using decision trees to make decision. The following section provides a step-by-step algorithm that's widely used to generate a decision tree from raw historical data.

A *decision tree* is an approach to analysis that can help you make decisions. Suppose, for example, that you need to decide whether to invest a certain amount of money in one of three business projects: a food-truck business, a restaurant, or a bookstore. A business analyst has worked out the rate of failure or success for each of these business ideas as percentages (shown in Table 7-1) and the profit you'd make in each case (shown in Table 7-2).

TABLE 7-1   **Business Success Percentages**

Business	Success Rate	Failure Rate
Food Truck	60 percent	40 percent
Restaurant	52 percent	48 percent
Bookstore	50 percent	50 percent

TABLE 7-2   **Business Value Changes**

Business	Gain (USD)	Loss (USD)
Food Truck	20,000	-7,000
Restaurant	40,000	-21,000
Bookstore	6,000	-1,000

From past statistical data shown in Table 7-1, you can construct a decision tree, as shown in Figure 7-1.

FIGURE 7-1:
Decision tree for
three business
ideas.

Using such a decision tree to decide on a business venture begins with calculating the *expected value* for each alternative — a numbered rank that helps you select the best one on average.

The expected value is calculated in such a way that includes all possible outcomes for a decision. Calculating the expected value for the food-truck business idea looks like this:

Expected value of food-truck business = (60 percent x 20,000 (USD)) + (40 percent * -7,000 (USD)) = 9,200 (USD)

Here the expected value reflects the average gain from investing in a food-truck business. In this scenario — working with hypothetical numbers, of course — if you attempt to invest in food-truck businesses several times (under the same circumstances each time), your average profit will be 9,200 (USD) per business.

Accordingly, you can calculate the expected values of a restaurant business and bookstore the same way, as follows:

Expected value of restaurant business = (52 percent x 40,000 (USD)) + (48 percent * -21,000 (USD)) = 10,720 (USD)

Expected value of bookstore business = (50 percent x 6,000 (USD)) + (50 percent * -1,000 (USD)) = 2,500 (USD)

The expected value of a restaurant business represents a prediction of how much profit you'd make (on average) if you invested in a restaurant business several times. Therefore, the expected value becomes one of the criteria you figure into your business decision making. In this example, the expected values of the three alternatives might incline you to favor investing in the restaurant business.

Decision trees can also be used to visualize classification rules (such as those mentioned in the earlier example of the online watch store).

In the watch-store example mentioned in the previous section, you want to predict whether a given customer will buy a watch from your store; the decision tree will be, essentially, a flow chart (refer to Figure 7-1): Each *node* of the decision tree represents an attribute identified in the data matrix. The leaves of the tree are the predicted decisions, as shown in Figure 7-2.

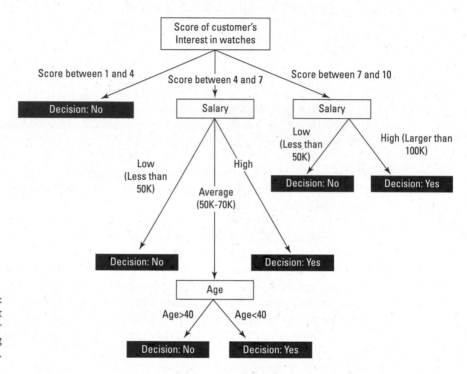

FIGURE 7-2: Decision tree that predicts customer interest in buying watches.

This decision tree predicts whether a customer might buy a given watch at the online store. The nodes in this decision tree represent some of the attributes you're analyzing; each is a score — of customer interest in watches, customer age, and customer salary.

Applying the model to a new Customer X, you can trace a path from the root of the tree down to a decision tree's leaf (yes or no) that indicates and maps how that customer would behave toward the watch being advertised.

In the preceding example, we showed you how a decision tree can be used as a useful management tool to make decisions. The following section will walk you through a step-by-step algorithm to generate a decision tree from raw customer data.

Algorithms for Generating Decision Trees

The longtime senior executive for the Walt Disney Company, Roy Disney once said: "It's not hard to make decisions when you know what your values are." This is indeed true especially when you have a decision tree in front of you, so how do can we automatically generate decision trees from historical data in order to predict the future?

A recent CNNMoney article titled "Would you wear a tracker to get an insurance discount?" explained that for the first time in the United States of America insurance companies are trying activity trackers for discounted rates. In other words, insurance companies may offer you a discount if you wear a fitness tracker that measures your lifestyle.

Imagine that you decided to wear the fitness tracker to get an insurance discount. The fitness tracker captures your personal data, your heart rate, your sleeping hours, your locations, your gym visits, and your favorite exercises among others. This data can be combined into a simple mathematical function that can generate a score to determine if you are maintaining a healthy lifestyle.

Imagine the insurance company has collected historical data, as shown in Table 7-3 (this is an imaginary dataset for the purpose of explaining the decision tree algorithm).

As shown in Table 7-3, the table represents each customer's name, zip code, age, lifestyle label (as inferred from the health tracker device), and awarded discount range.

TABLE 7-3 **Sample Historical Customer Personal and Fitness Tracker Data**

Customer Name	Zip Code	Age	Lifestyle (Health)	Discount
Sarah	10036	30-40	Average	1%-5%
Ana	10020	20-30	Good	1%-5%
Mariah	10018	30-40	Good	6%-15%
Mike	10011	40-50	Average	1%-5%
Zach	20052	20-30	Average	1%-5%
John	20037	30-40	Good	6%-15%

Consider this new customer to whom the insurance company is about to award a discount:

{customer name = David, age 20-30, lifestyle=good, **discount=?**}

The insurance company wants to decide what discount will be awarded to David. For that purpose, we will use the data in Table 7-3 to create a decision tree that will help in making this decision.

Before we dive into how we can automatically create a decision tree, you need to know an important concept known as *entropy* that is widely used in algorithms that generate decision trees.

In the world of information theory, the entropy measures the amount of information in a random variable. For instance, we can calculate the entropy of the variables (attribute) Lifestyle or Age shown in Table 7-3 to see how much information they can tell to predict the discount range for a given customer. The entropy can be used to select the nodes that will make the decision tree. In general, high entropy of an attribute X means that the attribute is from a uniform distribution; if the entropy of X is low, it means that the variable is from a varied and interesting distribution.

The entropy of a variable X can be calculated as follows:

$$Entropy\,(X) = \sum_{d \in Decisions}^{n} -P(d) * \log_2(P(d))$$

Where P(d) is the probability that represent the number of data items for decision (label) d divided by the total number of items.

In Table 7-3, there are two possible decisions to be taken for a given customer either to award them 6-15 percent discount or 1-5 percent discount. In order to better understand how to calculate the entropy of an attribute, here's the Age attribute as an example. It can be calculated as follows for three classes for ages: 20-30, 30-40, and 40-50. Based on Age, we can divide the data elements (rows) into three subsets. We will compute the entropy for each subset:

>> For ages 20-30, two customers received 1-5 percent discount. We are using log base two in the calculation below.

$$Entropy\,(Age\,(20-30)) = -\frac{2}{2} * \log\frac{2}{2} - \frac{0}{2} * \log\frac{0}{2} = 0$$

The entropy is zero because the outcome (discount) is certain along the age (20-30) dimension for the dataset shown in table 7-3.

>> For ages 30-40, two customers received 6-15 percent discount and one customer received 1-5 percent.

$$Entropy\,(Age\,(30-40)) = \frac{2}{3} * \log\frac{2}{3} - \frac{1}{3} * \log\frac{1}{3} = 0.918$$

>> For ages 40-50, one customer received 1-5 percent discount.

$$Entropy\,(Age\,(40-50)) = -\frac{1}{1} * \log\frac{1}{1} - \frac{0}{1} * \log\frac{0}{1} = 0$$

TECHNICAL STUFF

The log used in these the calculations is of base two.

The overall conditional entropy for attribute Age is:

$$Entropy\,(Age) = \frac{1}{6} * Entropy\,(Age\,(40-50))$$
$$+ \frac{3}{6} * Entropy\,(Age\,(30-40)) + \frac{2}{6} * Entropy\,(Age\,(20-30)) = 0.459$$

In order to construct a decision tree, it is important to determine which attributes (such as age and lifestyle) are most discriminating between the data classes. The following measure, Information Gain, can reveal the importance of a given attribute that can lead to the creation of the decision tree.

TECHNICAL STUFF

The zip code attribute was discarded in this analysis because in the sample data in Table 3-7 there is no clear mapping between zip values and discount (at least in the sample data). In a real data set ZIP code would almost always have too many possible categories to be useful as a nominal variable.

$$InformationGain\,(X) = Entropy(Label) - \sum_{x \in Values(X)} \frac{|label_x|}{|labelset|} \cdot Entropy(X)$$

Where

$$Entropy\,(Discount) = -\frac{2}{6} * \log\frac{2}{6} - \frac{4}{6} * \log\frac{4}{6} = 0.918$$

The information gain for the age attribute is

$$InformationGain\,(Age) = Entropy(Discount) - Entropy(Age) = 0.459$$

Similarly, the information gain for the Lifestyle attribute is

$$InformationGain\,(Lifestyle) = Entropy(Discount) - Entropy(Lifestyle) = 0.459$$

In this example, both attributes Lifestyle and Age are of the same information gain. In other cases, you might have different values for attributes. Because both features "Lifestyle" and "Age" have the same values of information gain, we can start with either one as a first node in the decision tree. We will choose Lifestyle as the root of the tree.

Because the variable "Lifestyle" has two possible values average and good, we will have two branches coming out of the root of the tree as shown in Figure 7-3.

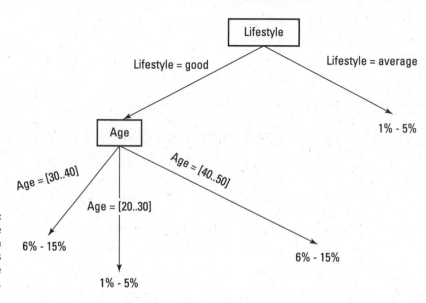

FIGURE 7-3:
Decision tree deciding on customer's insurance discount.

If the Lifestyle is average, then it's clear from historical data in Table 7-3 that discount is 1 percent to 5 percent, regardless of the age. If the Lifestyle is good, the discount will depend on the age attribute:

>> If the age is between 20 and 30, the discount is between 1 percent and 5 percent.

>> If the age is between 30 and 40, the discount is between 6 percent and 15 percent.

Because the historical data doesn't support the case where the lifestyle is good and the age is between 40-50, we assume that the discount is 6 percent to 15 percent (because most of the outcomes for good lifestyle are 6 percent to 15 percent).

The final decision tree is shown in Figure 7-3. Now that we derived the decision tree, we can easily decide on the discount we will give to customer David (introduced earlier):

{Customer Name = David, Age 20-30, Lifestyle = Good, **Discount** = ?}

If we follow the decision tree shown in Figure 7-3, David will be awarded a discount in the range of 1 percent to 5 percent.

Multiple algorithms that can automatically learn a decision from large amount of data. Some of the most widely used algorithms are

» ID3 (Iterative Dichotomiser 3)

» C4.5 (successor of ID3)

» CART (Classification and Regression Tree)

Most of these algorithms are implemented in R, RapidMiner, and Weka. With a matter of clicks, you can build a decision tree after you upload your historical data.

Support vector machine

The *support vector machine* (SVM) is a data-classification algorithm that assigns new data elements to one of labeled categories

SVM is, in most cases, a *binary* classifier; it assumes that the data in question contains two possible target values. Another version of the SVM algorithm, *multiclass SVM*, augments SVM to be used as classifier on a dataset that contains more than two classes (grouping or category). SVM has been successfully used in many applications such as image recognition, medical diagnosis, and text analytics.

Suppose you're designing a predictive analytics model that will automatically recognize and predict the name of an object in a picture. This is essentially the problem of *image recognition* — or, more specifically, face recognition: You want the classifier to recognize the name of a person in a photo.

Well, before tackling that level of complexity, consider a simpler version of the same problem: Suppose you have pictures of individual pieces of fruit and you'd like your classifier to predict what kind of fruit appears in the picture. Assume you have only two types of fruit: apples and pears, one per picture.

Given a new picture, you'd like to predict whether the fruit is an apple or a pear — without looking at the picture. You want the SVM to classify each picture as apple or pear. As with all other algorithms, the first step is to train the classifier.

Suppose you have 200 pictures of different apples, and 200 pictures of pears. The learning step consists of feeding those pictures to the classifier so it learns what an apple looks like and what a pear looks like. Before getting into this first step, you need to transform each image into a data matrix, using (say) the R statistical package (which is covered in detail in Chapter 14). A simple way to represent an image as numbers in a matrix is to look for geometric forms within the image (such as circles, lines, squares, or rectangles) and also the positions of each instance of each geometric form. Those numbers can also represent coordinates of those objects within the image, as plotted in a coordinate system.

As you might imagine, representing an image as a matrix of numbers is not exactly a straightforward task. A whole distinct area of research is devoted to image representation.

Figure 7-4 shows how a support vector machine can predict the class of a fruit (labeling it mathematically as *apple* or *pear*), based on what the algorithm has learned in the past.

FIGURE 7-4: A support vector machine that predicts a fruit class.

Suppose you've converted all the images into data matrices. Then the support vector machine takes two main inputs:

>> Previous (training) data: This set of matrices corresponds to previously seen images of apples and pears.

>> The new (unseen) data consists of an image converted to a matrix. The purpose is to predict automatically what is in the picture — an apple or a pear.

The support vector uses a mathematical function, often called a *kernel function* which is a math function that matches the new data to the best image from the training data in order to predict the unknown picture's label (apple or pear).

REMEMBER

In comparison to other classifiers, support vector machines produce robust, accurate predictions, are less affected by noisy data, and are less prone to overfitting (see Chapter 15 for more about overfitting). Keep in mind, however, that support vector machines are most suitable for binary classification — when you have only two categories (such as apple or pear).

Ensemble Methods to Boost Prediction Accuracy

As in the real world, so with the multiplicity of predictive models: Where there is unity, there is strength. Several models can be combined in different ways to make predictions. You can then apply the combined model — called an *ensemble model* — at the learning stage, at the classification stage, or at both stages.

Here's one way to use an ensemble model:

1. Split the training data into several sets.

2. Have each of the individual models that make up the ensemble model process parts of the data and learn from it.

3. Have each model produce its learning outcome from that data.

So far, so good. But in order to get the ensemble model to predict a future class or category label for new data and make a decision, you have to run the new data through all of the trained models; each model predicts a class label. Then, on the basis of the collective classification or prediction, you can generate an overall prediction.

You can generate that overall prediction by simply implementing a voting mechanism that decides the final result. One voting technique could use the label that the majority of the models predict as the label that the ensemble model produces as its result.

Suppose you want to build a model that will predict whether an incoming e-mail is spam. Assume that the training data consists of a set of e-mails in which some are spam and others are not. Then you can distribute that dataset to a number of models for training purposes.

Then the trained models process an incoming e-mail. If the majority of the models classify it as spam, then the ensemble model gives the e-mail the final label of spam.

Another way to implement an ensemble model is to weigh the accuracy of each model you're building into the ensemble model against the accuracy of all the other models in the *set*:

1. You assign a specific weight (accuracy) to each model.

   This weight will vary from one dataset to the next and from one business problem to the next.

2. After the models are trained, you can use test data where you know the classification of each data point in the test data.

3. Evaluate the prediction made by each model for each test case.

4. Increase the weight for the models that predicted correctly and decrease the weight for the models that classified the data incorrectly.

Naïve Bayes classification algorithm

Naïve Bayes is a data-classification algorithm that is based on probabilistic analysis. The term *probability* is often associated with the term *event*. So you often hear statements along these lines: "The probability of Event X is so and so."

Well, the probability of Event X is a numerical value. You can calculate this numerical value by dividing the number of times Event X can occur by the number of events that are possible in the same circumstances.

Probability as a grab bag

Consider a bag that contains seven fruits: three apples and four oranges. Imagine that you'll be pulling one fruit at a time out of the bag, without looking at the bag. What is the likelihood (the probability) that you'll pull out an orange? In this case, following the definition just mentioned, Event X is *picking an orange out of a bag that contains seven fruits.*

>> The number of times that the Event X in question *could* happen is four because there are four oranges in the bag.

>> The total number of *possible* events that can occur is seven because there are seven fruits in the bag.

>> Each time you pull a fruit out of the bag, it's considered an event. Thus the probability of picking an orange is four divided by seven.

>> If you follow the same reasoning, you can deduce that the probability of pulling an apple out of the fruit bag is the result of dividing three by seven.

> >> The probability of pulling out a banana from the same bag is zero because the number of times such an event can happen is zero, the total number of possible events is seven, and zero divided by seven equals zero.

Naïve Bayes algorithm and Bayes' Theorem

The Naïve Bayes classification algorithm is based on basic probabilities and on *Bayes' Theorem*, a powerful formula that can be used to calculate the probability of an event based on previous knowledge. Such previous knowledge is often referred to as *evidence*.

Let X be the event you want to calculate the probability for; let Y be the prior event that has happened (evidence). Bayes' Theorem states that

$$\text{Probability of}\left(\text{Event X given Y}\right) = \text{Probability of}\left(\text{Events X and Y occurring}\right) / \text{Probability of}\left(\text{Event Y}\right)$$

The same equation can be also written as follows: $\text{Prob}\left(X \mid Y\right) = [P\left(X\right) * P\left(Y \mid X\right)] / [P\left(X\right) * P\left(Y \mid X\right) + P\left(not\_X\right) * P\left(Y \mid not\_X\right)]$

where

> P (X) is the probability that Event X will happen.
>
> P (not_X) is the probability that Event X will not happen.
>
> P (X|Y) is the probability that Event X will happen, given that Event Y has happened.
>
> P (Y|X) is the probability that Event Y will happen, given that Event X has happened.
>
> P (Y|not_X) is the probability that Event Y will happen, given that X has not happened.

In practice, the preceding equation in the list is the one most often used when applying Bayes' Theorem.

Fundamentals of the Naïve Bayes classifier

Consider the scenario where you want to advertise Product X to a customer. You've gathered information about your customers, as shown in Figure 7-5. You want to predict whether the customer in question will buy Product X.

Figure 7-5 shows customer data you could possibly gather. Each customer has an ID, income, a credit rating, and a purchase history of similar products. Each customer record also has sentiment analysis of his or her social media text about Product X.

customer ID	Income (I)	Credit Rating (CR)	Sentiment Analysis on Social Media about the Product (SA)	Purchased Similar Products (SP)
3345	High	Fair	Neutral	Yes
3346	Medium	Excellent	Positive	Yes
3347	Poor	Fair	Positive	Yes
3348	Medium	Poor	Positive	No
3349	Medium	Excellent	Positive	Yes
3350	High	Poor	Negative	Yes
3351	Poor	Fair	Positive	No
3352	High	Fair	Negative	No
3353	High	Excellent	Positive	No
3354	High	Fair	Positive	Yes

FIGURE 7-5:
Customer data.

Consider the following probabilities definitions and notations:

P(X) is the probability of X being purchased.

P(not_X) is the probability of X not being purchased.

P(CR_fair|X) is the probability that a customer's credit rating is fair, given the customer purchases Product X.

P(CR_excellent|X) is the probability that a customer's credit rating is excellent, given the customer purchases Product X.

P(CR_poor|X) is the probability that a customer's credit rating is poor, given the customer purchases Product X.

P(CR_fair|not_X) is the probability that a customer's credit rating is poor, given the customer did not purchase Product X.

P(CR_excellent|not_X) is the probability that a customer's credit rating is excellent, given the customer did not purchase Product X.

P(CR_poor|not_X) is the probability that a customer's credit rating is poor, given the customer did not purchase Product X.

P(I_medium|X) is the probability that a customer's income is medium, given the customer did purchase Product X.

P(I_high|X) is the probability that a customer's income is high, given the customer did purchase Product X.

P(I_poor|X) is the probability that a customer's income is poor, given the customer did purchase Product X.

P(I_medium|not_X) is the probability that a customer's income is medium, given the customer did not purchase Product X.

P(I_high|not_X) is the probability that a customer's income is high, given the customer did not purchase Product X.

P(I_poor|not_X) is the probability that a customer's income is poor, given the customer did not purchase Product X.

P(SA_neutral|X) is the probability that a customer's sentiment on social media is neutral about Product X, give the customer did purchase Product X.

P(SA_positive|X) is the probability that a customer's sentiment on social media is positive about Product X, given the customer did purchase Product X.

P(SA_negative|X) is the probability that a customer's sentiment on social media is negative about Product X, given the customer did purchase Product X.

P(SA_neutral|not_X) is the probability that a customer's sentiment on social media is neutral about Product X, given the customer did not purchase Product X.

P(SA_positive|not_X) is the probability that a customer's sentiment on social media is positive about Product X, given the customer did not purchase Product X.

P(SA_negative|not_X) is the probability that a customer's sentiment on social media is negative about Product X, given the customer did not purchase Product X.

P(SP_yes|X): the probability that a customer has purchased a product similar to X, given the customer did purchase Product X.

P(SP_no|X) is the probability that a customer has not purchased a product similar to X, given the customer did purchase Product X.

P(SP_yes|not_X) is the probability that a customer has purchased a product similar to X, given the customer did not purchase Product X.

P(SP_no|not_X) is the probability that a customer has not purchased a product similar to X, given the customer did not purchase Product X.

Those probabilities can be calculated as follows, using the basic explanation of probabilities described at the beginning of this section:

$P(X) = 6/10 = 0.6$

$P(not\_X) = 4/10 = 0.4$

$P(CR\_fair|X) = 4/6 = 0.67$

$P(CR\_excellent|X) = 2/6 = 0.33$

$P(CR\_poor|X) = 0/6 = 0$

$P(CR\_fair|not\_X) = 1/4 = 0.25$

$P(CR\_excellent|not\_X) = 1/4 = 0.25$

$P(CR\_poor|not\_X) = 2/4 = 0.5$

$P(I\_medium|X) = 2/6 = 0.33$

$P(I\_high|X) = 3/6 = 0.5$

$P(I\_poor|X) = 1/6 = 0.17$

$$P(I\_medium \mid not\_X) = 1/4 = 0.25$$

$$P(I\_high \mid not\_X) = 2/4 = 0.5$$

$$P(I\_poor \mid not\_X) = 1/4 = 0.25$$

$$P(SA\_neutral \mid X) = 1/6 = 0.17$$

$$P(SA\_positive \mid X) = 4/6 = 0.67$$

$$P(SA\_negative \mid X) = 1/6 = 0.17$$

$$P(SA\_neutral \mid not\_X) = 0/4 = 0$$

$$P(SA\_positive \mid not\_X) = 3/4 = 0.75$$

$$P(SA\_negative \mid not\_X) = 1/4 = 0.25$$

$$P(SP\_yes \mid X) = 4/6 = 0.67$$

$$P(SP\_no \mid X) = 2/6 = 0.33$$

$$P(SP\_yes \mid not\_X) = 2/4 = 0.5$$

$$P(SP\_no \mid not\_X) = 2/4 = 0.5$$

Here comes a new customer, whose ID is 3356 and who has the features (evidence) shown in Figure 7-6.

customer ID	Income (I)	Credit Rating (CR)	Sentiment Analysis on Social Media about the product (SA)	Pushased Similar Products (SP)
3356	Medium	Fair	positive	Yes

FIGURE 7-6: New customer data.

Figure 7-6 shows the data belonging to the new customer (#3356). You want to know whether the company should spend money on advertising Product X to this new customer. In other words, you want to know the probability that the customer will purchase Product X, given what you know already: that the customer is of medium income, has a poor credit rating, has a positive sentiment analysis on social media about Product X, and has a history of purchasing similar products.

The classifier uses historical data (as shown in Figure 7-6) and Bayes' Theorem (mentioned earlier in this section) to label the new customer as a potential buyer of Product X . . . or not.

Let $P(X \mid Customer\#3356)$ be the probability that Product X will be purchased by Customer#3356, given the customer's features.

Let $P(not\_X \mid Customer\#3356)$ be the probability that Product X will not be purchased by Customer#3356, given the customer's features.

Following Bayes' Theorem, the following probabilities can be calculated:

P (X|Customer#3356) =

[P(X) * P(Customer#3356|X)] / [P(X) * P(Customer#3356|X) + P (not_X) * P (Customer#3356|not_X)]

P(not_X|Customer#3356) = [P(not_X) * P(Customer#3356|not_X)] /

[P (not_X) * P (Customer#3356|not_X) +P(X) * P(Customer#3356|X)]

Notice that those probabilities have the same denominator. Thus we focus on comparing the numerators, as follows:

P(Customer#3356|X) is the probability of having customers like Customer#3356, knowing that Customer#3356 purchased Product X.

P(Customer#3356|X) = P(CR_fair|X) * P(I_medium|X) * P(SA_positive|X) * P(SP_yes|X)

=0.67 * 0.33 * 0.67 * 0.67 = 0.0993

P(Customer#3356|not_X) = P(CR_fair|not_X) * P(I_medium|not_X) * P(SA_ positive|not_X) * P(SP_yes|not_X)

=0.25 * 0.25 * 0.75 * 0.5 = 0.0234

P(X|Customer#3356) = [P(X) * P(Customer#3356|X)] /

[P(X) * P(Customer#3356|X) + P (not_X) * P (Customer#3356|not_X)]

=0.6*0.0993/[P(X)*P(Customer#3356|X)+P(not_X)*P(Customer#3356|not_X)]

P(not_X|Customer#3356) = [P(not_X) * P(Customer#3356|not_X)] / [P(X) * P(Customer#3356|X) + P (not_X) * P (Customer#3356|not_X)]

=0.4*0.0234/[P(X)*P(Customer#3356|X)+P(not_X)*P(Customer#3356|not_X)]

Notice that both probabilities P(not_X/Customer#3356) and P(X/Customer#3356) have the same numerator. Through comparing the numerators, the following inequality can be deduced:

P(X|Customer#3356) > P(not_X|Customer#3356)

Thus we can conclude that Customer#3356 is more likely to buy Product X.

The Markov Model

The *Markov Model* is a statistical model that relies heavily on probability theory. (It's named after a Russian mathematician whose primary research was in probability theory.)

Here's a practical scenario that illustrates how it works: Imagine you want to predict whether Team X (let's say a soccer team) will win tomorrow's game. The first thing to do is collect previous statistics about Team X. The question that might arise is how far back you should go in history. Let's assume you were able to get to the last 10 past game outcomes in sequence. You want to know the probability of Team X winning the next game, given the outcomes of the past 10 games (for example, Team X won 3 times and then lost 7 times). The problem is that the further back in history you want to go, the harder and more complex the data collection and probability calculations become.

Believe it or not, the Markov Model simplifies your life by providing you with the *Markov Assumption*, which looks like this when you write it out in words:

> The probability that an event will happen, given *n* past events, is approximately equal to the probability that such an event will happen given just the last past event.

Written as a formula, the Markov Assumption looks like this:

$$P\,(event_t \mid event_{t-1}, event_{t-2}, \ldots, event_1) = P(event_t \mid event_{t-1})$$

Either way, the Markov Assumption means that you don't need to go too far back in history to predict tomorrow's outcome. You can just use the most recent past event. This is called the *first-order Markov prediction* because you're considering only the present event to predict the future event. A *second order Markov prediction* includes just the last two events that happen in sequence. From the equation just given, the following widely used equation can also be derived:

$$P(event_1, event_2, \ldots, event_n) = \prod_{i=2}^{n} P(event_i \mid event_{i-1})$$

This equation aims to calculate the probability that some events will happen in sequence: *event1* after *event2*, and so on. This probability can be calculated by multiplying the probability of each *event t* (given the event previous to it) by the next event in the sequence. For instance, suppose you want to predict the probability that Team X wins, then loses, and then ties.

A typical Markov Model prediction

Here's how a typical predictive model based on a Markov Model would work. Consider the same example: Suppose you want to predict the results of a soccer game to be played by Team X. The three possible outcomes — called *states* — are win, loss, or tie.

Assume that you've collected past statistical data on the results of Team X's soccer games, and that Team X lost its most recent game. You want to predict the outcome of the next soccer game. It's all about guessing whether Team X will win, lose, or tie — relying only on data from past games. So here's how you use a Markov Model to make that prediction.

1. Calculate some probabilities based on past data.

   For instance, how many times has Team X lost games? How many times has Team X won games? For example, imagine if Team X won 6 games out of ten games in total. Then, Team X has won 60 percent of the time. In other words, the probability of wining for Team X is 60 percent. You arrive at this figure by taking the number of victories and dividing by 10 (the total number of games), which results in a probability of 60 percent.

2. Calculate the probability of a loss, and then the probability of a tie, in the same way.

3. Use the probability equation mentioned in the previous Naïve Bayes section to calculate probabilities such as the following:

   - The probability that Team X will win, given that Team X lost the last game.

   - The probability that Team X will lose, given that Team X won the last game.

   Let's arbitrarily assign those probabilities. Note that you can easily calculate $P(X|Y)$ — the probability of X given Y — as shown earlier in the Naïve Bayes section of this chapter.

4. Calculate the probabilities for each state (win, loss, or tie).

   Assuming that the team plays only one game per day, the probabilities are as follows:

   - $P(Win|Loss)$ is the probability that Team X will win today, given that it lost yesterday.

   - $P(Win|Tie)$ is the probability that Team X will win today, given that it tied yesterday.

   - $P(Win|Win)$ is the probability that Team X will win today, given that it won yesterday.

5. Using the calculated probabilities, create a chart like the one shown in Figure 7-7.

A circle in this chart represents a possible state that Team X could attain at any given time (win, loss, tie); the numbers on the arrows represent the probabilities that Team X could move from one state to another.

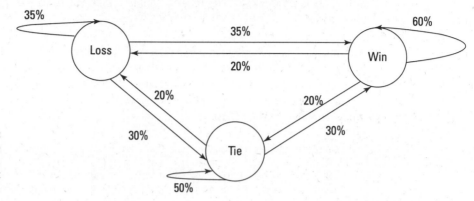

For instance, if Team X has just won today's game (its current state = win), the probability that the team will win again is 60 percent; the probability that they'll lose the next game is 20 percent (in which case they'd move from current state = win to future state = loss).

Suppose you want to know the chances that Team X will win two more games in a row and lose the third one. As you might imagine, that's not a straightforward prediction to make.

However, using the chart just created and the Markov assumption, you can easily predict the chances of such an event occurring. You start with the win state, walk through the win state twice, and record 60 percent twice; then you move to the loss state and record 20 percent. The chances that Team X will win twice and lose the third game become simple to calculate: 60 percent times 60 percent times 20 percent which equals 7.2 percent.

Using hidden Markov Models

A *hidden Markov Model* is a Markov Model in which a previous state from which the current state originated can be hidden or unknown. The main inputs to the model are the states transition probabilities and a number of observations. A hidden Markov Model takes observation states into consideration. Let us walk you through an example that predicts a future state on the basis of a previous state and some observations.

Suppose you're currently watching a game that Team X is playing and you make the following observation:

Team X is winning, so far, by 1 goal to zero (the current score over the first 30 minutes of the game).

Based on only one present observation, you want to predict a hidden future state: Will Team X win, lose, or tie?

Assume you know the past statistical probabilities for Team X, as mentioned earlier in the previous section (refer to Figure 7-7). Here are the steps to predict the next hidden (unknown) state — whether Team X will win, lose, or tie — on the sole basis of your current observation.

The first phase (as mentioned earlier) is the learning phase: You learn about Team X from past data and the outcomes of Team X's games. The following facts turn up:

» Team X won 55 percent of its past games, lost 40 percent of those games, and tied 5 percent of the time.

» In all past games, Team X won 60 percent of the time when they scored a goal within the first 30 minutes.

» In all past games, Team X lost 35 percent of the time when they scored a goal within the first 30 minutes.

» In all past games, Team X tied 5 percent of the time when they scored a goal within the first 30 minutes.

The statistics that reflect the learning outcomes from past games can be summarized like this:

	Win	Loss	Tie
P(X)	55 percent	40 percent	5 percent

The following table shows the probabilities of an outcome X, given observation Z.

	Z = scored a goal within the first 30 minutes
X=win	60 percent
X=loss	35 percent
X=tie	5 percent

Using a probability rule known as Bayes' Theorem (mentioned in the Naïve Bayes section) and the Markov Assumption just mentioned in the previous section, you can easily calculate the probability that Team X will win if you're currently observing that the team has scored a goal within the first 30 minutes of the game.

Similarly, you can calculate the probability that Team X will lose if you observe that the team has scored a goal within the first 30 minutes of the game. Also, assume that Team X ties in the previous game, and that the prior probability of Team X scoring in the first 30 minutes in any game is 40 percent. Given these facts and observations, what is the probability Team X will win the game?

Here's how to calculate the probability that Team X will win, given that Team X tied in the last game and you observe that the team scored within the first 30 minutes of the current game. This probability can be written as follows:

$$P(event_{t=future} = win | event_{t-1} = tie, observation = scored\ a\ goal\ in\ the\ first\ 30\ minutes)$$

For simplicity in the equations, consider the following notations:

$X : event_{t=future} = win$

$Y : event_{t-1} = tie$

$z : observation = scored\ a\ goal\ in\ the\ first\ 30\ minutes$

Now you can write that same probability — that Team X will win, given that Team X tied in the last game and you observe that the team scored within the first 30 minutes of the current game, and also given that Y and Z are independent — like this:

P(X|Y, Z) = P(X,Y|Z) / P(Y|Z)

= P(X,Y|Z) / P(Y)

Applying the Naïve Bayes rules explained earlier, we get this:

= P(Z|Y, X) * P(X, Y) / [P(Y) * P (Z)]

Applying Markov's Assumption equation (mentioned in the previous section) gives you this result:

= P(Z|X) * P(X, Y) / [P(Y) * P (Z)]

= P(Z|X) * P(X|Y) * P(Y) / [P(Y) * P (Z)]

= P(Z|X) * P(X|Y) / P (Z)

= (60 percent * 30 percent) / 40 percent = 45 percent

Written out, it looks like this:

$$P(event_{t=future} = win | event_{t-1} = tie, observation$$
$$= scored \, a \, goal \, in \, the \, first \, 30 \, minutes) = 45 \, percent$$

Hidden Markov Models have been successfully used in time series predictions and in practical applications such as speech recognition and biological sequence analysis.

Linear regression

Linear regression is a statistical method that analyzes and finds relationships between two variables. It can be used to predict a future numerical value of a variable.

Consider an example of data that contains two variables: past data consisting of the arrival times of a train and its corresponding delay time. Suppose you want to predict what the delay would be for the next train. If you apply linear regression to these two variables — the arrival and delay times — you can generate a linear equation such as

Delay = a + (b * Arrival time) + d

This equation expresses the relationship between delay time and arrival time. The constants *a* and *b* are the model's parameters. The variable *d* is the *error term* (also known as the *remainder*) — a numerical value that represents the mismatch between the two variables *delay* and *arrival time*.

If you're sitting at the train station, you can simply plug the arrival time into the preceding equation and you can compute the expected delay, using the linear regression model's given parameters *a*, *b*, and *d*.

Linear regression can be very sensitive toward outliers in the data points. The outliers in your data can have a significant impact on the model (for more about outliers, see Chapter 15). We recommend that you carefully remove those outliers from the training set if you're planning to use linear regression for your predictive model.

Neural networks

A complex algorithm, the *neural network*, is biologically inspired by the structure of the human brain. A neural network provides a very simple model in comparison to the human brain, but it works well enough for our purposes.

Widely used for data classification, neural networks process past and current data to estimate future values — discovering any complex correlations hidden in the data — in a way analogous to that employed by the human brain.

Neural networks can be used to make predictions on time series data, such as weather data. A neural network can be designed to detect pattern in input data and produce an output free of noise.

Figure 7-8 illustrates the structure of a neural-network algorithm and its three layers:

>> **The input layer** feeds past data values into the next (hidden) layer. The black circles represent *nodes* of the neural network.

>> **The hidden layer** encapsulates several complex functions that create predictors; often those functions are hidden from the user. A set of nodes (black circles) at the hidden layer represents mathematical functions that modify the input data; these functions are called *neurons*.

>> **The output layer** collects the predictions made in the hidden layer and produces the final result: the model's prediction.

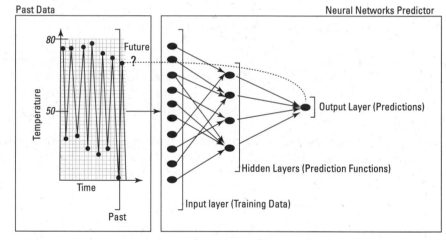

FIGURE 7-8: Neural networks create predictors in the second (hidden) layer of a three-layer structure.

Here's a closer look at how a neural network can produce a predicted output from input data. The hidden layer is the key component of a neural network because of the neurons it contains; they work together to do the major calculations and produce the output.

Each neuron takes a set of input values; each is associated with a *weight* (more about that in a moment) and a numerical value known as *bias*. The output of each neuron is a function of the output of the weighted sum of each input plus the bias.

Most neural networks use mathematical functions to activate the neurons. A *function* in math is a relation between a set of inputs and a set of outputs, with the rule that each input corresponds to an output. (For instance, consider the negative function where a whole number can be an input and the output is its negative equivalent.) In essence, a function in math works like a black box that takes an input and produces an output.

Neurons in a neural network can use *sigmoid* functions to match inputs to outputs. When used that way, a sigmoid function is called a *logistic function* and its formula looks like this:

$$f(input) = \frac{1}{1 + e^{output}}$$

Here *f* is the *activation function* that activates the neuron, and *e* is a widely used mathematical constant that has the approximate value of 2.718.

TECHNICAL STUFF

You might wonder why such a function is used in neurons. Well, most sigmoid functions have derivatives that are positive and easy to calculate. They're continuous, can serve as types of smoothing functions, and are also bounded functions. This combination of characteristics, unique to sigmoid functions, is vital to the workings of a neural network algorithm — especially when a derivative calculation (such as the weight associated with each input to a neuron) is needed.

The weight for each neuron is a numerical value that can be derived using either supervised training or unsupervised training, such as data clustering (see Chapter 6):

>> In the case of supervised training, weights are derived by feeding sample inputs and outputs to the algorithm until the weights are *tuned* (that is, there's a near-perfect match between inputs and outputs).

>> In the case of unsupervised training, the neural network is only presented with inputs; the algorithm generates their corresponding outputs. When we present the algorithm with new-but-similar inputs and the algorithm produces new outputs that are similar to previous outputs, then the neurons' weights have been tuned.

REMEMBER

Neural networks tend to have high accuracy, even if the data has a significant amount of noise. That's a major advantage; when the hidden layer can still discover relationships in the data despite noise, you may be able to use otherwise-unusable data.

Deep Learning

Deep learning algorithms are among the latest state-of-the-art innovations made in the field of machine learning.

Think of a deep learning algorithm as a black box that makes predictions. Consider a scenario where you have a picture that is first being converted to numbers and pixels. A deep learning algorithm can run a series of mathematical functions on those numbers and returns different numbers that can reveal the nature of the object in the image.

These mathematical functions are based on the neurons' parameters in a neural network. The biggest challenge with using neural networks has been to teach and train them on massive sets of inputs in order to derive the right neuron's parameters. This would lead to a better prediction accuracy.

The renaissance of neural networks

Deep learning algorithms are here to improve neural networks' ability to detect complex patterns. In fact, one of the key phases in the predictive analytics lifecycle involves the process of *Feature Extraction* explained in Chapter 9.

Feature Extraction, also known as Feature Engineering, is a time-consuming process that has to take place, in most cases, before applying a predictive model. It is also a process in the predictive analytics pipeline that has a lot of influence on the final model's accuracy.

Deep learning algorithms are designed so that they skip the feature extraction step of predictive analytics and machine learning. *Automatic learning of features relevant to the training data* is a major advantage of deep learning. In many cases, especially in the field of image pattern recognition, deep learning has outperformed the model accuracy of traditional feature extraction engineering algorithms.

Like any other predictive model, the choice of the training data set has a major effect on the accuracy of the deep learning algorithm.

Introducing deep learning

Deep learning is a novel sub-field of machine learning. It is often referred to as *deep structure learning, deep machine learning, or hierarchical learning.* Deep learning consists of algorithms that try to automatically learn multiple levels of abstractions of data. Those abstractions can help in the process of extracting insights and forward-insights.

Deep learning is about neural networks. As explained in the preceding section, a neural network is a graph of nodes called "neurons" that have edges between them. A neural network takes a set of numbers as inputs, then applies complex mathematical computations on those inputs and produces a set of outputs that could be used for data classification.

As we mention in the preceding section, a neural net is a network of nodes that are organized in layers. The first layer is called the *input layer* and the last layer is called the *output layer*. The layers in between are known as *"hidden layers."* Every node in the hidden layer can be seen as a classifier that takes an input and returns an output (which is also the input to another neuron in the subsequent hidden layers). The last outputs are a combination of the outputs from many neurons on the hidden layers of the neural network. This process of passing inputs from one layer to another through hidden layers until they reach the final output at the output layer is known as *forward propagation*.

You might wonder why each node in the hidden layers is producing a different output. The reason is that every node is associated with two values: a bias and weight. A *weight* is a numerical value by which an input is being multiplied; a *bias* is another numerical value that is being added to the output at every node. The weights and biases are critical to the classification accuracy in a neural network.

A neural network needs to be trained, like any other predictive model. Cross validation, for example, can be used to train the model. In other words, the ground truth output is compared to the output generated by the neural net, and the bias and weight values are adjusted accordingly each time there is a mistake on the output. The ultimate goal behind training a neural net is to reduce costs; the cost is the difference between the predicted value generated by the neural net and the actual known value in the training data.

The biases and weights are adjusted and tweaked through running the neural network across a large number of training data samples.

The reason why neural nets are complex is because multiple neurons, which can be viewed as classifiers, are being trained. For datasets of very complex patterns, neural nets tend to provide better prediction accuracy when compared with other classifiers, at the cost of training the neural network. However, with recent advancements in computing power, neural nets can be trained in relatively short amount of time.

Deep learning takes a divide-and-conquer approach to detect very complex patterns. In fact, a deep learning algorithm tries to break up the problem of detecting complex patterns into smaller parts. It does this by detecting a set of less complex sub-patterns that, collectively, will lead it to discover the original pattern.

In the previous fruits example, consider the data classification problem where the goal is to classify and determine whether the image is of a banana. In simple terms, a deep learning algorithm will try to detect the edges of the object, the shape, and the color. Next, it will calculate an output score that reflects a decision of whether this is a picture of a banana.

TIP

An analogy would be how we, as human beings, detect complex patterns. We tend to detect such patterns by finding smaller, simpler patterns that will lead us to make final decisions. Interestingly, the design of a deep neural network was inspired by the architecture of the human brain.

Deep learning algorithms are very robust and in most cases outperform all classifiers for detecting very complex patterns. However, deep learning networks take a very long time to be trained. For example, in some cases it might take about a week to train a deep network.

A neural network is trained through calculating a cost value. The cost is the difference between the actual value (ground truth and labeled training data) and the predictive value produced by the neural net. The cost is minimized by running several iterations of the training. The weights and biases at each neuron are adjusted accordingly to lower the cost.

The training process of neural networks utilizes a mathematical function called *gradient.* This measures how much the cost will change with respect to a change in biases, values, and weights. *Back propagation* is the process of training neural networks. This process can be seen as the reverse of forward propagations (discussed previously in this section). It starts with the last layer and moves towards the first layer. The gradients are being multiplied throughout the back propagation process. As the network becomes more complex, back propagation takes a lot of time to train the neural network and the accuracy deteriorates. While training a deep net, researchers have encountered a major problem known as the *vanishing gradient.* The vanishing gradient problem occurs as the values of the gradients become very small (multiplying numbers ranging from 0 to 1) until they vanish as we propagate back over the network.

These problems were addressed by researchers like Professor Yann LeCun, of New York Univerty's Courant Institute of Mathematical Sciences. He is also the director of Artificial Intelligence at Facebook.

Results from deep learning researchers' work and other teams led to the creation of the Restricted Boltzmann Machine (RBM). An RBM is considered a feature extractions neural network. In simple terms, an RBM is a neural network of two layers: the visible layer and the hidden layer. Each neuron (node) in the visible layer is connected to every neuron in the hidden layer. Nodes from the same layer can't be connected. The RBM converts the set of inputs into outputs in the forward pass, and tries to reconstruct the inputs from the output on the backward pass. Through this process, weights and biases on an RBM are being adjusted, and the RBM is trying to learn which inputs are more important than others through several iterations of backward and forward passes. An RBM doesn't necessarily require labeled data. The RBM has performed well for mining and classifying videos and images.

Combining multiple RBMs together can partially address the vanishing gradient problem. A set of combined RBMs can construct *deep belief networks*, another deep learning algorithm in the family of deep learning. Each RBMs' hidden layer is considered a visible layer of the subsequent RBM in the deep belief net structure. Because of its structure, deep belief networks would only need a reasonably small dataset to train.

There exist multiple deep learning algorithms known to work for different applications. Follow these guidelines to get started and make selections from available algorithms:

>> Recurrent nets algorithms are suitable for time series analysis.

>> Recursive neural tensor network algorithms are suitable for text mining problems for supervised learning.

>> In many cases, *Deep belief networks* and *convolutional neural networks* algorithms tend to perform well for supervised learning problems for image and object recognition.

>> *Restricted Boltzmann Machine* and *auto-encoder* algorithms are suitable for unsupervised learning, unlabeled data for the purpose of feature extraction.

>> *Deep belief networks* and *rectified linear units* (ReLU) algorithms are good for general-purpose data classification.

Remember:

>> In deep learning algorithms, data is being passed through a sequence of layers. Each layer takes some numbers and interprets those numbers, which are passed to another layer.

>> Each layer is trying to identify a subset of features in the input data. This data could be text, video, or images.

>> A neural network is being trained by calculating a cost value. The cost is the difference between the actual value (ground truth and labeled training data) and the predictive value produced by the neural net.

>> The cost is minimized through running several iterations of training. The weights and bias at each neuron are being adjusted accordingly to lower the cost.

>> For simple pattern detection, you might not need to use neural networks or deep learning algorithms; a simple classifier like linear regression or support vector machine would do the job.

>> For complex tasks such as facial recognition, deep learning algorithms are more appropriate.

>> To properly train a convolutional neural network (repeats), you need millions of images; otherwise, you may overfit the model.

>> Deep learning can be used in real-time speech recognition, natural language processing, text mining, video stream mining, and image recognition.

ALPHAGO: A GOOGLE DEEPMIND DRIVEN BY DEEP LEARNING

In 2013, a computer program called AlphaGo defeated a human opponent in the game of Go, a feat once thought to be impossible. Go is a board game that originated in China and is considered to be far more complex than chess. It's played on a board like a chess board, with one player taking control over black pieces and the other taking control over white pieces.

Each player's goal in the game of Go is to try to create a chain of pieces around the opponent player's stones. The score is based on the number of obstacles each player creates for the other.

Imagine a computer playing against a human being in Go. The complexity lies in the magnitude of possible moves for each stone. At iteration one, each player has about 360 possible moves, afterwards the number of possible moves increases exponentially at subsequent iterations. The very large number of possible moves makes it almost impossible for a computer to follow a brute force approach to figure out the outcomes from a possible move.

AlphaGo is a computer program that is based on a deep learning algorithm that predicts the quality of the move (poor or bad). AlphaGo judges the success of a possible moves based on a "policy network". The policy network used by AlphaGo takes an input of a 19-by-19 array that represents the board on which the game is played. The goal of the deep neural network is to predict the best move at any given iteration. The output layer shows all possible locations of a player's game piece and a score that represents the probability of successfully making each move.

Training AlphaGo required 30 million board configurations and games played by experts to adjust the parameters of the network. AlphaGo learned from experience to predict whether a given move was good or bad.

Deep learning is the future of artificial intelligence. It will lead applications in healthcare, automated translation, pattern recognition, and self-driving cars.

3 Developing a Roadmap

IN THIS PART . . .

Evaluating results

Creating proposals

Processing data

Building and maintaining models

Visualizing predictions and results

Chapter 8

Convincing Your Management to Adopt Predictive Analytics

P redictive analytics should be on every company's radar. If it isn't in your company's toolkit, take a good look at the surrounding competitive land-scape: Margins are thinner; customers are more demanding and selective; customers have more and more choices. Companies that thrive in this environ-ment are those that adapt to these changes and innovate to get ahead of the com-petition. They're lean; they're agile; they have embraced predictive analytics.

For examples of the effective use of predictive analytics, consider the success of Amazon, Netflix, LinkedIn, and Facebook. Amazon and Netflix have been around for about two decades, publicly traded for roughly half that time; LinkedIn and Facebook have been around for about a decade, publicly traded for only a few years. Although these companies are relatively new in comparison to blue-chip giants like Walmart or IBM, they are some of the biggest companies in the world.

In fact, Amazon and Facebook have both surpassed Walmart and IBM in market capitalization. One major reason: These companies have pioneered the use of data and predictive analytics to make business decisions.

The market has rewarded this new generation of companies with very high stock valuations — and equally high expectations. To justify those high valuations, these companies are expected to grow their earnings at a very rapid pace for the next several years. The velocity of growth in these young companies reflects the explosive growth in data generation — and the use of that data to grow.

Amazon and Netflix are not just any ordinary e-commerce companies; they have transformed how we shop and watch movies by their innovative use of predictive analytics to perfect the retail business. Facebook and LinkedIn started as companies that provided an online service. They smartly used the predictive analytics on the data they were generating to create an even better service that is used by millions of people every day. So in essence, their data is the core of their product.

All of these companies collect, analyze, and monetize their data by using it to understand their customers' needs and offer them compelling and customized products and services. Without using data in innovative and ingenious ways, these companies probably wouldn't have grown as fast and as large as they have.

So, if your company wants to follow suit, the questions to ask are

>> How did the analytics team or middle management (for companies that lacked data-science teams at the time) convince upper management to adopt predictive analytics?

>> How did the executive management team have (or acquire) the insight to create data science teams?

Nothing like that had been done before in the open, which makes it all the more remarkable. At least we don't have to worry about that now. You can use the success of the pioneering companies as a real-world example to convince your management about the importance of applying predictive analytics to your organization.

Making the Business Case

Many CMOs and CIOs may already be including predictive analytics in the company roadmap, but may not yet know how to incorporate it into their business. Others may not have even heard of predictive analytics, or may confuse it with traditional descriptive analytics. After reading this chapter, you'll have an understanding of that distinction. If you're a company executive, you'll have a handle on the benefits of predictive analytics as part of your overall business strategy.

If you're in a middle management role, you're probably looking for ways to make effective recommendations to upper management. You want to take advantage of the buzz surrounding big data and predictive analytics — and find out how you can use it to benefit your company. After reading this chapter, you'll be armed with what you need to propose a predictive analytics solution for decision management to the executive team.

Benefits to the business

The benefits of adopting predictive analytics can be achieved in any company. However, larger companies see greater benefits than smaller ones due to the multitude of inefficiencies that can be found in large corporations.

In general, more established companies see greater benefits and have greater opportunity to

>> Optimize their operations

>> Look for new opportunities

>> Acquire new customers

>> Retain current customers

>> Find new revenue streams from their current customer base

Startup companies may see a smaller benefit and defer adopting predictive analytics because their product roadmaps should already be prioritized for the next several months and should stay sharply focused on their current strategy. Smaller companies may also consider a predictive solution too costly and complex to implement. They may think differently later on: After all the core business strategies have been executed and the company has begun to search for ways to grow customer lifetime value and improve customer loyalty, the time is right to add predictive analytics to standard operations.

An exception to the preceding paragraph would be a startup company that has already centered its business on data and analytics. Whether such a company is already doing predictive analytics or already has the staff and tools to create a predictive analytics solution, cost and complexity may not be a barrier.

Companies are having a much more difficult time gaining an advantage over their competitors. Many competitive advantages that leading companies enjoyed were eventually eliminated as competitors adjusted or copied the leaders' practices. This is especially true for companies offering the same types of products.

Adopting predictive analytics is one of the last process enhancements that many companies pursue to gain a competitive edge. Most companies start with traditional business intelligence to answer:

>> What has happened in their business?

>> Why did it happen?

They use dashboards and ad hoc queries against their databases to create reports for the management team.

>> A *dashboard* is a graphical display where users, at a glance, can view summaries of predefined key information about the business.

>> *Ad hoc queries* are non-predefined and non-routine queries on the database, used when specific information is needed.

Using these tools just gives those businesses an understanding of what has happened in the past. It doesn't give them any insight as to what will happen in the future. You can, of course, use standard math and statistics to try to forecast the future by extrapolating from historical data. But sometimes that approach leads to incorrect or non-optimized results.

There is very little chance that a data analyst, using standard math or statistics, can find relationships among the hundreds or thousands of variables that can affect the outcome that he or she is trying to forecast. For example, using just a few predictor variables may lead the analyst to forecast an uptick in sales for the next few months for a product. But predictive analytics may present an entirely different picture.

By taking more variables into account, and faster, predictive analytics can provide a more reliable answer to the question that every business wants answered: What will happen in the future? In this case, suppose the predictive model has predicted a sales decline instead of an uptick for the next few months. The machine-learning algorithm discovered dozens of highly useful predictor variables that affect the outcome, sometimes too subtly to be easily understood as a contributing reason or cause. Not until a particular predictor has presented itself can the team think analytically about why the outcome would depend on it; here the subtler predictors were brought to light. The power you gain from predictive analytics is the insight to make better-informed decisions.

Even so, predictive analytics is still currently under-adopted (and incompletely understood) by many companies. Some companies that have invested the time and money to understand and implement a predictive solution for their operational processes have enjoyed a return on investment (ROI) double of that provided by non-predictive solutions.

In this tough competitive landscape, predictive analytics offer a way to differentiate from the competition.

Improving operational processes

The primary benefit of adopting predictive analytics is its ability to discover actionable insights that aren't easily found by the naked eye. With these insights, the company can optimize business processes.

Predictive analytics are typically applied to operational business decisions such as

- » Predicting trends in sales:
  - Forecasting sales of a particular product
  - Forecasting the revenue contribution of a company division
  - Lead scoring (predicting the value of a sales lead)
- » Predicting trends in marketing:
  - Target marketing: Predicting which customers will respond to advertisement
  - Cross-selling: Predicting which products a customer will also be interested in.
- » Predicting which customers will *churn* (leave the business relationship):
  - Predicting which customers will leave to a competitor
  - Predicting which customers will cancel a subscription
- » Prediction of fraud:
  - Predicting which retail transactions are likely to be fraudulent
  - Predicting unauthorized access to accounts
- » Predicting trends in employment:
  - Predicting which employees will quit their jobs
  - Predicting whether an applicant is the right fit for the job

REMEMBER

Historically, the specific applications of predictive analytics are usually associated with the particular industry a company does business in. However, predictive analytics can be applied to many more domains and problems. The applications are only limited to the imagination of your staff and available resources. Start small with a prototype and then scale up from there.

Using predictive analytics to make data-driven decisions provides a couple of major advantages:

>> It alleviates the stresses and inefficiencies of traditional processes.

   This relief not only optimizes decision-making throughout the organization, but also establishes a consistent decision, free of potentially harmful influences from other outside factors.

>> It frees up human resources to handle other operational issues that can't be (or haven't been) automated.

   The result is an improvement in the overall quality of operational processes, allowing the company to scale up its operations without having to add an equal amount of human resources.

Knowing the score

The predictive "score" is the best example of using predictive analytics to make data-driven decisions for operational processes. The best way to describe the score is in terms of a familiar example — the credit score created by the FICO company to help creditors make decisions on consumer loans. Several other credit companies create and sell their own credit scores, but the FICO Score is by far the most popular. Here are some examples of scoring decisions and their benefits:

>> Only contacting those sales leads in the CRM (customer relations management) database who have high lead scores.

   Sales managers save valuable time and money by not calling contacts who won't buy.

>> Only targeting a segment of the customer database that has high response scores for a particular marketing campaign.

   Saves marketing costs, decreases opt-out from email campaigns, and improves overall customer satisfaction rates by not contacting customers who aren't interested.

>> Contacting customers who have high churn scores.

   Send a retention offer, such as a discount, to prevent customers from defecting.

>> Fraud system will deny transaction and/or send inquiry to customer regarding the suspicious transaction with a high fraud score.

Saves fraudulent payments made to criminals and enhances customer loyalty.

Table 8-1 shows some typical uses of predictive scoring.

TABLE 8-1   ## Typical Uses of Predictive Analytics

Use Cases	Predictive Model	Output	Take Action
Mobile phone contracts, cable subscriptions	Churn model	Customer churn score	Send retention offer when score is high.
Insurance claims, e-commerce transactions	Fraud detection model	Transaction fraud score	Send claims to investigator or risk management when score is high.
Stock trading account	Risk model	Portfolio risk score	Send notification or route transaction to risk management when score is high.
e-commerce, marketing	Response model	Customer response score	Send advertisement to customers with high scores.

TIP

Operational decisions are generally scored along a range of numbers. If the range is from 0 to 100, you can treat each score value as a percentage and allow the user to make a decision based on that information. Or you can create a rule that tells the system always to take action when a score is higher than a particular number (provided your business rules allow it).

Sales and marketing teams are among the largest users of predictive analytics. A 2016 survey by Gartner reported that analytics and business intelligence form the top priority for CIOs. That result is almost certainly in response to the rapidly growing trend among sales and marketing teams to use big data to deliver business insights. One popular and widely respected CEO even goes so far as to cite a Gartner prediction that a company's chief marketing officer will spend more on technology than the chief information officer by 2017.

Building relationships with your customers

Company representatives spend many hours trying to get to know their customers and build a relationship. As the relationship grows, so does the *customer lifetime value* (CLV): Loyal customers will continue to add to future profits. Loyal customers also refer new customers to your business. Your cost of customer acquisition eases off and your revenues improve — the result is closer to an ideal business environment.

Obviously, it takes time to know each customer — and it's practically impossible to get to know each and every one of your customers in equal detail. Most businesses find the acquisition cost for each customer way too high using the one-at-a-time method.

Predictive analytics offers a way to get a virtual understanding of the customer by combining and analyzing data from

>> Registration forms filled out by customers

>> Customer surveys

>> Social networks

>> Customer purchase histories

The machine-learning algorithm learns and predicts the customers' behavior. The data can be thought of as the aggregate of the customers' experiences; thus the algorithm is learning from experiences of all the customers. By scoring each customer for churn or responses, you can optimize operational processes across all customer *touchpoints* (instances of company contact with the customer, whether in person or through a message conveyed by salespeople, store cashiers, call centers, websites, direct mail, television, radio, billboards, and the like). This is the competitive edge you gain by applying predictive analytics on the customer.

WARNING

Don't freak out your customer by obtaining or using data analytics in socially unacceptable ways. The result of doing so may be the complete opposite of what you're trying to accomplish. Customers are very sensitive to data privacy issues. For example, there was a big backlash when consumers found out that Target Corporation was using predictive analytics to predict pregnancy in customers.

IMPROVE CUSTOMER RETENTION

As the market becomes saturated, the cost of getting new customers (*customer acquisition cost*) generally increases. The supply of easy customers declines, so companies must work hard to keep the customers they spent so much to acquire.

Churn modeling is the application of predictive analytics for predicting a customer's propensity to leave the relationship with the company. If you know which customers are ready to leave, you can implement some type of retention program before they leave. It can be as simple as a discount offer for a product or service. The key is that you only offer these incentives to high-risk customers — keeping retention costs low and margins high.

Typical adopters of churn modeling are providers of service subscriptions such as those for mobile phone service. One implementation of such modeling is to integrate the churn score into the customer service application. Then the customer service representative can get a real-time notification to offer a discount for a new phone or service when the churn score is high, even during contact with the customer. The system can also generate a discount offer via text message, email or standard mail, if a customer's churn score is high when approaching renewal time.

IMPROVE RESPONSE RATES

Wouldn't it be nice to launch marketing campaigns that have higher response rates than you're used to? By applying predictive analytics, you can target customers with advertisements that make better sense in terms of expected return. The model can segment out a portion of your entire contact list with customers that have a high response score (those most likely to respond) for a particular product or marketing campaign. To increase response rates, companies must shift from mass marketing to such *segmented marketing*.

Segmented marketing also reduces the expensive side effects incurred by mass marketing. When enough ads miss the target, customers start to see your marketing messages as spam. Customers eventually become irritated and opt out of future contact. This in turn will reduce your contact list, customer satisfaction, and company image.

Many customers are only willing to spend a limited amount of money. By marketing products to them that are customized and have ranked high in the recommendation list, not only do you increase your response rate, you also increase customer satisfaction and loyalty.

REMEMBER

Check your data regularly. Customers often change their emails or create multiple user profiles with different emails (that get forwarded to their main email). Find the email that is valid and try not to pollute their inboxes with repetitions of the same advertisement. You don't want them to get irritated and opt out.

Gathering Support from Stakeholders

Most people don't like change; convincing management or other stakeholders to adopt change is hard. To make matters worse, the adoption of predictive analytics is low compared to other forms of analytics. Company executives either don't know what it is or they've heard of it but don't believe in its value, so convincing them to see the value in it will require some work.

The good news is that, as hard as it sounds to make the pitch, it can be accomplished. Many new CMOs, VPs, marketing directors and marketing managers are technically savvy and value the benefits of technology. Some companies have product management executives that are also engineering executives. Some software engineering managers are changing roles into engineering product managers. These executives are looking hard for technological ways to find an advantage over their competitors and using predictive analytics is an innovative and unique way to distinguish them from the competition.

In any case, starting a predictive analytics initiative begins with the leadership team, as shown in Figure 8-1.

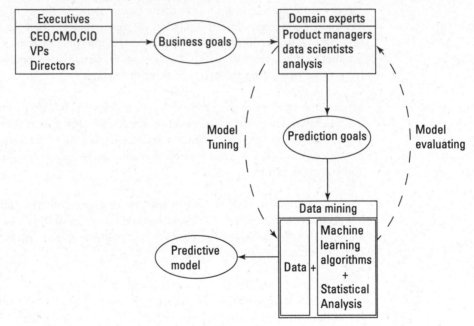

Working with your sponsors

In order to develop a successful and optimal predictive analytics initiative, the sponsors must think collectively about the problem(s) that they're trying to solve and how they will solve it. Developing a predictive analytics solution includes some indispensable activities:

» Thinking strategically

» Asking questions

>> Defining success as a group at the beginning of the process

>> Investing in human resources and tools

The upcoming subsections examine these developmental aspects.

STRATEGIC THINKING

As with most company initiatives, getting the executive team together in a room and having them agree on the strategy is critical to the success of this initiative. Doing so requires a lot of thinking about current objectives, business practices, investments, resources, and competition. Having a clearly defined plan from the executive team allows middle managers to prioritize and deploy the necessary resources to execute the plan.

ASKING THE RIGHT QUESTIONS

You need to know what insights you're looking for — and what operational decisions they help solve. If those aren't known right off the bat, then asking some concrete questions will help flesh out the answers. The executive team must answer these apparently simple questions in great detail:

>> What do you want to know?

>> Which actions will you take when you get the answers?

>> What is the expected outcome?

>> What are the success metrics?

These questions should lead to a series of follow-up questions. When the team is satisfied with the degree of detail in the answers, you should have a picture of the business problem they want most to solve. The time that the team invests in the beginning of this process — to define and clearly understand all aspects of the task — will contribute to the success of the project.

TIP

Try to think from the customers' point of view. Creating customer personas will help you understand who your customers are, their needs and *pain points* (problems that the business wants to solve). Ask questions that you think your customers would ask. Doing so helps identify the most important operational goals.

Defining success

To measure the expected ROI of the predictive analytics solution, you must be very specific when defining the prediction goals. Having an ambiguous definition of success can lead to misleading results and conflicting interpretations among stakeholders. Start with small projects that have clear outcomes. A clear win gives the executive team more confidence in predictive analytics generally, and can lead to additional projects of larger scope and value. A track record of success also boosts the confidence of the teams that work on the project, and can improve cross-functional and cross-organizational collaboration.

Time to market

Your first predictive analytics project will take some time, and that time will vary greatly depending on many factors such as the size of the company and what prediction goal is being attempted. Ask your marketing, analytics, IT, and engineering team to determine a timeframe for a small project. An alternative is to get an expert consultant who can discuss the project plan and review your infrastructure. Such a consultant can provide a cost estimate and a realistic timeframe.

Typically, most of the time spent is in data preparation. Most, if not all, commercial vendors provide capabilities to help you prepare your data for analysis. For example: After you load the data, you can explore the data and decide whether (and how) to handle columns that have missing data.

You may have the option to use your data in its current state — rather than having to spend precious time cleaning it — as you build a predictive model with. If you do so, your results may be less accurate than they'd be with thoroughly prepared data; it really depends on your specific situation. Your company may feel the time pressure to get the solution deployed quickly; dirty data may be less important than speed in such a case. Communicating to the leadership team that the results of the proof of concept may be dramatically different than a production-ready model is a must in this case.

Budgeting

Realistically, implementing a predictive analytics project will cost more than doing a non-predictive project. Such costs can include the addition of human resources in marketing, analytics, IT, and engineering. You need both people and tools to store the data, prepare the data, model the data, and deploy the model — which can make the whole undertaking appear too costly to many smaller companies. Larger companies can absorb the initial cost more easily, and may already have staff who can be reassigned to handle the task.

To determine whether to do a predictive analytics project, you have to evaluate whether the projected benefits exceed the costs. Predictive projects have returned up to two times the ROI realized by their non-predictive counterparts. If building a custom solution isn't feasible, products available from predictive analytics vendors can be of help.

Getting business and operations buy-in

After the strategy has been defined and the solution deployed, the key players in the success of the project will be the business and operations personnel.

You need people managers (such as program managers and project managers) to shepherd the team and coordinate with the other stakeholders. This group of people will keep the project on track, resolve road blocks, schedule cross-functional training, and help resolve any difficult cross-organizational issues that may arise.

Your product managers and analysts will have to create requirements, find meaning in the model's output (throughout the various stages of the project), and report the performance metrics to upper levels of management. Your customer operations team will make sure that the data is flowing smoothly between the company and the customer.

To get the full support of these people, you must be able to explain to them why these initiatives are being implemented — and why their routine operational processes are being altered. The project is about optimizing operational decisions, which targets the core of what many employees have been doing over time. The changes in their work requirements will take getting used to. They will also be the first people to feel the effects if the project is working — or if it's not.

Cross-organizational training

Cross-organizational training will be required for members who have customer contact, whether in person, by phone, or online. Salespeople will need to understand what the lead scores mean. And they may want to know how those scores were derived so they can use that information to strengthen their knowledge of the customer.

You must also train your customer support team not only to understand data scoring but also to apply it when the customer contact happens. Your customer service representatives must know how to respond to a high fraud score (ask for further verification or decline high-risk transactions) or a high churn score (offer a specific discount or freebie).

Standard operating procedures must be created to guide the interaction when such situations occur. To make things simpler, you can display the score as a color that shows the level of attention. You can also embed the correct decisions directly into the application.

A simple scenario between Customer Service and a mobile phone customer would look like this:

1. The customer calls Customer Service to inquire about her abnormally high bill this month.

2. In Customer Service, a red indicator on the screen shows that the churn score is high; the customer is predicted to cancel her service.

   The model scored this high because:

   - Her service contract has about one month left.

   - She has called numerous times in the past complaining about the high cost of service.

   - She has only been a customer for a year.

3. Action taken: The Customer Service representative offers a discount for a new phone if she renews for another year.

A more advanced version of this same scenario would change the churn score dynamically as the customer service representative inputs notes from the conversation. The model uses text and sentiment analysis to predict the likelihood that the customer will terminate her service contract.

Fostering a data-sharing environment

Being a data-driven company doesn't stop with using predictive analytics to create data in silos. The data should be shared across all business functions. As each team produces more data from the existing data they have, they should store it *and* make it readily available for other teams to use.

Another team may find just the piece of data they're looking for — which would otherwise be a waste of resources to redo the effort. Just as data should be shared, so should the techniques used to produce the data be shared. To make efficient use of the knowledge across the entire business ensures that the business reaps the maximum return on investment.

Getting IT buy-in

Predictive analytics is a science. To ensure that you get the best possible results, you need the talents and skill-sets of your engineering team. IT plays a critical role in the success of your predictive analytics projects.

In addition to data scientists (especially if your company lacks data scientists), you need computer scientists and software engineers who are experienced in machine learning, natural language processing, and data mining. They can help you choose the appropriate algorithm (say, a clustering or classification algorithm or decision tree) to build your predictive model. IT may also own the databases to which you would need access. They're the ones who set up access rights so the data doesn't get accidentally modified or deleted during the creation of the model. After building your predictive model, coordinating with IT again becomes necessary to deploy the model you've built.

From its inception, to data access, data integration with third-party vendors, data preparation, data mining and applying statistical analysis, and finally to model deployment and maintenance, getting IT buy-in will be critical to the success of your project.

Building a data-science team

Building a data-science team is an essential part of your predictive project. This is the team that helps you create the predictive model to solve the business problem.

You can hire new talent if your organization doesn't have qualified employees who can perform the task. Or you can recruit from within the organization. Recruiting personnel from within to be part of your data-science team may actually increase your chance of success; these people already have the much-needed business domain knowledge. Nevertheless, the team must have a strong lead member who has experience with the whole predictive analytics lifecycle.

The team's background should be diverse; the team should encompass business domain experts, data scientists, and IT personnel. All business departments should have representation in the makeup of your data-science team. Your data scientists should have deep mathematical knowledge and preferably proficiency in your line of business, and broader experience building different kinds of models. IT staff should include computer scientists who know machine-learning algorithms, software architects who can help in the design and implementation of the whole project, database and data warehouse experts, and personnel experienced in running IT operations.

If your organization lacks the skill-sets you need to produce a predictive analytics solution, you can look into the trade-off between hiring a consulting company versus building a team in-house. Many enterprise-level software solutions are available that managers and business analysts can use to build predictive models without having to know much about machine learning or algorithms. You can hire consultants to build the initial models with the software and also train your team to use the models. Your team can maintain and enhance the models.

Depending on your specific needs, it may be easier and more cost effective for you to buy a simple-but-powerful tool designed to enable business users to build predictive models. Such software products have built-in workflow templates for predictive modeling. The tools make assumptions based on the data you're loading into the program, which can get you started right away. This option may be faster than hiring specialized and diverse professionals to build your data-science team.

Choosing your tools

If you buy a software tool for your predictive analytics project, which tool should you use? As with all important business decisions, you have several factors to evaluate. Choosing the right tool(s) depends on

>> The budget

>> The scope of your project

>> The data you'll be analyzing

>> The main users of the tool

You may need to hire consultants to do a feasibility study for you to see what tools are available and which ones would work best for you, given the business questions you'd like to answer. Experienced consultants who have working knowledge of at least a few predictive analytics tools — who know the pros and cons of those tools, as well as the business problems they're built to solve — will be best able to help you choose a tool. Or you can have them build a pilot model if that's within your company's budget.

As with all information technologies, predictive analytics tools are getting more powerful and commodity hardware to store data are getting less expensive. This is an impressive trend, given that data is only getting bigger and more complex. Look for predictive analytics to become more widely adopted as data availability increases and the technology to analyze it becomes more accessible.

The tools are being built with user-friendly interfaces. They're easy to use and come already powered with all necessary features for managers with technical backgrounds and data analysts to start using them to derive value right away. Analysts can select the data, process it, run multiple algorithms on it, and view results as visualizations or reports; all in a few clicks.

There are also *open-source* tools available online: They're mostly free of charge and have active communities where you can discuss and post questions. Keep in mind, however, that open-source tools

>> Target more advanced users (some, for example, require programming knowledge).

>> Are often less user-friendly (some lack advanced graphical user interfaces).

>> Have limited capacity for handling big-data problems.

>> May run out of memory when handling big datasets.

>> May not be able to handle real-time analytics or streaming data.

>> Require that you invest time in learning them.

>> Usually don't have a professional services division for problems and needs. You will have to seek consulting help from third-party vendors.

TIP

The learning curve and lack of commercial support may make an open-source tool unsuitable for wide adoption in a large corporation. Using a commercial tool designed as an enterprise solution can lead to a much smoother deployment.

Having too little or too much data

Data is abundant and getting more so; *big data* has become a familiar buzzword. Everyone is collecting it and talking about the large amount of data that is available. Organizations are amassing more data than ever before.

In this environment, it's hard to imagine a scenario where a company has a shortage of data. Whether such a scenario exists, the quickest way to get more data is to ask your customers to fill out surveys, or ask your customers to rate the products they've already purchased. Here the goal is to generate valuable feedback that you can put to use for data analysis.

You should have already stored all past transactions that your business has conducted. Building a database that contains detailed profiles of your customers can be of great value to your predictive analytics model. You can even buy third-party data.

On the other hand, having too much data also poses challenges. How do you determine which items are important? Where do you begin? How do you handle the constant influx? Increasingly, software tools and industry literature are addressing such big-data issues. These challenges will continue to grow as data complexities, in terms of data velocity and data volume, deepen.

Leading software products in predictive analytics are making it much easier to use big data, rendering its analysis more manageable. By the same token, those same software leaders are providing tools that smaller companies can use and apply effectively, even on smaller datasets.

Employing data you're already storing

As a result of normal operations, your organization must have already collected a fair amount of data it can use for predictive analytics. That data may not be analysis-ready, but with some effort you can make that data work for you.

REMEMBER

One of the important steps in data preparation is to remove your duplicate entries. Make sure you don't have (for example) multiple IDs for the same customer profile. When you merged your data, you may have brought over the same customer with a different email address. The same customer may have registered multiple times by accident or through different channels. For openers, make sure that the email address you have for each customer is the most recent.

You can also buy third-party data, such as that derived from (and by) social media for the purpose of selling it to interested parties such as (perhaps) your company. Adding such data can help you build a better picture and richer profile of your customers — and it's readily available. Increasingly, data and its storage are affordable commodities.

TIP

To cut down on data preparation, you can enforce input checking at the time your customer information is collected, or (better yet) provide customers with multiple-choice surveys, and limited ranges of responses to choose from, to minimize data-input errors.

Buying data from third-party vendors

By itself, the data your company has may not be enough to provide you with a good basis for predictive analytics. For example, to produce actionable insights at today's ever-increasing pace, simply using demographics and basic inferences from your data isn't enough. The demographics of loyal customers may look exactly the same as demographics of churning customers.

You may also have transactional data from your operations to combine with customer profiles. But, in some cases, your existing customer base may be limited or belong to a specific segment of clientele. You might want to make predictions or target a whole different segment of customers; your transactional data may not be able to achieve that. Also, there are cases where you may have transactional data and very limited customer profile data. For example, you only have name and location, but you also want age, income, and gender.

To generate actionable insights, you'd need more complete data. To get it, you'd probably need to pull that data from various sources; one way of doing that is to buy it from third-party suppliers. Some suppliers offer what is called a DMP (data management platform). They can integrate your first-party data with third-party data to create personalization and segmentation models. If you can get hold of third-party data that's relevant to your predictive model, the next step is to integrate it into your existing datasets to create better models.

With the rise of social media, an abundance of data is being generated, some of which is collected by companies whose business model involves collecting this data, packaging it, and selling it. Such companies view that data as their product. Your company may have a use for that product.

Rapid prototyping

Predictive analytics is a complex science in every aspect. It requires a lot of strategic thinking by executives and domain experts. It requires technology and specialized skills. It requires time and money. When companies finally decide to take the plunge, they have to know where to start.

After the executive team has come to a consensus on what operational problem they want to solve, the spotlight is on you. You want to prove to them that predictive analytics will work. You want them to see some results in a month or two, not in six months to a year. Without their confidence in the science of predictive modeling, any attempt to launch a company-wide predictive initiative won't get off the ground.

When an executive wants something, time is your enemy. We know that most of the time creating a predictive model is in the data preparation. Don't spend that much time doing it. Creating a rapid prototype of the predictive model is the way to go. Such a prototype doesn't necessarily have to be pinpoint-accurate to be valuable; the idea is to prove the concept. You just want to build something for the executive team to see in action.

Take a clean subset of the data and use that for starters; that should be plenty for most prototypes. After the execs see the model at work, they may just get that "aha" moment that demonstrates the value of predictive analytics and makes a full adoption a lot more likely. Even if they don't get it right away, you may be buying some time with the demonstration. If they see that you're capable of building a predictive model, they'll probably wait a little longer to see clearer results.

You can build on the prototype and show incremental progress to the executive team. That way they can evaluate your progress and make recommendations along the way — which also firms up their relationship with the project. The investment is also allocated in small chunks instead of one big lump sum, which can make the decision to do the project much easier. Upper management loves small investments and quick returns.

Presenting Your Proposal

When you're ready to sit down with your executive management to propose a predictive analytics initiative, you must be able to explain predictive analytics clearly, and in simple terms. Granted, many executives already know about it (or have at least heard of it), but be prepared for those who have not. Be prepared to frame that explanation in many different ways.

Here are several definitions of predictive analytics that you can use for your specific needs:

>> A tool that uses data to assist a business to make smarter operational and strategic decisions.

>> A tool that uses advanced machine-learning and data-mining algorithms to extract hidden patterns that produce actionable business insights.

>> A tool that uses computer science to compute the best action from data.

>> Software that models future events based on historical data.

>> Software that allows you to simulate business decisions and see their predicted outcomes.

>> A technology that predicts customer behavior by using data from purchase histories, demographics, social media, and web logs.

Okay, here's another business truism: Executives are (by definition) busy, so they're generally pressed for time and skeptical of being sold to. You need to be concise. They got to where they are because they have been making decisions that got these results. They know what initiatives not to do, what initiatives to do, and probably have strong opinions about both. You had better have a thoroughly well-thought-out proposal.

With the right message, you may get their attention. To seal the deal, you'll have to wow them with a vision and a demo. When you have them interested, ask them to sponsor a rapid prototype.

Here are some tips on presenting the proposal.

>> This is a complex topic, so expect — and be prepared — to answer a lot of questions.

>> No presentation is complete without providing a summary and answering questions at the end. You can find answers to many of these questions in this chapter. Other questions will be specific to your situation. Generally you'll need to answer

- How will predictive analytics add value to the business?

- How long will it take?

- How much will it cost?

- Who's going to do it?

» Tell them at least one interesting story about who is using it and how they're reaping the benefits, before trotting out the details of how to implement predictive analytics.

» Be armed with success stories of predictive analytics as implemented by other companies — especially your competitors. If you can't find something specific to your domain, talk about these more famous success stories:

- Amazon's product recommendation engine

- Netflix's movie recommendation engine

- Facebook's recommendations based on users' "likes"

- LinkedIn's "people you may know" feature

» Show them a list of specific benefits that your company will get from applying predictive analytics.

For a refresher, see the "Benefits to the business" section of this chapter.

TIP

» You can frame the benefits in terms of an overarching goal: to gain a competitive advantage over your competitors by

- Optimizing company operations

- Looking for new business opportunities

- Acquiring new customers

- Retaining current customers

- Finding new revenue streams from your current customer base

» Show that the costs of missing these benefits are greater than the small cost of approving the pilot program.

» Have a list of employees (and the reasons why) you think are ideal prospective members of your data-science team.

The pilot program should be short-term and small in scope. The employees on your team can still work on their current projects if they can't be dedicated full-time to the predictive analytics pilot.

TIP

Employees may find it fun and rewarding to work on something new to the company. Finding meaning in data is very challenging and gratifying. Big data and predictive analytics form one of the hottest topics in technology right now — and employees are sure to dive right in to learn these new skills if given the opportunity.

» Ask them to sponsor you to build a pilot model in a short period of time.

TIP

Use open-source tools to create the predictive model to solve a simple problem. For example, build a simple recommendation engine that would address a small percentage of your overall web traffic or a small targeted mailing.

Chapter 9

Preparing Data

The roadmap to building a successful predictive model involves defining business objectives, preparing the data, and then building and deploying the model. This chapter delves into data preparation, which involves

>> Acquiring the data

>> Exploring the data

>> Cleaning the data

>> Selecting variables of interest

>> Generating derived variables

>> Extracting, loading, and transforming the data

>> Sampling the data into training and test datasets

Data is a four-letter word. It's amazing that such a small word can describe trillions of gigabytes of information: customer names, addresses, products, discounted versus original prices, store codes, times of purchase, supplier locations, run rates for print advertising, the color of your delivery vans. And that's just for openers. Data is, or can be, literally everything.

Not every source or type of data will be relevant to the business question you're trying to answer. Predictive analytics models are built from multiple data sources, and one of the first critical steps is to determine which sources to include in your model. If you're trying to determine (for example) whether customers who subscribe to e-magazines in the spring are more likely to purchase hardcover print books in the fall, you may decide to omit the January paperback sales records. Then you have to vet the specific records and attributes of each possible source for format, quantity, and quality. Data may be a small word, but it brings on a lot of big tasks.

Listing the Business Objectives

At this stage, presumably, you've already sat down with the business managers and collected the objectives they're after. Now you have to go into detail, evaluate what information sources will help achieve the objectives, and choose the variables you'll analyze for operational use.

Understanding what the stakeholders really want from the project is challenging; you may encounter multiple competing needs as well as limitations on what can be realistically done.

For this stage, you and the intended recipient of the results have to roll up your sleeves and brainstorm potential information sources. The goal is to determine what information, from which sources, will be relevant to reaching the type of concrete outcome that will provide true value for both the business and the customer. Without this in-the-trenches activity, your results may be no more than academic — of little practical value to your client. You may uncover fascinating inferences from (say) the accessory division's second-quarter sales records — and discover just how likely cross-dressers who wear flat shoes are to purchase faux leather purses — but this will fall on deaf ears if the accessories division is discontinuing its faux leather product line next quarter.

A business objective can be quantifiable and objective — for example, "identify two currently unknown major customer groups with a greater-than-50-percent likelihood of churning in the next six months" or "identify three supplier groups in Asia with decreasing delivery timeframes over the next five years." You might also list more subjective goals such as "provide valuable insights into the effectiveness of customer rewards incentives programs."

TIP

In the subjective cases, be sure to define what you mean by "valuable."

Identifying related objectives

Typically, there will be many subsets of business questions that the customer would like to address — any and all of which can provide insights into the main question. For example, the primary business goal might be to identify unhappy customers before they *churn* (move to a competing product). Related business questions could be: "How many times does a customer abandon a shopping cart online before purchasing from another online retailer?" "Does decreasing the threshold for free shipping from $100 to $75 prevent churn?" Table 9-1 shows some handy examples of primary and secondary business questions.

TABLE 9-1   **Primary and Secondary Business Questions**

Primary	Secondary
How do we increase print book sales?	Which percentage of people who bought or downloaded a fiction e-book in FY12 then bought a print fiction paperback in FY13?
How do we predict the effect of health-based decisions on fitness-related products more accurately?	If customers are buying fewer French fries this year, will they buy more or fewer yoga mats next year?
How will a new tablet affect sales of existing digital products?	Are iPad users less likely to purchase laptops?

Gathering user requirements

Okay, suppose the high-level objectives have been documented and now you're moving into the details. What are the project requirements and timeframes you'll need to fulfill and follow? What are the requirements for your business, project, system, models, and data?

In order to avoid mismatched expectations, project managers should meet with all relevant groups in the client department. For marketing, this could include social media marketing managers, marketing analytics specialists, or database marketing managers. Information sources to specify can include (for example) customer lists, budgets, schedules and other logistics.

Thorough documentation — and key management sign-off — are critical to ensure that everyone is embarking on the coming intensive effort with the same understanding, commitment, and expectations.

Processing Your Data

Don't be surprised if preparing your data to be fed into the predictive model is as tedious a task as it is crucial. Understanding data quality, availability, sources, and any existing constraints will have a direct effect on the successful implementation of your predictive analytics project.

The raw data usually has to be cleaned — and possibly integrated, combined with other datasets, and used to derive new data variables. Hence data quality and quantity should be carefully and thoroughly examined across all data sources used to build the model.

In this exploration phase, you'll gain intimate knowledge of your data — which in turn will help you choose the relevant variables to analyze. This understanding will also help you evaluate the results of your model.

Identifying the data

For your analytics project, you'll need to identify appropriate sources of data, pool data from those sources, and put it in a structured, well-organized format. These tasks can be very challenging and will likely require careful coordination among different data stewards across your organization.

You'll also need to select the variables you're going to analyze. This process must take data constraints, project constraints, and business objectives into consideration.

REMEMBER

The variables you select must have predictive power. Also, you need to consider variables that are both valuable and feasible for your project within the budget and timeframes. For example, if you're analyzing bank transactions in a criminal investigation, phone records for all parties involved may be relevant to the analysis but not accessible to the analysts.

Expect to spend considerable time on this phase of the project. Data collection, data analysis, and the process of addressing data content, quality, and structure can add up to a time-consuming to-do list.

During the process of data identification, it helps to understand your data and its properties; this knowledge will help you choose which algorithm to use to build your model. For example, time series data can be analyzed by regression algorithms; classification algorithms can be used to analyze discrete data.

Variable selection is affected by how well you understand the data. Don't be surprised if you have to look at and evaluate hundreds of variables, at least at first. Fortunately, as you work with those variables and start gaining key insights, you start narrowing them down to a few dozen. Also, expect variable selection to change as your understanding of the data changes throughout the project.

TIP

You may find it beneficial to build a data inventory that you can use to track what you know, what you don't know, and what might be missing. The data inventory should include a listing of the various data elements and any attributes that are relevant in the subsequent steps of the process. For example, you may want to document whether any segments are missing zip codes or missing records for a specific period of time.

REMEMBER

Your go-to people for business knowledge (also known as *domain knowledge experts*) will help you select the key variables that can positively influence the results of your project. They can help explain to you the importance of these variables, as well as where and how to get them, among other valuable input.

Cleaning the data

You'll need to make sure that the data is clean of extraneous stuff before you can use it in your model. This includes finding and correcting any records that contain erroneous values, and attempting to fill in any missing values. You'll also need to decide whether to include duplicate records (two customer accounts, for example). The overall goal is to ensure the integrity of the information you're using to build your predictive model. Pay particular attention to the completeness, correctness, and timeliness of the data.

TIP

It's useful to create *descriptive statistics* (quantitative characteristics) for various fields, such as calculating min and max, checking *frequency distribution* (how often something occurs) and verifying the expected ranges. Running a regular check can help you flag any data that is outside the expected range for further investigation. Any records showing retirees with birth dates in the 1990s can be flagged by this method. Also, cross-checking the information is important so that you make sure the data is accurate. For deeper analysis of the data characteristics and the identification of the relationship between data records, you can make use of *data profiling* (analyzing data availability and gathering statistics on the data quality), and visualization tools.

Missing data could be due to the fact that particular information was not recorded. In such a case, you can attempt to fill in as much as you can; suitable defaults can easily be added to fill the blanks of certain fields. For example, for patients in a hospital maternity ward where the gender field is missing a value, the application can simply fill it in as female. For that matter, for any male who was admitted to a hospital with a missing record for the pregnancy status, that record can similarly be filled in as not applicable. A missing zip code for an address can be inferred from the street name and the city provided in that address.

In the cases where the information is unknown or can't be inferred, then you would need to use values *other* than a blank space to indicate that the data is missing without affecting the correctness of the analysis. A blank in the data can mean multiple things, most of them not good or useful. Whenever you can, you should specify the nature of that blank by meaningful place filler. For numerical data made entirely of small and positive numbers (values between 0 and 100), the user, for example, can define the number -999.99 as place filler for missing data.

Just as it's possible to define a rose in a cornfield as a weed, outliers can mean different things to different analyses. It's common for some models to be built solely to track those outliers and flag them. Fraud-detection models and criminal activities monitoring are interested in those outliers, which in such cases indicate something unwanted taking place. So keeping the outliers in the dataset in cases like these is recommended. However, when outliers are considered anomalies within the data — and will only skew the analyses and lead to erroneous results — remove them from your data. What we don't want to happen is that our model will try to predict the outliers, and end up failing to predict anything else.

Duplication in the data can also be useful or a nuisance; some of it can be necessary, can indicate value, and can reflect an accurate state of the data. For example, a record of a customer with multiple accounts can be represented with multiple entries that are (technically, anyway) duplicate and repetitive of the same records. Another example would be a customer who has both a work phone and a personal phone with the same company and with the bill going to the same address – something that would be valuable to know. By the same token, when the duplicate records don't contribute value to the analysis and aren't necessary, then removing them can be of tremendous value. This is especially true for large datasets where removing duplicate records can simplify the complexity of the data and reduce the time needed for analysis.

TIP

You can pre-emptively prevent incorrect data from entering your systems by adopting some specific procedures:

>> Institute quality checks and data validation for all data being collected.

>> Allow your customers to validate and self-correct their personal data.

>> Provide your clients with possible and expected values to choose from.

>> Routinely run checks on the integrity, consistency, and accuracy of the data.

Generating any derived data

Derived attributes are entirely new records constructed from one or more existing attributes. An example would be the creation of records identifying books that are bestsellers at book fairs. Raw data may not capture such records — but for modeling purposes, those derived records can be important. Price-per-earnings ratio and 200-day moving average are two examples of derived data that are heavily used in financial applications.

Derived attributes can be obtained from simple calculation such as deducing age from birth date. Derived attributes can also be computed by summarizing information from multiple records. For example, converting a table of customers and their purchased books into a table can enable you to track the number of books sold via a recommender system, through targeted marketing, and at a book fair — and identify the demographic of customers who bought those books.

Generating such additional attributes brings additional predictive power to the analysis. In fact, many such attributes are created so as to probe their potential predictive power. Some predictive models may use more derived attributes than the attributes in their raw state. If some derived attributes prove especially predictive and their power is proven to be relevant, then it makes sense to automate the process that generates them.

REMEMBER

Derived records are new records that bring in new information and provide new ways of presenting raw data; they can be of tremendous value to predictive modeling. They are often considered the most important contribution that a modeler can make to the process.

Reducing the dimensionality of your data

The data used in predictive models is usually pooled from multiple sources. Your analysis can draw from data scattered across multiple data formats, files, and databases, or multiple tables within the same database. Pooling the data together and combining it into an integrated format for the data modelers to use is essential.

If your data contains any hierarchical content, it may need to be *flattened*. Some data has some hierarchical characteristics such as parent-child relationships, or a record that is made up of other records. For example, a product such as a car may have multiple makers; flattening data, in this case, means including each maker as an additional feature of the record you're analyzing. Another example is that a single customer can have multiple transactions.

Flattening data is essential when it merged from multiple related records to form a better picture. For example, analyzing adverse events for several drugs made by several companies may require that the data be flattened at the substance level. By doing so, you end up removing the *one-to-many relationships* (in this case, many makers and many substances for one product) that can cause too much duplication of data by repeating multiple substance entries that repeat product and maker information at each entry.

Flattening forces you to think about reducing the *dimensionality* of the data, which is represented by the number of features a record or an observation has. For example, a customer can have the following features: name, age, address, items purchased. When you start your analysis, you may find yourself evaluating records with many features, only some of which are important to the analysis. So you should eliminate all but the very few features that have the most predictive power for your specific project.

Reducing the dimensionality of the data can be achieved by putting all the data in a single table that uses multiple columns to represent attributes of interest. At the beginning of the analysis, of course, the analysis has to evaluate a large number of columns — but that number can be narrowed down as the analysis progresses. This process can be aided by reconstituting the fields — for example, by grouping the data in categories that have similar characteristics.

The resultant dataset — the cleaned dataset — is usually put in a separate database for the analysts to use. During the modeling process, this data should be easily accessed, managed, and kept up to date.

Applying principal component analysis

Principal component analysis (PCA) is a valuable technique that is widely used in data science. It studies a dataset to learn the most relevant variables responsible for the highest variation in that dataset. PCA is mostly used as a data reduction technique.

While building predictive models, you may need to reduce the number of features describing your dataset. It's very useful to reduce this high dimensionality of data through approximation techniques, at which PCA excels. The approximated data summarizes all the important variations of the original data.

For example, the feature set of data about stocks may include stock prices, daily highs and lows, trading volumes, 200-day moving averages, price-to-earning ratios, relative strength to other markets, interest rates, and strength of currencies.

Finding the most important predictive variables is at the core of building a predictive model. The way many have been doing it is by using a brute force approach. The idea is to start with as many relevant variables as you can, and then use a funnel approach to eliminating features that have no impact, or no predictive value. The intelligence and insight is brought to this method by engaging business stakeholders, because they have some hunches about which variables will have the biggest impact in the analysis. The experience of the data scientists engaged in the project is also important in knowing what variables to work with and what algorithms to use for a specific data-type or a domain-specific problem.

To help with the process, data scientists employ many predictive analytics tools that make it easier and faster to run multiple permutations and analyses on a dataset in order to measure the impact of each variable on that dataset.

Knowing that there is a large amount of data to work with, you can employ PCA for help.

TIP

Reducing the number of variables you look at is reason enough to employ PCA. In addition, by using PCA you're automatically protecting yourself from *overfitting* (see Chapter 15) the model.

Certainly, you could find correlation between weather data in a given country and the performance of its stock market. Or with the color of a person's shoes and the route she or he takes to the office, and the performance of their portfolio for that day. However, including those variables in a predictive model is more than just overfitting, it's misleading and leads to false predictions.

PCA uses a mathematically valid approach to determine the subset of your dataset that includes the most important features; in building your model on that smaller dataset, you will have a model that has predictive value for the overall, bigger dataset you're working with. In short, PCA should help you make sense of your variables by identifying the subset of variables responsible for the most variation with your original dataset. It helps you spot redundancy. It helps you find out that two (or more variables) are telling you the same thing.

Moreover, principal components analysis takes your multidimensional dataset and produces a new dataset whose variables are representative of the linearity of the variables in the original dataset. In addition, the outputted dataset has individually un-correlated variables, and their variance is ordered by their principal components where the first one is the largest, and so on. In this regard, PCA can also be considered as a technique for constructing features.

REMEMBER

While employing PCA or other similar techniques that help reduce the dimensionality of the dataset you're dealing with, you have to always exercise caution to not affect the performance of the model negatively. Reducing the size of the data should not come at the expense of negatively impacting the performance (the accuracy of the predictive model). Tread safely and manage your dataset with care.

REMEMBER

The increased complexity of a model doesn't translate to higher quality in the outcome.

To preserve the performance of the model, you may need to carefully evaluate the effectiveness of each variable, measuring its usefulness in the shaping of the final model.

Knowing that the PCA can be especially useful when the variables are highly correlated within a given dataset, then having a dataset with non-correlated predictive variables can only complicate the task of reducing the dimensionality of multivariate data. Many other techniques can be used here in addition to the PCA, such as forward feature selection and backward feature elimination (covered in this chapter).

WARNING

PCA is not a magic bullet that will solve all issues with multi-dimensional data. Its success is highly dependent on the data you're working with. The statistical variance may not align to variables with the most predictive values, even though it is safe to work with such approximations.

Leveraging singular value decomposition

Singular value decomposition (SVD) represents a dataset by eliminating the less important parts and generating an accurate approximation of the original dataset. In this regard, SVD and PCA are methods of data reduction.

SVD will take a matrix as an input and decompose it into a product of three simpler matrices.

An m by n matrix M can be represented as a product of three other matrices as follows:

$$M = U * S * V^T$$

Where U is an m by r matrix, V is an n by r matrix, and S is an r by r matrix; where r is the rank of the matrix M. The * represents matrix multiplication. ^{T} indicates matrix transposition.

In a data matrix where fewer concepts can describe the data, or can relate the data matrix's columns to its rows, then SVD is a very useful tool to extract those concepts. For example, a dataset might contains books' ratings, where the reviews are the rows and books the columns. The books can be grouped by type or domain, such as literature and fiction, history, biographies, children's or teen books. Those will be the concepts that SVD can help extract.

These concepts must be meaningful and conclusive. If we stick to only a few concepts or dimensions to describe a larger dataset, our approximation will not be as accurate. This is primarily why it's important to only eliminate concepts that are less important and not relevant to the overall dataset.

Latent semantic indexing is a data mining and natural language processing technique that is used in document retrieval and word similarity. Latent semantic indexing employs SVD to group documents to the concepts that could consist of different words found in those documents. The universe of words can be very large, and various words can be grouped into a concept. SVD helps reduce the noisy correlation between those words and their documents, and it gives us a representation of that universe using far fewer dimensions than the original dataset.

TIP

It is easier to see that documents discussing similar topics can use different words to describe those same topics. A document describing lions in Zimbabwe and another document describing elephants in Kenya should be grouped together. So we rely on concepts (wildlife in Africa, in this case), not words, to group these documents. The relation between documents and their words is established with those concepts or topics.

SVD and PCA have been used in classification and clustering (see Chapter 6 and Chapter 7). Generating those concepts is just a form of classification and grouping the data. Both have also been used for collaborative filtering (see Chapter 2).

Working with Features

When you have a dataset, selecting the most relevant features is what makes or breaks the model. The more predictive your features are, the more successful your model will be.

REMEMBER

In their quests to build predictive models, data scientists spend most of their time preparing the data and selecting the relevant features.

There are algorithms and tools that will help you with feature selection and feature extraction, and you may even need to look at ranking your features based on their importance. Doing so by relying solely on brute force is always an option; some scientists adopt a funnel approach and go through the set of features they have, one by one, and select the most relevant ones. However, this will be time consuming, may risk missing iterations, and will be more complex if features have high dependency among each other.

Very often, you won't be sure which feature to include and which to disregard. If you follow a trial and error approach, adding a feature or removing it (one at a time), you can witness that such addition or subtraction will have a major impact on the model you're building. The result will vary substantially by whether you include this feature or the other, and this approach becomes even more complex if one feature is only relevant in the presence of another one. It's a challenge to undergo such an approach if the features or variables are highly correlated. A feature can have a big impact on the analysis when grouped with another and yet that same feature has no effect by itself. The case where the effect of a feature is only manifested when combined with other features, and is absent in their absence or when not grouped with them.

Let's say you're building a decision tree as your model. That tree can grow larger or shrink, according to the features you include or exclude. Furthermore, often you won't be sure which model is better, especially if your dataset is small and you don't have enough data to test or make an informed decision about the outcome. In addition to the importance of spending the time necessary to get this part of the process right, it's here where experience and tools will make a difference. It's also at this step where we refer to this predictive analytics as a business and a discipline that is partly art and partly science.

TIP

The following are guidelines to keep in mind as you go about preparing your data and building your model:

>> Expect your data to have many features.

>> Allow plenty of time to prepare and understand your data.

>> Know the business domain represented in your data.

>> Allow yourself time to select the relevant features.

>> Employ tools and algorithms to help you with feature selection and feature extraction.

>> Avoid overfitting.

>> Avoid oversimplifying.

» Expect to go through many iterations as you select features and zero in building the model.

» Let the data analysis and the model's insights guide your decision.

Expect the data to be overwhelming. Only a handful of projects won't have enough data to build accurate models. Most projects will suffer from the abundance of the data. Nowadays, we are experiencing exponential growth in the data. This abundance applies equally to the sample size of the data as it does to its dimensionality. As such, the data may include a lot of noise. Differentiating the signal from the noise is at the core of what data scientists do.

In some applications, such as bioinformatics or document classification, it's common for a dataset to have thousands of features. Not all features are important for all problems. Feature selection and extraction are two methods that can help reduce the dimensionality of the data set and identify relevant features to work with.

Both feature extraction and feature selection will improve the predictive power of your model and speed up its performance.

Selecting features

Feature selection is the process of selecting a subset of features from the original features. The subset is selected without undergoing any transformation and while keeping the properties of the original features intact. For example, a scientist examining multiple proteins and their effects on a disease is looking to identify which proteins are most relevant in the analysis. For a loan application, your credit score is probably the most important deciding factor.

In a classification problem (see Chapter 7) where the training data is already labeled and the classes are known (like spam and non-spam emails), selecting the most important features determining whether an email is spam can be iterative. As long as the features you're selecting still produce the correct class, you're heading in the right direction.

REMEMBER

The goal is to identify which features you must keep and still get the labeled data classified correctly during the training phase.

Feature selection for classification aims at selecting a subset of the original feature without impacting the accuracy of the classifier. The subset of features should still be a good predictor of the classification, if all available features are included.

Feature selection is very complex and the degree of the difficulty will vary with the dimensionality of the data, the correlation level among features, whether they are highly dependent or independent, and the structure of the data.

REMEMBER

Identifying the right features will help in the performance of your model, both in terms of speed and accuracy of its prediction.

There are two widely used methods for feature selection:

>> **Forward selection** starts with one feature and adds one each iteration. It keeps adding one variable at a time, which helps decrease the error until further additions either do not improve the model or have no significance in decreasing the error.

>> **Backward selection** starts with all features in the dataset, then removes one feature at a time while making sure that the removal either decreases the error or only slightly increases it. A feature is removed if its removal produces the smallest increase in the error rate. When no further improvement to the model is achieved, or when the error is increased significantly, then the process stops.

There are three feature selection approaches:

>> **Filters:** Preprocessing techniques that compute a score for each feature, and then select features with high scores.

>> **Wrappers:** Techniques that use the learning algorithm to score subsets of features according to their usefulness to a given predictor. Multiple subsets of features are generated and evaluated.

>> **Embedded:** Techniques that perform the selection as part of the training algorithm or the learning procedure. The search for features is embedded into the classifier itself.

Extracting features

Feature extraction transforms your original features and creates a small subset of new ones, resulting in a much lower dimensionality. As shown in the preceding sections, dimensionality reduction can assist you in getting rid of redundant features, and noise in your data. Feature extraction projects and maps your features to a new set of features that is much smaller than the original.

We have discussed the idea of creating concepts when analyzing books and generating meaningful groups, such as fiction and literature, history, or biographies.

Then we can use those new concepts to analyze our data. This transformation from individual books to concepts, or *logical grouping,* is a kind of transformation that results in dimensionality reduction. However, these new generated features that are produced by feature extraction still need further analysis to fully make sense of the data, and eventually build your predictive model.

Another example of feature extraction, often used in text analytics, is the capability to transform text to a numerical representation. Like the ability to generate either

>> Term frequency (TF) of words

>> Term frequency inverse document frequency (TFIDF)

    TFIDF often is used to adjust for the fact that some words are more frequently used than others; the term frequency, or word count, is offset with the frequency of that word across documents.

REMEMBER

The key difference between features selection and features extraction is that the extraction reduces the dimensionality without necessarily preserving the actual attributes, such as units of the original features. Also, feature extraction can be a data transformation technique by taking a set of original features and transforming them to, or extracting, new ones.

Feature selection keeps the original set of features; it only lowers the number of the original features. Feature selection aims at eliminating redundancy and maximizing relevance.

Ranking features

When working with features, one thinks of ranking them. Don't you want to know which feature is the most important in your dataset? Which feature or set of features is the absolute indicator of a given class or a label? In the case of the biologist in her lab, it makes perfect sense to zero in on that one gene or a subset of genes responsible for a biological condition. The model then can easily watch for the existence of that gene or its expression to predict the expected behavior.

Ranking methods help select features and reduce dimensionality of the dataset. To rank features, you can choose from the following ranking methods:

>> Gain Ratio

>> Information Gain

>> Chi-square

>> SVM Ranker

These algorithms can be divided into two broad categories:

» **Statistical methods,** such as Chi-square, rely on the computation of the chi-squared statistic value for attributes to evaluate their ranking.

» **Entropy-based methods** measure the amount of information in a feature. The relevance of a feature, as indicated by its ranking score, is measured through the calculation of the expected value of the information contained in a message in relation to the output of that variable:

  • A high entropy value indicates that the variable belongs to a uniform distribution.

  • A low entropy value indicates that the variable belongs to a varied distribution.

In a decision-tree model, the importance of an attribute is measured using an entropy-based approach. The information gains in determining a given classification are used to select the features for the model. With such a process, a decision tree focuses on relevant features that lead to a given decision.

REMEMBER

The two highly ranked features aren't necessarily the best two for the overall model. In other words, if you rely on ranking algorithms alone to sort features based on the amount of information they hold (that is, entropy), you aren't necessary selecting the best features. A feature of high entropy may not contribute to a high accuracy if this feature is being combined with other features.

The forward selection algorithm uses a better approach to select features. At each iteration, the algorithm searches for the best features that provide high accuracy when joined together. The feature selection algorithms, such as forward selection or backward selection, are widely used, despite their relatively high computational time to complete.

TIP

You can use ranking algorithms first, such as Information Gain, to eliminate those features with no information on them (very low value of Information Gain); then you can apply feature selection algorithms on the remaining subset.

Structuring Your Data

Raw data is a potential resource, but it can't be usefully analyzed until it's been given a consistent structure. Data residing in multiple systems has to be collected and transformed to get it ready for analysis. The collected data should reside in a separate system so it won't interfere with the live production system. While building your model, split your dataset into a training dataset to train the model, and a test dataset to validate the model.

Extracting, transforming and loading your data

After it's initially collected, data is usually in a dispersed state; it resides in multiple systems or databases. Before you can use it for a predictive analytics model, you have to consolidate it into one place. Also, you don't want to work on data that resides in operational systems — that's asking for trouble. Instead, place a portion of it somewhere where you can work on it freely without affecting operations. *ETL (extract, transform and load)* is the process that achieves that desirable state.

Many organizations have multiple databases; your predictive model will likely utilize data from all of them. ETL is the process that collects all the information needed and places it in a separate environment where you can run your analysis. ETL is not, however, a once-and-for-all operation; usually it's an ongoing process that refreshes the data and keeps it up to date. Be sure you run your ETL processes at night or at other times when the load on the operational system is low.

>> **The extraction step** collects the desired data in its raw form from operational systems.

>> **The transformation step** makes the collected data ready to be used in your predictive model — merging it, generating the desired derived attributes, and putting the transformed data in the appropriate format to fit business requirements.

>> **The loading step** places the data in its designated location, where you can run your analysis on it — for example, in a data mart, data warehouse, or another database.

You should follow a systematic approach to build your ETL processes to fulfill the business requirements. It's a good practice to keep a copy of the original data in a separate area so you can always go back to it in case an error disrupts the transformation or the loading steps of the processes. The copy of the original data serves as a backup that you can use to rebuild the entire dataset employed by your analysis if necessary. The goal is to head off Murphy's Law and get back on your feet quickly if you have to rerun the entire ETL process from scratch.

Your ETL process should incorporate *modularity* — separating the tasks and accomplishing the work in stages. This approach has advantages in case you want to reprocess or reload the data, or if you want to use some of that data for a different analysis or to build different predictive models. The design of your ETL should be able to accommodate even major business requirement changes — with only minimal changes to your ETL process.

Keeping the data up to date

After the loading step of ETL, after you get your data into that separate database, data mart, or warehouse, you'll need to keep the data fresh so the modelers can rerun previously built models on new data.

Implementing a data mart for the data you want to analyze and keeping it up to date will enable you to refresh the models. You should, for that matter, refresh the operational models regularly after they're deployed; new data can increase the predictive power of your models. New data can allow the model to depict new insights, trends, and relationships.

Having a separate environment for the data also allows you to achieve better performance for the systems used to run the models. That's because you aren't overloading operational systems with the intensive queries or analysis required for the models to run.

Data keeps on coming — more of it, faster, and in greater variety all the time. Implementing automation and the separation of tasks and environments can help you manage that flood of data and support the real-time response of your predictive models.

REMEMBER

To ensure that you're capturing the data streams and that you're refreshing your models while supporting automated ETL processes, analytical architecture should be highly modular and adaptive. If you keep this design goal in mind for every part you build for your overall predictive analytic project, the continuous improvement and tweaking that go along with predictive analytics will be smoother to maintain and will achieve better success.

Outlining testing and test data

When your data is ready and you're about to start building your predictive model, it's useful to outline your testing methodology and draft a test plan. Testing should be driven by the business goals you've gathered, documented, and collected all necessary data to help you achieve.

Right off the bat, you should devise a method to test whether a business goal has been attained successfully. Because predictive analytics measure the likelihood of a future outcome — and the only way to be ready to run such a test is by training your model on past data, you still have to see what it can do when it's up against future data. Of course, you can't risk running an untried model on real future data, so you'll need to use existing data to simulate future data realistically. To do so, you have to split the data you're working on into training and test datasets.

TIP

Be sure that you select these two datasets at random, and that both datasets contain and cover all the data parameters you're measuring.

When you split your data into test and training datasets, you're effectively avoiding any overfitting issues that could arise from overtraining the model on the entire dataset and picking up all the noise patterns or specific features that only belong to the sample dataset and aren't applicable to other datasets. (See Chapter 15 for more on the pitfalls of overfitting.)

REMEMBER

Separating your data into training and test datasets, about 70 percent and 30 percent respectively, ensures an accurate measurement of the performance of the predictive analytics model you're building. You want to evaluate your model against the test data because it's a straightforward way to measure whether the model's predictions are accurate. Succeeding here is an indication that the model will succeed when it's deployed. A test dataset will serve as an independent set of data that the model hasn't yet seen; running your model against the test dataset provides a preview of how the model will perform when it goes live.

Chapter 10

Building a Predictive Model

S ome claims are fraudulent. Some customers will churn. Some transactions are fraudulent. Some investments will be a loss. Some employees will leave. But the burning question in everyone's mind is: Which ones?

Building a predictive analytics model can help your business answer such questions. The model will look at the data you have about your customers, for example, and tell you the probability of customer churning. But such questions merely touch upon the surface of what predictive analytics can do; the potential applications of this fascinating discipline are endless.

As mentioned earlier in the book, a *model* is a mathematical representation of a real-world phenomenon we're interested in making sense of. For example, you can use the data you have to build a model that mimics the stock market in which your firm is actively engaged in all sort of trades — and then your job is to sort out the winning trades from the losing ones. In such a case, your model helps you select a strategy to make money by trading on the stock market.

Building a predictive analytics model becomes vital when the consequences of not acting — or of making the wrong decision — would be costly. Fraudulent transactions, for example, can drain resources such as time, money, and personnel; they can break the financial health of a company. Using predictive analytics to detect and counteract fraud then becomes part of your risk management strategy — and again, this function only scratches the surface of the potential value that a predictive model can bring to your company.

Getting Started

A predictive model combines mathematics and data to solve a business problem. The goal is to train the model to learn and create a mapping function between input data and the desired output or a target variable. It's a three-step process:

1. Clearly define the business problem you're trying to solve.

2. Collect all historical data you can put your hands on.

   That data will need some preprocessing to be used as part of the training and test data for your model. There are many algorithms and techniques for modeling. All commercial and open-source tools come equipped with the most common ones (see Chapter 6 and Chapter 7). You need to choose which method (or combination of methods) best fits your business need.

3. Evaluate the model and measure its accuracy.

Predictive analytics aims at finding answers to business questions by examining data and presenting a range of possible outcomes, ranked with a score for each outcome. It helps organizations predict future outcomes and trends with confidence. It improves an organization's ability to plan, adopt, and execute strategies that improve its competitive edge. After your organization has put a predictive model in place, it then has the responsibility to act upon those findings.

Creating a successful predictive model involves these general steps:

1. Define the business objectives. (See Chapter 8.)

2. Prepare the data for use in the model. (See Chapter 9.)

3. Apply statistical and/or data-mining algorithms to the data. (See Chapters 6 and 7.)

4. Build, test, deploy, and maintain the model. (This chapter delves into this stage.)

Building a predictive model is the essence of predictive analytics. The specific model-building stage of the whole process is when you're ready to run some mathematical algorithms to see what interesting patterns and relationships you can find in the data. As you do so, keep these questions in mind:

>> How can you answer business questions?

>> What can you contribute to business decision-making?

>> How can you increase return on investment?

For you to be at this stage, you must already have convinced your management about the worthiness of predictive analytics. You've sealed the business case; met with management and stakeholders to ask all the relevant questions; and chosen to address one or a few related business questions. Then you've gathered a talented group of people: data scientists, IT personnel, and business experts, and formed your data analytical group.

Of course, the analytics team (which may consist of one person running from cubicle to office, verifying and asking questions at each step) have already done mighty deeds of preparation:

>> You've identified the data sources that you'll use to run the model. (See Chapter 3 and 9.)

>> You've performed any required data preprocessing (such as cleansing and integration), and created any derived data that you expect to have predictive power. (See Chapter 9 and 15.)

>> You've selected and identified all the variables. (See Chapter 9.)

At last, it's time to run the mathematical algorithm and see what you can learn from it.

The essential steps of the preparatory process leading up to this point are making the business case and preparing your data. Now for the fun part: running those specialized algorithms and see what you can learn.

We address a few practical questions here:

>> What is the process of running the algorithm?

>> How do I go about it?

>> Which algorithm do I choose?

>> How do I test my model?

>> What's next?

Building a predictive analytics model starts with clearly defining the business objectives you want it to attain, and then identifying and preparing the data that will be used to train and test the model.

Defining your business objectives

A predictive analytics model aims at solving a business problem or accomplishing a desired business outcome. Those business objectives become the model's goals. Knowing those ensures the business value of the model you build — which isn't to be confused with the accuracy of the model. After all, hypothetically you can build an accurate model to solve an imaginary business problem — but it's a whole other task to build a model that contributes to attaining business goals in the real world.

Defining the problem or the business need you want your model to solve is a vital first step in this process. A relevant and realistic definition of the problem will ensure that if you're successful in your endeavor of building this model and after it's used, it will add value to your business.

>> Which business problems would your stakeholders like to solve? Here are some immediately useful examples:

- Classify transactions into legitimate versus fraudulent.

- Identify the customers who are most likely to respond to a marketing campaign.

- Identify what products to recommend to your customers.

- Solve operational issues such as the optimal scheduling of employees' work — days or hours.

- Cluster the patients according to their different stages of the disease.

- Identify individualized treatments for patients.

- Pick the next best-performing stock for today, the quarter, or the year.

The preceding list can be addressed through the creation of supervised models that predict specific outcomes as they pertain to the business needs.

Clearly defining the business problem you're trying to solve will help you verify the result or the outcome produced by your model. It will give business stakeholders and data scientists a clear understanding of what they are after, allowing them to better evaluate the quality of the solution.

In addition to defining the business objectives and the overall vision for your predictive analytics model, you need to define the scope of the overall project. Here are some general questions that must be answered at this stage:

» If you develop your predictive model as a solution, you have another range of questions to address:

- What would stakeholders do with that solution?

- How would they use the model?

- What is the current status with no model in place?

- How is this business problem handled today?

- What are the consequences of predicting the wrong solution?

- What is the cost of a false positive?

- How will the model be deployed?

- Who is going to use the model?

- How will the output of the model be represented?

Preparing your data

When you've defined the objectives of the model, the next step is to identify and prepare the data you'll use to build your model. (Chapter 9 addresses this step in detail.) This section touches upon the most important activities. The general sequence of steps looks like this:

1. Identify your data sources.

Data could be in different formats or reside in various locations.

2. Identify how you will access that data.

Sometimes, you would need to acquire third-party data, or data owned by a different division in your organization, etc.

3. Consider which variables to include in your analysis.

One standard approach is to start off with a wide range of variables and eliminate the ones that offer no predictive value for the model.

TIP

4. Determine whether to use derived variables (See Chapter 9).

In many cases, a derived variable (such as the price-per-earning ratio used to analyze stock prices) would have a greater direct impact on the model than would the raw variable.

5. Explore the quality of your data, seeking to understand both its state and limitations.

The accuracy of the model's predictions is directly related to the variables you select and the quality of your data. You would want to answer some data-specific questions at this point:

- Is the data complete?

- Does it have any outliers?

- Does the data need cleansing?

- Do you need to fill in missing values, keep them as they are, or eliminate them altogether?

Understanding your data and its properties can help you choose the algorithm that will be most useful in building your model. For example:

>> Regression algorithms can be used to analyze time-series data.

>> Classification algorithms can be used to analyze discrete data.

>> Association algorithms can be used for data with correlated attributes.

Individual algorithms and predictive techniques have different weaknesses and strengths. Most important, the accuracy of the model relies on having both a great quantity and quality of data. Your data should have a sufficient number of records to provide statistically meaningful results.

Gathering relevant data (preferably many records over a long time period), pre-processing, and extracting the features with most predictive values will be where you spend the majority of your time. But you still have to choose the algorithm wisely, an algorithm that should be suited to the business problem.

Data preparation is specific to the project you're working on and the algorithm you choose to employ. Depending on the project's requirements, you will prepare your data accordingly and feed it to the algorithm as you build your model to address the business needs.

The dataset used to train and test the model must contain relevant business information to answer the problem you're trying to solve. If your goal is (for example) to determine which customer is likely to churn, then the dataset you choose must contain information about customers who have churned in the past in addition to customers who have not.

REMEMBER

Some models created to mine data and make sense of its underlying relationships — for example, those built with clustering algorithms — needn't have a particular end result in mind.

Two problems arise when dealing with data as you're building your model: underfitting and overfitting.

Underfitting

Underfitting is when your model can't detect any relationships in your data. This is usually an indication that essential variables — those with predictive power — weren't included in your analysis.

If the variables used in your model don't have high predictive power, then try adding new domain-specific variables and re-run your model. The end goal is to improve the performance of the model on the training data.

Another issue to watch for is *seasonality* (when you have seasonal pattern, if you fail to analyze multiple seasons you may get into trouble.) For example, a stock analysis that includes only data from a bull market (where overall stock prices are going up) doesn't account for crises or bubbles that can bring major corrections to the overall performance of stocks. Failing to include data that spans both bull *and* bear markets (when overall stock prices are falling) keeps the model from producing the best possible portfolio selection.

Overfitting

Overfitting is when your model includes data that has no predictive power but it's only specific to the dataset you're analyzing. *Noise* — random variations in the dataset — can find its way into the model, such that running the model on a different dataset produces a major drop in the model's predictive performance and accuracy. The accompanying sidebar provides an example.

THESE GENES FIT WRONG

A classic example of overfitting might cause trouble in a gene classification analysis that measures the proteins in particular genes. Imagine what happens when a lab technician calibrates the machine while it's taking measurements that turn out to be erroneous — or a particular machine used for the experiment suffers an electrical disruption, or a specific technique goes awry during the experiments: The erroneous measurements end up in the data, and the model's predictive potential goes out the window.

If your model performs well on a particular dataset and only underperforms when you test it on a different dataset, suspect overfitting. (For more about overfitting, see Chapter 15.)

Choosing an algorithm

Various statistical, data-mining, and machine-learning algorithms are available for use in your model. You're in a better position to select an algorithm after you've defined the objectives of your model and selected the data you'll work on. Some of these algorithms were developed to solve specific business problems, enhance existing algorithms, or provide new capabilities — which may make some of them more appropriate for your purposes than others. You can choose from a range of algorithms to address business concerns such as the following:

>> For customer segmentation and/or community detection in the social sphere, for example, you'd need clustering algorithms.

>> For customer retention or to develop a recommender system, you'd use classification algorithms.

>> For credit scoring or predicting the next outcome of time-driven events, you'd use a regression algorithm.

As time and resources permit, you should run as many algorithms of the appropriate type as you can. Comparing different runs of different algorithms can bring surprising findings about the data or the business intelligence embedded in the data. Doing so gives you more detailed insight into the business problem, and helps you identify which variables within your data have predictive power.

Some predictive analytics projects succeed best by building an *ensemble model*, a group of models that operate on the same data. An ensemble model uses a predefined mechanism to gather outcomes from all its component models and provide a final outcome for the user.

Models can take various forms — a query, a collection of scenarios, a decision tree, or an advanced mathematical analysis. In addition, certain models work best for certain data and analyses. You can (for example) use classification algorithms that employ decision rules to decide the outcome of a given scenario or transaction, addressing questions like these:

>> Is this customer likely to respond to our marketing campaign?

>> Is this money-transfer likely to be part of a money-laundering scheme?

>> Is this loan applicant likely to default on the loan?

You can use unsupervised clustering algorithms to find what relationships exist within your dataset. (For more about the use of unsupervised clustering, see Chapter 6.) You can use these algorithms to find different groupings among your customers, determine what services can be grouped together, or decide for example which products can be upsold.

Regression algorithms can be used to forecast continuous data, such as predicting the trend for a stock movement given its past prices.

Decision trees, support vector machines, neural networks, logistic, and linear regressions are some of the most common algorithms, explained in detail in Chapter 6 and Chapter 7. Although their mathematical implementations differ, these predictive models generate comparable results. The decision trees are more popular, because they're easy to understand; you can follow the path to a given decision.

Classification algorithms are great for the type of analysis when the target is known (such as identifying spam emails). On the other hand, when the target variable is unknown, clustering algorithms are your best bet. They allow you to cluster or group your data into meaningful groups based on the similarities among the group members.

These algorithms are widely popular. There are many tools, both commercial and open-source, that implement them. With data accumulation thriving and accelerating (that is, big data), and cost-efficient hardware and platforms (such as cloud computing and Hadoop), predictive analytics tools are experiencing a boom.

Data and business objectives aren't the only factors to consider when you're selecting an algorithm. The expertise of your data scientists is of tremendous value at this point; picking an algorithm that will get the job done is often a tricky combination of science and art. The art part comes from experience and proficiency in the business domain, which also plays a critical role in identifying a model that can serve business objectives accurately.

Developing and Testing the Model

Let the magic begin! Model development starts at this stage, followed by testing the results of the runs. You use training and test datasets to align the model more closely to its business objectives, and refine the model's output through careful selection of variables, further training, and evaluating the output.

Developing the model

Developing a predictive model almost can never be a one-time deal; it requires an iterative process. You have to narrow the list of variables you're working with — starting with more variables than you think you'll need, and using multiple runs on the training dataset to narrow down the variables to those that truly count.

TIP

Run each algorithm several times while tweaking and changing the input variables fed to that model. With each run, you're examining a new hypothesis, changing input variables, and digging deeper for better solutions and more accurate predictions.

Okay, an iterative process can be overwhelming; you can easily lose track of what you've changed, or of what combinations of hypotheses and variables you've already run. Be sure to document each experiment thoroughly. Include inputs, the algorithm, and the outputs of each experiment. In addition, document any relevant observations you may have such as the specific assumptions made, your initial assessment, and the next step planned. This way you can avoid duplicate efforts.

REMEMBER

Consulting with business domain experts at this stage can help you keep your model relevant while you're building it. Your domain experts can

>> Identify the variables that have greater predictive power.

>> Provide you with business language necessary for you to report your findings.

>> Help you explain the business significance of your preliminary results.

Testing the model

To be able to test the model you need to split your dataset into two sets: training and test datasets. These datasets should be selected at random and should be a good representation of the actual population.

TIP

Split your data: 70 percent to train the model and 30 percent to test the model. This ensures that the model is tested against data it hasn't seen before.

The following are guidelines as you split your data between training and test datasets:

>> Similar data should be used for both the training and test datasets.

>> Normally the training dataset is significantly larger than the test dataset.

>> Using the test dataset helps you avoid errors such as overfitting.

>> The trained model is run against test data to see how well the model will perform.

Some data scientists prefer to have a third dataset that has characteristics similar to those of the first two: a *validation dataset*. The idea is that if you're actively using your test data to refine your model, you should use a separate (third) set to check the accuracy of the model. Having a validation dataset, that wasn't used as part of the development process of your model, helps ensure a neutral estimation of the model's accuracy and efficacy.

TIP

If you've built multiple models using various algorithms, the validation sample can also help you evaluate which model performs best.

REMEMBER

Make sure you double-check your work developing and testing the model. In particular, be skeptical if the performance or the accuracy of the model seems too good to be true. Errors can happen where you least expect them. Incorrectly calculating dates for time series data, for example, can lead to erroneous results.

Employing cross-validation

Cross-validation is a popular technique you can use to evaluate and validate your model. The same principle of using separate datasets for testing and training applies here: The training data is used to build the model; the model is run against the testing set to predict data it hasn't seen before, which is one way to evaluate its accuracy.

In cross-validation, the historical data is split into X numbers of subsets. Each time a subset is chosen to be used as test data, the rest of the subsets are used as training data. Then, on the next run, the former test set becomes one of the training sets and one of the former training sets becomes the test set. The process continues until every subset of that X number of sets has been used as a test set.

For example, imagine we have a dataset that we have divided into 5 sets numbered 1 to 5. In the first run, we use set 1 as the test set and use sets 2, 3, 4 and 5 as the training set. Then, on the second run, we use set 2 as the test set and sets 1, 3, 4, and 5 as training set. We continue this process until every subset of the 5 sets has been used as a test set.

Cross-validation allows you to use every data point in your historical data for both training and testing. This technique is more effective than just splitting your historical data into two sets, using the set with the most data for training, using the other set for testing, and leaving it at that. When you cross-validate your data, you're protecting yourself against randomly picking test data that's too easy to predict — which would give you the false impression that your model is accurate. Or, if you happen to pick test data that's too hard to predict, you might falsely conclude that your model isn't performing as you had hoped.

TIP

Cross-validation is widely used not only to validate the accuracy of models but also to compare the performance of multiple models.

Balancing bias and variance

Bias and variance are two sources of errors that can take place as you're building your analytical model.

Bias is the result of building a model that significantly simplifies the presentation of the relationships among data points in the historical data used to build the model.

Variance is the result of building a model that is explicitly specific to the data used to build the model.

Achieving a balance between bias and variance — by reducing the variance and tolerating some bias — can lead to a better predictive model. This trade-off usually leads to building less complex predictive models. A model with high complexity tends to have high variance and low bias. On the other hand, a very simple model tends to have high bias and low variance. Your goal is to build predictive models that have both low bias and low variance.

Many data-mining algorithms have been created to take into account this trade-off between bias and variance.

Troubleshooting ideas

When you're testing your model and you find yourself going nowhere, here are a few ideas to consider that may help you get back on track:

» Always double-check your work. You may have overlooked something you assumed was correct but isn't. Such flaws could show up (for example) among the values of a predictive variable in your dataset, or in the preprocessing you applied to the data.

» If the algorithm you chose isn't yielding any results, try another algorithm. For example, you try several classification algorithms available and depending on your data and the business objectives of your model, one of those may perform better than the others.

>> Try selecting different variables or creating new derived variables. Be always on the lookout for variables that have predictive power.

>> Frequently consult with the business domain experts who can help you make sense of the data, select variables, and interpret the model's results.

Evaluating the model

At this stage, you're trying to make sure that your model is accurate, can meet its business objective, and can be deployed.

Before presenting your findings, make sure that the steps you took to build the model are all correct. Verification of those steps, from data processing to data analysis, is essential.

After partitioning your data into training and test sets and performing a cross-validation, you still need to evaluate whether the model meets its business objectives and interpret its results in familiar business terms; domain experts can help with that.

It is important that you evaluate the outcome of your model and make sure that it meets the business needs you sought to achieve. It's equally important that you should be able to explain the results of your model using business terms that managements can relate to. You should be able to explain how these perditions will affect your business, how the stakeholders can benefit from their insights, and they can use them to make informed decisions.

Here's where you address the model's performance in terms of its speed and accuracy when deployed. You want to know how well your model will run against larger datasets — especially in the production environment.

To determine what measures you can take so as to judge the quality of your model, start by comparing the outputs of multiple models (or multiple versions of the same model). You want to have confidence that the model you built is sound, and that you can defend its findings. Be sure you can explain and interpret the results in business terms that the stakeholders can readily understand and apply.

TIP

You should be able to pinpoint why your model gives a particular recommendation or prediction. Doing so makes the model's outputs transparent, which allows business stakeholders to transform the predictions more easily into actionable decisions. If you're lucky, you may stumble over some new insights that only make sense after the model brings them to light. Those are rare, but when you get such results, the rewards can be substantial.

Going Live with the Model

After developing the model and successfully testing it, you're ready to deploy it into the production environment.

Deploying the model

The ultimate goal of a predictive analytics project is to put the model you build into the production process so it becomes an integral part of business decision-making.

The model can be deployed as a standalone tool or as part of an application. Either way, deploying the model can bring its own challenges.

» Because the goal is to make use of the model's predictive results and act upon them, you have to come up with an efficient way to feed data to the model and retrieve results from the model after it analyzes that data.

» Not all predictive decisions are automated; sometimes human intervention is needed. If a model flags a claim as fraudulent or high-risk, a claim processor may examine the claim more thoroughly and find it to be sound, saving the company from the loss of opportunity.

 The higher the stakes of a predictive decision, the more necessary it is to incorporate human oversight and approval into those decisions.

TIP

The model accrues real value only when it's incorporated into business processes — and when its predictions are turned into actionable decisions that drive business growth higher. This becomes especially useful when the deployed model provides recommendations, some of them in real time, during customers' interactions — or assesses risk during transactions, or evaluates business applications. This business contribution is especially powerful when repeated across several transactions, seamlessly.

The Predictive Model Markup Language (PMML) is a predictive model interchange format that allows you to use your favorite tool to develop your model, then directly deploy it. It's widely supported by analytics tools. PMML offers you the flexibility to develop a model in one environment, then deploy it into another without the need to write code or modify the application. As such, PMML is a standard way to represent your model, or your predictive analytics solution, independently of the environment in which is it was built.

Monitoring and maintaining the model

The longer the model is deployed, the more likely it will lose its predictive relevance as the environment changes. Business conditions are constantly changing, new data keeps coming in, and new trends are evolving. To keep your model relevant, monitor its performance and refresh it as necessary:

» Run the deployed model on the newly acquired data.

» Use new algorithms to refine the model's output.

A model tends to degrade over time. A successful model must be revisited, revaluated in light of new data and changing conditions, and probably retrained to account for the changes. Refreshing the model should be an ongoing part of the overall planning process. Refreshing the model will vary from simply tweaking the deployed model to completely rebuilding a new model.

Chapter 11

Visualization of Analytical Results

Visualization is an art. In predictive analytics, it's the art of being able to analyze and tell a story from your data and analytical results. The story may not only be about the present or the past, but also about the future.

Quick, easy-to-generate visualizations would enhance the decision-making process, making it faster and more effective. Data visualization would also provide executives with a basis for asking better and smarter questions about the organization.

This chapter zooms in on the importance, benefits, and complexities of data visualization. You become familiar with four criteria you can use to evaluate a visualization of analytical results. You're also introduced to the different types of visualizations that you can deploy for different types of prediction models.

REMEMBER

This chapter focuses on the specific use of data visualization: making sense of the analytical results and using the visualization as part of your reporting back to the business stakeholders. See Chapter 4 for other data visualization techniques that can help you get a closer look at your data and understand it better.

Visualization as a Predictive Tool

Napoleon Bonaparte said, "A good sketch is better than a long speech." The reason for this truism is that the human brain finds pictures easier to digest than text or numbers. Since the early days, mankind has been relying on pictorial representations to communicate and share information. Maps were one of the very first widespread visualizations, becoming indispensable enough to originate the field of cartography. Maps have played a far-reaching role in sharing ideas and distributing them widely to many generations, reinforcing the human tendency to communicate information visually.

In predictive analytics, data visualization presents analytical results as a picture that can be easily used to build realistic, actionable narratives of possible futures; such narratives can be archived and transmitted throughout your organization, helping to form the basis of its approach to its business.

So, how does visualization figure into the lifecycle of predictive analytics? Read on.

Why visualization matters

Reading rows of spreadsheets, scanning pages and pages of reports, and going through stacks of analytical results generated by predictive models can be painstaking, time-consuming, and — let's face it — boring. Looking at a few graphs representing that same data is faster and easier, while imparting the same meaning. The graphs can bring more understanding more quickly, and drive the point home efficiently. Graphs can tell you more than tables. For example, summary statistics like mean and median don't allow you to spot a bimodal distribution without an accompanying chart. A lift chart is often better than a gains table or certainly better than a simple report of overall accuracy. Such advantages are behind the increased demand for data visualization. Companies are starving for visualization tools that can help them understand the key drivers of their businesses.

Arming your data analysts with visualization tools changes the way they analyze data: They can derive more insights and respond to risks more quickly. And they will be empowered to utilize imagination and creativity in their digging and mining for deeper insights. Additionally, through visualization tools, your analysts can present their findings to executives in a way that provides easy, user-friendly access to analytical results.

For example, if you're dealing with content analytics and have to analyze text, emails, and presentations (for openers), you can use visualization tools to convert the content and ideas mentioned in raw content (usually as text) into a clear pictorial representation.

One such visualization is the graphs shown in Figure 11-5; they represent the correlation between concepts mentioned in text sources. Think of it as a labor-saving device: Now someone doesn't have to read thousands of pages, analyze them, extract the most relevant concepts, and derive a relationship among the items of data.

Analytics tools provide such visualizations as output, which goes beyond traditional visualizations by helping you with a sequence of tasks:

1. Do the reading efficiently.

2. Understand lengthy texts.

3. Extract the most important concepts.

4. Derive a clear visualization of the relationship between those concepts.

5. Present the concepts in ways that your stakeholders find meaningful.

This process is known as *interactive data visualization*. It's different from a simple visualization because

» You can analyze and drill down into the data represented by the graphs and charts for more details and insights.

» You can dynamically change the data used in those charts and graphs.

» You can select the different predictive models or preprocessing techniques to apply to the data that generated the graph.

These visualization tools save the data analyst a tremendous amount of time when generating reports, graphs, and (most importantly) effective communication about the results of predictive analysis.

That effective communication includes getting people together in a room, presenting the visualizations, and leading discussions that emerge from questions such as these:

"What does that point in the graph mean?"

"Does everyone see what I see?"

"What would happen if we added or removed certain data elements or variables?"

"What would happen if we changed this or that variable?"

Such discussions could unveil aspects of the data that weren't evident before, remove ambiguity, and answer some new questions about data patterns.

Getting the benefits of visualization

Using visualizations to present the results of your predictive analytics model can save you a lot of time when you're conveying your ideas to management. Visualization can make the business case for you, providing an instant understanding of complex analytical results.

Another benefit of using charts and graphs is to ease the process of decision-making. For example, you can use visualizations to identify areas in your business that need attention, as when you show maps that present comparative sales of your product by location and can more easily identify areas that might need more advertising. Doing several such analyses and presentations over time can create a narrative of predicting sales volume by location.

Similarly, in political campaigns maps are powerful communication tools that can be used to convey visually the up-to-date status of votes and eventually help predict the chances of winning. They can also aid with rethinking the campaign strategy.

Walking into a meeting with eye-catching graphics in addition to spreadsheets of numbers can make your meeting more effective because visualizations are easy to explain to a diverse audience. Meetings can then become opportunities for discussion, focused imagination, and ingenuity, leading to the discovery of new insights.

Visualization can be used to confirm or disprove assumptions made about a specific topic or phenomenon in your data. It can also validate your predictive model by helping you determine whether the output of the model is in line with the business requirements, and the data supports the claims made for the model.

In summary, visualization

>> Is easy to understand

>> Is visually appealing

>> Simplifies the complexities of the analysis

>> Is an efficient medium for communicating results

>> Makes the business case

>> Validates the output of your model

>> Enables the decision-making process

Dealing with complexities

Let's face it: Visualization may help simplify communication, but making effective use of visualization isn't exactly simple. Using data visualization to draft the storylines of scenarios that portray the future of your organization can be both powerful and complex.

The complexities of using visualization in predictive analytics can crop up in various areas:

>> Visualization requires a wide range of multi-disciplinary skills in (for example) statistics, analysis, graphic design, computer programming, and narrative.

>> A large body of data that comes from a variety of sources can be unruly to handle. Finding innovative ways to plot all that data — and represent it to the decision-makers in ways they find meaningful — can be challenging.

>> Visualizing analytical results can accidentally convey misleading patterns or predictions. Different interpretations and various possible insights might come from the same visualization.

TIP

To head off this difficulty, you might want to have different analysts discuss these possibilities and their meanings beforehand, in depth; get them to agree on a single, consistent story derived from the visualization before you present it to management.

Evaluating Your Visualization

There are several ways to visualize data; but what defines a good visualization? The short answer: Whatever gets the meaning across is your best choice. To help you find that best choice, this section lists four criteria you can use to judge your visualization. This isn't a comprehensive list, but it should point you toward the best visualization to drive your idea home.

How relevant is this picture?

Your data visualization must have a clear, well-defined purpose — have a goal in mind and convey a clear idea of how to get there. That purpose could be the answering of the business need that brought you to apply predictive analytics in the first place. A subsidiary, immediately practical purpose could be your need to convey complex ideas through visualization. To answer both needs, first keep in mind that the data presented in the visualization has to be relevant to the overall theme of your analytics project. (That relevance won't be far to seek; your analytical project started with selecting the relevant data to feed into your predictive model.)

With the theme in mind, the next step is to create a narrative that presents the relevant data, highlights the results that point toward the goal, and uses a relevant visualization medium. (If your company has a room that's ideal for, say, PowerPoint presentations, consider that a big hint.)

How interpretable is the picture?

If you apply analytics to your data, build a predictive model, and then display your analytical results visually, you should be able to derive well-defined interpretations from your visualizations. Deriving those meaningful interpretations leads, in turn, to deriving insights, and that's the linchpin for the whole predictive analytics process.

The story you tell via your visualization medium must be clear and unambiguous. A roomful of conflicting interpretations is usually a sign that something is amiss. To keep the interpretation of the visualization on track, be sure you keep it firmly in line with the model's output — which in turn aligns the whole effort with the business questions that prompted the predictive analytics quest.

In cases where a visualization might allow several interpretations, those interpretations should converge to tell the same story in the end. As with many undertakings, multiple interpretations are often possible. Try to anticipate, discuss, and tweak them beforehand until they all convey the same underlying idea or support the same overarching concept.

Is the picture simple enough?

A visualization that's too complex or too simple can be misleading or confusing. To achieve effectiveness, your visualization needs clarity and elegance. For example, to make it very easy to read, you might be tempted to use two simple charts instead of one more complex one; if it isn't done well, makes the relationships harder to see. Sometimes a little starting at a well-crafted graphic for several minutes is worth the effort. The trick is not to distract with needless detail. Everything should work together to communicate the pattern.

You should always aim for clarity by adding as many *legends* (guides to what the parts of the image mean) as needed, and making them as clear as possible. You can use legends to define all the symbols, figures, axes, colors, data ranges, and other graphical components you have in your visualization.

Choosing the right combination of colors and objects to represent your data can enhance elegance. The medium you choose to present your data is also critical. The medium refers to the images, graphs, and charts in your presentations, in addition to the conference room, and to the visual aids you use to present your analytical results, such as TV screen, white board, or projector.

TIP

As a rule, the simpler the visualization and the more straightforward its meaning is, the better it is. You know you've succeeded when the visualization does the talking for you.

Does the picture lead to new actionable insights?

Your visualization should add something new to your predictive analytics project. Ideally, it should help you find new insights that weren't known before. During the building of your predictive analytics model, you can use visualization to fine-tune the output of your model, examine the data, and plot the result of the analysis. Visualization can be your guide to discovering new insights, or discerning and learning new relationships among items of data in the sea of data you're analyzing.

Visualization should help you seal the deal and erase any doubts about the analysis; it should support the findings and the output of the model. If it does so effectively, then presenting these findings to management will help them embrace and act upon the results.

Visualizing Your Model's Analytical Results

This section presents some ways to use visualization techniques to report the results of your models to the stakeholders.

Visualizing hidden groupings in your data

As discussed in Chapter 6, data clustering is the process of discovering hidden groups of related items within your data. In most cases, a *cluster* (grouping) consists of data objects of the same type such as social network users, text documents, or emails. One way to visualize the results of a data-clustering model is shown in Figure 11-1, where the graph represents social communities (clusters) that were discovered in data collected from social network users. In Figure 11-1, the data about customers was collected in a tabular format; then a clustering algorithm was applied to the data, and the three clusters (groups) were discovered: loyal customers, wandering customers, and discount customers. Assume that the X and Y axis represent the two principal components generated of the original data. Principal component analysis (PCA) is a data reduction technique. For more information about PCA, see Chapter 9.

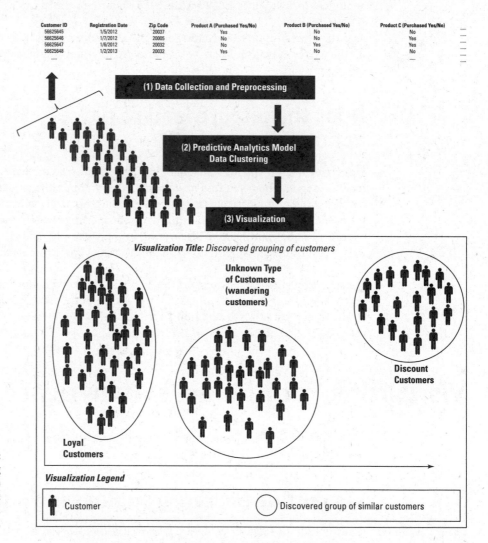

FIGURE 11-1:
Clustering
customers in
three groups:
loyal, wandering,
and discount.

Here the visual relationship among the three groups already suggests where enhanced and targeted marketing efforts might do the most good.

Visualizing data classification results

A classification model assigns a specific class to each new data point it examines. The specific classes, in this case, could be the groups that result from your clustering work (see the preceding section). The output highlighted in the graph (refer to Figure 11-1) can define your target sets. For any given new customer, a predictive classification model attempts to predict which group the new customer will belong to.

After you've applied a clustering algorithm and discovered groupings in the customer data, you come to a moment of truth: Here comes a new customer — you want the model to predict which type of customer he or she will be.

Figure 11-2 shows how a new customer's information is fed to your predictive analytics model, which in turn predicts which group of customers this new customer belongs to. In Figure 11-2, new Customers A, B, and C are about to be assigned to clusters according the classification model. Applying the classification model resulted in a prediction that Customer A would belong with the loyal customers, Customer B would be a wanderer, and Customer C was only showing up for the discount.

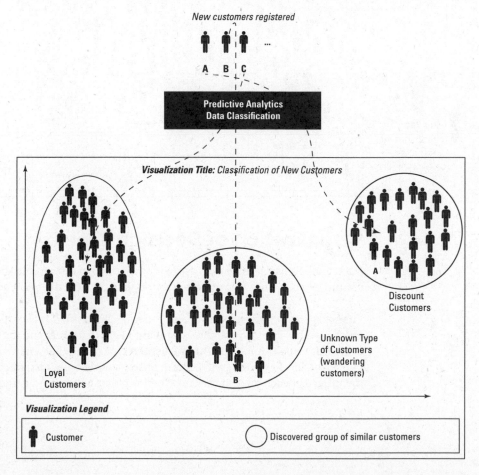

FIGURE 11-2:
Assigning Customers A, B, and C, to their classifications (clusters).

Visualizing outliers in your data

In the course of clustering or classifying new customers, every now and then you run into *outliers* (special cases that don't fit the existing divisions).

Figure 11-3 shows a few outliers that don't fit well into the predefined clusters. In Figure 11-3, six outlier customers have been detected and visualized. They behave differently enough that the model can't tell whether they belong to any of defined categories of customers.

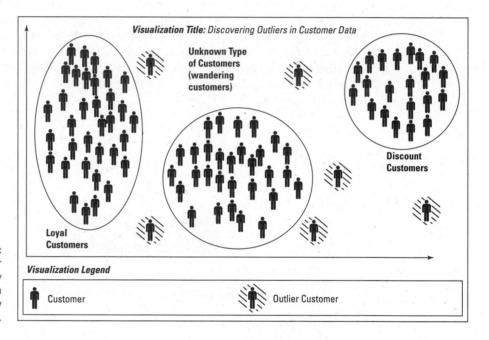

FIGURE 11-3:
Six outlier customers defy categorization just by showing up.

Visualization of Decision Trees

Many models use *decision trees* as their outputs: These diagrams show the possible results from alternative courses of action, laid out like the branches of a tree.

Figure 11-4 shows an example of a tree used as a classifier: It classifies baseball fans based on a few criteria, mainly the amount spent on tickets and the purchase dates. From this visualization, you can predict the type of fan that a new ticket-buyer will be: casual, loyal, bandwagon, diehard, or some other type. Attributes of each fan are mentioned at each level in the tree (total number of attended games, total amount spent, season); you can follow a path from a particular "root" to a specific "leaf" on the tree, where you hit one of the fan classes (c1, c2, c3, c4, c5). For more information on how to algorithmically generate a decision tree, see Chapter 7.

FIGURE 11-4:
Finding the class in which a particular baseball fan belongs.

Suppose we want to determine the type of baseball fan a customer is so that we can determine what type of marketing ads to send to the customer. We want to know whether the customer is a baseball fanatic or someone who just rides the bandwagon. Suppose we hypothesize that baseball fanatics and bandwagon fans can be persuaded to buy a new car (or other discretionary goods) when their team is doing well and headed for the playoffs. We may want to send marketing ads and discounts to persuade them to make the purchase. Further, suppose we hypothesize that bandwagon fans can be persuaded to vote in support of certain political issues. We can send them marketing ads asking them for that support. If you know what type of fan base you have, using decision trees can help you decide how to approach it as a range of customer types.

Visualizing predictions

Assume you've run an array of predictive analytics models, including decision trees, random forests, and flocking algorithms. You can combine all those results and present a consistent narrative that they all support, as shown in Figure 11-5. Here confidence is a numerical percentage that can be calculated using a mathematical function. The result of the calculation encapsulates a score of how probable a possible occurrence is. On the x axis, the supporting evidence represents the content source that was analyzed with content-analytics models that identified the possible outcomes. In most cases, your predictive model would have processed a large dataset, using data from various sources, to derive those possible outcomes. Thus you need show only the most important supporting evidence in your visualization, as depicted in Figure 11-5.

In Figure 11-5, a summary of the results obtained from applying predictive analytics is presented as a visualization that illustrates possible outcomes, along with a confidence score and supporting evidence for each one. Three possible scenarios are shown:

>> The inventory of Item A will not keep up with demand if you don't ship at least 100 units weekly to Store S. (Confidence score: 98 percent.)

>> The number of sales will increase by 40 percent if you increase the production of Item A by at least 56 percent. (Confidence score: 83 percent.)

>> A marketing campaign in California will increase sales of Items A and D but not Item K. (Confidence score: 72 percent.)

The confidence score represents the likelihood that each scenario will happen, according to your predictive analytics model. Note that they are listed here in descending order of likelihood.

Here the most important supporting evidence consists of how excerpts from several content sources are presented over the x axis. You can refer to them if you need to explain how you got to a particular possible scenario — and trot out the evidence that supports it.

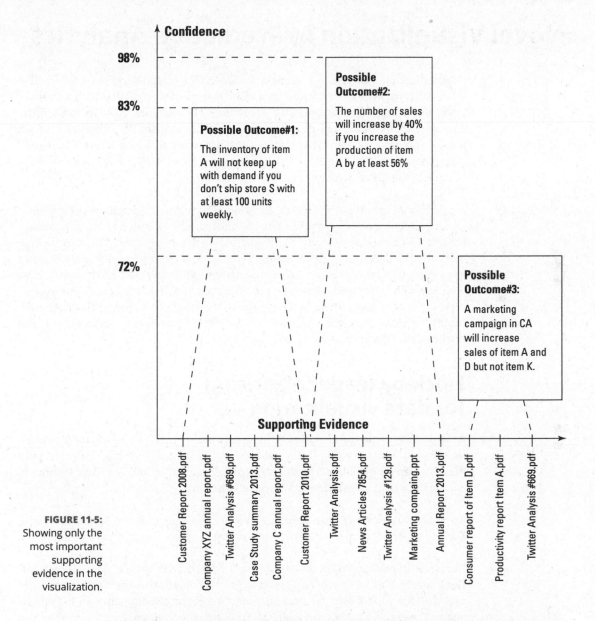

FIGURE 11-5:
Showing only the most important supporting evidence in the visualization.

The power behind this visualization is its simplicity. Imagine, after months of applying predictive analytics to your data, working your way through several iterations, that you walk into a meeting with the decision maker. You're armed with one slide visualization of three possible scenarios that might have a huge impact on the business. Such a visualization creates effective discussions and can lead management to "aha" moments.

Novel Visualization in Predictive Analytics

A visualization can also represent a *simulation* (a pictorial representation of a what-if scenario). You can follow up a visualization of a prediction with a simulation that overlaps and supports the prediction. For example, what happens if the company stops manufacturing Product D? What happens if a natural disaster strikes the home office? What happens if your customers lose interest in a particular product? You can use visualization to simulate the future behavior of a company, a market, a weather system — you name it.

A *dashboard* is another type of visualization you can use to display a comprehensive predictive analytics model. The dashboard will allow you, using a control button, to change any step in the predictive analytics pipeline. This can include selecting the data, data preprocessing, selecting a predictive model, and selecting the right evaluation versions. You can easily modify any part of the pipeline at anytime using the control button on the dashboard. A dashboard is an interactive type of visualization where you have control and you can change the diagrams, tables, or maps dynamically based on the inputs you choose to include in the analyses that generate those charts and graphs.

Flock-by-leader algorithm for data visualization

At least one predictive analytics technique is purely inspired by the natural phenomenon of birds flocking (refer to Chapter 2). The bird-flocking model not only identifies groupings in data, it shows them in dynamic action. The same technique can be used to picture hidden patterns in your data.

The model represents data objects as birds flying in a virtual space, following *flocking rules* that orchestrate how a migrating swarm of birds moves in nature.

Representing several data objects as birds reveals that similar data objects will flock together to form *subflocks* (groupings). The similarity among objects in the real world is what drives the movements of the corresponding birds in the virtual space. For example, as shown in Figure 11-6, imagine that you want to analyze the online data collected from several Internet users (also known as *netizens*).

Every piece of information (gleaned from such sources as social network user information and customer online transactions) will be represented as a corresponding bird in the virtual space, as shown in Figure 11-7.

FIGURE 11-6:
Using bird flocking to analyze the online behavior of Internet users.

Every netizen is modeled as a bird

Cyberspace	Bird Flocking Virtual Space

Bird Position on Y axis

Attraction vector

Initial Position

New Position

Netizen "X" interacts with Netizen "Y" on Facebook

Initial Position

Bird Position on X axis

FIGURE 11-7:
Two netizens flocking.

Simulating the birds' flocking behavior

If the model finds that two or more users interact with each other through email or chat, appear in the same online photo, buy the same product, or share the same interests, the model shows those two netizens as birds that flock together, following natural flocking rules.

The interaction (that is, how close the representative birds get to each other) is expressed as a mathematical function that depends on the frequency of social interaction, or the intensity with which the users buy the same products or share the same interests. This latest mathematical function depends purely on the type of analytics you're applying.

Figure 11-7 depicts the interaction on Facebook between Netizens X and Y in cyberspace as bird-flocking virtual space, where both X and Y are represented as birds. Because Netizens X and Y have interacted with each other, the next flocking iteration will show their two birds as closer together.

An algorithm known as "flock by leader," invented by Prof. Anasse Bari and Prof. Bellaachia (see the following references), was inspired by a recent discovery that revealed the leadership dynamics in pigeons. This algorithm can mine user input for data points that enable it to detect leaders, discover their followers, and initiate flocking behavior in virtual space that closely mimics what happens when flocks form naturally — except the flocks, in this case, are data clusters called *data flocks*.

This technique not only detects patterns in data, but also provides a clear pictorial representation of the results obtained by applying predictive analytics models. The rules that orchestrate natural flocking behavior in nature were extended to create new flocking rules that conform to data analytics:

>> **Data flock homogeneity:** Members of the flock show similarity in data.

>> **Data flock leadership:** The model anticipates information leaders.

TIP

Representing a large dataset as a flock of birds is one way to easily visualize big data in a dashboard.

This visualization model can be used to detect pieces of data that are outliers, leaders, or followers. One political application could be to visualize community outliers, community leaders, or community followers. In the biomedical field, the model can be used to visualize outliers' genomes and leaders among genetic samples of a particular disease (say, those that show a particular mutation most consistently).

A bird-flocking visualization can also be used to predict future patterns of unknown phenomena in cyberspace — civil unrest, an emerging social movement, a future customer's lineage.

The flocking visualization is especially useful if you're receiving a large volume of streamed data at high velocity: You can see the formation of flocking in the virtual space that contains the birds that represent your data objects. The results of data analytics are reflected (literally) on the fly on the virtual space. Reality given a fictional, yet observable and analytically meaningful, representation purely inspired from nature. Such visualizations can also work well as simulations or what-if scenarios.

In Figure 11-8, a visualization based on flocking behavior starts by indexing each netizen to a virtual bird. Initially, all the birds are idle. As data comes in, each bird starts flocking in the virtual space according to the analytics results and the flocking rules.

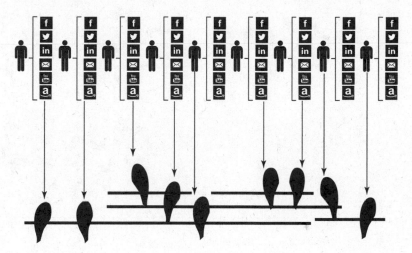

FIGURE 11-8:
Tracking the flocking netizens.

In Figure 11-9, the emerging flock is formed as the analytics are presented.

Simulating Flocking Behavior based on Netizen Cyberspace behavior at Time = t

FIGURE 11-9:
What the flock is doing.

After analyzing data over a large period of time ending at t+k, the results of this application of predictive analytics results can be depicted as shown in Figure 11-10: The flock-by-leader algorithm differentiates the members of the flock into three classes: a leader, followers, and outliers.

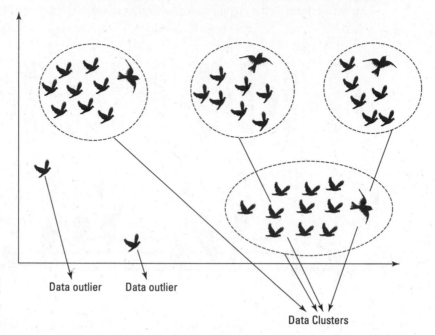

Simulating Flocking Behavior on Netizens Cyberspace behavior at <u>Time = t+k</u>

Data outlier   Data outlier

Data Clusters

FIGURE 11-10:
Flock-by-leader
subdivides
the flock.

TECHNICAL
STUFF

The flock–by–leader algorithm was invented by Dr.Bari and Dr.Bellaachia and it is explained in details in these resources:

>> "Flock by Leader: A Novel Machine Learning Biologically-Inspired Clustering Algorithm", IEEE International Conference of Swarm Intelligence, 2012.

This also appears as a book chapter in *Advances in Swarm Intelligence,* 2012 Edition – (Springer-Verlag).

>> "SFLOSCAN: A Biologically Inspired Data Mining Framework for Community Identification in Dynamic Social Networks", IEEE International Conference on Computational Intelligence, 2011 (SSCI 2011), 2011.

Big Data Visualization Tools

Big data has the potential to inspire businesses to make better decisions. It's important to be aware of the tools that can quickly help you create good visualization. You want to always keep your audience engaged and interested.

This section introduces some popular visualization tools for large scale enterprise analytics. Most of these tools don't require any coding experience and they are easy to use. If your raw data is in Excel sheets or resides in databases, you can load your data into these tools to visualize it for data exploration and analytics purposes. Alternatively, you may have the results from applying a predictive model on your data ready on spreadsheets, so (or and) you can also use these tools to visualize those results. (Examples of visualizations are illustrated in Chapter 4.)

Tableau

Tableau is a visualization tool for enterprise analytics. With Tableau, you can load your data and visualize it in charts, maps, tree maps, histograms, and word clouds. You can run Tableau as a desktop application a server, or a cloud-based solution.

Tableau integrates with many big-data platforms, such as R, RapidMiner, and Hadoop. Tableau pulls data from major databases and supports many file formats. Tableau for enterprise isn't free. For academic purposes, Tableau can provide free licenses.

For information about Tableau, visit `https://public.tableau.com/s` and `http://www.tableau.com`.

Google Charts

Google chart tools are free, and easy to use. They include histograms, geo charts, column charts, scatter charts, timeline charts, and organizational charts. Google Charts are interactive, zoomable, and can run on HTML5 and SVG. Google charts can also visualize real-time data.

For more information about Google Chart, visit `https://developers.google.com/chart`.

Plotly

Plotly is another visualization tool that your teams of developers can adopt using APIs. You can create charts and dashboard with Plotly.

Plotly is compatible with Python R and Matlab and its visualization can be embedded in web-based applications.

For more information about Plotly, visit `https://plot.ly`.

Infogram

This tool helps you create visualizations in a three-step process: choosing a template, adding charts to visualize your data, and then sharing your visualizations. A monthly fee is required to use the tool for a professional version, a business version, or an enterprise. The tool can support multiple accounts for your team.

For more information about Infogram, visit `https://infogr.am`.

4

Programming Predictive Analytics

IN THIS PART . . .

Installing software

Applying algorithms

Programming models with R

Maximizing accuracy

Applying predictive analytics to big data

IN THIS CHAPTER

Installing the machine-learning software

Working with a sample dataset

Creating simple predictive models

Visualizing and evaluating your results

Chapter 12

Creating Basic Prediction Examples

This chapter is about installing and setting up the machine-learning software and using the Python programming language to create a few simple predictive models. There are some modules to install and it will take a bit of time, so make sure you have plenty of battery life left if you're working on your laptop. If you already have Python installed prior to reading this book, make sure you're installing the correct versions of the machine-learning modules and dependencies for the Python version you're using.

In this book, Python version 2.7.11 is being used on a Windows 10 machine, but the installation instructions should work on older versions of Windows.

If you're following along in this chapter, you'll dive right in and start working with a sample dataset. Don't worry too much about the coding involved; most of the code will be provided and you can run it directly in the Python interactive interpreter, line by line. For most lines of code, you'll see what the output is. If, for some reason, an error crops up, you'll know exactly which line caused the error. Easy stuff.

Installing the Software Packages

The goal here is to build a couple of predictive models using different classification algorithms. To do that, you'll need to install Python, its machine-learning modules, and its dependencies. The setup process can take from 30 minutes to an hour, depending on your available Internet speed and your experience level in installing projects that require dependencies or multiple other projects.

You can choose from a variety of programming languages and add-on packages to create and run predictive models. Python, together with the `scikit-learn` module, is an easy and powerful combination of programming language and machine-learning package to use, learn, and get started with quickly.

Python is used widely in production systems, and is a requirement in many data science jobs.

Compared to other programming languages, Python is relatively easy to learn. Its syntax is straightforward and the code can be executed directly in an interactive console. You'll know immediately if you wrote a successful statement, and can learn quickly from trial and error in many cases.

Installing Python

Installing Python is an easy process that takes less than thirty minutes and just several clicks of the mouse. All of the default settings can be accepted during the installation process. You can install Python by downloading the installation program for Windows and other operating systems from the Python website at `www.python.org`. This chapter guides you through the installation process for the Windows operating system and Python release version 2.7.11. After you get to the Python website, you can look for the downloads link to get the file. After you've downloaded the file, just navigate to the folder where you downloaded it, then double-click on the file to begin the installation process.

Windows x86 MSI installer is available at

```
https://www.python.org/ftp/python/2.7.11/python-2.7.11.msi
```

To install Python, launch the installer and follow these steps:

1. **Choose which users you want to install Python for, then click Next.**

You can choose between all users or just yourself. Either choice is fine here. Figure 12-1 shows a prompt to select which user to install Python for. The default is to install for all users of the computer.

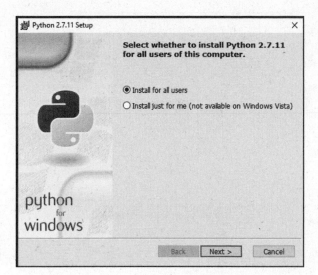

FIGURE 12-1:
A prompt to choose which user to install Python for.

2. **Choose the destination directory, then click Next.**

Figure 12-2 shows a prompt to select the location where you want Python to be installed.

FIGURE 12-2:
A prompt to choose the destination directory.

3. **Customize Python installation features, then click Next.**

For a new user, the default is fine. Figure 12-3 shows a prompt to select custom installation features and how much disk space is required for those features.

After a minute or so, the installation should be complete. Figure 12-4 shows that the installation of Python is complete. Click Finish.

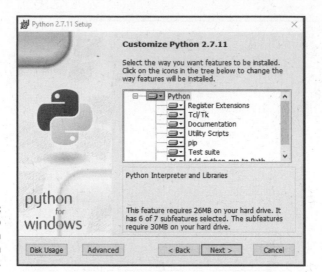

FIGURE 12-3:
A prompt to choose custom installation features.

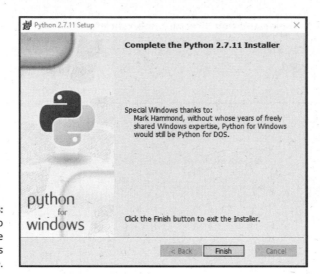

FIGURE 12-4:
A prompt to showing the installation is complete.

Installing the machine-learning module

If you're familiar with installing software packages, you can just download these files, then skip to the "Checking your installation" section:

>> Scikit-Learn

   https://sourceforge.net/projects/scikit-learn/files/scikit-learn-0.17.win32-py2.7.exe/download

>> Numpy

```
https://sourceforge.net/projects/numpy/files/NumPy/1.10.2/
numpy-1.10.2-win32-superpack-python2.7.exe/download
```

>> SciPy

```
https://sourceforge.net/projects/scipy/files/scipy/0.16.1/
scipy-0.16.1-win32-superpack-python2.7.exe/download
```

>> Matplotlib

```
https://sourceforge.net/projects/matplotlib/files/matplotlib/
matplotlib-1.2.1/matplotlib-1.2.1.win32-py2.7.exe/download
```

If you want to follow along with the same installation setup as used by this book, follow these instructions on the `scikit-learn` website (`http://scikit-learn.org`) to get the machine learning package:

1. **Click the link to the installation page.**

2. **Look for the information on installing the latest release.**

   You can follow the instructions listed on the site, which requires that you already have working installations of the dependent modules already or install a third-party distribution. However, the following steps will install everything you need.

   You can download the latest version of `scikit-learn` for your operating system from SourceForge, a source code repository website.

   Here is a direct link to the `scikit` project at SourceForge:

   ```
   https://sourceforge.net/projects/scikit-learn/files
   ```

   You'll be using the executable file `scikit-learn-0.17.win32-py2.7.exe` for your installation.

3. **Click the link with the executable filename.**

   Within about a minute, the download should be complete. Go to the download's folder or wherever your default download's folder is located. Double-click the file to start the installation process.

   WARNING

   Depending on the version of Windows and web browser you're using, you may receive a few warning prompts to download and execute the installer for these modules.

   The first prompt is a prompt to download the `scikit-learn` machine-learning module, as shown in Figure 12-5.

FIGURE 12-5:
A prompt to
download the
scikit-learn
machine-learning
module.

4. **Click the Save File button and wait for the download to finish.**

5. **When the download is finished, go to the folder where you saved the file and run the file by double-clicking the filename.**

This may open a series of prompts or warnings (similar to Figure 12-6 and Figure 12-7) that ask whether you want to proceed with running an executable file.

FIGURE 12-6:
System warning
that you're
opening an
executable file.

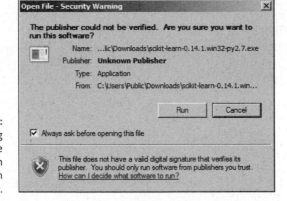

FIGURE 12-7:
System warning
that this software
is from an
unknown
publisher.

6. **Click the OK / Run button and continue.**

The next screen, shown in Figure 12-8, offers some important and useful information about the scikit-learn project.

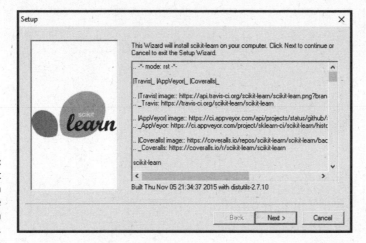

FIGURE 12-8:
Important
information
about the
scikit-learn
project.

7. **After you finish reading the information, click the Next button.**

During the installation process, the `scikit` installer may ask you to select some custom options. In most cases, accepting the default selections will be sufficient for running the examples.

TIP

When a screen asks where you want the module installed (as shown in Figure 12-9), we recommend accepting the default directory. Doing so simplifies the installation process, as there are other dependent modules you need to install. `C:\Python27\Lib\site-packages\` is the default installation directory for third-party modules.

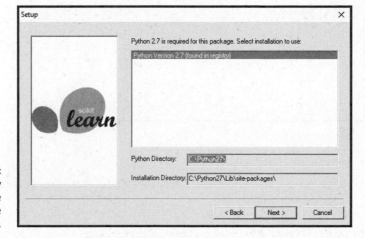

FIGURE 12-9:
The directory
where the
module is to be
installed.

8. **Click the Next button.**

You're now ready to install `scikit-learn`. Figure 12-10 shows one final prompt that appears before installation begins.

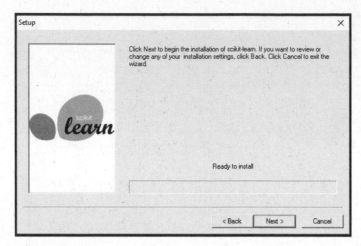

FIGURE 12-10:
Ready to install.

9. Click the Next button.

After the status bar is complete, you're notified that your installation is complete (as shown in Figure 12-11).

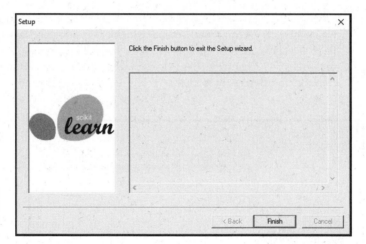

FIGURE 12-11:
Finished
installation
message.

10. Click the Finish button.

You're done installing the main module for `scikit`. You're now ready to install its dependencies.

Installing the dependencies

The `scikit-learn` module requires (or is dependent on) a few other modules to be installed before you can start using it. Modules that are dependent on other modules are called *dependencies*. In this case, the dependencies are `numpy`, `scipy`, and `matplotlib`.

REMEMBER

You need to install the following dependencies:

>> `numpy`

>> `scipy`

>> `matplotlib`

These packages may be available from several locations:

>> The Python Package Index website at `https://pypi.python.org/pypi`

>> The SourceForge website at `http://sourceforge.net`

>> The `matplotlib` website `http://matplotlib.org/downloads.html`

REMEMBER

Choosing the versions that have Windows installers will make the installation process quicker and as simple as possible.

Installing the dependencies is similar to installing `scikit-learn`. It's a series of prompts and clicks. To stay consistent across all dependencies, choose the default options.

Installing numpy

The following section details the steps needed to install `numpy`. You may download `numpy` from the SourceForge website.

1. From the SourceForge website, do a search for *numpy* in the search form.

Many listings show up. The needed module is `numpy-1.10.2`. If you search for it, it should appear as the top listing onscreen. To be sure that you have the same file, check to make sure it has the following description:

```
Numerical Python: Numerical Python adds a fast and
    sophisticated array facility to the Python language.
```

2. Click the *Numerical Python* link, then the *Files* tab link, then the *NumPy* folder link, then the *1.10.2* folder link to go to the folder with the latest binary distribution of `numpy`.

Here is a direct link to the download page:

`https://sourceforge.net/projects/numpy/files/NumPy/1.10.2`

3. **Click the** `numpy-1.10.2-win32-superpack-python2.7.exe` link.

Within a few seconds, the file `numpy-1.10.2-win32-superpack-python2.7.exe` should automatically start downloading.

4. **Go to your downloads folder (or wherever you saved the file) and run the file by double-clicking the filename.**

This may open a series of prompts or warnings that will ask whether you want to proceed with running an executable file. They'll be similar to those that show up when you install `scikit`.

5. **Click the OK/Run/Allow button and continue.**

A screen showing some important and useful information about the `numpy` project (similar to Figure 12-8) appears.

6. **Click the Next button.**

A screen similar to Figure 12-9 appears, asking where you want the `numpy` module installed.

7. **Accept the default location of the setup and click Next.**

A screen appears, displaying one final prompt before installation begins, as shown in Figure 12-10.

8. **Clicking Next begins the installation process.**

When the status bar is finished, you're notified that your installation is complete, as shown in Figure 12-11.

9. **Click the Finish button and then the Close button.**

That's it for this dependency — `numpy` is installed.

Installing scipy

The following section details the steps needed to install `scipy`. You may download `scipy` from the SourceForge website. The installation process is pretty much the same as the installation for `numpy`.

1. **From the SourceForge website, do a search for *scipy* in the search form.**

The top listing from the search should be

```
SciPy: Scientific Library for Python
```

2. **Click the *SciPy* link, then the *Files* tab link, then the *scipy* folder link, then the *0.16.1* folder link to go to the folder with the latest binary distribution of** `SciPy`.

Here is a direct link to the download page:

```
https://sourceforge.net/projects/scipy/files/scipy/0.16.1
```

3. **Click the** `scipy-0.16.1-win32.superpack-python2.7.exe link` **and wait for the download to finish.**

The rest of the installation process is the same as listed for numpy.

Installing matplotlib

The final module to install is matplotlib. To get the executable file, go to the SourceForge website search for matplotlib. The matplotlib version for this example is matplotlib 1.2.1. Once again, the rest of the installation process is the same as listed for numpy and scipy.

Here is a direct link to the download page:

```
https://sourceforge.net/projects/matplotlib/files/matplotlib/
matplotlib-1.2.1
```

Here is a direct link to the file:

```
https://sourceforge.net/projects/matplotlib/files/matplotlib/
matplotlib-1.2.1.win32-py2.7.exe/download
```

Checking your installation

When you've installed scikit-learn and all its dependencies, be sure you confirm that the installation went as expected. You want to avoid running into any problem or unexpected errors later on.

1. **Go to the Python interactive shell by choosing Windows Start button ⇨ Python2.7 ⇨ Python (command line).**

   The process is similar if you did a custom installation of Python.

2. **In the interactive shell, try running in the following statement to import all the modules that you installed:**

   ```
   >>> import sklearn, numpy, scipy, matplotlib
   ```

   If the Python interpreter returns no errors, then your installation succeeded, as shown in Figure 12-12.

```
C:\Python27\python.exe                                          −   □   ×
Python 2.7.11 (v2.7.11:6d1b6a68f775, Dec  5 2015, 20:32:19) [MSC v.1500 32 bit
(Intel)] on win32
Type "help", "copyright", "credits" or "license" for more information.
>>> import sklearn, numpy, scipy, matplotlib
>>>
```

REMEMBER

If you get an error like the one shown in Figure 12-13, then something went wrong in the installation process. You'll have to reinstall the module that is listed in the line that begins with ImportError.

```
C:\Python27\python.exe                                          −   □   ×
Python 2.7.11 (v2.7.11:6d1b6a68f775, Dec  5 2015, 20:32:19) [MSC v.1500 32 bit
(Intel)] on win32
Type "help", "copyright", "credits" or "license" for more information.
>>> import sklearn, numpy, scipy, matplotlib
Traceback (most recent call last):
  File "<stdin>", line 1, in <module>
ImportError: No module named matplotlib
>>>
```

Assuming everything went as planned, then you're ready to begin using scikit-learn to build a predictive model.

Preparing the Data

When you're learning a new programming language, it's customary to write the "hello world" program. For machine learning and predictive analytics, creating a model to classify the Iris dataset is its "hello world" equivalent program. This is a rather simple example, but it's very effective in teaching the basics of machine learning and predictive analytics.

Getting the sample dataset

To create our predictive model, you'll need to download the sample Iris dataset. This dataset is freely available from many sources, especially at academic institutions that have machine-learning departments. Fortunately, the folks at scikit-learn were nice enough to include some sample datasets and data-loading functions along with their package. So, for the purposes of these examples, you'll only need to run a couple of simple lines of code to load the data.

Labeling your data

Table 12-1 shows one observation and its features from each class of the Iris Flower dataset.

TABLE 12-1   **The Iris Flower Dataset**

Sepal Length	Sepal Width	Petal Length	Petal Width	Target Class/ Label
5.1	3.5	1.4	0.2	Setosa (0)
7.0	3.2	4.7	1.4	Versicolor (1)
6.3	3.3	6.0	2.5	Virginica (2)

The Iris Flower dataset is a real multivariate dataset of three classes of the Iris flower (*Iris setosa, Iris virginica,* and *Iris versicolor*) introduced by Ronald Fisher in his 1936 article, "The Use of Multiple Measurements in Taxonomic Problems." This dataset is best known for its extensive use in academia for machine learning and statistics. The dataset consists of 150 total instances, with 50 instances from each of the 3 classes of the Iris flower. The sample has 4 features (also commonly called *attributes*), which are the length and width measurements of the sepals and petals.

The interesting part of this dataset is that the three classes are somewhat linearly separable. The *Setosa* class can be separated from the other two classes by drawing a straight line on the graph between them. The *Virginica* and *Versicolor* classes can't be perfectly separated using a straight line — although it is close. This makes it a perfect candidate dataset to do classification analysis but not so good for clustering analysis.

The sample data was already labeled. The right column (Label) of Table 12-1 shows the names of each class of the Iris flower. The class name is called a *label* or a *target*; it's usually assigned to a variable named *y*. It's basically the outcome or the result of what is being predicted. In statistics and modeling, it is often referred to as the *dependent variable*. It depends on the inputs that correspond to sepal length and width and to petal length and width.

You may also want to know what's different about the `scikit` preprocessed Iris dataset, as compared to the original dataset. To find out, you need to obtain the original data file. You can do a Google search for *iris dataset* and download it or view it from any one of the academic institutions. The result that usually comes up first is the University of California Irvine's (UCI) machine-learning repository of datasets. Here is a direct link to the Iris dataset in its original state from the UCI machine-learning repository:

```
http://archive.ics.uci.edu/ml/machine-learning-databases/iris/iris.
data
```

If you download it, you should be able to view it with any text editor. Upon viewing the data in the file, you'll notice that there are five columns in each row. The first four columns are the measurements (referred to as the *features*) and the last column is the label. The label differs between the original and scikit version of the Iris dataset. Another difference is the first row of the scikit data file. It includes a header row used by the scikit data-loading function. It has no effect on the algorithms themselves.

TIP

Transforming features to numbers rather than keeping them as text makes it easier for the algorithms to process — and it's much more memory-efficient. This is especially evident if you run very large datasets with many features — which is often the case in real scenarios.

Table 12-2 shows sample data from both files. All the data columns are the same except for Col5. Note that scikit has class names with numerical labels; the original file has text labels.

TABLE 12-2   ## Sample Data

Source	Col1	Col2	Col3	Col4	Col5
scikit	5.1	3.5	1.4	0.2	0
original	5.1	3.5	1.4	0.2	Iris-setosa
scikit	7.0	3.2	4.7	1.4	1
original	7.0	3.2	4.7	1.4	Iris-versicolor
scikit	6.3	3.3	6.0	2.5	2
original	6.3	3.3	6.0	2.5	Iris-virginica

Making Predictions Using Classification Algorithms

You have all the tools and data necessary to start creating a predictive model. Now the fun begins.

In general, creating a learning model for classification tasks will entail the following steps:

1. Load the data.

2. Choose a classifier.

3. Train the model.

4. Visualize the model.

5. Test the model.

6. Evaluate the model.

Creating a supervised learning model with SVM

Supervised learning is a machine-learning task that learns from data that has been labeled. One way to think about supervised learning is that the labeling of data is done under the supervision of the modeler; *unsupervised learning*, by contrast, doesn't require labeled data. Supervised learning is commonly performed using a classification algorithm. In this section, you will use the Support Vector Machine classification algorithm to create a supervised learning model.

Loading your data

You need to load the data for your algorithms to use. Loading the Iris dataset in `scikit` is as simple as issuing a couple of lines of code because `scikit` has already created a function to load the dataset.

1. **Open a new Python interactive shell session.**

   Use a new Python session so there isn't anything left over in memory and you have a clean slate to work with.

2. **Enter the following code in the prompt and observe the output:**

   ```
   >>> from sklearn.datasets import load_iris
   >>> iris = load_iris()
   ```

   After running those two statements, you shouldn't see any messages from the interpreter. The variable `iris` should contain all the data from the `iris.csv` file.

Before you create a predictive model, it's important to understand a little about the new variable `iris` and what you can do with it. It makes the code easier to follow and the process much simpler to grasp. You can inspect the value of `iris` by typing it in the interpreter.

```
>>> iris
```

The output will be all the content from the iris.csv file, along with some other information about the dataset that the load_iris function loaded into the iris variable. The iris variable is a dictionary data structure with four main properties. The important properties of iris are listed on Table 12-3.

TABLE 12-3 **Main Properties of Iris Variable**

Property Name	Description
data	Contains all the measurements of the observations.
feature_name	Contains the name of the feature (attribute name).
target	Contains all the targets (labels) of the observations.
target_names	Contains the names of the iris classes.

TIP

You can print out the values in the interpreter by typing the variable name followed by dot followed by property name. An example is using iris.data to access the data property of iris, like this:

```
>>> iris.data
```

This is a standard way of accessing properties of an object in many programming languages.

To create an instance of the SVM classifier, type the following code in the interpreter:

```
>>> from sklearn.svm import LinearSVC
>>> svmClassifier = LinearSVC(random_state=111)
```

The first line of code imports the LinearSVC library into the session. The linear Support Vector Classifier (SVC) is an implementation of SVM for linear classification and has multi-class support. The dataset is somewhat linearly separable and has three classes, so it would be a good idea to experiment with LinearSVC to see how it performs. (You can read more about SVM in Chapter 7.)

The second line creates the instance using the variable svmClassifier. This is an important variable to remember; you'll see it used several more times in the chapter. The random_state parameter allows us to reproduce these examples and get the same results. If you didn't put in the random_state parameter, your results may differ from the ones shown here.

Running the training data

Before you can feed the SVM classifier with the data that was loaded, you must split the full dataset into a training set and test set.

Fortunately, scikit-learn has implemented a function that will help you to easily split the full dataset. The train_test_split function takes as input a single dataset and a percentage value. The percentage value is used to determine the size of the test set. The function returns two datasets: the test dataset (with its size specified) and the training dataset (which uses the remaining data).

Typically, one can take around 70-80 percent of the data to use as a training set and use the remaining data as the test set. But the Iris dataset is very small (only 150 instances), so you can take 90 percent of it to train the model and use the other 10 percent as test data to see how your predictive model will perform.

WARNING

In Python, the left indentation level of each statement is significant. In the interpreter, every new statement will begin with >>>. For the sample code in this book, if you don't see >>> in the beginning of a new line and it's indented, then it means it's a continuation of the preceding line and should be typed in as a single line (don't hit carriage return until the whole statement has been entered). If the next line doesn't have >>> in the beginning and it isn't indented, then it's the output from the interpreter. The code was formatted this way for better readability.

Type in the following code to split your dataset:

```
>>> from sklearn import cross_validation
>>> X_train, X_test, y_train, y_test =
        cross_validation.train_test_split(iris.data,
        iris.target, test_size=0.10, random_state=111)
```

The first line imports cross-validation library into your session. The second line creates the test set from 10 percent of the sample.

X_train will contain 135 observations and its features.

y_train will contain 135 labels in the same order as the 135 X_train observations.

X_test will contain 15 (or 10 percent) observations and its features.

y_test will contain 15 labels in the same order as the 15 X_test observations.

The following code verifies that the split is what you expected:

```
>>> X_train.shape
(135, 4)
```

```
>>> y_train.shape
(135,)
>>> X_test.shape
(15, 4)
>>> y_test.shape
(15,)
```

You can see from the output that there are 135 observations with 4 features and 135 labels in the training set. The test set has 15 observations with 4 features and 15 labels.

WARNING

Many beginners in the field of predictive analytics forget to split the datasets — which introduces a serious design flaw into the project. If the full 150 instances were loaded into the machine as training data, that would leave no unseen data for testing the model. Then you'd have to resort to reusing some of the training instances to test the predictive model. You'll see that in such a situation, the model always predicts the correct class — because you're using the same exact data you used to train the model. The model has already seen this pattern before; it will have no problem just repeating what it's seen. A working predictive model needs to make predictions for data that it hasn't seen yet.

When you have an instance of an SVM classifier, a training dataset, and a test dataset, you're ready to train the model with the training data. Typing the following code into the interpreter will do exactly that:

```
>>> svmClassifier.fit(X_train,y_train)
```

This line of code creates a working model to make predictions from. Specifically, a predictive model that will predict what class of Iris a new unlabeled dataset belongs to. The svmClassifier instance will have several methods that you can call to do various things. For example, after calling the fit method, the most useful method to call is the predict method. That's the method to which you'll feed new data; in return, it predicts the outcome.

Running the test data

Using 10 percent of the 150 instances from the dataset gives you 15 test-data points to run through the model. Let's see how your predictive model will perform. Type the following code listing into the interpreter:

```
>>> predicted = svmClassifier.predict(X_test)
>>> predicted
array([0, 0, 2, 2, 1, 0, 0, 2, 2, 1, 2, 0, 1, 2, 2])
```

The `predict` function in the first line of code is what does the prediction, as you may have guessed. It takes the test data as input and outputs the results into the variable `predicted`. The second line prints the output. The last line in the code section is the output, or prediction: an array of 15 — that is, 10 percent of the sample dataset, which is the size of the test dataset. The numbers in the array represent the Iris Flower classes.

Evaluating the model

To evaluate the accuracy of your model, you can compare the output array with the `y_test` array. For this small sample dataset, you can easily tell how it performed by seeing that the output array from the predict function is almost the same as the `y_test` array. The last line in the code is a simple equality check between the two arrays, sufficient for this simple test case. Here's the code:

```
>>> predicted
array([0, 0, 2, 2, 1, 0, 0, 2, 2, 1, 2, 0, 1, 2, 2])
>>> y_test
array([0, 0, 2, 2, 1, 0, 0, 2, 2, 1, 2, 0, 2, 2, 2])
>>> predicted == y_test
array([ True,  True,  True,  True,  True,  True,  True,
        True,  True,  True,  True,  True, False,  True,
        True], dtype=bool)
```

Looking at the output array with all the Boolean (`True` and `False`) values, you can see that the model predicted all but one outcome. On the thirteenth data point, it predicted 1 (Versicolor) when it should have been 2 (Virginica). The `False` value(s) indicate that the model predicted the incorrect Iris class for that data point. The percentage of correct predictions will determine the accuracy of the predictive model. In this case you can simply use basic division and get the accuracy:

correct outcomes / test size => 14 / 15 => 0.9333 or 93.33 percent

It's no surprise that the model failed to predict Virginica or Versicolor; they're clearly not separable by a straight line. A failure to predict Setosa, however, would be surprising because Setosa *is* clearly linearly separable. Still, the accuracy was 14 out of 15, or 93.33 percent.

For a test set with more data points, you may want to use the `metrics` module to do your measurements. The following code will get the accuracy of the model:

```
>>> from sklearn import metrics
>>> metrics.accuracy_score(y_test, predicted)
0.93333333333333335
```

The *mean absolute error* of the model is simply 1 − the accuracy score. In this case, it would be 1 − 0.9333. Here is the code to get this value:

```
>>> metrics.mean_absolute_error(y_test, predicted)
0.066666666666666666
```

Another useful measurement tool is the *confusion matrix*. Yes, it's real. It's a matrix (tabular format) that shows the predictions that the model made on the test data. Here is the code that displays the confusion matrix:

```
>>> metrics.confusion_matrix(y_test, predicted)
array([[5, 0, 0],
       [0, 2, 0],
       [0, 1, 7]])
```

The diagonal line from the top-left corner to the bottom-right corner is the number of correct predictions for each row. Each row corresponds to a class of Iris. For example: The first row corresponds to the Setosa class. The model predicted five correct test data points and had no errors predicting the Setosa class. If it had an error, a number other than zero would be present in any of the columns in that row. The second row corresponds to the Versicolor class. The model predicted two correct test data points and no errors. The third row corresponds to the Virginica class. The model predicted seven correct test data points but also had one error. The model mistakenly predicted one observation of Virginica for a Versicolor. You can tell that by looking at the column where the error is showing up. Column 1 (the second column, because Python arrays start at 0) belongs to Versicolor.

The accuracy of a predictive model's results will directly affect the decision to deploy that model; the higher the accuracy, the more easily you can gather support for deploying the model.

TIP

When creating a predictive model, start by building a simple working solution quickly — and then continue to build iteratively until you get the desired outcome. Spending months building a predictive model — and not being able to show your stakeholders any results — is a sure way to lose the attention and support of your stakeholders.

Here is the full listing of the code to create and evaluate a SVM classification model:

```
>>> from sklearn.datasets import load_iris
>>> from sklearn.svm import LinearSVC
>>> from sklearn import cross_validation
>>> from sklearn import metrics
```

```
>>> iris = load_iris()
>>> X_train, X_test, y_train, y_test =
        cross_validation.train_test_split(iris.data,
        iris.target, test_size=0.10, random_state=111)
>>> svmClassifier = LinearSVC(random_state=111)
>>> svmClassifier.fit(X_train, y_train)
>>> predicted = svmClassifier.predict(X_test)
>>> predicted
array([0, 0, 2, 2, 1, 0, 0, 2, 2, 1, 2, 0, 1, 2, 2])
>>> y_test
array([0, 0, 2, 2, 1, 0, 0, 2, 2, 1, 2, 0, 2, 2, 2])
>>> metrics.accuracy_score(y_test, predicted)
0.93333333333333335
>>> predicted == y_test
array([ True,  True,  True,  True,  True,  True,  True,
        True,  True,  True,  True,  True, False,  True,
        True], dtype=bool)
```

Visualizing the classifier

Looking at the decision surface area on the plot, as shown in Figure 12-14, it looks like some tuning has to be done. If you look near the middle of the plot, you can see that many of the data points belonging to the middle area (Versicolor) are lying in the area to the right side (Virginica).

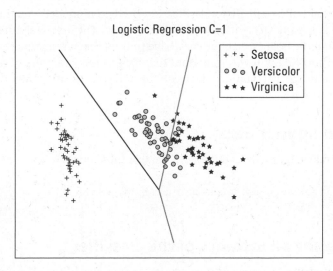

FIGURE 12-14:
Classification based on logistic regression with C=1.

Figure 12-15 shows the decision surface with a C value of 150. It visually looks better, so choosing to use this setting for your logistic regression model seems appropriate.

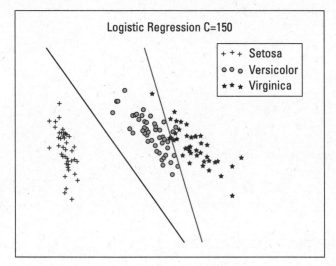

FIGURE 12-15:
Classification based on logistic regression with C=150.

Creating a supervised learning model with logistic regression

After you build your first classification predictive model, creating more models like it is a really straightforward task in scikit. The only real difference from one model to the next is that you may have to tune the parameters from algorithm to algorithm. We felt it was important to include a few examples of the classification technique so that you can feel comfortable trying other algorithms from the scikit library.

Loading your data

This code listing will load the iris dataset into your session:

```
>>> from sklearn.datasets import load_iris
>>> iris = load_iris()
```

Creating an instance of the classifier

The following two lines of code creates an instance of the classifier. The first line imports the logistic regression library. The second line creates an instance of the logistic regression algorithm.

```
>>> from sklearn import linear_model
>>> logClassifier = linear_model.LogisticRegression(C=1,
            random_state=111)
```

Notice the C parameter (regularization parameter) in the constructor. The *regularization parameter* is used to prevent overfitting (see Chapter 15 for more about overfitting). The parameter isn't strictly necessary (the constructor will work fine without it because it will default to C=1). In a later section, however, we'll be creating a logistic regression classifier, using C=150 because it creates a better plot of the decision surface, so we're just introducing it here. (You can see both plots in the "Visualizing the classifier" section in the chapter, in Figures 12-16 and 12-17.)

Running the training data

You'll need to split the dataset into training and test sets before you can create an instance of the logistic regression classifier. The following code will accomplish that task:

```
>>> from sklearn import cross_validation
>>> X_train, X_test, y_train, y_test =
        cross_validation.train_test_split(iris.data,
        iris.target, test_size=0.10, random_state=111)
>>> logClassifier.fit(X_train, y_train)
```

Line 1 imports the library that allows us to split the dataset into two parts.

Line 2 calls the function from the library that splits the dataset into two parts and assigns the now-divided datasets to two pairs of variables.

Line 3 takes the instance of the logistic regression classifier you just created and calls the fit method to train the model with the training dataset.

Running the test data

In the following code, the first line feeds the test dataset to the model and the third line displays the output:

```
>>> predicted = logClassifier.predict(X_test)
>>> predicted
array([0, 0, 2, 2, 1, 0, 0, 2, 2, 1, 2, 0, 2, 2, 2])
```

Evaluating the model

You can cross-reference the output from the prediction against the y_test array. As a result, you can see that it predicted all the test data points correctly. Here's the code:

```
>>> from sklearn import metrics
>>> predicted
array([0, 0, 2, 2, 1, 0, 0, 2, 2, 1, 2, 0, 2, 2, 2])
>>> y_test
array([0, 0, 2, 2, 1, 0, 0, 2, 2, 1, 2, 0, 2, 2, 2])
>>> metrics.accuracy_score(y_test, predicted)
1.0               # 1.0 is 100 percent accuracy
>>> predicted == y_test
array([ True,  True,  True,  True,  True,  True,  True,
        True,  True,  True,  True,  True,  True,  True,
        True], dtype=bool)
```

So how does the logistic regression model with parameter C=150 compare to that? It should do better because the visualization looked better, but you can't beat 100 percent. Here is the code to create and evaluate the logistic classifier with C=150:

```
>>> logClassifier_2 = linear_model.LogisticRegression(
        C=150, random_state=111)
>>> logClassifier_2.fit(X_train, y_train)
>>> predicted = logClassifier_2.predict(X_test)
>>> metrics.accuracy_score(y_test, predicted)
0.93333333333333335
>>> metrics.confusion_matrix(y_test, predicted)
array([[5, 0, 0],
       [0, 2, 0],
       [0, 1, 7]])
```

We expected better, but it was actually worse. There was one error in the predictions. The result is the same as that of the SVM model built earlier in the chapter.

Here is the full listing of the code to create and evaluate a logistic regression classification model with the default parameters:

```
>>> from sklearn.datasets import load_iris
>>> from sklearn import linear_model
>>> from sklearn import cross_validation
>>> from sklearn import metrics
>>> iris = load_iris()
```

```
>>> X_train, X_test, y_train, y_test =
        cross_validation.train_test_split(iris.data,
        iris.target, test_size=0.10, random_state=111)
>>> logClassifier = linear_model.LogisticRegression(,
        random_state=111)
>>> logClassifier.fit(X_train, y_train)
>>> predicted = logClassifier.predict(X_test)
>>> predicted
array([0, 0, 2, 2, 1, 0, 0, 2, 2, 1, 2, 0, 2, 2, 2])
>>> y_test
array([0, 0, 2, 2, 1, 0, 0, 2, 2, 1, 2, 0, 2, 2, 2])
>>> metrics.accuracy_score(y_test, predicted)
1.0            # 1.0 is 100 percent accuracy
>>> predicted == y_test
array([ True,  True,  True,  True,  True,  True,  True,
        True,  True,  True,  True,  True,  True,  True,
        True], dtype=bool)
```

Visualizing the classifier

The Iris dataset isn't easy to graph in its original form because you can't plot all four coordinates (from the features) of the dataset onto a two-dimensional screen. Therefore you can either pick two of the four features for visualization purposes or often better you can reduce the dimensions by applying a *dimensionality reduction* algorithm to the features. In this case, the algorithm you'll be using to do the data transformation (reducing the dimensions of the features) is called Principal Component Analysis (PCA).

The PCA algorithm takes all four features (numbers), does some math on them, and outputs two new numbers that you can use to do the plot. Think of PCA as following two general steps:

1. It takes as input a dataset with many features.

2. It reduces that input to a smaller set of features (user-defined or algorithm-determined) by transforming the components of the feature set into what it considers as the main (principal) components.

This transformation of the feature set is also called *feature extraction*. The following code does the dimension reduction:

```
>>> from sklearn.decomposition import PCA
>>> pca = PCA(n_components=2).fit(X_train)
>>> pca_2d = pca.transform(X_train)
```

TIP

If you've already imported any libraries or datasets listed in this code section, it isn't necessary to re-import or load them in your current Python session. If you do so, however, it shouldn't affect your program.

After you run the code, you can type the pca_2d variable in the interpreter and see that it outputs arrays with two items instead of four. These two new numbers are mathematical representations of the four old numbers. With the reduced feature set, you can plot the results by using the following code:

```
>>> import pylab as pl
>>> for i in range(0, pca_2d.shape[0]):
>>>    if y_train[i] == 0:
>>>       c1 = pl.scatter(pca_2d[i,0],pca_2d[i,1],c='r',
              marker='+')
>>>    elif y_train[i] == 1:
>>>       c2 = pl.scatter(pca_2d[i,0],pca_2d[i,1],c='g',
              marker='o')
>>>    elif y_train[i] == 2:
>>>       c3 = pl.scatter(pca_2d[i,0],pca_2d[i,1],c='b',
              marker='*')
>>> pl.legend([c1, c2, c3], ['Setosa', 'Versicolor',
              'Virginica'])
>>> pl.title('Iris training dataset with 3 classes and
              known outcomes')
>>> pl.show()
```

Figure 12-16 is a *scatter plot* — a visualization of plotted points representing observations on a graph. This particular scatter plot represents the known outcomes of the Iris training dataset. There are 135 plotted points (observations) from our training dataset. (You can see a similar plot, using all 150 observations, in Chapter 13.) The training dataset consists of

» 45 pluses that represent the Setosa class.

» 48 circles that represent the Versicolor class.

» 42 stars that represent the Virginica class.

You can confirm the stated number of classes by entering following code:

```
>>> sum(y_train==0)
45
>>> sum(y_train==1)
48
>>> sum(y_train==2)
42
```

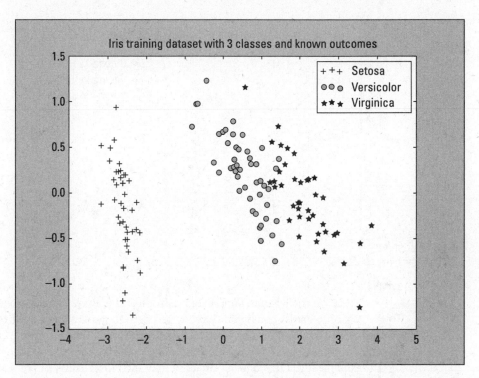

FIGURE 12-16:
Plotting data elements from the Iris dataset.

From this plot you can clearly tell that the Setosa class is linearly separable from the other two classes. While the Versicolor and Virginica classes aren't completely separable by a straight line, they aren't overlapping by very much. From a simple visual perspective, the classifiers should do pretty well.

Figure 12-17 shows a plot of the Support Vector Machine (SVM) model trained with a dataset that has been dimensionally reduced to two features. This isn't the same SVM model that you trained earlier in the preceding section; that SVM model used all four features. Four features is a small feature set; we want to keep all four so that the data can retain most of its useful information. The plot is shown here as a visual aid.

This plot includes the *decision surface* for the classifier — the area in the graph that represents the decision function that SVM uses to determine the outcome of new data input. The lines separate the areas where the model will predict the particular class that a data point belongs to. The left section of the plot will predict the Setosa class, the middle section will predict the Versicolor class, and the right section will predict the Virginica class.

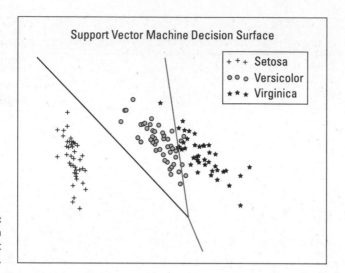

FIGURE 12-17:
Classification based on Support Vector Machine.

REMEMBER

The SVM model that you created didn't use the dimensionally reduced feature set. We only use dimensionality reduction here to generate a plot of the decision surface of the SVM model — as a visual aid. The full listing of the code that creates the plot is provided as reference. *It shouldn't be run in sequence with our current example if you're following along.* It may overwrite some of the variables that you may already have in the session. The code to produce this plot is based on the sample code provided on the `scikit-learn` website. You can learn more about creating plots like these at the `scikit-learn` website.

Here is the full listing of the code that creates the plot:

```
>>> from sklearn.decomposition import PCA
>>> from sklearn.datasets import load_iris
>>> from sklearn import svm
>>> from sklearn import cross_validation
>>> import pylab as pl
>>> import numpy as np
>>> iris = load_iris()
>>> X_train, X_test, y_train, y_test =
        cross_validation.train_test_split(iris.data,
        iris.target, test_size=0.10, random_state=111)
>>> pca = PCA(n_components=2).fit(X_train)
>>> pca_2d = pca.transform(X_train)
>>> svmClassifier_2d =
        svm.LinearSVC(random_state=111).fit(
        pca_2d, y_train)
>>> for i in range(0, pca_2d.shape[0]):
>>>     if y_train[i] == 0:
```

```
>>>         c1 = pl.scatter(pca_2d[i,0],pca_2d[i,1],c='r',
                s=50,marker='+')
>>>     elif y_train[i] == 1:
>>>         c2 = pl.scatter(pca_2d[i,0],pca_2d[i,1],c='g',
                s=50,marker='o')
>>>     elif y_train[i] == 2:
>>>         c3 = pl.scatter(pca_2d[i,0],pca_2d[i,1],c='b',
                s=50,marker='*')
>>> pl.legend([c1, c2, c3], ['Setosa', 'Versicolor',
        'Virginica'])
>>> x_min, x_max = pca_2d[:, 0].min()&#x00A0;- 1,
        pca_2d[:,0].max() + 1
>>> y_min, y_max = pca_2d[:, 1].min()&#x00A0;- 1,
        pca_2d[:, 1].max() + 1
>>> xx, yy = np.meshgrid(np.arange(x_min, x_max, .01),
        np.arange(y_min, y_max, .01))
>>> Z = svmClassifier_2d.predict(np.c_[xx.ravel(),
        yy.ravel()])
>>> Z = Z.reshape(xx.shape)
>>> pl.contour(xx, yy, Z)
>>> pl.title('Support Vector Machine Decision Surface')
>>> pl.axis('off')
>>> pl.show()
```

Creating a supervised learning model with random forest

The random forest model is an ensemble model; it takes an ensemble (selection) of decision trees to create its model. The idea is to take a random sample of weak learners (a random subset of the training data) and have them vote to select the strongest and best model. The random forest model can be used for either classification or regression. In the following example, the random forest model is used to classify the Iris species.

Loading your data

This code listing will load the iris dataset into your session:

```
>>> from sklearn.datasets import load_iris
>>> iris = load_iris()
```

Creating an instance of the classifier

The following two lines of code create an instance of the classifier. The first line imports the random forest library. The second line creates an instance of the random forest algorithm:

```
>>> from sklearn.ensemble import RandomForestClassifier
>>> rf = RandomForestClassifier(n_estimators=15,
            random_state=111)
```

The n_estimators parameter in the constructor is a commonly used tuning parameter for the random forest model. The value is used to build the number of trees in the forest. It's generally between 10 and 100 percent of the dataset, but it depends on the data you're using. Here, the value is set at 15, which is 10 percent of the data. Later in the *Evaluating the model* section, you will see that changing the parameter value to 150 (100 percent) produces the same results.

The n_estimators is used to tune model performance and overfitting. The greater the value, the better the performance but at the cost of overfitting. The smaller the value, the higher the chances of not overfitting but at the cost of lower performance. Also, there is a point where increasing the number will generally degrade in accuracy improvement and may dramatically increase the computational power needed. The parameter defaults to 10 if it is omitted in the constructor.

As with the other classifiers created earlier in this chapter (Creating a supervised learning model with Support Vector Machines; Creating a supervised learning model with logistic regression), the steps to train, test, and evaluate are similar.

Running the training data

You'll need to split the dataset into training and test sets before you can create an instance of the random forest classifier. The following code will accomplish that task:

```
>>> from sklearn import cross_validation
>>> X_train, X_test, y_train, y_test =
            cross_validation.train_test_split(iris.data,
            iris.target, test_size=0.10, random_state=111)
>>> rf = rf.fit(X_train, y_train)
```

1. Line 1 imports the library that allows us to split the dataset into two parts.

2. Line 2 calls the function from the library that splits the dataset into two parts and assigns the now-divided datasets to two pairs of variables.

3. Line 3 takes the instance of the random forest classifier you just created,then calls the fit method to train the model with the training dataset.

Running the test data

In the following code, the first line feeds the test dataset to the model, then the third line displays the output:

```
>>> predicted = rf.predict(X_test)
>>> predicted
array([0, 0, 2, 2, 2, 0, 0, 2, 2, 1, 2, 0, 1, 2, 2])
```

Evaluating the model

You can cross-reference the output from the prediction against the y_test array. As a result, you can see that it predicted two test data points incorrectly. So the accuracy of the random forest model was 86.67 percent.

Here's the code:

```
>>> from sklearn import metrics
>>> predicted
array([0, 0, 2, 2, 2, 0, 0, 2, 2, 1, 2, 0, 1, 2, 2])
>>> y_test
array([0, 0, 2, 2, 1, 0, 0, 2, 2, 1, 2, 0, 2, 2, 2])
>>> metrics.accuracy_score(y_test, predicted)
0.8666666666666667      # 1.0 is 100 percent accuracy
>>> predicted == y_test
array([ True,  True,  True,  True,  False,  True,  True,
        True,  True,  True,  True,  True,  False,  True,
        True], dtype=bool)
```

How does the random forest model perform if we change the n_estimators parameter to 150? It looks like it won't make a difference for this small dataset. It produces the same result:

```
>>> rf = RandomForestClassifier(n_estimators=150,
            random_state=111)
>>> rf = rf.fit(X_train, y_train)
>>> predicted = rf.predict(X_test)
>>> predicted
array([0, 0, 2, 2, 2, 0, 0, 2, 2, 1, 2, 0, 1, 2, 2])
```

Comparing the classification models

The logistics regression and SVM classification models perform rather well using the Iris dataset. The logistic regression model with parameter C=1 was perfect in its predictions, while the SVM model and the logistic regression model with C=150 missed only one prediction. The random forest model missed two predictions and was the least accurate of the three models, but obtaining over 86 percent accuracy is still pretty good.

Indeed, the high accuracy of all three models is a result of having a small dataset that has data points that are pretty close to linearly separable. At the same time, the dataset is so small that the small differences in performance easily can be influenced by subtle randomness.

Interestingly, the logistic regression model with C=150 had a better-looking decision surface plot than the one with C=1, but it didn't perform better. That isn't such a big deal, considering that the test set is so small. If another random split between training set and test set had been selected, the results could have easily been different.

This reveals another source of complexity that crops up in model evaluation: the effect of sampling, and how choosing the training and testing sets can affect the model's output. Cross-validation techniques (see Chapter 15) can help minimize the impact of random sampling on the model's performance.

REMEMBER

For a larger dataset with non-linearly separable data, you would expect the results to deviate even more. In addition, choosing the appropriate model becomes increasingly difficult due to the complexity and size of the data. Be prepared to spend a great deal of time tuning your parameters to get an ideal fit.

TIP

When creating predictive models, try a few algorithms and exhaustively tune their parameters until you find what works best for your data. Then compare their outputs against each other. Almost all modeling algorithms have these kinds of parameters, and fine tuning them can have a measurable impact on the final result.

Chapter 13

Creating Basic Examples of Unsupervised Predictions

This chapter is about creating a few simple predictive models using unsupervised learning with clustering algorithms such as K-means, DBSCAN, and mean shift. These examples use the Python programming language, version 2.7.4, on a Windows machine. See Chapter 12 if you need instructions on installing Python and the `scikit-learn` machine-learning package.

No prior knowledge of supervised learning is required to understand the concepts of unsupervised learning. *Supervised learning* is when the output categories are known in the historical data; *unsupervised learning* is when the output categories are unknown. Chapter 12 covers examples of supervised learning with classification and regression algorithms.

You can read Chapters 12 and 13 independently. One advantage of reading both chapters in the same session is that you'll be able to reuse the work that you did to load the Iris dataset into the Python *interpreter* (the command line where you enter the code statements or commands). So if you're continuing from Chapter 12, you may skip the next section.

Getting the Sample Dataset

The sample Iris dataset is included in the installation of scikit-learn — along with a set of functions that load data into the Python session.

To load the Iris dataset, follow these steps:

1. **Open a new Python interactive shell session.**

   Use a new Python session so there isn't anything left over in memory and you have a clean slate to work with.

2. **Paste the following code at the prompt and press Enter:**

   ```
   >>> from sklearn.datasets import load_iris
   >>> iris = load_iris()
   ```

   After you run those two statements, you shouldn't see any messages from the interpreter. The variable iris should contain all the data from the iris.csv file.

3. **Enter the following command to confirm that variable iris contains the data:**

   ```
   >>> iris
   ```

   The command prints out a verbose description of the Iris dataset, followed by a list of all the data members. Please refer to Table 12-3 for the main properties and descriptions of the iris variable.

REMEMBER

You don't use a training dataset for an unsupervised learning task because you normally don't know the outcomes. Hence the dataset isn't labeled and the clustering algorithm doesn't accept a target value in its creation.

Using Clustering Algorithms to Make Predictions

In general, the use of clustering algorithms to create an unsupervised learning model entails the following general steps:

1. Prepare and load the data.

2. Fit the model.

3. Visualize the clusters.

4. Tune the parameters.

5. Repeat Steps 2 to 4 until you get the clustering output that you think yields the best results.

6. Evaluate the model.

Comparing clustering models

Unsupervised learning has many challenges — including not knowing what to expect when you run an algorithm. Each algorithm will produce different results; until you try a variety of solutions, you can't know which solution will work, but when you've really nailed it, you will know it when you see it. Either it will either provide value or it won't. Because that is through the lens of the business problem, at the end of the process you will know.

In the case of the Iris dataset, you know what the outcomes should be; as a result, you can tweak the algorithms to produce the desired outcomes. In real-world datasets, you won't have this luxury. You'll have to depend on some prior knowledge of the data (or intuition by the domain expert) to decide which initialization parameters and algorithms to use as you create your model.

We are starting with the famous Iris dataset because it makes the patterns especially easy to see, but you will face more challenges in real world situations; the outcomes are unknown and the desired result is difficult to find. For example, in K-means, choosing the right number of clusters is the key problem. If you find the right number of clusters, your data will yield insights with which you can make highly accurate predictions. On the flip side, choosing the wrong number of clusters may yield subpar results.

K-means algorithm is a good choice for datasets that have a small number of clusters with proportional sizes and linearly separable data — and you can scale it up to use the algorithm on very large datasets.

Think of *linearly separable* data as a bunch of points in a graph that can be separated using a straight line. If the data isn't linearly separable, then more advanced versions of K-means will have to be employed — which will become more expensive computationally and may not be suitable for very large datasets. In its standard implementation, the complexity to compute the cluster centers and distances is low.

K-means is widely employed to solve big-data problems because it's simple to use, effective, and highly scalable. No wonder most commercial vendors use the K-means algorithm as a key component of their predictive analytics packages.

The DBSCAN (Density-Based Spatial Clustering of Applications with Noise) and mean-shift implementations in `scikit-learn` don't require any user-defined initialization parameters to create an instance. You can override the default parameters during initialization if you want. Unfortunately, if you're using the default parameters, the algorithms can't provide a close match to the desired outcome.

That said, neither DBSCAN nor mean shift perform well with the Iris dataset. Even after exhaustive tweaking of the initialization parameters, it's still very hard to get an output that mimics the known outcomes for Iris. DBSCAN is better suited for datasets that have disproportional cluster sizes, and whose data can be separated in a non-linear fashion. While mean shift can handle arbitrary shapes and sizes very well, its standard implementation isn't very scalable, as it is a $O(n^2)$ algorithm, and may not work well on high-dimensional data. Like K-means, DBSCAN is scalable, but using it on very large datasets requires more memory and computing power. You get a closer look at DBSCAN and mean shift in action later in this chapter.

Creating an unsupervised learning model with K-means

The K-means algorithm normally expects one initialization parameter from the user in order to create an instance. It needs to know how many K clusters to use to perform its work. The K-means implementation in Python will use the default of $K=8$ if the user doesn't provide it.

Because you're using the Iris dataset, you already know that it has three clusters. As described in Chapter 12, the Iris dataset has three classes of the Iris flower (Setosa, Versicolor, and Virginica). In general, when you're creating an unsupervised learning task with a clustering algorithm, you wouldn't know how many clusters to specify. Some algorithms try to determine the best number of clusters by iterating through a range of clusters and then selecting the number of clusters that best fits its mathematical criteria.

The best way to get immediate results is to make an educated guess about the number of clusters to use — basing your estimate on features present in the data (whether one or multiple features), or on some other knowledge of the data you may have from the business domain expert.

This falling back on guesswork (even educated guesswork) is a major limitation of the K-means clustering algorithm. An upcoming section explores a couple of other clustering algorithms, DBSCAN and mean shift, that don't need the number of clusters in order to do their work.

Running the full dataset

To create an instance of the K-means clustering algorithm and run the data through it, type the following code in the interpreter.

```
>>> from sklearn.cluster import KMeans
>>> kmeans = KMeans(n_clusters=3, random_state=111)
>>> kmeans.fit(iris.data)
```

The first line of code imports the KMeans library into the session. The second line creates the model and stores it in a variable named kmeans. The model is created with the number of clusters set to 3. The third line fits the model to the Iris data. Fitting the model is the core part of the algorithm, where it will produce the three clusters with the given dataset and construct a mathematical function that describes the line or curve that best fits the data. To see the clusters that the algorithm produces, type the following code.

```
>>> kmeans.labels_
```

The output should look similar to this:

```
array([1, 1, 1, 1, 1, 1, 1, 1, 1, 1, 1, 1, 1, 1, 1, 1, 1,
       1, 1, 1, 1, 1, 1, 1, 1, 1, 1, 1, 1, 1, 1, 1, 1, 1,
       1, 1, 1, 1, 1, 1, 1, 1, 1, 1, 1, 1, 1, 1, 1, 0,
       0, 2, 0, 0, 0, 0, 0, 0, 0, 0, 0, 0, 0, 0, 0, 0,
       0, 0, 0, 0, 0, 0, 0, 0, 0, 2, 0, 0, 0, 0, 0, 0, 0,
       0, 0, 0, 0, 0, 0, 0, 0, 0, 0, 0, 0, 0, 0, 2, 0,
       2, 2, 2, 2, 0, 2, 2, 2, 2, 2, 2, 0, 0, 2, 2, 2, 2,
       0, 2, 0, 2, 0, 2, 2, 0, 0, 2, 2, 2, 2, 2, 0, 2, 2,
       2, 2, 0, 2, 2, 2, 0, 2, 2, 2, 0, 2, 2, 0])
```

This is how the K-means algorithm labels the data as belonging to clusters, without input from the user about the target values. Here the only thing K-means knew was what we provided it: the number of clusters. This result shows how the algorithm viewed the data, and what it learned about the relationships of data items to each other — hence the term *unsupervised learning*.

You can see right away that some of the data points were mislabeled. You know, from the Iris dataset, what the target values should be:

» The first 50 observations should be labeled the same (as 1s in this case).

  This range is known as the *Setosa class*.

» Observations 51 to 100 should be labeled the same (as 0s in this case).

  This range is known as the *Versicolor class*.

» Observations 101 to 150 should be labeled the same (as 2s in this case).

  This range is known as the *Virginica class*.

It doesn't matter whether K-means labeled each set of 50 with a 0, 1, or 2. As long as each set of 50 has the same label, it accurately predicted the outcome. It's up to you to give each cluster a name and to find meaning in each cluster. If you run the K-means algorithm again, it may produce an entirely different number for each set of 50 — but the meaning would be the same for each set (class).

TECHNICAL
STUFF

You can create a K-means model that can generate the same output each time by passing the `random_state` parameter with a fixed seed value to the function that creates the model. The algorithm depends on randomness to initialize the cluster centers. Providing a fixed seed value takes away the randomness. Doing so essentially tells K-means to select the same initial data points to initialize the cluster centers, every time you run the algorithm. It's possible to get a different outcome by removing the `random_state` parameter from the function.

Visualizing the clusters

REMEMBER

As mentioned in Chapter 12, the Iris dataset isn't easy to graph in its original form. Therefore, you have to reduce the number of dimensions by applying a *dimensionality reduction algorithm* that operates on all four fields and outputs two new numbers (that represent the original four fields) that you can use to do the plot.

You can see that the current shape of the Iris dataset is 150 rows, with each row having 4 fields. You can find the shape by entering this line of code:

```
>>> iris.data.shape
(150, 4)
```

The following code will do the dimension reduction:

```
>>> from sklearn.decomposition import PCA
>>> pca = PCA(n_components=2).fit(iris.data)
>>> pca_2d = pca.transform(iris.data)
```

After you run the dimensionality reduction code, you can see that the transformed iris data will be stored into a new variable name, pca_2d. You can verify that the shape has been transformed to two dimensions:

```
>>> pca_2d.shape
(150, 2)
```

You can also type the pca_2d variable into the interpreter and it will output arrays (think of an *array* as a container that stores items in a list) with two fields instead of four. Now that you have the reduced feature set, you can plot the results with the following code:

```
>>> import pylab as pl
>>> pl.figure('Figure 13-1')
>>> for i in range(0, pca_2d.shape[0]):
>>>     if iris.target[i] == 0:
>>>         c1 = pl.scatter(pca_2d[i,0],pca_2d[i,1],c='r',
                marker='+')
>>>     elif iris.target[i] == 1:
>>>         c2 = pl.scatter(pca_2d[i,0],pca_2d[i,1],c='g',
                marker='o')
>>>     elif iris.target[i] == 2:
>>>         c3 = pl.scatter(pca_2d[i,0],pca_2d[i,1],c='b',
                marker='*')
>>> pl.legend([c1, c2, c3], ['Setosa', 'Versicolor',
                'Virginica'])
>>> pl.title('Iris dataset with 3 clusters and known
                outcomes')
>>> pl.show()
```

The output of this code is a plot that should be similar to Figure 13-1. This is a plot representing how the known outcomes of the Iris dataset should look like. It's what you would like the K-means clustering to achieve. The figure shows a scatter plot, which is a graph of plotted points representing an observation on a graph, of all 150 observations. As indicated on the graph plots and legend:

» There are 50 pluses that represent the *Setosa class*.

» There are 50 circles that represent the *Versicolor class*.

» There are 50 stars that represent the *Virginica class*.

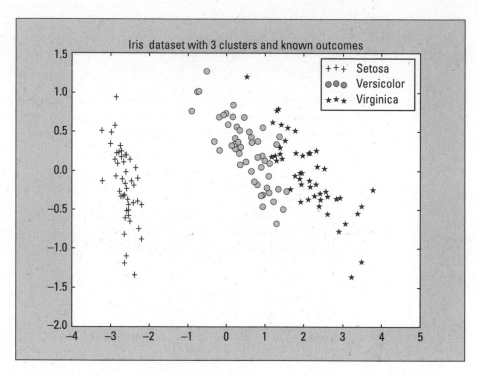

FIGURE 13-1:
Plotting data
elements from
the Iris dataset.

Figure 13-2 shows a visual representation of the data that we are asking K-means to cluster: a *scatter plot* with 150 data points that haven't been labeled (hence all the data points are the same color and shape). The K-means algorithm doesn't know any target outcomes. The actual data that we're going to run through the algorithm hasn't had its dimensionality reduced yet.

The following lines of code create this scatter plot, using the X and Y values of pca_2d and coloring all the data points black (c='black' sets the color to black).

```
>>> pl.figure('Figure 13-2')
>>> pl.scatter(pca_2d[:,0],pca_2d[:,1],c='black')
>>> pl.title('Iris dataset without labels as seen by K-means')
>>> pl.show()
```

If you try fitting the two-dimensional data that was reduced by PCA, the K-means algorithm will fail to cluster the Virginica and Versicolor classes correctly. Using PCA to preprocess the data will destroy too much information that K-means needs.

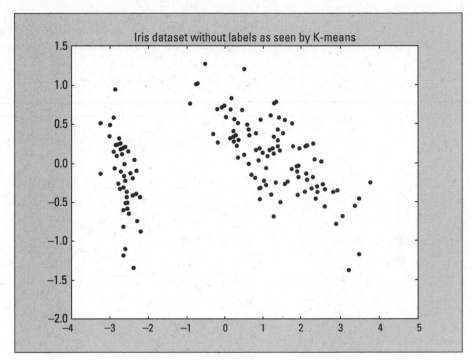

FIGURE 13-2:
Visual represen-
tation of data fed
into the K-means
algorithm.

After K-means has fitted the Iris data, you can make a scatter plot of the clusters
that the algorithm produced; just run the following code:

```
>>> pl.figure('Figure 13-3')
>>> for i in range(0, pca_2d.shape[0]):
>>>    if kmeans.labels_[i] == 1:
>>>       c1 = pl.scatter(pca_2d[i,0],pca_2d[i,1],c='r',
              marker='+')
>>>    elif kmeans.labels_[i] == 0:
>>>       c2 = pl.scatter(pca_2d[i,0],pca_2d[i,1],c='g',
              marker='o')
>>>    elif kmeans.labels_[i] == 2:
>>>       c3 = pl.scatter(pca_2d[i,0],pca_2d[i,1],c='b',
              marker='*')
>>> pl.legend([c1, c2, c3],['Cluster 1', 'Cluster 0',
              'Cluster 2'])
>>> pl.title('K-means clusters the Iris dataset into 3
              clusters')
>>> pl.show()
```

Recall that K-means labeled the first 50 observations with the label of 1, the
second 50 with label of 0, and the last 50 with label of 2. In the preceding code,

the lines with the `if`, `elif`, and `legend` statements reflects those labels. This change was made to make it easy to compare with the actual results.

The output of the scatter plot is shown in Figure 13-3.

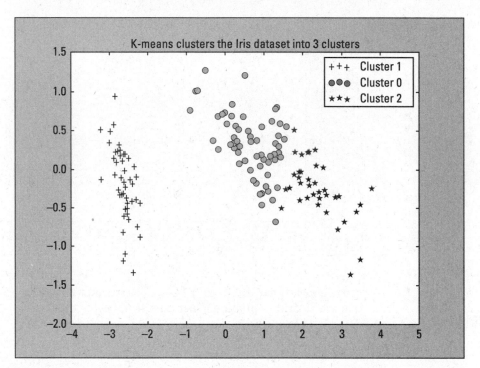

FIGURE 13-3:
The K-means
algorithm outputs
three clusters.

Compare the K-means clustering output (shown in Figure 13-3) to the original scatter plot (refer to Figure 13-1) — which provides labels because the outcomes are known. You can see that the two plots resemble each other. The K-means algorithm did a pretty good job with the clustering. Although the predictions aren't perfect, they come close. That's a win for the algorithm.

In unsupervised learning, you rarely get an output that's 100 percent accurate because real-world data is rarely that simple. You won't know for sure how many clusters to choose (or other initialization parameter(s) for other clustering algorithms). You will have to handle outliers (data points that don't seem consistent with others) and complex datasets that are dense, highly dimensional, and not linearly separable.

REMEMBER

You can only get to this point if you know how many clusters the dataset has. You don't need to worry about which features to use or reducing the dimensionality of a dataset that has so few features (in this case, four) to fit the model. We only reduced the dimensions for the sake of visualizing the data on a graph. We didn't fit the model with the dimensionality reduced dataset.

Here's the full listing of the code that creates both scatter plots and color-codes the data points:

```
>>> from sklearn.decomposition import PCA
>>> from sklearn.cluster import KMeans
>>> from sklearn.datasets import load_iris
>>> import pylab as pl
>>> iris = load_iris()
>>> pca = PCA(n_components=2).fit(iris.data)
>>> pca_2d = pca.transform(iris.data)
>>> pl.figure('Reference Plot')
>>> pl.scatter(pca_2d[:, 0], pca_2d[:, 1], c=iris.target)
>>> kmeans = KMeans(n_clusters=3, random_state=111)
>>> kmeans.fit(iris.data)
>>> pl.figure('K-means with 3 clusters')
>>> pl.scatter(pca_2d[:, 0], pca_2d[:, 1], c=kmeans.labels_)
>>> pl.show()
```

Repeating the runs with a different K-value

A common outcome for clustering the Iris dataset is a two-cluster solution: one cluster contains the Setosa class and the other contains both the Versicolor and Virginica classes.

If you didn't have prior knowledge of how many clusters the Iris dataset has, you may have chosen to use two clusters with the K-means algorithm. With two clusters, K-means correctly clusters the Setosa class and combines the Virginica and the Versicolor classes into a single cluster.

The following code uses K-means to create two clusters, after which it displays a scatter plot of the results. Figure 13-4 shows the output of the K-means two-cluster solution.

```
>>> kmeans2 = KMeans(n_clusters=2, random_state=111)
>>> kmeans2.fit(iris.data)
>>> pl.figure('Figure 13-4')
>>> for i in range(0, pca_2d.shape[0]):
```

```
>>>    if kmeans2.labels_[i] == 1:
>>>        c1 = pl.scatter(pca_2d[i,0],pca_2d[i,1],c='r',
               marker='+')
>>>    elif kmeans2.labels_[i] == 0:
>>>        c2 = pl.scatter(pca_2d[i,0],pca_2d[i,1],c='g',
               marker='o')
>>> pl.legend([c1, c2], ['Cluster 1', 'Cluster 2'])
>>> pl.title('K-means clusters the Iris dataset into 2
           clusters')
>>> pl.show()
```

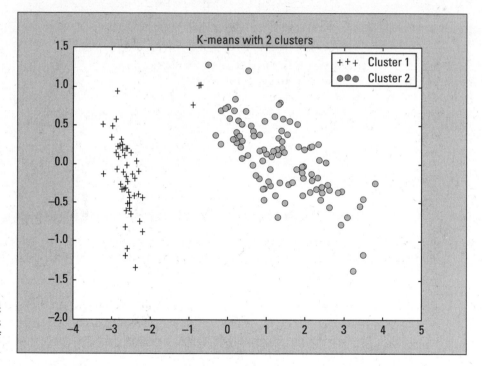

FIGURE 13-4:
Here's a K-means output of two clusters.

At first glance, the results seem to be within reason — and a potential candidate you might use to create your model. In fact, if you did use those results to make your predictive model, your success rate would be around 67 percent — not bad for a very basic model that uses unsupervised learning and a wrong guess for the number of clusters. You would have expected the accuracy to be around 67 percent because the algorithm is very accurate at clustering the linearly separable Setosa class (33.3 percent of the data). Clustering the remaining data into a single class would automatically give it an additional 33.3-percent accuracy because it only has two possibilities to choose from.

A four-cluster solution may yield a result that has one large cluster on the left (Setosa) and one on the right that's separated into three clusters (as shown in Figure 13-5). As you start increasing the value of *K* (the number of clusters), however, your results become less meaningful.

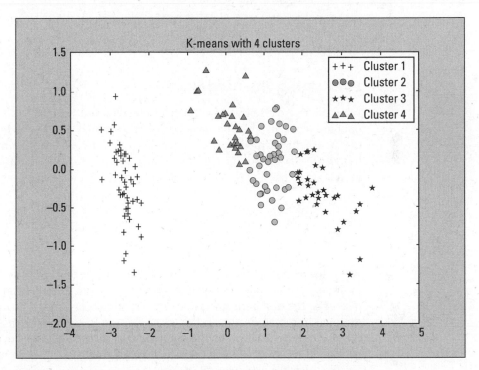

FIGURE 13-5:
Here's a K-means
output of
four clusters.

The following code creates a four-cluster model with K-means:

```
>>> kmeans4 = KMeans(n_clusters=4, random_state=111)
>>> kmeans4.fit(iris.data)
>>> pl.figure('Figure 13-5')
>>> for i in range(0, pca_2d.shape[0]):
>>>    if kmeans4.labels_[i] == 1:
>>>        c1 = pl.scatter(pca_2d[i,0],pca_2d[i,1],c='r',
               marker='+')
>>>    elif kmeans4.labels_[i] == 0:
>>>        c2 = pl.scatter(pca_2d[i,0],pca_2d[i,1],c='g',
               marker='o')
>>>    elif kmeans4.labels_[i] == 2:
>>>        c3 = pl.scatter(pca_2d[i,0],pca_2d[i,1],c='b',
               marker='*')
```

```
>>>    elif kmeans4.labels_[i] == 3:
>>>        c4 = pl.scatter(pca_2d[i,0],pca_2d[i,1],c='c',
            marker='^')
>>> pl.legend([c1, c2, c3, c4], ['Cluster 1', 'Cluster 2',
    'Cluster 3', 'Cluster 4'])
>>> pl.title('K-means clusters the Iris dataset into 4
            clusters')
>>> pl.show()
```

Evaluating the model

When you've chosen your number of clusters and have set up the algorithm to populate the clusters, you have a predictive model. The following example uses the three-cluster model previously built in this chapter. You can make predictions based on new incoming data by calling the predict function of the K-means instance and passing in an array of observations. It looks like this:

```
>>> # to call the predict function with a single observation
>>> kmeans.predict([[5.1,  3.5,  1.4,  0.2]])
array([1])
```

When the predict function finds the cluster center that the observation is closest to, it outputs the index of that cluster center's array. Python arrays are indexed at 0 (that is, the first item starts at 0). Observations closest to a cluster center will be grouped into that cluster. In this example, the K-means algorithm predicts that the observation belongs to Cluster 1 (Setosa in this case) — an easy prediction because the Setosa class is linearly separable and far away from the other two classes. Also, we just selected the very first observation from the dataset to make the prediction verifiable and easy to explain. You can see that the attributes of the observation we're trying to predict are very close to the second cluster center's attributes (kmeans.cluster_centers_[1]).

The new observation that we are trying to predict [5.1, 3.5, 1.4, 0.2] is closest to the second cluster center [5.006, 3.418,1.464, 0.244].

To see all the cluster centers, type the following code:

```
>>> kmeans.cluster_centers_
array([[ 5.9016129 ,  2.7483871 ,  4.39354839,  1.43387097],
       [ 5.006      ,  3.418      ,  1.464      ,  0.244      ],
       [ 6.85        ,  3.07368421,  5.74210526,  2.07105263]])
```

You can also use the `predict` function to evaluate a set of observations, as shown here:

```
>>> # to call the predict method with a set of data points
>>> kmeans.predict([[ 5.1,   3.5,   1.4,   0.2 ],
                    [ 5.9,   3.0,   5.1,   1.8 ]])
array([1,0])
```

The result is an array with a list of predictions. The first observation is predicted to be Cluster 1, and the second is predicted to be Cluster 0.

To see the cluster labels that the K-means algorithm produces, type the following code:

```
>>> kmeans.labels_
array([1, 1, 1, 1, 1, 1, 1, 1, 1, 1, 1, 1, 1, 1, 1, 1,
       1, 1, 1, 1, 1, 1, 1, 1, 1, 1, 1, 1, 1, 1, 1, 1,
       1, 1, 1, 1, 1, 1, 1, 1, 1, 1, 1, 1, 1, 1, 1, 0,
       0, 2, 0, 0, 0, 0, 0, 0, 0, 0, 0, 0, 0, 0, 0, 0,
       0, 0, 0, 0, 0, 0, 0, 0, 0, 2, 0, 0, 0, 0, 0, 0,
       0, 0, 0, 0, 0, 0, 0, 0, 0, 0, 0, 0, 0, 0, 2, 0,
       2, 2, 2, 2, 0, 2, 2, 2, 2, 2, 0, 0, 2, 2, 2, 2,
       0, 2, 0, 2, 0, 2, 2, 0, 0, 2, 2, 2, 2, 2, 0, 2, 2,
       2, 2, 0, 2, 2, 2, 0, 2, 2, 2, 0, 2, 2, 0])
```

Although you know that the three-cluster solution is correct, don't be surprised if intuitively the two-cluster solution seems to look the best and the four-cluster solution also looks quite reasonable. If you increase the number of clusters beyond three, your predictions' success rate starts to break down. With a little bit of luck (and some educated guessing), you'll choose the best number of clusters. Consider the process as mixing a little bit of art with science. Even the algorithm itself uses randomness in its selection of the initial data points it uses to start each cluster. So even if you're guessing, you're in good company.

For this toy dataset, we can measure how well K-means clustered the 150 observations, because we know the outcomes. We can look at the labels K-means created and see how the clusters were formed. We know that the first 50 observations should be the same cluster (Cluster 1), the second 50 should be the same cluster (Cluster 0), and the last 50 should be the same cluster (Cluster 2). Here are the actual results:

>> K-means clustered the first 50 together.

>> For the second group of 50, a couple of 2's were mixed in; for that group, the error was 2/50, or 4 percent.

» For the third group of 50, there was a mix of 0's and 2's. The 0's belonged to the second cluster. So 14 out of 50 (28 percent) were incorrectly clustered with this group.

» The total error is 16/150, or 10.67 percent.

Evaluating the performance of an algorithm requires a label that represents the *expected* value and a *predicted* value to compare it with. Remember that when you apply a clustering algorithm to an unsupervised learning model, you don't know what the expected values are — and you don't give labels to the clustering algorithm. The algorithm puts data points into clusters on the basis of which data points are most similar to one another by finding the closest cluster center for each observation. For the Iris dataset, K-means has no concept of Setosa, Versicolor, or Virginica classes; it only knows it's supposed to cluster the data into three clusters and name them randomly from 0 to 2.

The purpose of unsupervised learning with clustering is for data exploration; to find meaningful relationships in the data, preferably where you couldn't have seen them otherwise. Did the model form distinct and interpretable groups of clusters for a market segmentation project? It's up to you to decide whether those relationships are a good basis for an actionable insight.

Creating an unsupervised learning model with DBSCAN

As mentioned earlier, DBSCAN is a popular clustering algorithm used as an alternative to K-means. It doesn't require that you input the number of clusters in order to run. But in exchange, you have to tune two other parameters. The scikit-learn implementation provides a default for the two parameters, eps and min_samples, but you're generally expected to tune those. The eps parameter is the maximum distance between two data points to be considered in the same neighborhood. The min_samples parameter is the minimum amount of data points in a neighborhood to be considered a cluster.

One advantage that DBSCAN has over K-means is that DBSCAN isn't restricted to a set number of clusters during initialization. The algorithm will determine a number of clusters based on the density of a region. Keep in mind, however, that the algorithm depends on the eps and min_samples parameters to figure out what the density of each cluster should be. The thinking is that these two parameters are much easier to choose for some clustering problems.

TIP

In practice, you should test with multiple clustering algorithms.

Because the DBSCAN algorithm has a built-in concept of noise, it's commonly used to detect outliers in the data — for example, fraudulent activity in credit cards, e-commerce, or insurance claims.

Running the full dataset

You'll need to load the Iris dataset into your Python session. If you're continuing from the preceding section and already have it loaded, you can skip Steps 1 and 2. Here's the procedure:

1. **Open a new Python interactive shell session.**

Use a new Python session so that memory is clear and you have a clean slate to work with.

2. **Paste the following code in the prompt and observe the output:**

```
>>> from sklearn.datasets import load_iris
>>> iris = load_iris()
```

After running those two statements, you shouldn't see any messages from the interpreter. The variable iris should contain all the data from the iris.csv file.

3. **Create an instance of DBSCAN. Type the following code into the interpreter:**

```
>>> from sklearn.cluster import DBSCAN
>>> dbscan = DBSCAN()
```

The first line of code imports the DBSCAN library into the session for you to use. The second line creates an instance of DBSCAN with default values for eps and min_samples.

4. **Check which parameters were used by typing the following code into the interpreter:**

```
>>> dbscan
DBSCAN(algorithm='auto', eps=0.5, leaf_size=30,
    metric='euclidean', min_samples=5, p=None,
    random_state=None)
```

5. **Fit the Iris data into the DBSCAN clustering algorithm by typing the following code into the interpreter:**

```
>>> dbscan.fit(iris.data)
```

6. To check the outcome, type the following code into the interpreter:

```
>>> dbscan.labels_
array([ 0.,  0.,  0.,  0.,  0.,  0.,  0.,  0.,  0.,  0.,
        0.,  0.,  0.,  0.,  0.,  0.,  0.,  0.,  0.,  0.,
        0.,  0.,  0.,  0.,  0.,  0.,  0.,  0.,  0.,  0.,
        0.,  0.,  0.,  0.,  0.,  0.,  0.,  0.,  0.,  0.,
        0., -1.,  0.,  0.,  0.,  0.,  0.,  0.,  0.,  0.,
        1.,  1.,  1.,  1.,  1.,  1.,  1., -1.,  1.,  1.,
       -1.,  1.,  1.,  1.,  1.,  1.,  1.,  1., -1.,  1.,
        1.,  1.,  1.,  1.,  1.,  1.,  1.,  1.,  1.,  1.,
        1.,  1.,  1.,  1.,  1.,  1.,  1., -1.,  1.,  1.,
        1.,  1.,  1., -1.,  1.,  1.,  1.,  1., -1.,  1.,
        1.,  1.,  1.,  1.,  1., -1., -1.,  1., -1., -1.,
        1.,  1.,  1.,  1.,  1.,  1.,  1., -1., -1.,  1.,
        1.,  1., -1.,  1.,  1.,  1.,  1.,  1.,  1.,  1.,
        1., -1.,  1.,  1., -1., -1.,  1.,  1.,  1.,  1.,
        1.,  1.,  1.,  1.,  1.,  1.,  1.,  1.,  1.,  1.])
```

If you look very closely, you'll see that DBSCAN produced three groups (-1, 0, and 1).

Visualizing the clusters

Let's get a scatter plot of the DBSCAN output. Type the following code:

```
>>> import pylab as pl
>>> from sklearn.decomposition import PCA
>>> pca = PCA(n_components=2).fit(iris.data)
>>> pca_2d = pca.transform(iris.data)
>>> for i in range(0, pca_2d.shape[0]):
>>>     if dbscan.labels_[i] == 0:
>>>         c1 = pl.scatter(pca_2d[i,0],pca_2d[i,1],c='r',
                marker='+')
>>>     elif dbscan.labels_[i] == 1:
>>>         c2 = pl.scatter(pca_2d[i,0],pca_2d[i,1],c='g',
                marker='o')
>>>     elif dbscan.labels_[i] == -1:
>>>         c3 = pl.scatter(pca_2d[i,0],pca_2d[i,1],c='b',
                marker='*')
>>> pl.legend([c1, c2, c3], ['Cluster 1', 'Cluster 2',
            'Noise'])
>>> pl.title('DBSCAN finds 2 clusters and noise)
>>> pl.show()
```

The scatter plot output of this code is shown in Figure 13-6.

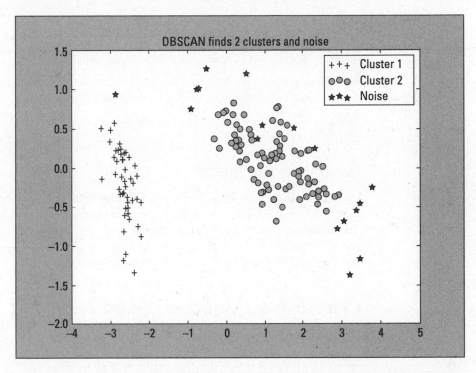

FIGURE 13-6:
DBSCAN finds
two clusters
and noise.

You can see that DBSCAN produced three groups. Note, however, that the figure closely resembles a two-cluster solution: It shows only 17 instances of label –1. That's because it's a two-cluster solution; the third group (–1) is noise (outliers).

In addition to enhancing marketing campaigns, predictive analytics can serve as a tool to fight fraud. Many industries are plagued with fraud — which is costly to combat on a large scale. The noise in the DBSCAN results can indicate that there is something abnormal or suspicious with those occurrences. The thinking is that fraud is unusual, and won't happen as commonly as normal transactions. Thus an *outlier detection* algorithm looks for events that fall outside regular patterns to detect fraud.

You can increase the distance parameter (eps) from the default setting of 0.5 to 0.9, and it will become a two-cluster solution with no noise. The distance parameter is the maximum distance an observation is to the nearest cluster. The greater the value for the distance parameter, the fewer clusters are found because clusters eventually merge into other clusters. The -1 labels are scattered around Cluster 1 and Cluster 2 in a few locations:

TIP

>> Near the edges of Cluster 2 (Versicolor and Virginica classes)

>> Near the center of Cluster 2 (Versicolor and Virginica classes)

The graph only shows a two-dimensional representation of the data. The distance can also be measured in higher dimensions.

>> One instance above Cluster 1 (the Setosa class)

Evaluating the model

In this example, DBSCAN didn't produce the ideal outcome with the default parameters for the Iris dataset. Its performance was pretty consistent with other clustering algorithms that end up with a two-cluster solution. The Iris dataset doesn't take advantage of DBSCAN's most powerful features — noise detection and the capability to discover clusters of arbitrary shapes.

Creating an unsupervised learning model with mean shift

Another clustering algorithm offered in `scikit-learn` is the mean shift algorithm. This algorithm, like DBSCAN, doesn't require you to specify the number of clusters, or any other parameters, when you create the model. The primary tuning parameter for this algorithm is called the `bandwidth` parameter. You can think of `bandwidth` like choosing the size of a round window that can encompass the data points in a cluster. Choosing a value for bandwidth isn't trivial, so we'll go with the default.

Running the full dataset

The steps to create a new model with a different algorithm is essentially the same each time. If you've been following along in this chapter or Chapter 12, you'll most likely have everything nearly set up. The steps are similar to the steps for creating the model with K-means:

1. **Open a new Python interactive shell session.**

Use a new Python session so that memory is clear and you have a clean slate to work with.

2. **Paste the following code in the prompt and observe the output:**

```
>>> from sklearn.datasets import load_iris
>>> iris = load_iris()
```

3. **Create an instance of mean shift. Type the following code into the interpreter:**

```
>>> from sklearn.cluster import MeanShift
>>> ms = MeanShift()
```

Mean shift created with default value for bandwidth.

4. **Check which parameters were used by typing the following code into the interpreter:**

```
>>> ms
MeanShift(bandwidth=None, bin_seeding=False,
    cluster_all=True, min_bin_freq=1, n_jobs=1,
    seeds= None)
```

5. **Fit the Iris data into the mean shift clustering algorithm by typing the following code into the interpreter:**

```
>>> ms.fit(iris.data)
```

6. **To check the outcome, type the following code into the interpreter:**

```
>>> ms.labels_
array([1, 1, 1, 1, 1, 1, 1, 1, 1, 1, 1, 1, 1, 1, 1, 1, 1,
       1, 1, 1, 1, 1, 1, 1, 1, 1, 1, 1, 1, 1, 1, 1, 1, 1,
       1, 1, 1, 1, 1, 1, 1, 1, 1, 1, 1, 1, 1, 1, 1, 1, 0,
       0, 0, 0, 0, 0, 0, 0, 0, 0, 0, 0, 0, 0, 0, 0, 0, 0,
       0, 0, 0, 0, 0, 0, 0, 0, 0, 0, 0, 0, 0, 0, 0, 0, 0,
       0, 0, 0, 0, 0, 0, 0, 0, 0, 0, 0, 0, 0, 1, 0, 0, 0,
       0, 0, 0, 0, 0, 0, 0, 0, 0, 0, 0, 0, 0, 0, 0, 0, 0,
       0, 0, 0, 0, 0, 0, 0, 0, 0, 0, 0, 0, 0, 0, 0, 0, 0,
       0, 0, 0, 0, 0, 0, 0, 0, 0, 0, 0, 0, 0, 0, 0, 0])
```

Mean shift produced two clusters (0 and 1).

Visualizing the clusters

A scatter plot is a good way to visualize the relationship between a large number of data points. It's useful for visually identifying clusters of data and finding data points that are distant from formed clusters.

Let's produce a scatter plot of the DBSCAN output. Type the following code:

```
>>> import pylab as pl
>>> from sklearn.decomposition import PCA
>>> pca = PCA(n_components=2).fit(iris.data)
>>> pca_2d = pca.transform(iris.data)
>>> pl.figure('Figure 13-7')
>>> for i in range(0, pca_2d.shape[0]):
>>>     if ms.labels_[i] == 1:
>>>         c1 = pl.scatter(pca_2d[i,0],pca_2d[i,1],c='r',
                marker='+')
>>>     elif ms.labels_[i] == 0:
>>>         c2 = pl.scatter(pca_2d[i,0],pca_2d[i,1],c='g',
                marker='o')
>>> pl.legend([c1, c2], ['Cluster 1', 'Cluster 2')]
>>> pl.title('Mean shift finds 2 clusters)
>>> pl.show()
```

The scatter plot output of this code is shown in Figure 13-7.

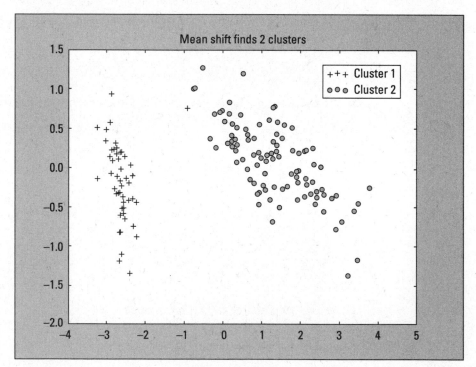

FIGURE 13-7: Mean shift finds two clusters.

Figure 13-7 shows that mean shift found two clusters. You can try to tune the model with the bandwidth parameter to see if you can get a three-cluster solution. Mean shift is very sensitive to the bandwidth parameter:

» If the chosen value is too big, then the clusters will tend to combine and the final output will be a smaller number of clusters than desired.

» If the chosen value is too small, then the algorithm may produce too many clusters and it will take longer to run.

Evaluating the model

Mean shift didn't produce the ideal results with the default parameters for the Iris dataset, but a two-cluster solution is in line with other clustering algorithms. Each project has to be examined individually to see how well the number of cluster fits the business problem. The obvious benefit of using mean shift is that you don't have to predetermine the number of clusters. In fact, you can use mean shift as a tool to find the number of clusters for creating a K-means model. Mean shift is often used for computer vision applications because it's good at lower dimensions, accommodates clusters of any shape, and accommodates clusters of any size.

Chapter 14

Predictive Modeling with R

A book covering the major facets of predictive analysis isn't complete unless it covers the R programming language. Our goal is to get you up and running as quick as possible. That goal entails getting you started making predictions and experimenting with predictive analysis, using standard tools such as R and the algorithms data scientists and statisticians use to make predictive models.

So do you have to know how to program to create predictive models? We would answer, "probably not, but it surely helps." Relax. We think you'll have fun learning R. Granted, this chapter is pretty high-level, so you may read it just to boost your understanding of how data scientists and statisticians use R.

In an enterprise environment, you'll most likely use commercial tools available from industry vendors. Getting familiar with a free, open-source, widely used, powerful tool like R prepares you to use the commercial tools with ease. By that point, you'll have gotten a big dose of the terminology, understand how to handle the data, and know all the steps of predictive modeling. After doing all those steps "by hand," you'll be well prepared to use the commercial tools.

Open-source R has memory and computational limits for enterprise-level big data analysis. Even so, open-source R is more than capable of handling most datasets for learning on a standard personal computer. On a powerfully equipped machine, it can handle datasets up to a few gigabytes. Beyond a few gigabytes, the computer may either run out of memory or take a very long time to run the machine learning algorithms.

Commercial enterprise tools with R aim to smooth out all the complexities of storing, analyzing, and processing big data; they even choose the algorithms for you. Learning some R helps you understand what the software tools are doing under the hood. That may give you the confidence to experiment even more by adjusting the default values and tweaking stuff here and there to see how it changes your predictive model.

R is an easy language with which to start learning programming. It has most, if not all, the same features you'll find in most of the programming languages commonly used for commercial software — Java, C++, Python, and such. So if you already have a programming language under your belt, this should be a cakewalk.

If R is the first programming language you've been exposed to, it'll still be easy, but it'll require some time spent playing around with it. But that's the beauty of the R language: You can play around with it and learn as you go. There is no boilerplate code that you have to remember to put in your code to make it work. You don't have to compile the program for it to work. It just works.

R is an *interpreted* language, which means you can run it interactively. You can run each line of code one by one and get an instant output (provided the code isn't for an intensive operation, and most operations in R shouldn't be intensive).

We also introduce you to the RStudio integrated development environment (IDE). Using an IDE to write code will give you further help in learning R. IDEs have a vast number of features that even the most seasoned developers depend on. Using a commercial IDE for a software development class may seem over the top to seasoned programmers who prefer a plain text editor like vi or emacs with programming language support and syntax highlighting. Professional software development benefits from the use an IDE because the volume of production-level code is enormous. Even if you wrote the entire code base, there's no way to fully understand and navigate through all that code without an IDE. An IDE also lets you to do things much faster and easier.

Programming in R

R is a programming language originally written for statisticians to do statistical analysis. It's open-source software, used extensively in academia to teach such disciplines as statistics, bio-informatics, and economics. From its humble beginnings, it has since been extended to do data modeling, data mining, and predictive analysis.

R has a very active community; free code contributions are being made constantly and consistently. One of the benefits of using an open-source tool such as R is that most of the data analysis that you'll want to do has already been done by someone. Code samples are posted on many message boards and by universities. If you're stuck with some problematic code, simply post a question on a message board (such as stack-exchange or stack-overflow) and you'll have an answer in no time.

Because R is free to use, it's the perfect tool to use to build a rapid prototype to show management the benefits of predictive analytics. You don't have to ask management to buy anything in order to get started right away. Any one of your data scientists, business analysts, statisticians, or software engineers can do the prototype without any further investment in software.

Therefore R can be an inexpensive way to experiment with predictive analytics without having to purchase enterprise software. After you prove that predictive analytics can add (or is adding) value, you should be able to convince management to consider getting a commercial-grade tool for your newly minted data-science team.

Installing R

Installing R is an easy process that takes less than thirty minutes. Most of the default settings can be accepted during the installation process. You can install R by downloading the installation program for Windows and other operating systems from the R project website at `https://cran.r-project.org`. From there, you can choose any one of the download mirrors to get the R installation binary. The mirror for this example is `https://cran.rstudio.com`.

This chapter guides you through the installation process for the Windows 10 operating system and the latest R release (version R-3.3.1). After you get to the RStudio website, look for the downloads link to get the file. After you've downloaded the file, just double-click it to begin the installation process.

Here is a direct link to the download page:

```
https://cran.rstudio.com/bin/windows/base/
```

After you install R, there should be two icons for R on your desktop: a 32-bit version and a 64-bit version. Choose the appropriate version for your computer. You can find the system type of your machine by going to the system settings and looking for the "About" tab. This computer is a 64-bit operating system, x64-based processor. Click the R x64 3.3.1 icon to confirm that the installation was successful.

If your installation succeeded, you should see the R Console, as shown in Figure 14-1.

FIGURE 14-1:
RGui console.

Installing RStudio

After you've finished the R installation process, you may install RStudio. Installing the RStudio IDE is just as easy as installing R. You can download RStudio Desktop open-source edition from their website at www.rstudio.com. You'll want to install the desktop version appropriate for your operating system (for example, RStudio version 0.99.902 for Windows 10). After you've downloaded the file, just double-click it to begin the installation process.

Here is a direct link to the download page:

www.rstudio.com/products/rstudio/download

If your installation succeeded, the RStudio program should have been added to the Start menu. If you can't find it, use the search tool to look for "RStudio."

Getting familiar with the environment

RStudio is a graphical user interface for developing R programs. The default interface (the way it looks when you first start the program) has three window panes. Go to the file menu and create a new R script by going to File -> New File -> R Script, or simply press Control+Shift+N. You'll see a screen similar to what is shown in Figure 14-2. You'll use all four of them frequently; we describe what each one is used for and how to use it.

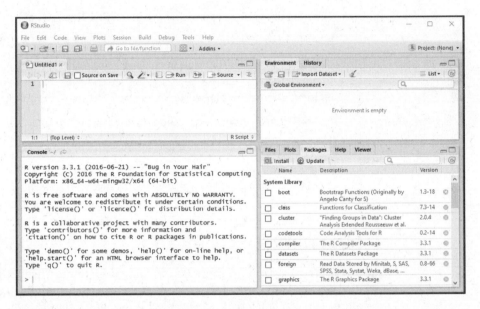

FIGURE 14-2:
RStudio in
the default view
of the graphical
user interface.

>> **The top-left window is your script window.**

This is where you can copy and paste R code. You can run the code line-by-line or in chunks by highlighting the lines you want to execute. The script window is also where you can view the values of data frames. When you click a data frame from the workspace pane, it will open a new tab in the script pane with the data frame values.

>> **The bottom-left window is your console window.**

This is where you can type your R code one line at a time. It will execute each line immediately after you press carriage return, unlike the script window where you have to click the Run button to execute line(s) of code. The output (if there is any) is printed on the next line right after the command finishes execution.

>> **The top-right window is your workspace and history window.**

It has two tabs:

- The History tab stores the history of all the code you've executed in the current session.

- The Environment tab lists all the variables in the memory. Here you can click the variables to see their values and (if you so choose) load datasets interactively.

>> **The bottom-right window is where you'll find five tabs of interest:**

- A Help tab offers documentation such as descriptions of functions.

- The Packages tab shows all the packages installed and available to load by your program. The checked packages are the ones that have been loaded for your program to use. You can search and install new packages here.

- The Plots tab is where the output of any plots will appear.

- The Files tab is your file explorer inside RStudio.

- The Viewer tab is used to display local web content. It's like a web browser that can display either local web files or local web applications.

Learning just a bit of R

It doesn't take much to program something useful in R. The nice thing about R is that you can learn just what you need at the moment. And if you need something more, you can learn that, as you need it. So, at minimum, you'll need to know how to:

>> Assign values to variables

>> Do operations on those variables

>> Access and manipulate data types and structures

>> Call a function to do something

The upcoming subsections detail these operations. Everything else you can learn as you go.

Assigning variables

Variables can be assigned in several ways in R. The convention for R is to use the less-than sign (<) and the minus sign (−) together, making an arrow-like sign (<−). Another way (standard for other programming languages) is to use just the equal sign (=). One other feature in R is that you may assign a variable in either direction using less-than and greater-than symbols with the minus sign to make the arrow-like sign (<– or –>).

As described in the preceding paragraph, you can assign a value to a variable in one of three ways:

```
> x <- "hello there"
> x = "hello there"
> "hello there" -> x
```

The preceding three lines of code all do the same thing; knowing all the different ways will come in handy because you'll surely come across all of them when you start reading other people's code. As mentioned previously, the preferred way in R is the first one shown.

To print out the value of the variable, simply type the variable and then press Enter, like this:

```
> x
[1] "hello there"
```

In the RStudio console pane, a line that has a number between [ ] symbols shows you the output from the execution of the preceding line(s) of code.

TECHNICAL
STUFF

The R interpreter has a leading > sign as the command prompt in the console window. You can't copy and paste whole sections of code in that window because the > command prompt will be interpreted as part of the code. It will output an error if you do. You must use the script window of RStudio if you want to copy and paste sections of code.

Operating on variables

For most of its arithmetic and logical operators, R uses syntax that is standard to most other programming languages:

» These are examples of the arithmetic operators in R:

```
> w <- 5 + 5    # addition
> x <- w * 5    # multiplication
> y <- x / 5    # division
> z <- y - 5    # subtraction
```

The # symbol is the start of a comment; the R interpreter ignores comments. You can print out the values by using the concatenate function, like this:

```
> c(w,x,y,z)
[1] 10 50 10 5
```

A function is called when its name is followed by either parameters or arguments inside enclosing parenthesis. In the preceding example, c is the name for the concatenate function, followed by arguments w, x, y, z.

» These are examples of the logical operators in R:

```
w == y      # is equal to
x > z       # is greater than
y >= 10     # is greater than or equal to
z < w       # is less than
10 <= y     # is less than or equal to
```

All these comparisons evaluate to TRUE values; you can see the results by executing them:

```
> w == y
[1] TRUE
> x > z
[1] TRUE
> y >= 10
[1] TRUE
> z < w
[1] TRUE
> 10 <= y
[1] TRUE
```

Working with data types and structures

Data *types* are sometimes confused with data *structures*. Each variable in the program memory has a data type. Sure, you can get away with having several variables in your program and still be manageable. But that probably won't work so well if you have hundreds (or thousands) of variables; you have to give every variable a name so you can access it. It's more efficient to store all those variables in a logical collection.

For example, if you have a million customers, you can use the vector data structure (as shown in the "Data structures" section later in this chapter) to store the names of all your customers and give the vector a name of *customer*. That's one variable (customer) with a data type of character that stores all million customer names. You can use array notation to access each customer. (For more about array notation, flip to the upcoming subsection's discussion of data structures.)

DATA TYPES

Like other full-fledged programming languages, R offers many data types and data structures. You'll only be working with just a handful of them in this chapter. There is no need to specify the type that you're assigning to a variable; the interpreter will do that for you. However, you can specify or convert the type if the need arises; this is called *casting*. You'll see examples of casting when you load the dataset in a later section of this chapter. The data types that we'll be dealing with in this chapter are as follows:

» **Numerical:** These are your typical decimal numbers. These are called *floats* (short for *floating-point numbers*) or *doubles* in other languages.

» **Characters:** These are your strings formed with combinations of letters, characters, and numbers. They aren't meant to have any numerical meaning. These are called *strings* in other languages.

» **Logical:** TRUE or FALSE. Always capitalize these values in R. These values are called *Booleans* in other languages.

TECHNICAL
STUFF

Comparing a string of numbers to a numerical number results in the interpreter converting the string of numbers into a numerical and then doing a numerical comparison.

Examples of data types are as follows:

```
> i <- 10        # numeric
> j <- 10.0      # numeric
> k <- "10"      # character
> m <- i == j    # logical
> n <- i == k    # logical
```

After you execute those lines of code, you can find out their values and types by using the structure function str(). It displays the data type and value of the variable. That operation looks like this:

```
> str(i)
 num 10
> str(j)
 num 10
> str(k)
 chr "10"
```

```
> str(m)
  logi TRUE
> str(n)
  logi TRUE
```

TECHNICAL STUFF

The expression in the n assignment is an example of the interpreter temporarily converting the data type of k into a numeric to do the evaluation between numeric i and character k.

DATA STRUCTURES

R will need a place to store groups of data types in order to work with it efficiently. These are called *data structures*. A real-life example of this concept is a parking garage: It's a structure that stores automobiles efficiently. It's designed to park as many automobiles as possible, and allows for automobiles to efficiently enter and exit the structure (in theory, at least). Also, no other objects besides automobiles should be parked in a parking structure. The data structures we use in this chapter are as follows:

>> **Vectors:** Vectors store a set of values of a single data type. Think of it as a weekly pillbox. Each compartment in the pillbox can only store a certain type of object. After you put some pills in one of the compartments, all the other compartments must also be filled with either zero pills or more pills. You can't put coins in that same box; you have to use a different "pill box" (vector) for that. Likewise, once you store a number in a vector, all future values should also be numbers. Otherwise the interpreter converts all your numbers to characters.

>> **Matrices:** A *matrix* looks like an Excel spreadsheet: Essentially it's a table consisting of rows and columns. The data populates the empty cells by row or column order, in which you specify when you create the matrix.

REMEMBER

All columns in a matrix must have the same data type.

>> **Data frames:** A data frame is similar to a matrix, except a data frame's columns can contain different data types. The datasets used in predictive modeling are loaded into data frames and stored there for use in the model.

>> **Factors:** A *factor* is like a vector with a limited number of distinct values. The number of distinct values is referred to as its *level*. You can use factors to treat a column that has a limited and known number of values as categorical values. By default, character data is loaded into data frames as factors.

REMEMBER

You access vectors, matrices, and data frames by using *array notation*. For example, you would type **v[5]** to access the fifth element of vector *v*. For a two-dimensional matrix and data frame, you put in the row number and column number, separated by a comma, inside the square brackets. For example, you type **m[2,3]** to access the second row, third column value for matrix *m*.

REMEMBER

R vectors, matrices, and data frames start indexing at 1. Python and many other programming languages index at 0.

Data structures are an advanced subject in computer science. For now, we're sticking to the practical. Just remember that data structures were built to store specific types of data and they have functions for data insertion, deletion, and retrieval.

Calling a function

Functions are lines of code that do something useful and concrete. Because these operations are often repeated, they are usually saved with a name so you can *call* (use) them again. Typically a function takes an input parameter, does something with it, and outputs a value. You save functions in your own programs or libraries for future use.

There are many built-in functions in the R programming language for developers to use. You've already used the str() function to find out the structure of a variable. It can be used to find the structure of data objects like data frames, vectors, and matrices, not just simple data types like numerical, characters, and logicals. The following section shows an example of using the structure function on a data frame.

You can use the built-in help function to find out more about R commands and functions. In the RStudio console, typing in help with the parameter of str will bring up documentation on the str function in the bottom-right pane. The command looks like this:

```
> help(str)
```

REMEMBER

Calling a function will always be in the same form: the function name followed by parentheses. (Inside the parentheses is the parameter list that may or may not be empty).

Whenever you start to suspect that the operation you're doing must be common, check to see whether a function exists already that does it for you. Getting to know all the built-in functions in R will greatly improve your productivity and your code. Having a cheat sheet or reference card of all the built-in functions is handy when you're learning a new language. Here is a link to an R reference card:

http://cran.r-project.org/doc/contrib/Short-refcard.pdf

Making Predictions Using R

We use R to make three predictive models in this chapter. All the R commands are entered into the RStudio console (the bottom-left pane onscreen) for execution. The first predictive model uses a regression algorithm to predict an automobile's fuel economy as miles per gallon. The second and third predictive models use decision tree and random forest classifiers to predict which category of wheat a particular seed belongs to.

Predicting using regression

A crucial task in predictive analytics is to predict the *future* value of something — such as the value of a house, the price of a stock at a future date, or sales you want to forecast for a product. You can do such tasks by using *regression analysis* — a statistical method that investigates the relationship between variables.

Introducing the data

The dataset we use to make a prediction on is the Auto-MPG dataset. This dataset has 398 observations and nine attributes plus the label. The *label* is the expected outcome; it's used to train and evaluate the accuracy of the predictive model. The outcome that we're trying to predict is the expected mpg (attribute 1) of an automobile when given the values of the attributes.

Here are the attributes and label in the column order in which they are provided:

1. mpg
2. cylinders
3. displacement
4. horsepower
5. weight
6. acceleration
7. model year
8. origin
9. car name

You can get the dataset from the UCI machine-learning repository at

http://archive.ics.uci.edu/ml/datasets/Auto+MPG

To get the dataset from the UCI repository and load it into memory, type the following command into the console:

```
> autos <-
    read.csv("http://archive.ics.uci.edu/ml/machine-
    learning-databases/auto-mpg/auto-mpg.data",
    header=FALSE, sep="", as.is=TRUE)
```

You'll see that the dataset was loaded into memory as the data frame variable autos, by looking at your workspace pane (the top-right pane). Click the autos variable to view the data values in the source pane (the top-left pane). Figure 14-3 shows how the data looks in the source pane.

	V1	V2	V3	V4	V5	V6	V7	V8	V9
1	18	8	307.0	130.0	3504	12.0	70	1	chevrolet chevelle malibu
2	15	8	350.0	165.0	3693	11.5	70	1	buick skylark 320
3	18	8	318.0	150.0	3436	11.0	70	1	plymouth satellite
4	16	8	304.0	150.0	3433	12.0	70	1	amc rebel sst
5	17	8	302.0	140.0	3449	10.5	70	1	ford torino
6	15	8	429.0	198.0	4341	10.0	70	1	ford galaxie 500
7	14	8	454.0	220.0	4354	9.0	70	1	chevrolet impala
8	14	8	440.0	215.0	4312	8.5	70	1	plymouth fury iii
9	14	8	455.0	225.0	4425	10.0	70	1	pontiac catalina
10	15	8	390.0	190.0	3850	8.5	70	1	amc ambassador dpl

FIGURE 14-3: View of the autos data loaded into memory.

TECHNICAL STUFF

The data is from Bache, K. & Lichman, M. (2013). UCI Machine Learning Repository [http://archive.ics.uci.edu/ml]. Irvine, CA: University of California, School of Information and Computer Science.

Using the head and tail functions can come in handy sometimes if you just want to see the first and last five rows of the data. This is also a quick way to verify that you actually loaded the correct file and it was read correctly. The summary function can give you basic statistics on each column of the data. You can copy and paste the following three lines of code, separately, into the source pane and have the output shown in the console:

```
head(autos,5)
tail(autos,5)
summary(autos)
```

The output of `head` and `tail` isn't shown here. This is the output of the `summary` function:

```
         V1              V2              V3              V4
 Min.   : 9.00   Min.   :3.000   Min.   : 68.0   Length:398
 1st Qu.:17.50   1st Qu.:4.000   1st Qu.:104.2   Class :character
 Median :23.00   Median :4.000   Median :148.5   Mode  :character
 Mean   :23.51   Mean   :5.455   Mean   :193.4
 3rd Qu.:29.00   3rd Qu.:8.000   3rd Qu.:262.0
 Max.   :46.60   Max.   :8.000   Max.   :455.0
         V5              V6              V7              V8
 Min.   :1613    Min.   : 8.00   Min.   :70.00   Min.   :1.000
 1st Qu.:2224    1st Qu.:13.82   1st Qu.:73.00   1st Qu.:1.000
 Median :2804    Median :15.50   Median :76.00   Median :1.000
 Mean   :2970    Mean   :15.57   Mean   :76.01   Mean   :1.573
 3rd Qu.:3608    3rd Qu.:17.18   3rd Qu.:79.00   3rd Qu.:2.000
 Max.   :5140    Max.   :24.80   Max.   :82.00   Max.   :3.000
         V9
 Length:398
 Class :character
 Mode  :character
```

Preparing the data

You have to get the data into a form that the algorithm can use to build a model. To do so, you have to take some time to understand the data and to know the structure of the data. Type in the `str` function to find out the structure of the `autos` data. The command and its output look like this:

```
> str(autos)

'data.frame':    398 obs. of  9 variables:
 $ V1: num  18 15 18 16 17 15 14 14 14 15 ...
 $ V2: int  8 8 8 8 8 8 8 8 8 8 ...
 $ V3: num  307 350 318 304 302 429 454 440 455 390 ...
 $ V4: chr  "130.0" "165.0" "150.0" "150.0" ...
 $ V5: num  3504 3693 3436 3433 3449 ...
 $ V6: num  12 11.5 11 12 10.5 10 9 8.5 10 8.5 ...
 $ V7: int  70 70 70 70 70 70 70 70 70 70 ...
 $ V8: int  1 1 1 1 1 1 1 1 1 1 ...
 $ V9: chr  "chevrolet chevelle malibu" "buick skylark 320" "plymouth satellite"
           "amc rebel sst" ...
```

From looking at the structure, we can tell that there is some data preparation and cleanup to do. Here's a list of the needed tasks:

>> **Rename the column names.**

This isn't strictly necessary, but for the purposes of this example, it's better to use column names we can understand and remember.

>> **Change the data type of predictor variable V4** (horsepower) **to a** numeric **data type.**

In this example, horsepower is supposed to be a continuous numerical value and not a character data type that the function loaded it as by default.

>> **Handle missing values.**

Here horsepower has six missing values. You can find this by looking for "?" in the V4 column. Here is the code and output for that:

```
> sum(autos["V4"] == "?")
[1] 6
```

>> **Change the attributes that have discrete values to factors.**

Here cylinders, modelyear, and origin have discrete values.

>> **Discard the V9** (carname) **attribute.**

Here carname doesn't add value to the model that we're creating. If the origin attribute weren't given, we could have derived the origin from the carname attribute.

To rename the columns, type in the following code:

```
> colnames(autos) <-
        c("mpg","cylinders","displacement","horsepower",
        "weight","acceleration","modelYear","origin",
        "carName")
```

Next, we change the data type of horsepower to numeric with the following code:

```
> autos$horsepower <- as.numeric(autos$horsepower)
```

The program will complain because not all the values in horsepower were string representations of numbers. There were some missing values that were represented as the "?" character. That's fine for now because R converts each instance of ? into NA. The following line of code confirms that six missing values were converted into NA:

```
> sum(is.na(autos["horsepower"]))
[1] 6
```

A common way to handle the missing values of continuous variables is to replace each missing value with the mean of the entire column. The following line of code does that:

```
> autos$horsepower[is.na(autos$horsepower)] <-
        mean(autos$horsepower,na.rm=TRUE)
```

It's important to have na.rm=TRUE in the mean function. It tells the function not to use columns with null values in its computation. Without it, the function will return NA. The following line of code verifies that the operation worked there are no missing values for the horsepower attribute.

```
> sum(is.na(autos["horsepower"]))
[1] 0
```

Next, we change the attributes with discrete values to factors. We have identified three attributes as discrete. The following three lines of code change the attributes.

```
> autos$origin <- factor(autos$origin)
> autos$modelYear <- factor(autos$modelYear)
> autos$cylinders <- factor(autos$cylinders)
```

Finally, we remove the carname attribute from the data frame with this line of code:

```
> autos$carName <- NULL
```

At this point, the data is prepared for the modeling process. The following is a view of the structure after the data-preparation process:

```
> str(autos)

'data.frame':   398 obs. of  8 variables:
 $ mpg        : num  18 15 18 16 17 15 14 14 14 15 ...
 $ cylinders  : Factor w/ 5 levels "3","4","5","6",..:
            5 5 5 5 5 5 5 5 5 5 ...
```

```
$ displacement: num   307 350 318 304 302 429 454 440 455
              390 ...
$ horsepower  : num   130 165 150 150 140 198 220 215 225
              190 ...
$ weight      : num   3504 3693 3436 3433 3449 ...
$ acceleration: num   12 11.5 11 12 10.5 10 9 8.5 10 8.5
              ...
$ modelYear   : Factor w/ 13 levels "70","71","72",..:
              1 1 1 1 1 1 1 1 1 1 ...
$ origin      : Factor w/ 3 levels "1","2","3":
              1 1 1 1 1 1 1 1 1 1 ...
```

In the preceding output, you can see that the attributes cylinders, modelYear, and origin are now factors and the attribute carName has been removed.

Creating the model

We want to create a model that we can evaluate by using known outcomes. To do that, we're going to split our autos dataset into two sets: one for training the model and one for testing the model. A 70/30 split between training and testing datasets will suffice. The next two lines of code calculate and store the sizes of each set:

```
> trainSize <- round(nrow(autos) * 0.7)
> testSize <- nrow(autos) - trainSize
```

To output the values, type in the name of the variable used to store the value and press Enter. Here is the output:

```
> trainSize
[1] 279
> testSize
[1] 119
```

This code determines the sizes of the datasets that we intend to make our training and test datasets. We still haven't actually created those sets yet. Also, we don't want simply to call the first 279 observations the training set and call the last 119 observations the test set. That would create a bad model because the autos dataset appears ordered. Specifically, the modelYear column is ordered from smallest to largest.

From examining the data, you can see that most of the heavier, eight-cylinder, larger-displacement, greater-horsepower autos reside on the top of the dataset. From this observation, without having to run any algorithms on the data, you can already tell that (in general for this dataset) older cars compared to newer cars as follows:

>> Are heavier

>> Have eight cylinders

>> Have larger displacement

>> Have greater horsepower

Okay, obviously many people know something about automobiles, so a guess as to what the correlations are won't be too farfetched after you see the data. Someone with a lot of automobile knowledge may have already known this without even looking at the data. This is just a simple example of a domain (cars) that many people can relate to. If this was data about cancer, however, most people wouldn't immediately understand what each attribute means.

TIP

This is where a domain expert and a data modeler are vital to the modeling process. Domain experts may have the best knowledge of which attributes may be the most (or least) important — and how attributes correlate with each other. They can suggest to the data modeler which variables to experiment with. They can give bigger weights to more important attributes and/or smaller weights to attributes of least importance.

So we have to make a training dataset and a test dataset that are truly representative of the entire set. One way to do so is to create the training set from a random selection of the entire dataset. Additionally, we want to make this test reproducible so we can learn from the same example. Thus we set the seed for the random generator so we'll have the same "random" training set. The following code does that task:

```
> set.seed(123)
> training_indices <- sample(seq_len(nrow(autos)),
        size=trainSize)
> trainSet <- autos[training_indices, ]
> testSet <- autos[-training_indices, ]
```

Because the same seed was used to create the random sample of training indices, your output should be like this:

```
> training_indices
 [1] 115 313 162 349 371  18 208 395 216 178 372 176 262 221  40 345
[17]  95  17 125 362 337 386 241 373 246 265 203 385 107  55 355 332
[33] 253 291   9 174 275  79 398  84  52 148 357 131  54  49  83 164
[49]  94 300  16 154 277  43 193  71  44 257 305 127 225  32 130  92
```

```
[65]  273 150 269 367 263 145 248 206 232    1 155   72 123 197 113   36
[81]   78 212 132 249   33 137 308 278 379 369   41 201 106 307   98   57
[97]  237   29 141 153 179   99 329 282 142 261 268 389 120 383 270   87
[113] 393 271 205 312 324 331 351 320 181   89   85   61 102 281   42   25
[129]   39 186 166 239 180 196 138 363 390 327 255 114   81 306    3   47
[145] 215   59 310   20   62 183 211 322   96 252   28 382 139   53 370 376
[161] 290 359 347 346 302 380 172 358 243 245 144 272 375 168 333 264
[177] 352 118 344 128 184   68 299 303 219 103 254 238 192 189   58   67
[193] 204 214 210 230 222 133   31 360   48 190 394 101 361 170   70   56
[209] 314 321   91 198 283 233 364 129   65   75 356 165   51 171 315 121
[225]   10   69 202 374 119 295 104 323   90 330 289 182 209 134 285 284
[241] 287 338   27 297 353 111 229 147 146 109 288 396 158 266   77 279
[257]   24 392 207 175 159 242 335 387 293 228   45   46 256 163 112 325
[273] 298   21 177 188 220 317 218
```

The training set `trainSet` contains 279 observations, along with the outcome (`mpg`) of each observation. The regression algorithm uses the outcome to train the model by looking at the relationships between the predictor variables (any of the seven attributes) and the response variable (`mpg`).

The test set `testSet` contains the rest of the data (that is, the portion not included in the training set). You should notice that the test set also includes the response (`mpg`) variable. When you use the `predict` function (from the model) with the test set, it ignores the response variable and only uses the predictor variables as long as the column names are the same as those in the training set.

To create a linear regression model, we will use the `lm` function, which stands for linear models. The `lm` function uses the `mpg` attribute as the response variable and all the other variables as predictor variables, type in the following line of code:

```
> model <- lm( formula=trainSet$mpg ~ . , data=trainSet)
```

Explaining the results

To see some useful information about the model you just created, type in the following code:

```
> summary(model)
```

The output provides information that you can explore if you want to tweak your model further. For now, we'll leave the model as it is. Here are the last two lines of the output:

```
Multiple R-squared: 0.8741, Adjusted R-squared: 0.8633
F-statistic: 80.82 on 22 and 256 DF,  p-value: < 2.2e-16
```

A couple of data points stand out here:

» The `Multiple R-squared` value tells you how well the regression line fits the data (goodness of fit). A value of 1 means that it's a perfect fit. So an r-squared value of 0.874 is good; it says that 87.4 percent of the variability in mpg is explained by the model.

» The `p-value` tells you how significant the predictor variables affect the response variable. A `p-value` of less than (typically) 0.05 means that we can reject the null hypothesis that the predictor variables collectively have no effect on the response variable (mpg). The `p-value` of 2.2e-16 (that is, 2.2 with 16 zeroes in front of it) is much smaller than 0.05, so the predictors clearly have an effect on the response.

With the model created, we can make predictions against it with the test data we partitioned from the full dataset. To use this model to predict the mpg for each row in the test set, you issue the following command:

```
> predictions <- predict(model, testSet,
          interval="predict", level=.95)
```

This is the code and output of the first six predictions:

```
> head(predictions)

    fit       lwr      upr
2 16.48993 10.530223 22.44964
4 18.16543 12.204615 24.12625
5 18.39992 12.402524 24.39732
6 12.09295  6.023341 18.16257
7 11.37966  5.186428 17.57289
8 11.66368  5.527497 17.79985
```

The output is a matrix that shows the predicted values in the `fit` column and the prediction interval in the `lwr` and `upr` columns — with a confidence level of 95 percent. The higher the confidence level, the wider the range, and vice versa. The predicted value is in the middle of the range; so changing the confidence level doesn't change the predicted value. The first column is the row number of the full dataset.

To see the actual and predicted values side by side so we can easily compare them, you can type in the following lines of code:

```
> comparison <- cbind(testSet$mpg, predictions[,1])
> colnames(comparison) <- c("actual", "predicted")
```

The first line creates a two-column matrix with the actual and predicted values. The second line changes the column names to actual and predicted. Type in the first line of code to get the output of the first six lines of comparison, as follows:

```
> head(comparison)

  actual predicted
2     15  16.48993
4     16  18.16543
5     17  18.39992
6     15  12.09295
7     14  11.37966
8     14  11.66368
```

We also want to see a summary of the two columns to compare their means. This is the code and output of the summary:

```
> summary(comparison)

     actual            predicted
 Min.   :10.00    Min.   : 8.849
 1st Qu.:16.00    1st Qu.:17.070
 Median :21.50    Median :22.912
 Mean   :22.79    Mean   :23.048
 3rd Qu.:28.00    3rd Qu.:29.519
 Max.   :44.30    Max.   :37.643
```

Next we use the *mean absolute percent error* (mape), to measure the accuracy of our regression model. The formula for mean absolute percent error is

$$(\Sigma(|Y-Y'|/|Y|)/N)*100$$

where Y is the actual score, Y' is the predicted score, and N is the number of predicted scores. After plugging the values into the formula, we get an error of only 10.94 percent. Here is the code and the output from the R console:

```
> mape <- (sum(abs(comparison[,1]-comparison[,2]) /
          abs(comparison[,1]))/nrow(comparison))*100
> mape
[1] 10.93689
```

The following code enables you to view the results and errors in a table view:

```
> mapeTable <- cbind(comparison, abs(comparison[,1]-
        comparison[,2])/comparison[,1]*100)
> colnames(mapeTable)[3] <- "absolute percent error"
> head(mapeTable)

    actual predicted      absolute percent error
2       15  16.48993                    9.932889
4       16  18.16543                   13.533952
5       17  18.39992                    8.234840
6       15  12.09295                   19.380309
7       14  11.37966                   18.716708
8       14  11.66368                   16.688031
```

Here's the code that enables you to see the percent error again:

```
> sum(mapeTable[,3])/nrow(comparison)
                        [1] 10.93689
```

Making new predictions

To make predictions with new data, you simply use the predict function with a list of the attribute values. We don't have any new test observations so we'll just make up some values for the attributes. The following code does that job:

```
> newPrediction <- predict(model,
        list(cylinders=factor(4), displacement=370,
        horsepower=150, weight=3904, acceleration=12,
        modelYear=factor(70), origin=factor(1)),
        interval="predict", level=.95)
```

This is the code and output of the new prediction value:

```
> newPrediction
    fit      lwr      upr
1 14.90128 8.12795 21.67462
```

What you have here is your first real prediction from the regression model. The model predicts that this fictional car will have around 14.90 miles per gallon. Because it's from unseen data and you don't know the outcome, you can't compare it against anything else to find out whether it is correct.

After you've evaluated the model with the testing dataset, and you're happy with its accuracy, you'd be confident that you built a good predictive model. You'll have to wait for business results to measure the effectiveness of your predictive model.

TIP

There may be optimizations you can make to build a better and more efficient predictive model. By experimenting, you may find the best combination of predictors to create a faster and more accurate model. One way to construct a subset of the features is to find the correlation between the variables and remove the highly correlated variables. Removing the redundant variables that add nothing (or add very little information) to the fit, you can increase the speed of the model. This is especially true when you're dealing with many observations (rows of data) where processing power or speed might be an issue. For a big dataset, more attributes in a row of data will slow down the processing. So you should try to eliminate as much redundant information as possible.

Using classification to predict

Another task in predictive analytics is to classify new data by predicting what class a target item of data belongs to, given a set of independent variables. You can, for example, classify a customer by type — say, as a high-value customer, a regular customer, or a customer who is ready to switch to a competitor — by using a decision tree.

Setting up the environment

The party package is one of several packages in R that creates decision trees. It isn't installed by default in the base package of R. Other common decision-tree packages include rpart, tree, and randomForest. The randomForest package is used at the end of this chapter. The first step is to set up the environment by installing the party package and load it into the R session.

Type the following lines of code to install and load the party package:

```
> install.packages("party")
> library(party)
```

The party package may take a couple of minutes to download and install. You will see a message on the console after the package has been downloaded and loaded into RStudio.

Introducing the data

The dataset we use to make a prediction on is the Seeds dataset. This dataset has 210 observations and 7 attributes plus the label. The label is the expected outcome and is used to train and evaluate the accuracy of the predictive model. The outcome that we're trying to predict is the type of seed (attribute 8), given the values of the seven attributes. The three possible values for the seed type are labeled 1, 2, and 3, and represent the Kama, Rosa, and Canadian varieties of wheat.

The attributes in the column order they are provided are the following:

1. area
2. perimeter
3. compactness
4. length of kernel
5. width of kernel
6. asymmetry coefficient
7. length of kernel groove
8. class of wheat

You can get the dataset from the UCI machine-learning repository at

```
http://archive.ics.uci.edu/ml/datasets/seeds
```

To get the dataset from the UCI repository and load it into memory, type the following command into the console:

```
> seeds <-
        read.csv("http://archive.ics.uci.edu/ml/machine
        -learning-databases/00236/seeds_dataset.txt",
        header=FALSE, sep="", as.is=TRUE)
```

You see that the dataset was loaded into memory as the data frame variable *seeds*, by looking at your workspace pane (the top-right). Click the *seeds* variable to see the data values in the source pane (the top-left). Figure 14-4 shows how the data looks in the source pane.

FIGURE 14-4:
View of the
seeds data
loaded into
memory.

You can find more information about the data you just loaded by using the
summary() function.

```
> summary(seeds)

        V1                V2                V3
 Min.   :10.59    Min.   :12.41    Min.   :0.8081
 1st Qu.:12.27    1st Qu.:13.45    1st Qu.:0.8569
 Median :14.36    Median :14.32    Median :0.8734
 Mean   :14.85    Mean   :14.56    Mean   :0.8710
 3rd Qu.:17.30    3rd Qu.:15.71    3rd Qu.:0.8878
 Max.   :21.18    Max.   :17.25    Max.   :0.9183
...
```

Preparing the data

You have to get the data into a form that the algorithm can use to build a model.
To do that, you have to take some time to understand the data and to know its
structure. Type in the str function to find out the structure of the seeds data.
Here's what it looks like:

```
> str(seeds)

'data.frame':   210 obs. of  8 variables:
 $ V1: num  15.3 14.9 14.3 13.8 16.1 ...
 $ V2: num  14.8 14.6 14.1 13.9 15 ...
 $ V3: num  0.871 0.881 0.905 0.895 0.903 ...
 $ V4: num  5.76 5.55 5.29 5.32 5.66 ...
 $ V5: num  3.31 3.33 3.34 3.38 3.56 ...
 $ V6: num  2.22 1.02 2.7 2.26 1.35 ...
 $ V7: num  5.22 4.96 4.83 4.8 5.17 ...
 $ V8: int  1 1 1 1 1 1 1 1 1 1 ...
```

From looking at the structure, we can tell that the data needs one pre-processing step and one convenience step:

>> **Rename the column names.** Once again, this isn't strictly necessary, but it makes sense to provide meaningful column names that we can understand and remember.

>> **Change the attribute with categorical values to a factor.** The label has three possible categories.

To rename the columns, type in the following code:

```
> colnames(seeds) <-
         c("area","perimeter","compactness","length",
         "width","asymmetry","length2","seedType")
```

Next, we change the attribute that has categorical values to a factor. (We've identified the label as categorical.) The following code changes the data type to a factor:

```
> seeds$seedType <- factor(seeds$seedType)
```

This command finishes the preparation of the data for the modeling process. The following is a view of the structure after the data-preparation process:

```
> str(seeds)

'data.frame':  210 obs. of  8 variables:
 $ area       : num  15.3 14.9 14.3 13.8 16.1 ...
 $ perimeter  : num  14.8 14.6 14.1 13.9 15 ...
 $ compactness: num  0.871 0.881 0.905 0.895 0.903 ...
 $ length     : num  5.76 5.55 5.29 5.32 5.66 ...
 $ width      : num  3.31 3.33 3.34 3.38 3.56 ...
 $ asymmetry  : num  2.22 1.02 2.7 2.26 1.35 ...
 $ length2    : num  5.22 4.96 4.83 4.8 5.17 ...
 $ seedType   : Factor w/ 3 levels "1","2","3":
              1 1 1 1 1 1 1 1 1 1 ...
```

Creating the model

We want to create a model that we can evaluate using known outcomes. To do that, we're going to split our `seeds` dataset into two sets: one for training the model and one for testing the model. We'll use a 70/30 split between training and testing datasets. The next two lines of code calculate and store the sizes of each dataset:

```
> trainSize <- round(nrow(seeds) * 0.7)
> testSize <- nrow(seeds) - trainSize
```

To output the values, type in the name of the variable that we used to store the value and press Enter. Here is the output:

```
> trainSize
[1] 147
> testSize
[1] 63
```

This code determines the sizes for the training and testing datasets. We haven't actually created the sets yet. Also, we don't just want the first 147 observations to be the training set and the last 63 observations to be the test set. That would create a bad model because the seeds dataset is ordered in the label column.

Thus we have to make both the training set and the test set representative of the entire dataset. One way to do that is create the training set from a random selection of the entire dataset. Additionally, we want to make this test reproducible so we can learn from the same example. We can do that by setting the seed dataset for the random generator so we have the same "random" training set, like this:

```
> set.seed(123)
> training_indices <- sample(seq_len(nrow(seeds)),
          size=trainSize)
> trainSet <- seeds[training_indices, ]
> testSet <- seeds[-training_indices, ]
```

Because the the same seed was used to create the random sample of training indices, your output should be like this:

```
> training_indices
  [1]  61 165  86 183 194  10 108 182 112  92 192  91 135 113  21
 [16] 176  48   9  63 207 170 131 121 186 122 132 101 109  53  27
 [31] 174 162 123 141   5  84 185  38  55  40  25  71  70  62  26
 [46]  23  39  76  44 139   8 169 127  20  88  33 157 116 137  57
 [61] 100  15 151  41 119  66 117 144 197 200 106 156  99   1  65
 [76]  30  51  82  47 149  32  87  54 184  13 172 178 110 191  22
 [91]  16  78 147  77 173 188  90  11 203 148 145  37 202 103  52
[106]  94  96 177  42 189 105 198   6 201 168  14 140  89 128 187
[121]  59  29  28 154 130 175 126 160  12  56  50 159 204 111 171
[136]  80 210  58  79 208 115  93 152  85  81 120 136
```

The training set `trainSet` we get from this code contains 147 observations along with an outcome (`seedType`) of each observation. When we create the model, we'll tell the algorithm which variable is the outcome. The classification algorithm uses those outcomes to train the model by looking at the relationships between the predictor variables (any of the seven attributes) and the label (`seedType`).

The test set `testSet` contains the rest of the data, that is, all data not included in the training set. Notice that the test set also includes the label (`seedType`). When you use the `predict` function (from the model) with the test set, it ignores the label and only uses the predictor variables, as long as the column names are the same as they are in the training set.

```
Now it's time to train the model. The next step is to use the
    party package to create a decision-tree model, using seedType
    as the target variable and all the other variables as
    predictor variables. Type in the following line of code:>
    model <- ctree(seedType ~ . , data=trainSet)
```

Explaining the results

To see some useful information about the model you just created, type in the following code:

```
> summary(model)
    Length       Class      Mode
        1 BinaryTree        S4
```

The `Class` column tells you that you've created a decision tree. To see how the splits are being determined, you can simply type in the name of the variable in which you assigned the model, in this case `model`, like this:

```
> model

Conditional inference tree with 6 terminal nodes

Response:  seedType
Inputs:  area, perimeter, compactness, length, width,
            asymmetry, length2
Number of observations:  147

1) area <= 16.2; criterion = 1, statistic = 123.423
   2) area <= 13.37; criterion = 1, statistic = 63.549
      3) length2 <= 4.914; criterion = 1, statistic = 22.251
         4)*  weights = 11
```

```
   3) length2 > 4.914
      5)* weights = 45
   2) area > 13.37
      6) length2 <= 5.396; criterion = 1, statistic = 16.31
         7)* weights = 33
      6) length2 > 5.396
         8)* weights = 8
1) area > 16.2
   9) length2 <= 5.877; criterion = 0.979, statistic =
         8.764
      10)* weights = 10
   9) length2 > 5.877
      11)* weights = 40
```

Even better, you can visualize the model by creating a plot of the decision tree with this code:

```
> plot(model)
```

You can see the output in the plots tab (bottom-right) of RStudio. (Click the zoom button to make it look more to scale.)

Figure 14-5 shows a graphical representation of a decision tree. You can see that the overall shape mimics that of a real tree. It's made of *nodes* (the circles and rectangles) and *links* or *edges* (the connecting lines). The very first node (starting at the top) is called the *root node* and the nodes at the bottom of the tree (rectangles) are called *terminal nodes*. There are five decision nodes and six terminal nodes.

FIGURE 14-5:
Decision tree of
the seeds model.

At each node, the model makes a decision based on the criteria in the circle and the links, and chooses a way to go. When the model reaches a terminal node, a verdict or a final decision is reached. In this particular case, two attributes, the length2 and the area, are used to decide whether a given seed type is in class 1, 2 or 3.

For example, take observation #2 from the seeds dataset. It has a length2 of 4.956 and an area of 14.88. We can use the tree we just built to decide which particular seed type this observation belongs to. Here's the sequence of steps:

1. We start at the root node, which is node 1 (the number is shown in the small square at the top of the circle). We decide based on the area attribute: Is the area of observation #2 less than or equal to (denoted by <=) 16.2? The answer is yes, so we move along the path to node 2.

2. At node 2, the model asks: Is the area <= 13.37? The answer is no, so we try the next link which asks: Is the area > 13.37? The answer is yes, so we move along the path to node 6. At this node the model asks: Is the length2 <= 5.396? It is, and we move to terminal node 7 and the verdict is that observation #2 is of seed type 1. And it is, in fact, seed type 1.

   The model does that process for all other observations to predict their classes.

3. To find out whether we trained a good model, we check it against the training data. We can view the results in a table with the following code:

```
> table(predict(model),trainSet$seedType)

     1   2   3
 1  45   4   3
 2   3  47   0
 3   1   0  44
```

   The results show that the error (or misclassification rate) is 11 out of 147, or 7.48 percent.

4. With the results calculated, the next step is to read the table.

   The correct predictions are the ones that show the column and row numbers as the same. Those results show up as a diagonal line from top-left to bottom-right; for example, [1,1], [2,2], [3,3] are the number of correct predictions for that class. So for seed type 1, the model correctly predicted it 45 times, while misclassifying the seed 7 times (4 times as seed type 2, and 3 times as type 3). For seed type 2, the model correctly predicted it 47 times, while misclassifying it 3 times. For seed type 3, the model correctly predicted it 44 times, while misclassifying it only once.

We find that this is a good model. So now we evaluate it with the test data. Here is the code that uses the test data to predict and store it in a variable (testPrediction) for later use:

```
> testPrediction <- predict(model, newdata=testSet)
```

To evaluate how the model performed with the test data, we view it in a table and calculate the error, for which the code looks like this:

```
> table(testPrediction, testSet$seedType)
testPrediction  1   2   3
             1 18   4   4
             2  0  15   0
             3  3   0  19
```

The results show that the error is 11 out of 63, or 17.46 percent. This is a bit worse than what was produced with the training data.

Making new predictions

To make predictions with new data, you simply use the predict function with a list of the seven attribute values for the seed type. It was just a coincidence that we are using seven attributes as we did for the autos dataset. There can be any number of attributes in a dataset. The following code does that:

```
> newPrediction <- predict(model, list(area=11,
         perimeter=13, compactness=0.855, length=5,
         width=2.8, asymmetry=6.5, length2=5))
```

This is the code and output of the new prediction value.

```
> newPrediction
```

```
  [1] 3
Levels: 1 2 3
```

The prediction was seed type 3, which isn't surprising because values were deliberately chosen that were close to observation #165.

We can also get this prediction value by walking through the decision tree shown in Figure 14-5. Here are the steps:

1. Start at the root node and look at what attribute the node wants to evaluate. Is area > 16.2 or area <= 16.2. The value of area is 11, so the answer is <=. So we go to the left child, node #2.

2. At node #2, we are asked if area is > 13.37 or area <= 13.37. The answer is <=. So we go to the left child, node #3.

3. At node #3, we are asked if length2 is > 4.914 or length2 <= 4.914. The value of length2 is 5, so the answer is >. So we go to the right child, node #5.

4. At terminal node #5, you can see in the bar chart, that the bar is the highest for 3. So the decision tree model predicts that the data it was given belongs to seed type 3.

Classification by random forest

The last model in this chapter is the random forest model. The random forest algorithm uses an ensemble technique to build its model. (To learn more about ensemble techniques, refer to Chapter 7.) This example continues from the preceding section by creating a random forest model to classify the Seeds dataset.

You've already done the all the hard work in setting up the data in the last section on decision trees, so this section mostly repeat that process. Trying a different classification algorithm is just a matter of changing a few lines of code. The steps are much the same from model to model. Most time will be spent on data preparation. However, you need to know the required parameters for each algorithm. To get better performance, you need to dive deeper into the algorithms to tune them.

Preparing the data

Before we can create the model, let's take the steps to get the data ready for modeling. The steps will look similar to the preceding section on decision trees:

1. **Install the randomForest package and load it into RStudio.**

```
> install.packages("randomForest")
> library(randomForest)
```

2. **Load the data.**

```
> seeds <-
        read.csv("http://archive.ics.uci.edu/ml/machine
        -learning-databases/00236/seeds_dataset.txt",
        header=FALSE, sep="", as.is=TRUE)
```

3. **Prepare the data.**

Rename the variables to meaningful names.

```
> colnames(seeds) <-
        c("area","perimeter","compactness","length",
        "width","asymmetry","length2","seedType")
```

Change the label to a factor data type.

```
> seeds$seedType <- factor(seeds$seedType)
```

4. **Split the data into training and test sets.**

```
> trainSize <- round(nrow(seeds) * 0.7)
> testSize <- nrow(seeds) – trainSize
> set.seed(123)
> training_indices <- sample(seq_len(nrow(seeds)),
        size=trainSize)
> trainSet <- seeds[training_indices, ]
> testSet <- seeds[-training_indices, ]
```

With the preprocessing steps completed, you're ready to create the random forest model.

Creating the model

To create the random forest model, enter the following code into the console:

```
> set.seed(123)
> model <- randomForest(seedType ~ . , data=trainSet)
```

There are many tuning parameters for the random forest algorithm. The most commonly used parameter is ntree, which specifies the number of trees to grow (or number of voters). The default value for ntree is 500. To learn more about the ntree parameter, refer to the random forest section (n_estimators parameter) in Chapter 12. You can find a list of all the parameters for the random forest algorithm by using the help function, as shown below.

```
> help(randomForest)
```

Evaluating the results

When the random forest model has been fitted, you can enter the `model` variable into the console to find the estimate of error rate:

```
> model
Call:
 randomForest(formula = seedType ~ ., data = trainSet)
               Type of random forest: classification
                     Number of trees: 500
No. of variables tried at each split: 2

        OOB estimate of error rate: 8.16%
Confusion matrix:
    1  2  3 class.error
1 43  2  4  0.12244898
2  2 49  0  0.03921569
3  4  0 43  0.08510638
```

The model estimates that it will have an error rate of 8.16 percent (or be 91.8 percent accurate, if you're a positive sort of person). It also gives the error rate of each class in the confusion matrix. Each class is represented by a row:

» Class 1 has an error rate of 12.2 percent.

» Class 2 has an error rate of 3.9 percent.

» Class 3 has an error rate of 8.5 percent.

The random forest algorithm allows the error rate of the trees to be plotted, as shown in Figure 14-6. The plot shows the number of trees on the x-axis and the error rate on the y-axis. Because the forest has 500 trees, the limit on the x-axis is 500. There are four color-coded curves that show the error for each class and the overall error rate, from top to bottom:

» Class 1 (the highest error rate)

» Class 3 (about 8.51 percent).

» Overall error rate (about 8.16 percent)

» Class 2 (the lowest error rate)

To create the plot, enter the following code:

```
> plot(model)
```

FIGURE 14-6:
Error rate plot
of random
forest model.

Now you can check the test dataset. Enter the following code into the console:

```
> testPrediction <- predict(model, newdata=testSet)
> table(testPrediction, testSet$seedType)
testPrediction  1  2  3
            1 20  1  0
            2  0 18  0
            3  1  0 23
```

The results show that the error is 2 out of 63, or 3.17 percent. This is much better than expected, as the error rate was predicted to be around 8.16 percent. The results of the random forest model also is better than the results of the decision tree previously created in this chapter with the party package.

Making new predictions

After you have created the model and then determined that it's the model you will deploy, you'll feed it with new and unlabeled data to get predictions on what type of seed it is. Because we don't have any more new data, we'll use the same attribute values that we made up for the decision tree in the earlier section of this chapter. This will give us the opportunity to make a simple comparison of the decision tree model and the random forest model.

The following code makes a new prediction:

```
> newPrediction <- predict(model, list(area=11,
        perimeter=13, compactness=0.855, length=5,
        width=2.8, asymmetry=6.5, length2=5))
```

This is the code and output of the new prediction value:

```
> newPrediction
1
3
Levels: 1 2 3
```

The prediction was seed type 3, as shown in the second row of the output. (You can ignore the value in the first row and the last row; it's the row number of the list and the possible outcomes, respectively.) The result is the same as the prediction from the party decision tree. That isn't surprising as this should be an easy prediction because the attribute values were very close to the attributes values of observation #165. Of the two classification tree models created in this chapter, the random forest model performed better with the default parameters on the Seeds dataset, because it has a lower error rate.

Making new predictions on seeds data may seem a bit abstract and it may be difficult to understand how it relates to solving business problems. A real-life example of using classification you may be able to relate to is email spam detection.

This is a simplified example of creating and deploying a spam detection model. Suppose you're the operator of an email service and the business problem you want to solve is to determine if the email a customer receives is spam. Customers hate receiving spam email because it's annoying, wastes time, and it wastes disk space. So you want a model that produces the least amount of errors.

You create a spam detection model using a labeled spam email dataset. After you're confident with the model's results on the test data, you will deploy it to the production servers. Now, for every new email that is sent to the customer, the model will make a prediction on whether the email is spam before it's delivered. So the email will be either put into the customer's inbox or spam folder (if there are no other predefined filters already set). If spam email lands in the inbox or if valid email lands in the spam folder, it would be considered an error or misclassification.

By allowing customers to mark email as spam when they land in the inbox or not-spam if it lands in the spam folder, the customers are essentially labeling the data for you to measure the models results. Obviously not all customers will spend the time to mark any or all misclassified emails, but you have enough to work with and you can also use internal emails to measure the results.

IN THIS CHAPTER

Examining your data

Exploring your data potential problems

Dealing with outliers and fitting data to a curve

Evaluating your technical analysis

Describing the limitations of a predictive model

Chapter 15

Avoiding Analysis Traps

I n the quest for building a predictive model, you'll need to make decisions every step of the way — and some decisions are harder than others. Informed decisions — and an awareness of the common mistakes that most analysts make while building their predictive models — give you your best shot at success.

This chapter offers insights on the issues that could arise when you embark on a journey toward the effective use of predictive analytics. At the outset, consider this general definition:

> A *predictive model* is a system that can predict the next possible outcome, and assign a realistic probability to that outcome.

As you build your predictive model, you're likely to run into problems in two areas — the data and the analysis. This chapter delves into both types of problems to help you strengthen your safeguards, and allow you to stay on top of your project.

How well you handle both the data and the analysis at the core of your predictive model defines the success of your predictive analytics project. Data issues are more prominent now because *big data* (massive amounts of analyzable data generated online) is all the rage — and only getting bigger, thanks to explosive growth of data in the digital and social media worlds.

The more data you have, however, the more diverse the cases that generate it. Your job as a modeler can be harder if the data you're using contains *outliers* (extreme cases): Then your model must take into account

>> How rare those outliers are

>> How much complexity they add to your model

>> Whether to create risk management components to deal with them

Modeling requires that you choose which variables to report on — and that you understand not only the variables but also their impact on the business (for example, how an unusually active storm season might affect a fishery). Right off the bat, you need to consult someone with *domain knowledge* (expertise in the business) so you can identify those variables accurately. After all, the model should reflect the real world in which the business is operating. The model's predictions should be accurate enough to improve return on investment for the business — by helping its decision-makers answer tough questions and make bold, informed decisions.

REMEMBER

People with expert-level domain knowledge are best qualified to analyze the data in a comprehensive and meaningful way. *Hint:* You'll want to make sure your analysis has appropriate degrees of data validity, variety, *velocity* (the speed at which the data changes), and volume — all addressed at length in Chapter 4.

Data Challenges

Data mining is more than just gathering, generating, or retrieving data. It's a first step in treating data as a resource for your business, and it raises more issues:

>> Which type of analysis or analyses to adopt

>> Which algorithms to employ

>> Which data points to include and exclude and why

>> How to prepare your data for use in your model

>> How to select your variables for building your model

>> Which data to use for training and testing your model

Data is at the center of predictive analytics. Data quality is crucial to the effectiveness of the predictions. As a data analyst, you have to get familiar enough with the data to examine its limitations (if any). Here's a quick list of questions to ask about the data:

>> Where is it located?

>> How can I retrieve it?

>> Is it well documented?

>> Does it contain errors?

>> Are there any missing values?

>> Does it need to be *cleaned* of corrupt or inaccurate records?

>> Does it contain outliers?

>> Does it need *smoothing* to have individual aberrations minimized?

>> Does it require any kind of preprocessing before use in the model?

TIP

When the data is collected from multiple sources, potential problems — such as formatting issues, data duplication, and consolidation of similar data — become more likely. In view of all these questions and uncertainties, don't be surprised if your incoming data requires some preprocessing before you can run it through your model and use it in a meaningful analysis.

Data preparation (see Chapter 9 for more details) is tedious and time-consuming. At this stage of developing your predictive model, expertise and tools in data preparation can be essential to the success of your project.

Data preparation will take up to 80 percent of your time to build a predictive analytics model. Expect to spend most of your time getting your data ready so you can apply analysis. Collecting relevant variables, data cleansing, and preprocessing of the data (such as generating derived variables, integrating data from multiple sources, and data mapping) will take the majority of your time.

Outlining the limitations of the data

As with many aspects of any business system, data is apt to have some limits on its usability when you first obtain it. Here's an overview of some limitations you're likely to encounter:

>> **The data could be incomplete.** Missing values, even the lack of a section or a substantial part of the data, could limit its usability. Missing data is having

empty fields for some variables that you're analyzing. When your data spans multiple seasons, it may need extra attention; even though your data may not have any missing values, but if it only spans a particular season or phase and it doesn't represent other seasons, then your data isn't complete. For example, your data might cover only one or two conditions of a larger set that you're trying to model — as when a model built to analyze stock market performance only has data available from the past 5 years, which skews both the data and the model toward the assumption of a bull market. The moment the market undergoes any correction that leads to a bear market, the model fails to adapt — simply because it wasn't trained and tested with data representing a bear market.

TIP

Make sure you're looking at a time frame that gives you a complete picture of the natural fluctuations of your data; your data shouldn't be limited by *seasonality*.

>> **If you're using self-reported data, keep in mind that people don't always provide accurate information.** Not everyone will answer truthfully about (say) how many times they exercise — or how many alcoholic beverages they consume — per week. People may not be dishonest so much as self-conscious, but the data is still skewed.

>> **Data collected from different sources can vary in quality and format.** Data collected from such diverse sources as surveys, emails, data-entry forms, and the company website will have different attributes and structures. For example, data embedded within pdf files or scattered across various publications will need to be extracted, assembled, and preprocessed before you can include it in any analysis. Data from various sources may not have much compatibility among data fields. Such data requires major preprocessing before it's analysis-ready. The accompanying sidebar provides an example.

WHAT'S THE DATE WHERE YOU ARE?

Different sources format data differently — and many fields may have different weights. A date collected from an American website (for example) could have the format mm/dd/yyyy — while the same company, collecting that same data in Europe, uses the dd/mm/yyyy format. Thus, in source documents from the American and European branch offices of the same company, the numerical date 05/11/2014 would mean (respectively) May 11, 2014 or 5 November 2014.

REMEMBER

Data collected from multiple sources may have differences in formatting, duplicate records, and inconsistencies across merged data fields. Expect to spend a long time cleaning such data — and even longer validating its reliability.

To determine the limitations of your data, be sure to:

» Verify all the variables you'll use in your model.

» Assess the scope of the data, especially over time, so your model can avoid the seasonality trap.

» Check for missing values, identify them, and assess their impact on the overall analysis.

» Watch out for extreme values (outliers) and decide on whether to include them in the analysis.

» Confirm that the pool of training and test data is large enough.

» Make sure *data type* (integers, decimal values, or characters, and so forth) is correct and set the upper and lower bounds of possible values.

» Pay extra attention to data integration when your data comes from multiple sources.

REMEMBER

Be sure you understand your data sources and their impact on the overall quality of your data.

» Choose a relevant dataset that is representative of the whole population.

» Choose the right parameters for your analysis.

Even after all this care and attention, don't be surprised if your data will still need preprocessing before you can analyze it accurately. In practice, you will find that you will do at least one or two of the tasks listed below. Preprocessing often takes a long time and significant effort because it has to address several issues related to the original data — these issues include:

» Any values missing from the data.

» Any inconsistencies and/or errors existing in the data.

» Any duplicates or outliers in the data.

» Any normalization or other transformation of the data.

» Any derived data needed for the analysis.

Dealing with extreme cases (outliers)

Your data may contain *outliers* — extreme values that are often significant but atypical. You'll have to deal with these outliers — maintaining data integrity without affecting your predictive model negatively. It's a key challenge.

Part of your data preparation is to determine whether the values and data types of your data are what you expected. Check for

>> The expected minimum and maximum values

>> The data types and the expected values for a given field

>> Any anomaly in the values and/or data types

Outliers caused by outside forces

Be sure you check carefully for outliers *before* they influence your analysis. Outliers can distort both the data and data analysis. For example, any statistical analysis done with data that leaves outliers in place ends up skewing the means and variances. Some techniques, such as Trees, are more robust to outliers than others.

Unchecked or misinterpreted outliers may lead to false conclusions. Say your data that shows that a stock that was traded for a whole year at a price above $50 — but for only a few minutes out of that whole year the stock was traded at $20. The $20 price — an obvious exception — is the outlier in this dataset.

Now you have to decide whether to include the $20 stock price in your analysis; if you do, it has ramifications for the overall model. But what do you consider normal? Was the "flash crash" that took the stock market by surprise on May 6, 2010 a normal event or an exception? During that brief time, the stock market experienced a sharp decline in prices across the board — which knocked the sample stock price down from $50 to $20, but had less to do with the stock than with wider market conditions. Does your model need to take the larger fluctuations of the stock market into account?

Anyone who's lost money on brief moments of free-fall market considers those few minutes real and normal (even if they felt like an eternity to go through). A portfolio that diminishes in milliseconds due to a rapid decline, albeit short-lived, is clearly real. Yet the flash crash is an anomaly, an outlier that poses a problem for the model.

Regardless of what's considered normal (which can change anyway), data sometimes contains values that don't fit the expected values. This is especially true in the stock market, where virtually any event may send the market flying or plunging. You don't want your model to fail when the reality changes suddenly — but a model and a reality are two different things. As a data scientist, you should strive to build models that account for the unexpected and be able to address it in a way that strengthens the business.

Outliers caused by errors in the system

When we rely on technology or instrumentation to conduct a task, a glitch here or there can cause these instruments to register extreme or unusual values. If sensors register observational values that fail to meet basic quality-control standards, they can produce real disruptions that are reflected in data.

Someone performing data entry, for example, can easily add an extra 0 at the end of a value by mistake, taking the entry out of range and producing an outlier. If you're looking at observational data collected by a water sensor installed in Baltimore Harbor — and it reports a water height of 20 feet above mean sea level — you've got an outlier. The sensor is obviously wrong unless Baltimore is completely covered by water.

Data can end up having outliers because of external events or an error by a person or an instrument. If a real event such as a flash crash is traced to an error in the system, its consequences are still real — but if you know the source of the problem, you may conclude that a flaw in the data, not your model, was to blame if your model didn't predict the event. Such problems can be addressed outside the model, such as instituting risk management for your portfolio in case of financial data.

REMEMBER

Knowing the source of the outlier will guide your decision on how to deal with it. Outliers that were the result of data-entry errors can easily be corrected after consulting the data source. Outliers that reflect a changed reality may prompt you to change your model.

There's no one-size-fits-all answer when you're deciding whether to include or disregard extreme data that isn't an error or glitch. Your response depends on the nature of the analysis you're doing — and on the type of the model you're building. In a few cases, the way to deal with those outliers is straightforward:

>> If you trace your outlier to a data-entry error when you consult the data source, you can easily correct the data and (probably) keep the model intact.

>> If that water sensor in Baltimore Harbor reports a water height of 20 feet above mean sea level, and you're in Baltimore, look out your window:

- If Baltimore isn't completely covered by water, the sensor is obviously wrong.

- If you see a fish looking in at you, the reality has changed; you may have to revise your model.

>> The flash crash may have been a one-time event (over the short term, anyway), but its effects were real — and if you've studied the market over the longer term, you know that something similar may happen again. If your business is in finance and you deal with the stock market all the time, you want your model to account for such aberrations.

In general, if the outcome of an event normally considered an outlier can have a significant impact on your business, consider how to deal with those events in your analysis. Keep these general points in mind about outliers:

>> The smaller dataset is, the more significant the impact outliers can have on the analysis.

>> As you develop your model, be sure you also develop techniques to find outliers and to systematically understand their impact on your business.

>> Detecting outliers can be a complex process; there is no simple way of identifying them.

>> A *domain expert* (someone who knows the field you're modeling) is your best go-to person to verify whether a data point is valid, an outlier you can disregard, or an outlier you have to take into account. The domain expert should be able to explain what factors created the outlier, what its range of variability is, and its impact on the business.

>> Visualization tools can help you spot outliers in the data. Also, if you know the expected range of values you can easily query for data that falls outside that range.

Keeping the outliers in the analysis — or not

Deciding to include outliers in the analysis — or to exclude them — will have implications for your model.

WARNING

Keeping outliers as part of the data in your analysis may lead to a model that isn't applicable — either to the outliers or to the rest of the data. If you decide to keep an outlier, you'll need to choose techniques and statistical methods that excel at handling outliers without influencing the analysis. One such technique is to use mathematical functions such as natural algorithms and square root to reduce the gap between the outliers and the rest of the data. These functions, however, only work for numerical data that is greater than zero — and other issues may arise. For example, transforming the data may require interpretations of the relationship between variables in the newly transformed data that differ from the interpretation that governs those variables in the original data.

REMEMBER

The mere presence of outliers in your data can provide insights into your business that can be very helpful in generating a robust model. Outliers may draw attention to a valid business case that illustrates an unusual but significant event.

Looking for outliers, identifying them, and assessing their impact should be part of data analysis and preprocessing. Business domain experts can provide insight and help you decide what to do with unusual cases in your analysis. Although sometimes common sense is all you need to deal with outliers, often it's helpful to ask someone who knows the ropes.

TIP

If you're in a business that benefits from rare events — say, an astronomical observatory with a grant to study Earth-orbit-crossing asteroids — you're more interested in the outliers than in the bulk of the data.

Outliers can be a great source of information. Deviating from the norm could be a signal of suspicious activity, breaking news, or an opportunistic or catastrophic event. You may need to develop models that help you identify outliers and asses the risks they signify.

TIP

It's prudent to conduct two analyses: one that includes outliers, and another that omits them. Then examine the differences, try to understand the implications of each method, and assess how adopting one method over the other would influence your business goals.

Data smoothing

Data smoothing is, essentially, trying to find the "signal" in the "noise" by discarding data points that are considered "noisy". The idea is to sharpen the patterns in the data and highlight trends the data is pointing to.

Figure 15-1 shows a typical graph that results from data smoothing.

The implication behind data smoothing is that the data consists of two parts: one part (consisting of the *core data points*) that signifies overall trends or real trends, and another part that consists mostly of deviations (*noise*) — some fluctuating points that result from some volatility in the data. Data smoothing seeks to eliminate that second part.

FIGURE 15-1:
A graph showing smoothed data.

Turning down the noise

Data smoothing operates on several assumptions:

» That fluctuation in data is likeliest to be noise.

» That the noisy part of the data is of short duration.

» That the data's fluctuation, regardless of how varied it may be, won't affect the underlying trends represented by the core data points.

Noise in data tends to be random; its fluctuations shouldn't affect the overall trends drawn from examining the rest of the data. So reducing or eliminating noisy data points can clarify real trends and patterns in the data — in effect, improving the data's "signal-to-noise ratio."

Provided you've identified the noise correctly and then reduced it, data smoothing can help you predict the next observed data point simply by following the major trends you've detected within the data. Data smoothing concerns itself with the majority of the data points, their positions in a graph, and what the resulting patterns predict about the general trend of (say) a stock price, whether its general direction is up, down, or sideways. This technique won't accurately predict the exact price of the next trade for a given stock — but predicting a general trend can yield more powerful insights than knowing the actual price or its fluctuations.

REMEMBER

A forecast based on a general trend deduced from smoothed data assumes that whatever direction the data has followed thus far will continue into the future in a way consistent with the trend. In the stock market, for example, past performance is no definite indication of future performance, but it certainly can be a general guide to future movement of the stock price.

Methods, advantages, and downsides of data smoothing

Data smoothing focuses on establishing a fundamental direction for the core data points by

>> Ignoring any noisy data points

>> Drawing a smoother curve through the data points that skips the wriggling ones and emphasizes primary patterns — trends — in the data, no matter how slow their emergence

In a numerical time series, data smoothing serves as a form of filtering.

TECHNICAL STUFF

Data smoothing is not be confused with *fitting a model*, which is part of the data analysis consisting of two steps:

1. Find a suitable model that represents the data.

2. Make sure that the model fits the data effectively.

For details of the model-fitting process, see Chapter 12.

Data smoothing can use any of the following methods:

>> **Random walk** is based on the idea that the next outcome, or future data point, is a random deviation from the last known, or present, data point.

>> **Moving average** is a running average of consecutive, equally spaced periods. An example would the calculation of a 200-day moving average of a stock price.

>> **Exponential smoothing** assigns exponentially more weight, or importance, to recent data points than to older data points.

- **Simple:** This method should be used when the time series data has no trend and no seasonality.

- **Linear:** This method should be used when the time series data has a trend line.

- **Seasonal:** This method should be used when the time series data has no trend but seasonality.

What these smoothing methods all have in common is that they carry out some kind of averaging process on several data points. Such averaging of adjacent data points is the essential way to zero in on underlying trends or patterns.

The advantages of data smoothing are

>> It's easy to implement.

>> It helps identify trends.

>> It helps expose patterns in the data.

>> It eliminates data points that you've decided aren't of interest.

>> It helps predict the general direction of the next observed data points.

>> It generates nice smooth graphs.

But everything has a downside. The disadvantages of data smoothing are

>> It may eliminate valid data points that result from extreme events.

>> It may lead to inaccurate predictions if the test data has only one season and isn't fully representative of the reality that generated the data points.

>> It may shift or skew the data, especially the peaks, resulting in a distorted picture of what's going on.

>> It may be vulnerable to significant disruption from outliers within the data.

>> It may result in a major deviation from the original data.

If data smoothing does no more than give the data a mere facelift, it can lead to a fundamentally wrong path in the following ways:

>> It can introduce errors through distortions that treat the smoothed data as if it were identical to the original data.

>> It can skew interpretation by ignoring — and hiding — risks embedded within the data.

>> It can lead to a loss of detail within your data — which is one way that a smoothed curve may deviate greatly from that of the original data.

How seriously data smoothing may affect your data depends on the nature of the data at hand, and which smoothing technique was implemented on that data. For example, if the original data has more peaks in it, then data smoothing will lead to major shifting of those peaks in the smoothed graphs — most likely a distortion.

REMEMBER

Here are some cautionary points to keep in mind as you approach data smoothing:

>> It's a good idea to compare smoothed graphs to untouched graphs that plot the original data.

>> Data points removed during data smoothing may not be noise; they could be valid data points that result from rare, but real, events.

>> Data smoothing can be helpful in moderation, but its overuse can lead to a misrepresentation of your data.

By applying your professional judgment and your business knowledge expertise, you can use data smoothing effectively. Removing noise from your data — without negatively affecting the accuracy and usefulness of the original data — is at least as much an art as a science.

Curve fitting

Curve fitting, as mentioned earlier, is a process distinct from data smoothing: Here the goal is to create a curve that depicts the mathematical function that best fits the actual (original) data points in a data series. In general, you smooth time series data, and curve fit regression relationships.

The curve can either pass through every data point or stay within the bulk of the data, ignoring some data points in hopes of drawing trends from the data. In either case, one single mathematical function is assigned to the entire body of data, with the goal of fitting all data points into a curve that delineates trends and aids predictions.

Figure 15-2 shows a typical graph that results from curve-fitting a body of data.

Curve fitting can be achieved in one of three ways:

>> By finding an exact fit for every data point (a process called *interpolation*)

>> By staying within the bulk of the data while ignoring some of data points in hopes of drawing trends out of the data

>> By employing data smoothing to come up with a function that represents the smoothed graph

Curve fitting can be used to fill in possible data points to replace missing values or help analysts visualize the data.

FIGURE 15-2:
An example of curve fitting.

WARNING

When you're working to generate a predictive analytics model, avoid tailoring your model to fit your data sample perfectly. Such a model will fail — miserably — to predict similar yet varying datasets outside the data sample. Fitting a model too closely to a particular data sample is a classic mistake called *overfitting*.

The woes of overfitting

In essence, overfitting a model is what happens when you train the model to represent only your sample data — which isn't a good representation of the data as a whole. Without a more realistic dataset to go on, the model can then be plagued with errors and risks when it goes operational — and the consequences to your business can be serious.

Overfitting a model is a common trap because people want to create models that work — and so are tempted to keep tweaking variables and parameters until the model performs perfectly — on too little data. To err is human. Fortunately, it's also human to create realistic solutions.

REMEMBER

To avoid overfitting your model to your sample dataset, be sure to have a body of test data available that's separate from your sample data. Then you can measure the performance of your model independently before making the model operational. Thus one general safeguard against overfitting is to divide your data to two parts: training data and test data. The model's performance against the test data will tell you a lot about whether the model is ready for the real world.

Another best practice is to make sure that your data represents the larger population of the domain you're modeling for. All that an overtrained model knows is the specific features of the sample dataset it's trained for. If you train the model only on (say) snowshoe sales in winter, don't be surprised if it fails miserably when it's run again on data from any other season.

Avoiding overfitting

It's worth repeating: Too much tweaking of the model is apt to result in overfitting. One such tweak is including too many variables in the analysis. Keep those variables to a minimum. Start by including variables that you see as absolutely necessary — those you believe will make a significant difference to the outcome. This insight comes from intimate knowledge of the business domain you're in. That's where the expertise of domain experts can help keep you from falling into the trap of overfitting. In addition, we can obtain such insight through the modeling process; the data more often than not manages to surprise us.

Here's a checklist of best practices to help you avoid overfitting your model:

>> Chose a dataset to work with that is representative of the population as a whole.

>> Divide your dataset into two parts: training data and test data.

>> Keep the variables analyzed that have predictive value.

>> Enlist the help of domain knowledge experts.

In the stock market, for example, a classic analytical technique is *back-testing* — running a model against historical data to look for the best trading strategy. Suppose that, after running his new model against data generated by a recent bull market, and tweaking the number of variables used in his analysis, the analyst creates what looks like an optimal trading strategy — one that would yield the highest returns *if* he could go back and trade only during the year that produced the test data. Unfortunately, he can't. If he tries to apply that model in a current bear market, look out below: He'll incur losses by applying a model too optimized for a narrow period of time and set of conditions that doesn't fit current realities. (So much for hypothetical profits.) The model worked only for that vanished bull market because it was overtrained, bearing the earmarks of the context that produced the sample data — complete with its specifics, outliers, and shortcomings. All the circumstances surrounding that dataset probably won't be repeated in the future, or in a true representation of the whole population — but they all showed up in the overfitted model.

REMEMBER

If a model's output is too accurate, consider that a hint to take a closer look. Enlist the help of domain knowledge experts to see whether your results really are too good to be true, and run that model on more test data for further comparisons.

Keeping the assumptions to a minimum

In spite of everything we've all been told about assumptions causing trouble, a few assumptions remain at the core of any predictive analytics model. Those assumptions show up in the variables selected and considered in the analysis — and those variables directly affect the accuracy of the final model's output. Therefore your wisest precaution at the outset is to identify which assumptions matter most to your model — and to keep them to an absolute minimum.

Creating a predictive model that works well in the real world requires an intimate knowledge of the business. Your model starts out knowing only the sample data — in practical terms, almost nothing. So start small and keep on enhancing the model as necessary. Probing possible questions and scenarios can lead to key discoveries and/or can shed more light on the factors at play in the real world. This process can identify the core variables that could affect the outcome of the analysis. In a systematic approach to predictive analysis, this phase — exploring "what-if" scenarios — is especially interesting and useful. Here's where you change the model inputs to measure the effects of one variable or another on the output of the model; what you're really testing is its forecasting capability.

Improving the model's assumptions — by testing how they affect the model's output, probing to see how sensitive the model is to them, and paring them down to the minimum — will help you guide the model toward a more reliable predictive capability. Before you can optimize your model, you have to know the *predictive variables* — features that have a direct impact on its output.

You can derive those decision variables by running multiple simulations of your model — while changing a few parameters with each run — and recording the results, especially the accuracy of the model's forecasts. Usually you can trace variations in accuracy back to the specific parameters you changed.

At this point, the twenty-first century can turn to the fourteenth for help. William of Ockham, an English Franciscan friar and scholastic philosopher who lived in the 1300s, developed the research principle we know as Occam's Razor: You should cut away unnecessary assumptions until your theory has as few of them as possible. Then it's likeliest to be true.

Too many assumptions weigh down your model's forecasts with uncertainties and inaccuracies. Eliminating unnecessary variables leads to a more robust model, but it isn't easy to decide which variables to include in the analysis — and those decisions directly affect the performance of the model. But here's where the analyst can run into a dilemma: Including unnecessary factors can skew or distort the output of the model, but excluding a relevant variable leaves the model incomplete. So when it comes time to select those all-important decision variables, call in your domain knowledge experts. When you have an accurate, reality-based set of decision variables, you don't have to make too many assumptions — and the result can be fewer errors in your predictive model.

Analysis Challenges

Predictive modeling is gaining popularity as a tool for managing many aspects of business. Ensuring that data analysis is done right will boost confidence in the models employed — which, in turn, can generate the needed buy-in for predictive analytics to become part of your organization's standard toolkit.

Perhaps this increased popularity comes from the ways in which a predictive analytics project can support decision-making by creating models that describe datasets, discover possible new patterns and trends (as indicated by the data), and predict outcomes with greater reliability.

To accomplish this goal, a predictive analytics project must deliver a model that best fits the data by selecting the decision variables correctly and efficiently. Some vital questions must be answered in pursuit of that goal:

>> Which are the minimum assumptions and decision variables that enable the model to best fit the data?

>> How does the model under construction compare to other applicable models?

>> Which criteria are best for evaluating and scoring this model?

Once again, you can call the voice of experience to the rescue: Domain knowledge experts can discuss these questions, interpret any results that show hidden patterns in the data, and help verify and validate the model's output. They can also help you navigate the tricky aspects of predictive analytics described in the upcoming sections of this chapter.

Supervised analytics

In *supervised analytics,* both input and historical output are part of the training data. The model is presented with the correct results as part of its learning process. Such supervised learning assumes pre-classified examples: The goal is to get the model to learn from the previously known classification so it can correctly label the next unknown data point based on what it has learned.

When the model's training is complete, a mathematical function is inferred by examining the training data. That function will be used to label new data points.

For this approach to work correctly, the training data — along with the test data — must be carefully selected. The trained model should be able to predict the correct label for a new data point quickly and precisely, based on the data type(s) the model has seen in the training data.

Supervised analytics offer some distinct advantages:

>> The analyst is in charge of the process.

>> Labeling is based on known classifications.

>> Labeling errors can be easily resolved.

The flip side of these advantages is an equally distinct set of potential disadvantages:

>> Any mistakes at the training phase will be reinforced later on.

>> The classification provided by the analyst may not describe the whole population adequately.

>> The model may be unable to detect classes that deviate from the original training set.

>> The assumption that the clusters within the data don't overlap — and that they can easily be separated — may not prove valid.

Relying on only one analysis

As you probably guessed, predictive analytics isn't a one-size-fits-all activity — nor are its results once-and-for-all. For the technique to work correctly, you have to apply it again and again over time — so you'll need an overall approach that fits your business well. The success of your predictive analytics project depends on multiple factors:

>> The nature of your data

>> The nature of your business and its culture

>> The availability of the in-house expertise

>> Access to appropriate analytical tools

The approach you choose will influence the model's output, the process of analyzing its results, and the interpretation of its forecasts. And choosing an approach is no walk in the park. There are many things that can go wrong, many traps that you can fall into, and misleading paths you can take.

Happily, you can defend against these pitfalls by adopting a couple of wise practices early on:

>> **Continuously test the results of your predictive analytics model.** Don't rely on the results of one single analysis; instead, run multiple analyses in parallel — and compare their outcome.

>> **Run, test, compare, and evaluate multiple models and their outcomes.** Use as many simulations as you can, and check as many permutations as you can. Some limitations in your data can only come to light when you compare the results you get from your model to those you get from other models. Then you can assess the impact of each model's results vis-à-vis your business objectives.

Use multiple models to identify as many relevant patterns as possible in your data.

REMEMBER

Describing the limitations of the model

Any predictive analytic model has certain limitations based on the algorithms it employs and the dataset it runs on. You should be aware of those limitations and make them work to your advantage; those related to the algorithms include

>> Whether the data has nonlinear patterns (doesn't form a line)

>> How highly correlated the variables are (statistical relationships between features)

>> Whether the variables are independent (no relationships between features)

>> Whether the scope of the sample data makes the model prone to overfitting (as described earlier in this chapter)

To overcome the limitations of your model, use sound *cross-validation* techniques to test your models. Start by dividing your data into training and test datasets, and run the model against each of those datasets separately to evaluate and score the predictions of the model.

Testing and evaluating your model

No model can produce 100-percent accurate forecasts; any model has the potential to produce inaccurate results. Be on the lookout for any significant variation between the forecasts your model produces and the observed data — especially if the model's outputs contradict common sense. If it looks too good, bad, or extreme to be true, then it probably isn't true (to reality, anyway).

In the evaluation process, thoroughly examine the outputs of the models you're testing and compare them to the input variables. Your model's forecast capability should answer all stated business goals that drove its creation in the first place.

If errors or biases crop up in your model's output, try tracing them back to

>> The validity, reliability, and relative seasonality of the data

>> Assumptions used in the model

>> Variables that were included or excluded in the analysis

The preceding factors will directly influence the accuracy of your model. If your data isn't appropriate for the model you're building, then your model is bound to fail to answer its business needs. If the data is good but flawed, like absent representation of a type of data due to seasonality, or that the data isn't valid or reliable, your data will not account for all cases that the model should be aware of and address when similar situations arise in the future.

As part of building the model, the data scientists or business stakeholders may make some assumptions either about the data used to create the model, or the business environment in which the model will run. If those assumptions are wrong, the model will be less or inaccurate.

The decision to include a variable or exclude it from the analysis has a direct impact on the outcome of the model. Some variables may only be effective and their predictive powers may only come in play in the presence of other variables. The decision to whether include or exclude a variable from an analysis is at the core of building predictive analytics models. Business stakeholders, data scientists' experience, tools, and quality data should be of tremendous help in building successful predictive analytics models.

REMEMBER

Work with business users to evaluate every step of your model's process; make sure that the model outputs can be easily interpreted and used in a real-world business situation. Balance the accuracy and reliability of the model with how easily the model's outputs can be interpreted and put to practical use.

The ability to easily interpret the model and for that interpretation to make sense to the business stakeholders is essential. That interpretation may be new, but you should be able to explain why this variable, or that variable, or a combination of variable will allow your business to make an accurate prediction.

Avoiding non-scalable models

When you're building a model, always keep scalability in mind. Always check the performance, accuracy, and reliability of the model at various scales. Your model should be able to change its scale — and scale up as big as necessary — without falling apart or outputting bad predictions.

Scalability is quite a challenge. Predictive models can take a long time to build and to run. In the past, the datasets the models ran on were small, and the data was expensive to collect, store, and search. But that was all in the "pre-big data" era.

Today big data is cheap, plentiful, and growing. In fact, another potential problem looms: The formidable data volume and data velocity, and the rate of the incoming data currently available and possible, may negatively affect the model and degrade its performance, outdating the model in a relatively short period of time. Properly implemented, scalability can help "future-proof" your model.

The future isn't the only threat. Even in the present online era, streamed data can overwhelm a model — especially if the streams of data increase to a flood.

If the model refreshes at a rate slower than the incoming data, then the model's predictions are almost obsolete for the data; the universe it represents has already changed and the model needs to play catch up to address the new reality.

Data volume alone can cause the decision variables and predicting factors to grow to giant numbers that require continuous updating to the model. So yes, your model had better be scalable — rapidly scalable.

Scoring your predictions accurately

When analyzing the quality of a predictive model, you'll want to measure its accuracy. The more accurate a forecast the model makes, the more useful it is to the business, which is an indication of its quality. This is all good — except for when the predicted event is rare. In such case, the high accuracy of the predictive model may be meaningless.

For example if the probability of rare event to occur is 5 percent, a model that simply answers "no" all the time when asked whether the rare event has occurred would be right 95 percent of the time. But how useful would such a model be? Thus, if your business is interested in predicting and handling rare events, don't rely on accuracy alone as a measure of your model's reliability.

In such a case, you can evaluate the efficacy and the quality of a predictive model in the light of the how likely the rare event is to take place. A useful metric to follow is to specify which types of errors you can accept from the model and which you cannot.

Here's a quick list of other ways to evaluate your model:

>> Check to see whether the model's output meets your evaluation criteria.

>> Devise a testing strategy so you can test your model repeatedly and consistently.

>> Measure how well the model meets the business goals for which it was built.

>> Assess the risks of deploying the model live.

REMEMBER

Help stamp out overfitting. When building a predictive model, keep in mind that your dataset is only a sample of the whole population. There will always be unknown factors that your data can't account for, no matter what.

Approach the analysis of your predictive model with care, starting with this quick checklist:

>> Prepare your data with the utmost diligence before using it to train your model.

>> Carefully consider outliers before including or excluding them.

>> Remain vigilant in repeated testing and evaluation.

>> Cross-check sample data and test data to steer away from overfitting.

>> Consult your domain knowledge experts often and appropriately.

5

Executing Big Data

Chapter 16

Targeting Big Data

At a broad level, *big data* is the mass of data generated at every moment. It includes — for openers — data emerging in real time from

>> Online social networks such as Facebook

>> Micro-blogs such as Twitter

>> Online customer-transaction data

>> Climate data gathered from sensors

>> GPS locations for every device equipped with GPS

>> User queries on search engines such as Google

And that list barely scratches the surface; think of big data as a growing worldwide layer of data. What to do with it all? Answer: Start by using predictive analytics as a means to extract valuable information from the mass of big data, find patterns in the data, learn new insights, and predict future outcomes.

Here's a familiar example: You might have noticed ads appearing on websites while you're browsing that "just happen" to mention products that you already intended to buy. No magic at work here; the sites that show such ads are utilizing predictive analytics to *data-mine* (dig up insights from) big data: your buying patterns leave a trail of valuable data online; the well-targeted ads show that someone is using that data.

This chapter shows you how predictive analytics can crack the big-data nut and extract the nutmeat. First we guide you through a number of trends in the predictive analytics market — in particular, predictive analytics as a service — that offer significant applications for businesses. You're also introduced to some aspects of predictive analytics and how it can be used to tame big data:

>> Utilize big data to predict future outcomes

>> Explore predictive analytics as a service

>> Apply free, open-source tools to fuse, and make use of data from different sources

>> Prepare to build a predictive analytics model

>> Build and test a proof-of-concept predictive analytics model

Major Technological Trends in Predictive Analytics

Traditional analytical techniques can only provide insights on the basis of historical data. Your data — both past and incoming — can provide you with a reliable predictor that can help you make better decisions to achieve your business goals. The tool for accomplishing those goals is predictive analytics.

Companies that adopt and apply this tool extensively are looking not only for insights, but also for usable *forward-looking insights* from multiple sources of data. Using a wide range of data, companies want to predict their customer's next action before it occurs, to predict marketing failures, detect fraud, or predict the likelihood that future business decisions will succeed.

Exploring predictive analytics as a service

As the use of predictive analytics has become more common and widespread, an emerging trend is (understandably) toward greater ease of use. Arguably the easiest way to use predictive analytics is as software — whether as a standalone product or as a cloud-based service provided by a company whose business is providing predictive analytics solutions for other companies.

If your company's business is to offer predictive analytics, you can provide that capability in two major ways:

» **As a standalone software application with an easy-to-use graphical user interface:** The customer buys the predictive analytics product and uses it to build customized predictive models.

» **As a cloud-based set of software tools that help the user choose a predictive model to use:** The customer applies the tools to fulfill the requirements and specifications of the project at hand, and the type of data that the model will be applied to. The tools can offer predictions quickly, without involving the client in the workings of the algorithms in use or the data management involved. These services don't require that the user have prior knowledge of the inner workings of the provided models and services. Cloud-based services allow for third-party integration with no need for client interaction, and also offer a marketplace for other services.

A simple example can be as straightforward as these three steps:

1. A client uploads data to your servers, or chooses data that already resides in the cloud.

2. The customer applies some of the available predictive model to that data.

3. The customer reviews visualized insights and predictions from the results of the analysis or service.

Aggregating distributed data for analysis

A growing trend is to apply predictive analytics to data gathered from diverse sources. Deploying a typical predictive analytics solution in a distributed environment requires collecting data — sometimes big data — from different sources; an approach that must rely on data management capabilities. Data needs to be collected, pre-processed, and managed *before* it can be considered usable for generating actionable predictions.

The architects of predictive analytics solutions must always face the problem of how to collect and process data from different data sources. Consider, for example, a company that wants to predict the success of a business decision that affects one of its products by evaluating one of the following options:

» To put company resources into increasing the sales volume

» To terminate manufacture of the product

» To change the current sales strategy for the product

The predictive analytics architect must engineer a model that helps the company make this decision, using data about the product from different departments (as illustrated in Figure 16-1):

>> **Technical data**: The engineering department has data about the product's specifications, its lifecycle, and the resources and time needed to produce it.

>> **Sales data**: The sales department has information about the product's sales volume, the number of sales per region, and profits generated by those sales.

>> **Customer data from surveys, reviews, and posts**: The company may have no dedicated department that analyzes how customers feel about the product. Tools exist, however, that can automatically analyze data posted online and extract the attitudes of authors, speakers, or customers toward a topic, a phenomenon, or (in this case) a product. The process is known as *sentiment analysis* or *opinion mining*.

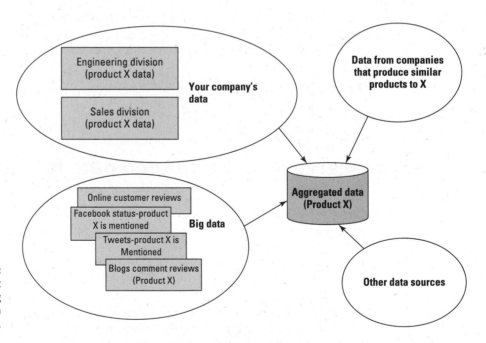

FIGURE 16-1:
Data about Product X being aggregated from different sources.

For example, if a user posts a review about Product X that says, "I really like Product X and I'm happy with the price," a *sentiment extractor* automatically labels this comment as positive. Such tools can classify responses as "happy," "sad," "angry," and so on, basing the classification on the words that an author uses in text posted online. In the case of Product X, the predictive analytics solution would need to aggregate customer reviews from external sources (such as social networks and micro-blogs) with data derived from internal company sources.

Figure 16-1 shows such an aggregation of data from multiple sources, both internal and external — from the engineering and sales divisions (internal), and from customer reviews gleaned from social networks (external data that isn't found in the data warehouse) — which is also an instance of using big data in predictive analytics. A standard tool that can be used for such aggregation is Hadoop — a big-data framework that enables building predictive analytics solutions from different sources. (More about Hadoop in the next section.)

Real-time data-driven analytics

Delivering insights as new events occur in real time is a challenging task because so much is happening so fast. Modern high-speed processing has shifted the quest for business insight away from traditional data warehousing and toward real-time processing. But the volume of data is also high — a tremendous amount of varied data, from multiple sources, generated constantly and at different rates. Companies are eager for scalable predictive analytics solutions that can derive real-time insights from a flood of data that seems to carry "the world and all it contains."

The demand is intensifying for analyzing data in real time *and* generating predictions quickly. Consider the real-life example (mentioned earlier in this chapter) of encountering an online ad placement that corresponds to a purchase you were already about to make. Companies are interested in predictive analytics solutions that can provide such capabilities as the following:

>> Predict — in real time — the specific ad that a site visitor would most likely click (an approach called *real-time ad placement*).

>> Speculate accurately on which customers are about to quit a service or product in order to target those customers with a retention campaign (*customer retention and churn modeling*).

>> Identify voters who can be influenced through a specific communication strategy such as a home visit, TV ad, phone call, or email. (You can imagine the impact on political campaigning.)

In addition to encouraging buying and voting along desired lines, real-time predictive analytics can serve as a critical tool for the automatic detection of cyber-attacks. For example, RSA — a well-known American computer and network security company — has recently adopted predictive analytics and big-data visualization as part of a web-threat detection solution. The tool analyzes a large number of websites and web users' activities to predict, detect, visualize, and score (rate) cyber-threats such as denial-of-service attacks and malicious web activities such as online banking fraud.

Applying Open-Source Tools to Big Data

This section highlights two major open source Apache projects that are important and relevant to big data. The most important one is Apache Hadoop, a framework that allows storing and processing various datasets using parallel processing on a cluster of computers bundled together. The other project is Apache Spark, which is a recently developed computational engine that is responsible for distribution, scheduling, and managing large-scale data applications across many nodes in your cluster. It is designed to be flexible and relatively fast by trying to perform as much computations as possible in-memory (rather than going to disk).

Apache Hadoop

Apache Hadoop is a free, open-source software platform for writing and running applications that process a large amount of data. It enables a distributed parallel processing of large datasets generated from different sources. Essentially, it's a powerful tool for storing and processing big data.

Hadoop stores any type of data, structured or unstructured, from different sources — and then aggregates that data in nearly any way you want. Hadoop handles heterogeneous data using distributed parallel processing — which makes it a very efficient framework to use in analytic software dealing with big data. No wonder some large companies are adopting Hadoop, including Facebook, Yahoo!, IBM, Twitter, and LinkedIn (who developed Hadoop's components to solve big data problems that they were facing internally).

Before Hadoop, companies were unable to take advantage of big data, which wasn't analyzed and almost unusable. The cost to store that data in a proprietary relational database and create a structured format around it didn't justify the benefits of analyzing that data and making use of it. Hadoop, on the other hand, is making that task seamless — at a fraction of the cost — allowing companies to find valuable insights in the abundant data they have acquired and are accumulating.

The power of Hadoop lies in handling different types — in fact, any type — of data: text, speech, emails, photos, posts, tweets, you name it. Hadoop takes care of aggregating this data, in all its variety, and provides you with the ability to query all of the data at your convenience. You don't have to build a schema before you can make sense of your data; Hadoop allows you to query that data in its original format.

In addition to handling large amounts of varied data, Hadoop is fault-tolerant, using simple programs that handle the scheduling of the processing distributed over multiple machines. These programs can detect hardware failure and divert a task to another running machine. This arrangement enables Hadoop to deliver high availability, regardless of hardware failure.

Hadoop uses two main components to do its job: MapReduce and Hadoop Distributed File System. The two components work co-operatively:

» **MapReduce**: Hadoop's implementation of MapReduce is based on Google's research on programming models to process large datasets by dividing them into small blocks of tasks. MapReduce uses distributed algorithms, on a group of computers in a cluster, to process large datasets. It consists of two functions:

- **The** Map( ) **function** which resides on the master *node* (networked computer). It divides the input query or task into smaller subtasks, which it then distributes to *worker nodes* that process the smaller tasks and pass the answers back to the master node. The subtasks are run in parallel on multiple computers.

- **The** Reduce( ) **function** collects the results of all the subtasks and combines them to produce an aggregated final result — which it returns as the answer to the original big query.

» **Hadoop Distributed File System (HDFS)**: HDFS replicates the data blocks that reside on other computers in your data center (to ensure reliability) and manages the transfer of data to the various parts of your distributed system.

Consider a database of two billion people, and assume you want to compute the number of social friends of Mr. X and arrange them according to their geographical locations. That's a tall order. The data for two billion people could originate in widely different sources such as social networks, email contact address lists, posts, tweets, browsing histories — and that's just for openers. Hadoop can aggregate this huge, diverse mass of data so you can investigate it with a simple query.

You would use MapReduce programming capabilities to solve this query. Defining Map and Reduce procedures makes even this large dataset manageable. Using the tools that the Hadoop framework offers, you would create a MapReduce implementation that would do the computation as two subtasks:

» Compute the average number of social friends of Mr. X.

» Arrange Mr. X's friends by geographical location.

Your MapReduce implementation program would run these subtasks in parallel, manage communication between the subtasks, and assemble the results. Out of two billion people, you would know who Mr. X's online friends are.

Hadoop provides a range of Map processors; which one(s) you select will depend on your infrastructure. Each of your processors will handle a certain number of records. Suppose, for example, that each processor handles one million data records. Each processor executes a Map procedure that produces multiple records of key-value pairs ‹G, N› where G (key) is the geographical location a person (country) and N (value) is the number of contacts the person has.

Suppose each Map processor produces many pairs of the form ‹*key, value*›, such as the following:

    Processor Map#1: ‹France, 45›

    Processor Map#2: ‹Morocco, 23›

    Processor Map#3: ‹USA, 334›

    Processor Map#4: ‹Morocco, 443›

    Processor Map#5: ‹France, 8›

    Processor Map#6: ‹Morocco, 44›

In the Reduce phase, Hadoop assigns a task to a certain number of processors: Execute the Reduce procedure that aggregates the values of the same keys to produce a final result. For this example the Reduce implementation sums up the count of values for each key — geographical location. So, after the Map phase, the Reduce phase produces the following:

    ‹Morocco, 23+44+443=510› → ‹Morocco, 510›

    ‹France, 8+45=53› → ‹France, 53›

Clearly, Mr. X is a popular guy — but this was a very simple example of how MapReduce can be used. Imagine you're dealing with a large dataset where you want to perform complex operations such as clustering billions of documents as mentioned in Chapter 6 where the operation and the data is just too big for a single machine to handle. Hadoop is the tool to consider.

Latest versions of Hadoop decouple MapReduce programming model and Cluster Resources Management by introducing a new technology called Yarn within the Hadoop framework.

Apache Yarn

Yarn stands for*Yet Another Resource Negotiator,* which is a new component in the Hadoop framework. Yarn is responsible for cluster management and scheduling. Cluster resource management, as its name implies, manages the resources (such as memory and CPU) of the different clusters, including data nodes. In recent versions of Hadoop, Yarn took over cluster resource management; MapReduce is now only responsible for data processing.

TECHNICAL STUFF

Yarn is sometimes referred to as the operating system of Hadoop, because Yarn manages Hadoop resources and ensures high availability of Hadoop features.

Yarn was introduced to overcome major limitations of scalability in earlier versions of Hadoop. Users of the earliest version of Hadoop experienced major scalability, job tracker concurrency issues, and malfunctioning for a cluster of over about 3000 data nodes. Yarn handles job scheduling functionality as a separate generic application. The later allows the coexistence of different processing models with MapReduce. For example, with Yarn you can run machine learning algorithms, MapReduce programs, and stream processing.

Yarn is responsible for two main tasks:

>> Answering to a client request by allocating processes (known as *containers*) that will run on physical machines

>> Managing containers that were allocated for each application

Yarn can free some of the containers if they aren't being used or if they are complete, and allocates the freed resources to another application by client request. MapReduce in Hadoop 1.0 relied on a fixed number of Maps and Reduce processes that are allowed to run on a single node. This wasn't the best way to maximize the utilization of nodes in cluster. In later versions of Hadoop, Yarn allows clients' applications to request resources of different memory and CPU sizes. A Yarn application has full control over the resources needed to fulfill its work.

Hadoop ecosystem at a glance

The word *ecosystem* was invented in 1930 by botanist Roy Clapham, The word refers to physical and biological components that include plants, rocks, minerals, soil, water, and human beings, among other components, that interact with a unit. Each component has a specific role and exists to support other components. The same analogy applies to Hadoop.

Hadoop framework is made up of components that can interacts with each other's and work as a unit to provide a Hadoop-based data analytics solution.

Figure 16-2 shows an overview of the up-to-date software components available in Hadoop Ecosystem. Some of the components, like Spark and Mahout, are explained later in this chapter. The Hadoop ecosystem is frequently changing. Figure 16-2 gives an overview of the components you can adopt on Hadoop for such purposes as predictive analytics, data processing, and SQL-like processing. Apache's website maintains an up-to-date list of the Hadoop ecosystem: http://hadoop.apache.org

FIGURE 16-2: Hadoop Ecosystem.

Apache Mahout

Apache Mahout is a machine-learning library that includes large-scale versions of the clustering, classification, collaborative filtering, and other data-mining algorithms that can support a large-scale predictive analytics model. A highly recommended way to process the data needed for such a model is to run Mahout in a system that's already running Hadoop (see the preceding section). Hadoop designates a master machine that orchestrates the other machines (such as Map machines and Reduce machines) employed in its distributed processing. In most cases, Mahout should be installed on the server it will run on (for example, master node).

Imagine you have large amount of streamed data — Google news articles — and you would like to cluster by topic, using one of the clustering algorithms mentioned in Chapter 6. After you install Hadoop and Mahout, you can execute one of the algorithms — such as K-means — on your data.

The implementation of K-means under Mahout uses a MapReduce approach, which makes it different from the normal implementation of K-means (described earlier in Chapter 6). Mahout subdivides the K-means algorithm into these sub-procedures:

- >> **KmeansMapper** reads the input dataset and will assign each input point to its nearest initially selected means (cluster representatives).

- >> **KmeansCombiner** procedure will take all the records — <key, value> pairs — produced by KmeansMapper and produces partial sums to ease the calculation of the subsequent cluster representatives.

- >> **KmeansReducer** receives the values produced by all the subtasks (combiners) to calculate the actual centroids of the clusters which is the final output of K-means.

- >> **KmeansDriver** handles the iterations of the process until all clusters have converged. The output of a given iteration, a partial clustering output, is used as the input for the next iteration. The process of mapping and reducing the dataset until the assignment of records and clusters show no further changes. (For more about K-means, see Chapter 6.)

Apache Mahout is a recently developed project; its functionality still has a lot of space to accommodate extensions. In the meantime, Mahout already uses MapReduce to implement classification, clustering, and other machine-learning techniques — and can do so on a large scale.

Installing Hadoop

For a very straightforward installation of Hadoop, adopt Cloudera's distribution. Cloudera's Hadoop Distribution (CDH) is an integrated Apache Hadoop that contains pre-installed and configured components for a Hadoop production environment. CDH is free and is available on different formats of Linux packages, virtual machine images, and in tar files. You can also run CDH on the cloud. Everything in CDH is installed and ready to go. You can download the image type that corresponds to your preferred virtual machine tool. To download and get started on Hadoop installation, visit `www.cloudera.com/downloads.html` three modes:

- >> **Fully-distributed mode:** Normal mode with namenodes and datanodes.

- >> **Pseudo-distributed mode:** In this mode, there can be several mappers and reducers, but all daemons run on one machine (your local machine) using HDFS protocol.

  This mode is very useful for developers to mimic a Hadoop environment for testing purposes.

>> **Hadoop in standalone mode:** All jobs will run as one mapper and one reducer in your local file system (not HDFS). Running Hadoop in standalone mode is known to be a practical model for developers that can allow them to write and debug applications developed in the MapReduce programming paradigm.

Apache Spark

Originally developed at the University of California Berkeley in 2009, Apache Spark has quickly emerged as a big data analytics processing engine. It's positioned to become part of the next generation of data analytics processing engines that can improve and co-exist with Hadoop in certain circumstances.

Cloudera (one of the main players in the big data Hadoop distribution arena) announced that Spark was going to be their default selection. They have positioned Spark as replacement for MapReduce in the Hadoop ecosystem where data analytics workloads will be processed. Last year, IBM endorsed and supported Apache Spark as *"the most important new open source project in a decade that is being defined by data"*. IBM also committed to educate over a million data scientists on Spark technology.

eBay uses Spark for analyzing and aggregating logs of transactional data. OpenTable uses Spark to support extract transfer and load (ETL) jobs (see chapter 9), it's also being used to power a recommender system (see Chapter 2) that leverages MLliB Spark' component. Elsevier labs are evaluating Spark to build a machine learning pipeline to support content as a service, and many other companies are flocking to adopt Spark. So, what is Apache Spark?

Apache Spark is a relatively fast open source engine for general large scale processing. It's a computational engine that is responsible for scheduling, distributing tasks and managing applications across many nodes in the computing cluster.

Apache Spark is designed to be relatively fast, to support implicit data parallelism, to serve as a general workloads platform, and to provide fault-tolerance.

Spark is an extension of the MapReduce software paradigm. It adds the support of two main features:

>> Interactive queries over your data in lieu of exploring data and performing computations that could take hours

>> Ability to process data streams

The Spark framework runs complex data computations in memory which makes it, in most cases, more efficient and faster than MapReduce's computations running on disk. It makes it easy to combine a heterogonous array of data processing types that can be part of a data analytics pipeline (streaming, interactive queries, and iterative machine learning algorithms).

Spark can run in a Hadoop cluster and it can integrate different data sources. It provides several application programming interfaces in Java, Scala, Python and SQL.

Having the ability to support multiple data processing types and integration capabilities with different data sources, such as Cassandra, Amazon S3, or Hadoop HBase, Spark helps mitigate the burden of maintaining separate tools for specific processing types. In fact, Spark was designed as a unified stack that encapsulates multiple integrated components.

The elegance of Spark allows data scientists to combines and invoke multiple components, which are defined in Spark (such as Spark SQL, Spark Streaming, and MLlib for machine learning), in the same manner and ease as invoking libraries in a software development project. For example, a large-scale software application for an international bank was developed using the Spark framework. The application relied on the graph library provided by Spark, known as GraphX, to perform graph-based computations (such as PageRank and Dijkstra algorithms) from a large dataset modeled as a graph. The dataset was streamed live using the streaming library on Spark. The same application was used by business users to perform queries on the graph-structured data and on the discovered insights thanks to the Spark SQL library – all in one software application.

Under Spark's integration and comprehensive unified stack, the team had to maintain only one software application that offers multiple services, including analytics, ingesting data streams, and interactive queries.

Spark's main abstraction is based on resilient distributed datasets, known as RDDs. RDDs are created by either parallelizing collections in your program or referencing a dataset in an external storage.

The term collection (also known as *container)* in computer programming often refers to an object that combines a set of elements into a single unit. A collection is defined and used to apply operations to manipulate, store, and retrieve data. For example, in Java, using Spark, you can parallelize a collection that you define in your program (line 3) using the Spark framework. Here's a simple example:

1.
```
SparkConf conf = new SparkConf().setAppName(name).
setMaster(master);
```

2.
```
JavaSparkContext sparkContext = new JavaSparkContext(conf);
```

3. `List<Integer> dataset = Arrays.asList(10, 30, 60, 33);`

4. `JavaRDD<Integer> distributedData = sparkContext.`
`parallelize(dataset);`

Lines 1 and 2 are used to initialize the Spark configuration and context. In lines 3 and 4, a collection of four numbers (dataset) is being paralleled by SparkContext and converted in an RDD named distributedData that can be operated on in parallel. To learn more about the operations that can now be applied to the RDD, visit `http://spark.apache.org/docs/latest/programming-guide.html#resilient-distributed-datasets-rdds`

RDDs also can be also created by referencing a dataset in an external storage. Spark creates RDDs from datasets residing in any storage supported by Hadoop including text files.

SparkContext defined in Spark Application Programming Interfaces (API) is used to create text file RDD by calling textFile method. Consider the following Java:

```
SparkConf conf = new SparkConf().setAppName(name).setMaster(master);

JavaSparkContext sparkContext = new JavaSparkContext(conf);

JavaRDD<String> distributedFile = sparkContext.textFile("dataset.txt");
```

The data in dataset.txt file was converted to an RDD named distributedFile that you can apply all distributed operations like the map and reduce operations.

For more information about RDDs, visit `http://spark.apache.org/docs/latest/programming-guide.html#resilient-distributed-datasets-rdds`

Main Components of Spark

The main components of Apache Spark are

>> **Spark Core.** This is the main component in the Spark framework that consists of the API for creating and applying operations on the RDDs. Spark Core also is responsible for interacting with data sources, task scheduling, fault tolerance and recovery, and managing memory.

>> **Spark Streaming.** This is the component that is responsible for enabling your application to process live streams of data, such as logs of transactional data. Spark Streaming was designed to offer scalability and fault-tolerance.

>> **Spark SQL.** This is the component that is responsible for querying structured data. It supports SQL and Hive Query Language (HQL). It can be used to run queries on a variety of data sources and formats, such as JSON and Hive tables.

- » **Spark MLlib.** MLlib encapsulates a set of machine learning algorithms, such as data classification algorithms, data clustering algorithms, recommender systems algorithms, algorithms for predictive model evaluations and dimensionality reduction algorithms.

- » **Spark GraphX.** GraphX allows you to create graphs. These can be graphs of urban data or graphs of a social network. The Graph X component also includes algorithms that can be applied to analyze graphs, such as the PageRank algorithm.

In addition to the capabilities of the component as previously explained, Spark can run on several cluster managers, including Hadoop Yarn, Apache Mesos, and Spark scheduler. The cluster manager allows Spark to scale from a few nodes to several thousand.

Choosing a framework

The data science legend and inventor Amr Awadallah co-founded Cloudera, the most widely used Hadoop distribution in the industry. He was right when he said in an interview published at Kdnugget: "I have no favorites among the projects in our distribution, I love them all equally. It is the combined power of these projects, the platform, where the true power lies."

We believe that newer versions of Hadoop framework, along with more new components including new versions of Spark, will emerge and more new technologies will be invented. Sometimes, it is hard to keep up with the new trends. For example, Hadoop and Spark coexist and can support your enterprise in providing a comprehensive solution.

In leadership meetings at a large organization where we were evaluating Hadoop distributions, we were overwhelmed by the sales presentations that highlight the technologies being presented. However, behind closed doors and together with leadership, we decided to focus on these points that would help us pick our choice:

- » High availability
- » Fault tolerance
- » Scalability
- » Data availability
- » Federation
- » Multi-programming paradigm support, including MapReduce
- » Security
- » Data privacy

Chapter 17

Getting Ready for Enterprise Analytics

I n the world of enterprise architecture for data analytics, there are no clear standards. The design of an architecture depends on the data science problem you're addressing for your business.

This chapter introduces high-level requirements that you might need to consider for your enterprise architecture for big data.

There's also a summary of the most widely adopted tools for enterprise analytics, including RapidMiner, KNIME, Google Analytics, IBM Watson, and Microsoft Revolution R Enterprise. The end of this chapter presents the fundamentals of getting ready to build a rapid prototype for your predictive analytics efforts for your organization.

Enterprise Architecture for Big Data

In perspective, the goal for designing an architecture for data analytics comes down to building a framework for capturing, sorting, and analyzing big data for the purpose of discovering actionable results, as shown in Figure 17-1.

FIGURE 17-1:
Thinking of the
architecture that
will transform
big data into
actionable
results.

There is no one correct way to design the architectural environment for big data analytics. However, most designs need to meet the following requirements to support the challenges big data can bring. These criteria can be distributed mainly over six layers, as shown in Figure 17-2, and can be summarized as follows:

FIGURE 17-2:
The layers of
enterprise data
architecture.

>> Your architecture should include a big data platform for storage and computation, such as Hadoop or Spark, which is capable of scaling out.

>> Your architecture should include large-scale software and big data tools capable of analyzing, storing, and retrieving big data. These can consist of the components of Spark (discussed earlier in this chapter), or the components of Hadoop ecosystem (such as Mahout and Apache Storm). You might also want to adopt a big data large-scale tool that will be used by data scientists in your business. These include Radoop from RapidMiner, IBM Watson, and many others.

>> Your architecture should support virtualization. Virtualization is an essential element of cloud computing because it allows multiple operating systems and applications to run at the same time on the same server. Because of this capability, virtualization and cloud computing often go hand in hand. You might also adopt a private cloud in your architecture. A private cloud offers the same architecture as a public cloud, except the services in a private cloud are restricted to a certain number of users through a firewall. Amazon Elastic Computer Cloud is one of the major providers of private cloud solutions and storage space for businesses, and can scale as they grow.

>> Your architecture might have to offer real-time analytics if your enterprise is working with fast data (data that is flowing in streams at a fast rate). In a scenario where, you would need to consider an infrastructure that can support the derivation of insights from data in near real time without waiting for data to be written to disk. For example, Apache Spark's streaming library can be glued with other components to support analytics on fast data streams.

>> Your architecture should account for Big Data security by creating a system of governance around the supply of access to the data and the results. The big data security architecture should be in line with the standard security practices and policies in your organization that govern access to data sources.

If you're looking for a robust tool to help you get started on data analytics without the need for expertise in the algorithms and complexities behind building predictive models, then you should try KNIME (www.knime.org), RapidMiner (http://rapidminer.com), or IBM Watson (www.ibm.com/analytics/watson-analytics), among others.

Most of the preceding tools offer a comprehensive, ready-to-use toolbox that consists of capabilities that can get you started. For example, RapidMiner has a large number of algorithms from different states of the predictive analytics life-cycle, so it provides a straightforward path to quickly combining and deploying analytics models.

With RapidMiner, you can quickly load and prepare your data, create and evaluate predictive models, use data processes in your applications and share them with your business users. With very few clicks, you can easily build a predictive analytics model as simple as shown in Figure 17-3.

FIGURE 17-3: Drag-and-drop analytics with RapidMiner.

Data Analytics Process

Predictive Analytics Model

RapidMiner can be used by both beginners and experts. RapidMiner Studio is an open-source predictive analytics software that has an easy-to-use graphical interface where you can drag and drop algorithms for data loading, data preprocessing, predictive analytics algorithms, and model evaluations to build your data analytics process.

RapidMiner was built to provide data scientists with a comprehensive toolbox that consists of more than a thousand different operations and algorithms. The data can be loaded quickly, regardless of whether your data source is in Excel, Access, MS SQL, MySQL, SPSS, Salesforce, or any other format that is supported by RapidMiner. In addition to data loading, predictive model building and model evaluation, this tool also provides you with data visualization tools that include adjustable self-organizing maps and 3-D graphs.

RapidMiner offers an open extension application programming interface (API) that allows you to integrate your own algorithms into any pipeline built in RapidMiner. It's also compatible with many platforms and can run on major operating systems. There is an emerging online community of data scientists that use RapidMiner where they can share their processes, and ask and answer questions.

Another easy-to-use tool that is widely used in the analytics world is KNIME. KNIME stands for the Konstanz Information Miner. It's an open source data analytics that can help you build predictive models through a data pipelining concept. The tool offers drag-and-drop components for ETL (extraction, Transformation and Loading) and components for predictive modeling as well as data visualization. KNIME and RapidMiner are tools that you can arm your data science team to easily get started building predictive models. For an excellent use case on KNIME, we invite you to go over the paper "The Seven Techniques for Dimensionality Reduction" published at www.knime.org/files/knime_seventechniquesdatadimreduction.pdf.

RapidMiner Radoop for Big Data

RapidMiner Radoop is a product by RapidMiner that extends predictive analytics toolbox on RapidMiner Studio to run on Hadoop and Spark environments. Radoop encapsulates MapReduce, Pig, Mahout, and Spark. After you define your workflows on Radoop, then instructions are executed in Hadoop or Spark environment, so you don't have to program predictive models but focus on model evaluation and development of new models.

For security, Radoop supports Kerberos authentication and integrates with Apache Ranger and Apache Sentry.

For more information about RapidMiner, visit www.rapidminer.com

Analytics as a Service

Imagine living in a world where you can order customized *a la carte* analytics solutions, as depicted in Figure 17-4, which will fit your business needs and improve your return on investment (ROI). We almost live in that world of *analytics-as-a-service* (AAAS).

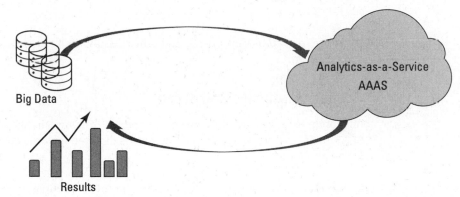

FIGURE 17-4:
Cloud-based
Analytics Services.

Big Data

Analytics-as-a-Service
AAAS

Results

The AAAS world has arrived, and it spans across an array of services that include storage, deployment, cloud based analytics, AB testing-based analytics (see Chapter 2), data-at-rest analytics and fast data analytics. According to a recent report by *Research and Markets*, the AAAS market is projected to grow from $5.9 billion in 2015 to $22 billion in 2020. For more information on the report, you can visit www.researchandmarkets.com/research/nz612h/global

According to the same report, primary users of AAAS will include retail, healthcare, manufacturing, and government. The main players in this space are Amazon, Google, Microsoft, IBM, and Intel.

Google Analytics

Google offers a suite of products that provide analytics services: Google Prediction API, Google Analytics 360 suite, and Google Big Query. We will give an over overview of each product that you may want to adopt in your enterprise architecture.

Google Prediction API

Google offers cloud-based services for large scale machine learning that can integrate into your application. The machine learning services offered by Google consist of, but aren't limited to, sentiment analysis (also known as opinion mining) on customer data, spam email detection, fraud detection, document and email classification, and recommendation systems (see Chapter 2). Using the representational state transfer (REST) Application Programming Interface (API), you can leverage Google's cloud services to build software applications that derive predictions of class labels or numerical values. This service can be used for different formats and data types. We encourage you to start with the basic "Hello World" of Google Prediction API at `https://cloud.google.com/prediction/docs/hello_world`

For more information on pricing and other details, visit `https://cloud.google.com/prediction`

Google Analytics 360 suite

In March 2016, Google announced the birth of a game changer in the world of AAAS. This product, Google Analytics 360, is directed towards customer segmentation and targeting.

Google Analytics 360 suite is a newer version of the Google Analytics product. It consists of six products. These are three of the most relevant components:

>> **Google Audience Center:** This component can help your marketing department find customers among similar lines of business. It serves as a data management platform (DMP). We speculate that the backbone of the data is based on Gmail, search data and traffic, and the Android platform, which is the dominant mobile operating system.

>> **Google Optimize:** This product is an analytics-based A/B testing platform (see Chapter 2) that is an extension of Google Experiments. Your marketers can use this product to create several versions of your site, log the behavior of customers on your site and optimize your site to target customers, and create better experiences for them.

>> **Google Analytics:** This product analyzes customer data from different sources to power the ad products in support of marketing campaigns.

Google BigQuery

Through a cloud-based service named Google BigQuery, you can query large datasets and apply analytics to your data hosted on Google's machines. BigQuery allows you to load, query, view, and manage big datasets on Google's infrastructure. BigQuery offers a REST API that will allow you to make calls in your application using Java, Python, or .NET to query your data. BigQuery also offers a web-based, user-friendly interface and command-line tool.

For more information on how to get started on BigQuery, visit `https://cloud.google.com/bigquery`

IBM Watson

The IBM Watson Developer Cloud can offer you an array of services that can be part of your analytics toolset. IBM Watson offers services including, but not limited to, entity and entity-relationship recognition, speech-to-text conversion, and personality insights that can extract a set of features from people's text that define their personality characteristics, among many other machine learning services.

For more information about Watson services, you will need to visit the IBM Watson services catalog at

`www.ibm.com/smarterplanet/us/en/ibmwatson/developercloud/services-catalog.html`

IBM Watson services can be accessed via a Representational State Transfer (REST) Application Programming Interface (API).

Bluemix is another IBM cloud platform where Watson-based applications can be deployed. Bluemix offers Apache Spark, Big Insights for Apache Hadoop, Cloud-based NoSQL databases, time series databases, and many others under the IBM cloud infrastructure.

Microsoft Revolution R Enterprise

If you happen to know R, think of Revolution R as an R++, a bigger R, or an R for Big Data Analytics. Revolution R Enterprise was recently acquired by Microsoft. The services offered include predictive analytics algorithms and statistical models that are compatible with R language and suitable for massive data.

Revolution R Enterprise provides a scalable R that allows programs written in R to be deployed in enterprise clusters including Hadoop environments. Revolution R offers a free, open-source suite of models known as Microsoft R Open. It contains the most up-to-date R packages from R Foundation for Statistical Computing. It provides a high-performance R engine that is based on multi-threaded processing. Revolution R Enterprise is another product by Revolution R that provides distributed R algorithms known as ScaleR that you will need in the data science lifecycle. For more details, visit `www.revolutionanalytics.com`

Preparing for a Proof-of-Value of Predictive Analytics Prototype

This section addresses briefly the steps needed to build a prototype for a proof-of-concept and a proof-of-value predictive model. (For more details on how to build a predictive model, refer to Chapters 8 to 11.)

Prototyping for predictive analytics

A good model needs a prototype as proof of concept. To build a prototype for your predictive analytics model, start by defining a potential *use case* (a scenario drawn from the typical operations of your business) that illustrates the need for predictive analytics.

Fitting the model to the type of decision

Business decisions take diverse forms. As you undertake to build a predictive analytics model, you're concerned with two main types of decision:

>> **Strategic decisions** often aren't well defined, and focus only on the big picture. Strategic decisions have an impact on the long-term performance of your company — and correlate directly with your company's mission and objectives. Senior managers are usually the ones who make strategic decisions.

>> **Operational decisions** focus on specific answers to existing problems and define specific future actions. Operational decisions usually don't require a manager's approval, although they generally have a standard set of guidelines for the decision-makers to reference.

The two classes of decisions require different predictive analytics models:

>> The chief financial officer of a bank might use predictive analytics to gauge broad trends in the banking industry that require a company-wide response (strategic).

>> A clerk in the same bank might use a predictive analytic model to determine credit-worthiness of a particular customer who is requesting a loan (operational).

With these two major types of decisions in mind, you can identify colleagues at your company who make either operational or strategic decisions. Then you can determine which type of decision is most in need of predictive analytics — and design an appropriate prototype for your model.

Defining the problem for the model to address

The basic objective of a predictive analytics model is make your business do better. You may find that a prototype of your model will work best if you apply it to operational examples and then link those results to solving broad, high-level business issues. Here is a list of general steps to follow next:

1. Focus on the operational decisions at your company that can have a major impact on a business process. One of the biggest reasons for this is that operational decisions are the kinds of decisions that are more likely deployed into an automated system.

2. Select those processes that have a direct effect on overall profitability and efficiency.

3. Conduct one-to-one interviews with the decision-makers whose support you want to cultivate for your project. Ask about

   - The process they go through to make decisions.

   - The data they use to make decisions.

   - How predictive analytics would help them make the right decisions.

4. Analyze the stories you gathered from the interviews, looking for insights that clearly define the problem you're trying to solve.

5. Pick one story that defines a problem of a small scope that your prototype model should be able to address it. Scaling down for a prototype is harder than it seems. For example, in the example that follows, the complete model might send the optimal promotion to each customer, the prototype model might only focus on handling one promotion.

   For example, suppose you interviewed a marketing specialist who is struggling to decide which customers to send a specific product ad. He or she has a limited budget for the ad campaign, and needs to have high confidence in the decision. If predictive analytics could help focus the campaign and generate the needed confidence, then you have an appropriate problem for your prototype to address.

Defining your objectives

An effective way to state your business objectives clearly is as a bulleted list of user decisions. Then run your prototype to generate predictions and scores for each possible decision. For example, in the earlier example of Product X, you could list your objectives as a range of possible business decisions to be assessed:

» Increase the sales volume of Product X.

» Terminate manufacture of Product X.

» Change the marketing strategy behind Product X:

- Increase ads in a specific geographical location.

- Increase ads for specific customers.

The predictive model will evaluate these decisions according to their future likelihood of successful profitability. The output might indicate, for example, that the company has an 80-percent chance of increasing profit by increasing the sales volume of Product X.

Find the right data

After you've clearly stated the business objective and the problem you're willing to tackle, the next step is to collect the data that your predictive model will use. In this phase, you have to identify your data source(s). For example, if you're developing a prototype for predicting the right decision on a specific product, then you need to gather both internal and external data for that product. You shouldn't restrict the type or source of data, as long as it's relevant to the business goal.

If (say) your company is considering the introduction of a new hybrid sports car, you can contact the sales department and gather information about the sales data generated by similar products. You can contact the engineering department to find out how much the components cost (how about those longer-lasting batteries?), as well as the resources and time needed to produce the product (any retooling needed?). You might also include data about previous decisions made about a similar product (say, an overpowered convertible introduced some years ago), and their outcome (market conditions and fuel prices depressed sales).

TIP

You might want to consider using big data related to the product in question. For example, download customer reviews about company products, tweets or Facebook posts where the products are mentioned. One way to do that is to use application programming interfaces (APIs) provided by those companies. For example, if you want to gather tweets that contain a specific word, Twitter provides a set of APIs that you could use to download such tweets. There's a limit to how much data you can capture free of charge; in some cases, you might have to pay to keep downloading the needed data from Twitter.

When you've determined the most relevant data and the most useful source from which to get it, start storing the data you intend to use for your predictive model. Data may need to undergo some preprocessing, for which you'd use techniques mentioned in Chapter 9.

Design your model

For a prototype, your input could be a data matrix (see Chapter 6) that represents known factors derived from historical data.

Such a data matrix, when analyzed, can produce output that looks something like this:

> 57.6 percent of customers stated they were unhappy with the product.
>
> The product requires three hours on average to produce.
>
> Positive sentiment on the product is 80 percent.

Inputs to the prototype model could include historical data about similar products, the corresponding decisions made about them, and the impact of those decisions on your business processes. The prototype's output would be predictions and their corresponding scores as possible actions toward attaining the objectives you've set.

To get a usable prototype, you have to employ a mixture of techniques to build the model. For example, you could use DBSCAN or K-means algorithm as one of the data clustering algorithms; you could use it to build clusters like these:

» Products that were terminated — and that decision's impact on profit

» Products that were increased in volume and that decision's impact on profit

» Products whose marketing strategy was changed and that decision's impact profit

Then you could use classification algorithms such as a decision tree or Naïve Bayes (see Chapter 7) that would classify or predict missing values (such as sales profit value) for the product in question (Product X).

Testing your predictive analytics model

This section introduces testing your model by using a test dataset that's similar to your training dataset. (See Chapter 10 for more on testing and evaluating your model.)

Identify your test data

To evaluate your predictive analytics model, you have to run the model over some test data that it hasn't seen yet. You could run the model over several historical datasets as input and record how many of the model's predictions turn out correctly.

Run the model on test data

Evaluating your predictive model is an iterative process — essentially trial and error. Effective models rarely result from a mere first test. If your predictive model produces 100-percent accuracy, consider that result too good to be true; suspect something wrong with your data or your algorithms. For example, if the first algorithm you use to build your prototype is the Naïve Bayes classifier and you aren't satisfied with the predictions it gives you when you run the test data, try another algorithm such as the Nearest Neighbor classifier (see Chapter 6). Keep running other algorithms until you find the one that's most consistently and reliably predictive.

During the testing, you might find out that you need to revisit the initial data that you used to build the prototype model. You might need to find more relevant data for your analysis.

REMEMBER

Consider adding to your checklist before closing the prototype lifecycle:

>> Always verify that the steps involved in building the model are correct.

>> Comparing the output of the model on the test dataset to the actual results will help you evaluate the accuracy of your model.

The higher the confidence in the results of your predictive model, the easier it is for the stakeholders to approve its deployment.

To make sure that your model is accurate, you need to evaluate whether the model meets its business objectives. Domain experts can help you interpret the results of your model.

6

The Part of Tens

IN THIS PART . . .

Important selling features

Simple steps

Popular suppliers

Chapter 18

Ten Reasons to Implement Predictive Analytics

B usiness competition is fierce and global, which leads companies to employ everything in their power to survive and thrive. In such an environment, companies are seeking to increase their revenues while keeping the operating cost to a minimum.

Predictive analytics is a business enabler that helps accomplish the very essence of increasing companies' return on investments. If implemented successfully, it will drive your company's profits higher. It will help you turn your data into valuable information you can capitalize on, and it will give you the competitive edge you need to outperform your competition.

Predictive analytics enables companies to use the massive data they've accumulated from their operations as a refined resource to advance their businesses.

Identifying Business Goals

Predictive analytics can help you solve many business problems more effectively, but the crucial step toward that advantage is to identify specific business goals so you can choose the appropriate analytical tools to achieve them.

The process is twofold: The business goals you define help you build your predictive analytics project, and the completed model helps you measure how successfully your company is moving toward the goals. At the heart of this process is the development of your predictive model by running real data — both historical and incoming — against it.

Set project goals that you can accomplish in a relatively short time frame and can measure — concrete steps toward the company's general vision and overall mission. Depending on your current strategies and which phase of market development your business is in, your business goals may change — which is why it's important to evaluate your project goals periodically and adjust them accordingly. Here are examples:

>> If you're after increasing your customer base, then your predictive analytics model should help you run targeted marketing campaigns to acquire new customers.

>> If you want to reduce the operational costs of your business, your predictive analytics model should help you balance the workload across departments, efficiently distribute resources, skills, and raw material, and accurately predict product demand.

>> If you seek to identify fraud, then the model should be designed to rapidly and accurately evaluate whether a transaction is fraudulent — and react accordingly.

TIP

Industries that already use predictive analytics to detect fraud include healthcare, finance, and insurance.

Knowing Your Data

The quality of your predictive models is dependent on the quality and relevance of your data. Predictive analytics explores your data through well-defined algorithms and techniques, mines the data, searches for hidden patterns or trends you were unaware of, and uncovers valuable facts about your business. But you have to feed good data to the model to make that happen.

Data can be a big driver of predictive analytics. To ensure that your data is the best resource possible, your organization needs to know

>> Which data is needed for a given analysis

>> Where the data resides

>> How to put the data to use in the analytic model

>> How the model's predictions can empower the business

REMEMBER

Volume of data is no substitute for relevance; you want your relevant data to have ample history. It should span enough of an extended period of time that you can track changes and spot any marked seasonality in your business.

Poor data quality — generally incomplete or irrelevant data — can skew your predictions' results and lead to much wasted energy and work by your experts to distinguish between real patterns and false signals and noise in the data.

REMEMBER

It's obvious that you need good data to build predictive models. However, the modeling process requires that you address any issues with your data, which, in itself, is a very important gain.

The model helps you improve the quality of the data; the better the data, the more useful the predictions. The better the predictions, the better you know your data. One feeds into the other.

Knowing your data will lead to better predictive analytics. Fortunately, establishing a predictive analytics project will lead to better knowledge of your data. In the course of that process, the output of your model helps you uncover relationships within your data that you were unaware of — giving you a much firmer foundation from which to embark on the predictive analytics journey.

Organizing Your Data

Transforming your data into knowledge — and transforming that knowledge into actionable decisions — is the core promise of predictive analytics.

Raw data will need to undergo extraction, cleaning, and transformation before the model can use it to create useful predictions.

It's important to clean your data of any errors, inconsistencies, and missing values. And ensure it has enough records, spans an extended period of time, and comprises all the necessary fields required by the analysis.

In addition to historical data, however, your predictive model needs some up-to-date input, and you may need to derive data from existing data points. To analyze and evaluate a stock's performance, for example, you might calculate a 200-day moving average of the stock price.

Preprocessing your data is a prerequisite for modeling data analytics; so is sampling your datasets. You'll need at least two datasets:

>> A *training dataset* on which to run your experiments while you're building your model. This dataset usually comprises historical data with known inputs and outputs.

>> A *testing dataset* consisting of data that the model hasn't seen before. This dataset helps you avoid overfitting the model to the training dataset. (See Chapter 15 for more about overfitting.)

Organizing your data is more of a challenge when the data comes from multiple sources. It's essential to closely examine each data source for quality and relevance.

When data is coming in from multiple sources, data integration and consolidation is crucial to the success of your model. Modelers need one pooled, cleansed dataset that is ready to be used in their modeling project.

Satisfying Your Customers

Global competition drives companies to lower prices to attract new customers. Companies strive to please their customers and gain new ones; customers increasingly demand high-quality products at cheaper prices. In response to these pressures, businesses strive to deliver the right balance of quality and price, at the right time, through the right medium, to the people most likely to buy.

Customers' experience of a product, if publicized through the power of the Internet — essentially a vast medium of communications — can make or break a business.

The Internet is a two-way street; companies have been gathering valuable information about their customers through transactional data that includes

>> Counting the number of items bought by customers

>> Tracking methods of payment used

>> Identifying customers' demographics

>> Collecting customers' responses to filled-out surveys

To complete the picture, other sources of information come from business operations — for example, the amount of time customers spend on the company websites and the customers' browsing histories.

All that data can be combined and analyzed to answer some important questions:

>> What are the demographics of your customers?

>> What drives the sales of your products?

>> How can your business improve the customer experience?

>> How can you retain existing customers and attract new customers?

>> What would your customers like to buy next?

>> What can you recommend to a particular customer?

Any information that can shed light about how customers think and feel can bring insight to understanding them and anticipating their needs.

Predictive analytics can also help improve your customers' experience by enhancing such processes as these:

>> Creating successful marketing campaigns

>> Building programs to reward customers' loyalty

>> Building recommender systems

- >> Reducing operational costs
- >> Delivering relevant service and products to your customers

Predictive analytics can also help you focus on identifying significant segments within your customer base — and make accurate predictions about their future behaviors. It can allow you offer relevant products to them with competitive prices, build targeted marketing campaigns, and enable you develop strategies to retain your customers and attract new ones.

Many online businesses use predictive analytics to manage customer relations. They harvest information about their customers, identify attributes that are the best predictors of customer behaviors, and use that information to make recommendations in real time. The result is that their customers get specialized and personalized service and attention, from marketing and cross-selling to customer retention.

Reducing Operational Costs

Predictive analytics is an effective tool for more than customer management. It can help you reduce cost in many ways and at different levels of the organization — planning resources, increasing customer retention, managing inventories — and that's just for openers.

Predictive analytics is especially useful for reducing operational costs in these areas:

- >> Balancing the workload across departments
- >> Effectively allocating available skills and raw materials
- >> Accurately estimating demand for your products
- >> Positioning your products correctly in the pricing war waged by the competition
- >> Purchasing raw materials and hedging against market fluctuations
- >> Predictive maintenance will help you address problems before they occur, thereby allowing you to save time and money while avoiding any downtime.
- >> Producing better forecasts of your inventory needs and efficiently managing resources

Predictive models can reduce operational costs by helping you decide when to make new orders, when to increase your marketing campaigns, as well as how to correctly price your products, manage inventories, and obtain a clear view (and a solid grasp) of your supply-and-demand chains.

By making more accurate decisions that correctly anticipate your business needs, you gain an advantage over businesses that manage their operations as a guessing game.

Increasing Returns on Investments (ROI)

Predictive analytics can help you increase return on investment (ROI) through

>> Targeted marketing campaigns

>> Improved risk assessment and management

>> Reducing operational costs

>> Making actionable decisions

By implementing predictive analytics, companies can accurately assess the present state of the business, optimize their operations, and compete more effectively in gaining market share. By scoring the predictive outcomes of future events, and using that information to their advantage, companies can improve their revenue and enhance the business performance as a whole. Deploying successful predictive models can help companies minimize risk and increase revenue across the board.

TIP

When embarking on your predictive analytics projects, be sure to document everything meticulously and methodically. It's equally important to establish a baseline before launching so you can accurately measure the ROI after the launch. You can calculate the improvement in ROI by measuring the enhancements of business processes and the improvement to the overall production as a result of implementing predictive analytics.

REMEMBER

Automating predictive analytics and extending it to all areas of business are two important and strategic ways to increase ROI. Sharing and co-ordinating the results of predictive analytics conducted by any one department with results obtained by other departments increases the benefits of those analytical projects. Among the different departments, synergies emerge that you can capitalize on.

Increasing the number of successful business decisions always leads to better performance. Informed decisions — backed up with accurate predictive scores — increase the confidence of management in decisions that resulted from deploying predictive analytics models. Better decision-making, on the basis of more accurate information, is the core of predictive analytics.

Gaining Rapid Access to Information

Predictive analytics enables business to make smarter decisions, some of which take place in real time. It allows businesses to improve all aspects of decision-making — including confidence in decisions based on insights derived from the in-depth analysis of trusted information.

Predictive analytics helps your organization predict future events with confidence and make optimal decisions to improve business outcomes. It automatically gives your organization an edge over competitors who are still using guesswork to manage their operations.

Predictive analytics models can evaluate complex scenarios and make real-time decisions quickly — and more accurately — in anticipating your business needs. The more such results accumulate, the more you boost confidence in the model and its predictive capability.

The automation of this decision-making, backed by thorough testing and refined by feedback from operational deployment, allows for greater consistency of those decisions that require precision. The effect is to avoid the subjective analysis or emotional attachment that can often lead to biased decisions.

Deriving actionable information from the use of analytics promotes faster response to rapidly changing business environments and external conditions. This process empowers your business with the agility to better position itself, taking advantage of emergent business opportunities while managing risks and reducing costs.

Companies that adopt predictive analytics undergo a cultural change that affects every area of the business. Making more informed decisions provides them with the confidence necessary to adopt those decisions and develop better strategic plans. The larger result is that they become more efficient, increase their profitability, and position themselves to play a more competitive role in the marketplace.

Making Informed Decisions

Predictive analytics, properly developed and applied, turns your data into key insights, and enables you to take action by making informed decisions about many areas of your business — based on extensive analysis of your data. Greater accuracy in predicting future events is an advantage unto itself — in part because it can be applied to so many areas.

Sometimes the ultimate objective of a predictive model is the automation of certain business decisions. An example is an automated trading system that places real-time trades on your behalf, manages your portfolio (money and assets) and any financial leverage you may have. The goal is to make the best decision as quickly as possible — automatically — taking into consideration the many complex factors that affect money management in response to existing market dynamics.

TIP

Business can also use predictive analytics to build a model that analyzes various aspects of not only a particular decision, but also its aftermath and possible scenarios — and then suggest the optimal decision for the circumstances.

Models' outputs can help a company make decisions affecting many aspects of the business, from supply-chain management to identifying opportunities and budgeting.

Companies use predictive analytics models to identify effective strategies that are effective and optimized to handle future events automatically, their actions guided by strategies based on knowledge acquired from thorough and exhaustive analysis.

A functioning predictive model can lead to making informed decisions guided by data analysis. If the model does its job well, its results are reinforced through testing — and validated by the feedback generated in response to its deployment, then when faced with new events, the business can rely on models that were built to handle them — especially if the events are unprecedented and unfolding in real time.

Gaining Competitive Edge

Making decisions with confidence based on predictive analytics models can provide your business with an edge over the competition by enabling you to

>> Exploit new opportunities

>> Navigate hidden risks

>> Recommend best choices for your customers

>> Quickly adapt to a changing business environment

>> Reduce operational costs

REMEMBER

Accumulating data isn't enough in itself. Mining that data to extract insightful information, uncover hidden patterns and relationships in that data and making informed decisions will enable you create competitive advantages for your business.

Predictive analytics can also play an important role in your planning, giving you the agility you need to stay ahead of your competitors. You can no longer afford to rely only on past experiences and executives' intuitions to run your business. Instead, predictive analytics can help you turn your wealth of data into a wealth of actionable insights and informed decisions (some of them made in real time).

Improving the Business

Predictive analytics can free your company from taking a scattershot approach to improving performance by boosting various areas of the business:

>> Increased cross-selling

>> Retention and acquisition of customers

>> Agility in the planning process

>> Inventory management

>> Accurate risk calculation

>> Effective resource allocation

Because predictive analytics models can also improve the reliability of business data and the agility of responses to emergent conditions, companies see a range of improvements:

>> Better, more accurate business decisions

>> Better understanding of internal business processes and external market conditions

>> Better management of customer relations

>> Better, faster response to real-time windows of opportunity

Chapter 19

Ten Steps to Build a Predictive Analytic Model

This chapter discusses best practices in building predictive analytics models. You'll get a handle on the importance of defining the business objectives early on — and on getting the leaders of your business to champion your project.

Building a Predictive Analytics Team

To assemble your predictive analytics team, you'll need to recruit business analysts, data scientists, and information technologists. Regardless of their particular areas of expertise, your team members should be curious, engaged, motivated, and excited to dig as deep as necessary to make the project — and the business — succeed.

Getting business expertise on board

Business analysts serve as your domain experts (see Chapter 15): They provide the business-based perspective on which problems to solve — and give valuable insight on all business-related questions. Their experience and domain knowledge give them an intuitive savvy about what approaches might or might not work, on where to start and what to look at to get something going.

REMEMBER

A model is only as relevant as the questions you use it to answer. Solid knowledge of your specific business can start you off in the right direction; use your experts' perspectives to determine:

>> Which are the right questions? (Which aspects of your business do you want predictive analytics to improve?)

>> Which is the right data to include in the analysis? (Should your focus be on the efficiency of your business processes? The demographics of your customers? Which body of data stands out as the most critical?)

>> Who are the business stakeholders and how can they benefit from the insights gained from your predictive analytics project?

Hiring analytical team members who understand your line of business will help you focus the building of your predictive analytics solutions on the desired business outcomes.

Firing up IT and math expertise

Data scientists can play an important role linking together the worlds of business and data to the technology and algorithms while following well-established methodologies that are proven to be successful. They have a big say in developing the actual models and their views will affect the outcome of your whole project. This role will require expertise in statistics such as knowledge of regression/non-regression analysis and cluster analysis. (*Regression analysis* is a statistical method that investigates the relationships between variables.) The role also requires the ability to correctly choose the right technical solutions for the business problem and the ability to articulate the business value of the outcome to the stakeholders.

Your data scientists should possess knowledge of advanced algorithms and techniques such as machine learning, data mining, and natural language processing.

Then you need IT experts to apply technical expertise to the implementation, monitoring, maintenance, and administration of the needed IT systems. Their job is to make sure the IT infrastructure and all IT strategic assets are stable, secure, and available to enable the business mission. An example of this is making sure the computer network and database work smoothly together.

When data scientists have selected the appropriate techniques, then (together with IT experts) they can oversee the overall design of the system's architecture, and improve its performance in response to different environments and different volumes of data.

TIP

In addition to the usual suspects — business experts, math and statistical modelers, and computer scientists — you may want to spice up your team with specialists from other disciplines such as physics, psychology, philosophy, or liberal arts to generate fresh ideas and new perspectives.

Setting the Business Objectives

To give your predictive analytics project its best shot at success, be sure to set out specific business goals right from the start. Is the company adding to its product line? Targeting new customers? Changing its overall business model? Whatever the major focus is, pay particular attention to how your project will make a positive impact on the bottom line. This practical perspective will help you get your stakeholders to champion your project — which in turn generates the confidence you need to go forward.

In the early phase of the project, your analytics team should gather relevant business information by meeting with the stakeholders to understand and record their business needs — and their take on the issues that the project is expected to solve. The stakeholders' domain knowledge and firsthand insights can

>> Help the team evaluate possible solutions

>> Identify attainable, quantifiable business objectives

>> Provide a practical perspective for prioritizing the project's goals

Preparing Your Data

This step in building your predictive analytics project is as crucial as it is unavoidably time-consuming and tedious: data preparation. The actual needed steps vary from one project to the next; they depend on the initial state of your data and the requirements for your project.

REMEMBER

You'll need to outline a strategy on how to handle these common data issues:

>> Which variables do you want to include in the analysis?

>> How will you check the correctness of certain field values?

>> How do you handle missing values in your data?

>> Will you include or exclude outliers?

>> Will you normalize some fields? Which ones?

>> Will you need to derive new variables from the existing data?

>> Will you need to include third-party data?

>> Does your data comprise enough records and variables?

Sampling Your Data

To ensure that you can accurately measure the performance of the predictive analytics model you're building, separate your historical business data into training and test datasets:

>> **The training dataset:** This dataset comprises the majority (about 70 percent) of the data. You'll use it to train the predictive model.

>> **The test dataset:** This is a smaller percentage (about 30 percent) of the data, used to test and measure the model's performance. It's an independent set of data that the model hasn't yet seen.

Splitting historical data into training and test datasets helps protect against overfitting the model to the training data. (See Chapter 15 for more about overfitting.) You want your model to identify true signals, patterns, and relationships, and to avoid any false ones that could be attributed to the noise within the data. The essence of overfitting is as follows: When a model is tuned to a specific dataset, there is a higher chance that any uncovered patterns are only true for that dataset;

the same model may not perform as well on other datasets. Use your testing dataset to help eliminate these dataset-specific patterns (which are considered mostly noise), and your predictive model will become more accurate.

TIP

For better model development, make sure your training and test datasets are similar enough to each other to minimize inconsistencies in data quality, relevance, and time coverage. One common way to get a true representation of similar data in both datasets is to choose these data samples at random.

Avoiding "Garbage In, Garbage Out"

More data doesn't necessarily mean better data. A successful predictive analytics project requires, first and foremost, relevant and accurate data.

Keeping it simple isn't stupid

If you're trying to address a complex business decision, you may have to develop equally complex models. Keep in mind, however, that an overly complex model may degrade the quality of those precious predictions you're after, making them more ambiguous. The simpler you keep your model, the more control you have over the quality of the model's outputs.

Limiting the complexity of the model depends on knowing what variables to select before you even start building it — and that consideration leads right back to the people with domain knowledge. Your business experts are your best source for insights into what variables have direct impact on the business problem you're trying to solve. Also, you can decide empirically on what variables to include or exclude.

Use those insights to ensure that your training dataset includes most (if not all) the possible data that you expect to use to build the model.

Data preparation puts the good stuff in

To ensure high data quality as a factor in the success of the model you're building, data preparation and cleaning can be of enormous help. When you're examining your data, pay special attention to

» Data that was automatically collected (for example, from web forms)

» Data that didn't undergo thorough screening

>> Data collected via a controlled process

>> Data that may have out-of-range values, data-entry errors, and/or incorrect values

REMEMBER

Common mistakes that lead to the dreaded "garbage in, garbage out" scenario include these classic goofs:

>> Including more data than necessary

>> Building more complex models than necessary

>> Selecting bad predictor variables or features in your analysis

>> Using data that lacks sufficient quality and relevance

Creating Quick Victories

An *iterative* approach to building the model — trying a version of the model, fine-tuning it in light of your results, and then trying the improved version — will allow you to evaluate the variables and algorithms used in your model, and choose those best suited to your final solution. Building your model iteratively may help you make some decisions and choices:

>> Determining whether to include other data types

>> Determining whether to aggregate some of the data fields

>> Clearly identifying a rollout plan

>> Identifying any data gaps early enough to improve the processes involved

>> Evaluating your model's scalability for bigger transactions and larger volume of data

REMEMBER

You can show the value of the analytics for your business by implementing a small pilot project and showing quick victories. Delivering a specific solution can bring you the buy-in necessary to build larger-scale solutions and more powerful models. Creating quick victories early in the process will allow you to understand pressing business questions, and when you provide solutions to those questions, you can reinforce the buy-in from the business stakeholders. Success breeds success — and it doesn't have to be overnight. By establishing a track record of success for your model, you can help foster the cultural change needed for a widespread adoption of predictive analytics within your organization.

Fostering Change in Your Organization

Impressive past performance doesn't guarantee an equally impressive future for an organization. It isn't enough to look at how the business has been done thus far. Instead, organizations should look at how predictive analytics can transform the way they're doing business in response to a rapidly changing present environment. For that to happen, business leaders need a major shift in the way they think and operate the business. Your predictive analytics project is a good place for them to start that shift.

Granted, the old guard — traditional business leaders who have been operating their businesses on gut feelings — can be close-minded at first, reluctant to adopt new technologies and trust the predictions and recommendations that come from them. You should expect some degree of organizational resistance to the deployment of your new model. This is especially true when an analytical system detects a major shift in trends — or a bigger crisis than anticipated — prompting the business leaders to distrust the system's recommendations and rely on historical analysis. If the business managers aren't willing to act on the recommendations of the predictive model, the project will fail.

REMEMBER

Creating cultural changes that promote the use of predictive analytics to drive business decisions isn't only essential to the success of your project, but also — if you've built the model well — to the success of your business. You have to build not only a working model, but also an in-house culture that champions the use of predictive analytics as an aspect of business intelligence.

When you've demonstrated that your analytics program can guide the organization effectively toward achieving its business goals, be sure you clearly communicate — and widely publicize — those results within the organization. The idea is to increase awareness and buy-in for the program. Educating stakeholders about the benefits of predictive analytics entails emphasizing the possible loss of both opportunities and competitive edge if this tool isn't developed and deployed. Maintaining focus on such business values can have a direct and positive impact on creating a cultural change that favors predictive analytics.

The process of educating and training may take time to bear fruit; most organizational changes require time to implement and to be adopted. Be sure you recruit business team members who have both an understanding of and experience in managing organizational change and developing internal communications strategy.

Building Deployable Models

In order to ensure a successful deployment of the predictive model you're building, you'll need to think about deployment very early on. The business stakeholders should have a say in what the final model looks like. Thus, at the beginning of the project, be sure your team discusses the required accuracy of the intended model and how best to interpret its results.

Data modelers should understand the business objectives the model is trying to achieve, and all team members should be familiar with the metrics against which the model will be judged. The idea is to make sure everyone is on the same page, working to achieve the same goals, and using the same metrics to evaluate the benefits of the model.

Keep in mind that the model's operational environment will most likely be different from the development environment. The differences can be significant, from the hardware and software configurations, to the nature of the data, to the footprint of the model itself. The modelers have to know all the requirements needed for a successful deployment in production before they can build a model that will actually work on the production systems. Implementation constraints can become obstacles that come between the model and its deployment.

Understanding the limitations of your model is also critical to ensuring its success. Pay particular attention to these typical limitations:

- >> The time the model takes to run
- >> The data the model needs; sources, types, and volume
- >> The platform on which the model resides

REMEMBER

Ideally, the model has a higher chance of getting deployed when

- >> It uncovers some patterns within the data that were previously unknown.
- >> It can be easily interpreted to the business stakeholders.
- >> The newly uncovered patterns actually make sense businesswise and offer an operational advantage.

Evaluating Your Model

Your goal, of course, is to build an analytical model that can actually solve the business objectives it was built for. Expect to spend some time evaluating the accuracy of your model's predictions so as to prove its value to the decision-making process — and to the bottom line.

Evaluate your model from these two distinct angles:

>> **Business:** The business analyst should evaluate the model's performance and the accuracy of its predictions in terms of how well they address business objectives. Are the insights derived from the model making it easier for you to make decisions? Are you spending more time or less time in meetings because of these new insights?

>> **Technical:** The data scientists and IT professionals should evaluate the algorithms used and the statistical techniques and methods applied. Are the algorithms chosen optimal for the model's purpose? Are the insights being generated fast enough to produce actionable advantages?

REMEMBER

In addition to closely examining the data used, selecting variables with the most predictive power, and the algorithms applied, the most critical test is to evaluate whether the model meets business needs and whether it adds value to the business.

TIP

Test your model in a test environment that closely resembles the production environment. Set the metrics to evaluate the success of the model at the beginning of the project. Specifying the metrics early makes the model easier to validate later on.

Updating Your Model

Successful deployment of the model in production is no time to relax. You'll need to closely monitor its accuracy and performance over time. A model tends to degrade over time (some faster than others); and a new infusion of energy is required from time to time to keep that model up and running. To stay successful, a model must be revisited and re-evaluated in light of new data and changing circumstances.

If conditions change so they no longer fit the model's original training, then you'll have to retrain the model to meet the new conditions. Such demanding new conditions include

>> An overall change in the business objective

>> The adoption of — and migration to — new and more powerful technology

>> The emergence of new trends in the marketplace

>> Evidence that the competition is catching up

Your strategic plan should include staying alert for any such emergent need to refresh your model and take it to the next level, but updating your model should be an ongoing process anyway. You'll keep on tweaking inputs and outputs, incorporating new data streams, retraining the model for the new conditions and continuously refining its outputs. Keep these goals in mind:

>> Stay on top of changing conditions by retraining and testing the model regularly; enhance it whenever necessary.

>> Monitor your model's accuracy to catch any degradation in its performance over time.

>> Automate the monitoring of your model by developing customized applications that report and track the model's performance.

Automation of monitoring, or having other team members involved, would alleviate any concerns a data scientist may have over the model's performance and can improve the use of everyone's time.

TIP

Automated monitoring saves time and helps you avoid errors in tracking the model's performance.

Index

About the Authors

Dr. Anasse Bari holds a Ph.D. in Computer Science with a focus on Data Mining from George Washington University. He is an entrepreneur and a Fulbright scholar. Dr. Bari is a clinical assistant professor of computer science at New York University, Courant Institute of Mathematical Sciences. He was previously professor of computer science at George Washington University where he was awarded the computer science Professor of the Year award in 2014, and was recognized by the Carnegie Foundation for the Advancement of Teaching for his nomination for the United States Professor of the Year Award.

Anasse has over ten years of experience in designing large-scale software applications and engineering analytics frameworks under different platforms for both the public and private sectors.

Dr. Bari has recently worked closely with leadership of the World Bank Group for many years as a data scientist where he was leading enterprise data analytics projects. Dr. Bari was the recipient of the World Bank Spot award for his extraordinary efforts in service of the organization. While at the World Bank, he attended an executive design thinking program at Stanford University. Dr. Bari is a renowned speaker and his research has been focused on predictive analytics, data mining, and information retrieval. He is the author of several research publications published at peer-reviewed venues on data mining with practical applications in financial analytics, social network analytics, bioinformatics and text mining.

Anasse lives in Manhattan in New York City.

Mohamed Chaouchi has a master's degree in computer science from the George Washington University. He has over 15 years of experience in software development and project management in the public and private sectors.

He is an application architect and technical lead, responsible for building software applications with high business impact and visibility. His technical expertise includes service-oriented architecture, web services, and application security.

Mohamed has extensive experience working with management and IT leadership, participates in information technology governing boards, and represents his division at inter-organizational conferences.

Mohamed has conducted extensive research using predictive analytics and data mining in both the health and financial domains. He has published several papers in peer-reviewed journals in cancer research and ocean-data integration.

He is also an inventor of an issued patent for a data-mining platform to analyze cancer development.

Mohamed currently lives in Kensington, MD, with his wife Jennifer and his son Zacharia.

Tommy Jung holds a bachelor's degree in computer science. He is an entrepreneur, investor, and consultant. He spends most of his time building software and analyzing data.

Tommy has over 15 years of professional experience in technology. He has worked extensively on natural language processing and machine learning in his days at a speech recognition company and then turned his focus to web applications, optimization, and analytics. He was the head of operations at UmeVoice, where he played various roles inside the organization, including operations, engineering, and marketing. He has also worked at several Fortune 500 companies as a software engineer or consultant. His expertise encompasses predictive analytics, data mining, natural language processing, web development, A/B testing, database marketing, search engine optimization, and search engine marketing.

While not working, Tommy enjoys playing chess face-to-face with his daughters, online with his friends, and sometimes elsewhere (he may pick up a game or two on a downtown bench). He currently lives in Silicon Valley with his wife and two young daughters.

Dedication

Dr. Anasse Bari: I dedicate this book to my parents Rachida Bargach and Ali Bari, and to my siblings Nima and Mounir Bari.

Mohamed Chaouchi: This book is dedicated to my wife, Jennifer, my son Zacharia, and my parents, Fatima El Bote and Mohamed Chaouchi.

Tommy Jung: This book is dedicated to my daughters, Tiffany and Victoria. To Tiffany, thanks for keeping me on track with my chapters and always thinking about me. To Victoria, thanks for keeping me company late at night (way past your bedtime!) and making me laugh.

Author's Acknowledgments

We were able to write this book thanks to the help and support of the great people at John Wiley & Sons. Thank you to Susan Spilka for getting the conversation started. Thank you to our acquisition editor Amy Fandrei, whose idea it was to write this book, and for her guidance, support, and encouragement. We greatly appreciate the support and advice of our project editor, Pat O'Brien, who kept us on target throughout the writing of the book.

Thank you to Barry Childs-Helton for his valuable edits, and to Dr. Smita Rajpal Kachroo, and Keith McCormick for their technical review. We are grateful to Steve Hayes for helping us whenever we needed it. And thanks to all the other members of the Wiley team that we did not have direct contact with and who have helped produce this book.

Dr. Anasse Bari: My thanks and deepest appreciation goes to Professor Abdelghani Bellaachia of the George Washington University who introduced me to, and sparked my interest in, data mining since day one of my doctoral degree. His guidance and ingenuity has profoundly influenced me as a scientist. I would also like to thank Jennifer Fulton for providing invaluable insights and extensive revisions, and José Pablo Cambronero and Usayd Casewit for their helpful reviews. I would like to thank my dear friends the Casewit family, Elvina Kamalova, Daron Bedrosyan, Adil Abaz, and Amine Chergui, for their support. I would also like to thank my co-authors (and friends) for their dedication and hard work that enabled us to meet all deadlines.

Mohamed Chaouchi: I would like to thank my beloved wife, Jennifer Fulton, for being my first sounding board, asking me great questions, and providing invaluable suggestions. And my amazing son, Zacharia: You are my source of joy and my inspiration for everything!

I would like to also thank my co-authors (and friends) for their effort and commitment to this project.

Tommy Jung: I would like to thank my beautiful wife Jenine, and kids Tiffany and Victoria, for always making each day special. Thank you again for giving up some of our precious weekend family time to allow me to write this second edition. Thanks for always being by my side and encouraging me to write. I would like to thank my parents, Michael and Holly Jung, for always encouraging me to make a difference, to work hard, and to take on new challenges with open arms. I would like to thank my father and mother in-law, Jerry and Joellyn Gor, for being there for my kids when Jenine was on business travel and I needed some extra time to do some writing. I would like to thank my brother Jimmy Jung for his ideas and feedback. If he can understand what I wrote, then anyone can (of course, we brothers *never* tease each other).

I'd like also to thank my co-authors (and friends) for being so easy to work with. It's always a pleasure to work with you guys in every capacity.

Publisher's Acknowledgments

Project Manager: Pat O'Brien
Technical Editor: Keith McCormick
Sr. Editorial Assistant: Cherie Case

Project Editor: Tamilmani Varadharaj
Cover Image: wongwean/Shutterstock